A History of Rome
Through the Fifth Century

Volume II: The Empire

A volume
in
DOCUMENTARY HISTORY
of
WESTERN CIVILIZATION

DOCUMENTARY HISTORY OF WESTERN CIVILIZATION
Edited by Eugene C. Black and Leonard W. Levy

ANCIENT AND MEDIEVAL HISTORY OF THE WEST

Morton Smith: ANCIENT GREECE

A. H. M. Jones: A HISTORY OF ROME THROUGH THE FIFTH CENTURY
Vol. I: The Republic   HR/1364
Vol. II: The Empire   HR/1460

Deno Geanakoplos: BYZANTINE EMPIRE

Marshall W. Baldwin: CHRISTIANITY THROUGH THE THIRTEENTH CENTURY   HR/1468

Bernard Lewis: ISLAM THROUGH SULEIMAN THE MAGNIFICENT

David Herlihy: HISTORY OF FEUDALISM

William M. Bowsky: RISE OF COMMERCE AND TOWNS

David Herlihy: MEDIEVAL CULTURE AND SOCIETY   HR/1340

EARLY MODERN HISTORY

Hanna H. Gray: CULTURAL HISTORY OF THE RENAISSANCE

Florence Edler de Roover: MONEY, BANKING,
AND COMMERCE, THIRTEENTH THROUGH SIXTEENTH CENTURIES

V. J. Parry: THE OTTOMAN EMPIRE

Ralph E. Giesey: EVOLUTION OF THE DYNASTIC STATE

J. H. Parry: THE EUROPEAN RECONNAISSANCE: *Selected Documents*   HR/1345

Hans J. Hillerbrand: THE PROTESTANT REFORMATION   HR/1342

John C. Olin: THE CATHOLIC COUNTER REFORMATION

Orest Ranum: THE CENTURY OF LOUIS XIV

Thomas Hegarty: RUSSIAN HISTORY THROUGH PETER THE GREAT

Marie Boas Hall: NATURE AND NATURE'S LAWS   HR/1420

Barry E. Supple: HISTORY OF MERCANTILISM

Arthur J. Slavin: IMPERIALISM, WAR, AND DIPLOMACY, 1550-1763

Herbert H. Rowen: THE LOW COUNTRIES

C. A. Macartney: THE HABSBURG AND HOHENZOLLERN DYNASTIES
IN THE SEVENTEENTH AND EIGHTEENTH CENTURIES   HR/1400

Lester G. Crocker: THE AGE OF ENLIGHTENMENT   HR/1423

Robert and Elborg Forster: EUROPEAN SOCIETY IN THE EIGHTEENTH CENTURY   HR/1404

REVOLUTIONARY EUROPE, *1789-1848*

Paul H. Beik: THE FRENCH REVOLUTION

David L. Dowd: NAPOLEONIC ERA, 1799-1815

René Albrecht-Carrié: THE CONCERT OF EUROPE   HR/1341

John B. Halsted: ROMANTICISM   HR/1387

R. Max Hartwell: THE INDUSTRIAL REVOLUTION

Mack Walker: METTERNICH'S EUROPE   HR/1361

Douglas Johnson: THE ASCENDANT BOURGEOISIE

John A. Hawgood: THE REVOLUTIONS OF 1848

NATIONALISM, LIBERALISM, AND SOCIALISM, *1850-1914*

Eugene C. Black: VICTORIAN CULTURE AND SOCIETY   HR/1426

Eugene C. Black: BRITISH POLITICS IN THE NINETEENTH CENTURY   HR/1427

Denis Mack Smith: THE MAKING OF ITALY, 1796-1870   HR/1356

David Thomson: FRANCE: *Empire and Republic*, 1850-1940   HR/1378

Theodore S. Hamerow: BISMARCK'S MITTELEUROPA

Eugene O. Golob: THE AGE OF LAISSEZ FAIRE

Roland N. Stromberg: REALISM, NATURALISM, AND SYMBOLISM:
Modes of Thought and Expression in Europe, 1848-1914   HR/1355

Melvin Kranzberg: SCIENCE AND TECHNOLOGY

Jesse D. Clarkson: TSARIST RUSSIA: *Catherine the Great to Nicholas II*

Philip D. Curtin and John R. W. Smail: IMPERIALISM

Massimo Salvadori: MODERN SOCIALISM   HR/1374

THE TWENTIETH CENTURY

Jere C. King: THE FIRST WORLD WAR

S. Clough, T. and C. Moodie : ECONOMIC HISTORY OF EUROPE:
Twentieth Century   HR/1388

W. Warren Wagar: SCIENCE, FAITH, AND MAN:
European Thought Since 1914   HR/1362

Paul A. Gagnon: INTERNATIONALISM AND DIPLOMACY BETWEEN THE WARS, 1919-1939

Henry Cord Meyer: WEIMAR AND NAZI GERMANY

Michal Vyvyan: RUSSIA FROM LENIN TO KHRUSHCHEV

Charles F. Delzell: MEDITERRANEAN TOTALITARIANISM, 1919-1945

Donald C. Watt: THE SECOND WORLD WAR

A History of Rome Through the Fifth Century

Volume II: The Empire

edited by

A. H. M. JONES

Harper & Row, Publishers
New York, Evanston, and London

A HISTORY OF ROME THROUGH THE FIFTH
CENTURY: VOLUME II: THE EMPIRE

Introduction, editorial notes, chronological table,
bibliography, and translations by the editor,
copyright © 1970 by A. H. M. Jones.

Printed in the United States of America.

First HARPER PAPERBACK. edition, Harper & Row, Publishers,
Inc., 49 East 33rd Street, New York, N.Y. 10016.

A clothbound edition of this book is published in the
United States and Canada by Walker and Company.

Library of Congress Catalog Card Number: 68-13332.

Contents

VII. THE PROVINCES

VIII. THE CITIES

IX. TAXATION

X. JUSTICE

XI. STATUS

XII. ECONOMIC AFFAIRS

XIII. RELIGION

Acknowledgments

The translations of the *Res Gestae Divi Augusti* (No. 1) and most of the papyri (Nos. 55–56, 59, 61, 86, 96, 102–04, 120, 126) are by kind permission of the Harvard University Press taken from the Loeb Classical Library. The versions of the Theodosian Code (Nos. 48–52, 69–75, 89, 115–18, 130–34, 155, 159–63, 182–84) are by kind permission of Professor C. Pharr, taken from his *The Theodosian Code and Novels, and the Sirmondian Constitutions* (Princeton, 1952); I am particularly grateful to him for waiving any royalty payment. The translations of Tacitus, *Annals* (Nos. 12, 21–22, 25–26, 28, 36, 53, 67, 85, 125, 135, 165, 167–68) are adapted from A. J. Church and W. J. Brodribb (London, 1876), those of his *Histories* (No. 15) from A. J. Church and W. J. Brodribb (London, 1876), those of his *Agricola* (Nos. 29, 80) from the same translators' *The Agricola and the Germania* (London, 1874). The translations of Suetonius (Nos. 10, 13–14) are adapted from Alexander Thomson, *The Lives of the First Twelve Caesars* (London, 1796); those of Pliny's *Letters* (Nos. 24, 35, 37, 54, 60, 82–84, 95, 107–11, 136, 144, 169) from William Melmoth, *The Letters of Pliny the Consul* (London, 1796). The versions of Cassius Dio (Nos. 4–7, 11) are adapted from H. B. Foster, *Dio's Rome, a Historical Narrative Composed in Greek and Now Presented in English* (Troy, N.Y., 1905); those of Eusebius (Nos. 171, 173, 175–78) from A. C. McGiffert and B. C. Richardson in *The Nicene and Post-Nicene Fathers*, vol. I (London, 1890). The translations of Ammianus Marcellinus (Nos. 17–20, 34, 76, 90, 92, 129) are adapted from C. D. Yonge, *The Roman History of Ammianus Marcellinus* (London, 1862). The two passages from the Acts of the Apostles (Nos. 142–43) are adapted from the Revised Version.

I have myself translated the passages from Velleius Paterculus (No. 2), Strabo (Nos. 3, 77–78), Frontinus (No. 91), Fronto (Nos. 38, 45, 81), Cyprian (No. 172), Lactantius (Nos. 16, 127), Optatus (Nos. 174, 179, 180), Zosimus (No. 68), the Digest (Nos. 79, 105, 121, 137), the Codex Justinianus (Nos. 156–58), a few papyri (Nos. 46, 57, 122, 128, 138, 145, 170), and all the inscriptions except the *Res Gestae* (Nos. 8, 9, 23, 27, 30–33, 39–44, 47, 58, 62–66, 87–88, 93–94, 97–101, 106, 112–14, 119, 123–24, 139–41, 146–54, 164, 166, 181).

NOTE: It must be remembered that two or more emperors might reign simultaneously as colleagues, e.g. Lucius Verus was colleague of Marcus Aurelius during the first eight years of the latter's reign, and Commodus, son of Marcus, was his colleague during his father's last six years. This practice became normal in the later empire. The list includes the more important "usurpers," who are difficult to distinguish from "legitimate" emperors. The letter A denotes Augustus (full emperor), C, Caesar (subordinate emperor).

27 B.C.–A.D. 14	Augustus
A.D. 14–37	Tiberius
37–41	Caligula
41–54	Claudius
54–68	Nero
68–69	Galba
69	Otho
69	Vitellius
69–79	Vespasian
79–81	Titus
81–96	Domitian
96–98	Nerva
98–117	Trajan
117–138	Hadrian
138–161	Antoninus Pius
161–180	Marcus Aurelius
161–169	Lucius Verus
176–192	Commodus
193	Pertinax
193	Didius Julianus
193–211	Septimius Severus
193–197	Clodius Albinus
193–194	Pescennius Niger
198–217	Caracalla
209–212	Geta
217–218	Macrinus
218	Diadumenianus
218–222	Elegabalus
222–235	Severus Alexander

235–238	Maximinus
238	Gordian I
238	Gordian II
238	Balbinus
238	Pupienus
238–244	Gordian III
244–249	Philip the Arab
249–251	Decius
251–253	Trebonianus Gallus
251–253	Volusianus
253	Aemilianus
253–260	Valerian
253–268	Gallienus
268–270	Claudius II Gothicus
270	Quintillus
270–275	Aurelian
275–276	Tacitus
276	Florianus
276–282	Probus
282–283	Carus
283–285	Carinus
283–284	Numerianus

WEST		EAST	
C. 285–86 A. 286–305, 307–10	Maximian	A. 284–305	Diocletian
C. 293–305 A. 305–06	Constantius I	C. 293–305 A. 305–11	Galerius
C. 306–08 A. 308–37	Constantine	C. 305–08 A. 308–13	Maximin
A. 306–07	Severus		
A. 307–12	Maxentius	A. 308–24	Licinius
A. 308–11	Alexander	C. 317–23	Licinianus
C. 317–25	Crispus	C. 324	Martinianus
C. 317–37 A. 337–40	Constantine II	A. 324–37 C. 324–37 A. 337–61	Constantine Constantius
C. 333–37 A. 337–50	Constans		

WEST		EAST	
C. 335–37	Dalmatius		
A. 350–53	Magnentius	C. 350–54	Gallus
A. 350	Vetranio		
A. 350	Nepotianus		
A. 351–61	Constantius II		
A. 355	Silvanus		
C. 355–60	Julian		
A. 360–63		A. 361–63	Julian
A. 363–64	Jovian	A. 363–64	Jovian
A. 364–75	Valentinian I	A. 364–78	Valens
A. 372	Firmus	A. 365	Procopius
A. 375–83	Gratian		
A. 383–87	Maximus	A. 379–95	Theodosius I
A. 383–92	Valentinian II		
A. 392–94	Eugenius		
A. 394–95	Theodosius I		
A. 395–423	Honorius	A. 395–408	Arcadius
A. 397	Gildo		
A. 407–11	Constantine	A. 408–50	Theodosius II
C. 408–10	Constans		
A. 408–10	Attalus		
A. 412–13	Jovinus		
A. 421	Constantius III		
A. 423–25	John		
A. 425–55	Valentinian III	A. 450–57	Marcian
A. 455	Petronius Maximus		
A. 455–56	Avitus		
A. 457–61	Majorian	A. 457–74	Leo I
A. 461–65	Libius Severus		
A. 467–72	Anthemius		
A. 472	Olybrius		
A. 473	Glycerius		
A. 473–80	Julius Nepos	A. 474	Leo II
A. 475–76	Romulus	A. 474–91	Zeno

A History of Rome
Through the Fifth Century
Volume II: The Empire

Introduction

The great achievement of the Roman empire was in the art of government. The emperors succeeded for nearly five centuries in holding together a state which extended from the Atlantic to the Arabian desert, and from the Danube to the Sahara, protecting it from the attacks of its often aggressive enemies, and giving it orderly administration, equitable justice based on a uniform and enlightened body of law, and a well-organized system of taxation, in short, peace, order, and prosperity. Finally they converted what had originated as a subject empire ruled by a conquering people into a uniform state, whose citizens, whether Italians or Britons or Egyptians, all enjoyed the same political status and were subject to the same law. There were of course bad periods of civil war, foreign invasion, and financial collapse, but these were relatively brief. There was also a growing discrimination not only in wealth but in legal status between the rich and the poor, and much corruption and extortion in the administration. But on the whole the population of the countries which composed the empire had never before enjoyed such good government, and were not to enjoy it again for centuries after the empire's fall.

Among the major achievements of the empire, the law, the army, taxation, and local and provincial government are prominent. A comprehensive, rational, and subtle body of law was gradually built up from the decisions and enactments of the emperors and the systematic treatises of the great jurists who advised them. In the military sphere the emperors created the first standing army in history—and the last until the eighteenth century—whose soldiers were for five centuries regularly recruited, trained, armed, paid, fed, and clothed, and finally pensioned by the state. In the financial sphere the empire, with occasional lapses, regularly raised adequate revenue by uniform taxes, equitably assessed and efficiently collected, and even achieved under Diocletian, for the first time in history, a flexible budget, in which expenditure was annually estimated in advance and the rate of tax adjusted accordingly. In the field of administration the empire worked out a practical system in which central control was combined with local self-government.

As against these achievements the political history of the Roman empire is not very interesting. It was from the beginning an autocracy tempered by assassination and military rebellion, and politics consisted mainly of obscure court intrigues. The republican façade set up by Augustus is of some constitutional interest; it was designed to placate senatorial and equestrian republican sentiment, and succeeded in doing so. Thereafter there was one difficulty only and one point of dissension, the succession. The bulk of the lower classes in Italy, the rank and file of the army, and provincials of all ranks favored a hereditary succession. Senators thought it improper that the empire should pass like a private estate, and desired the rule of the "best man"; when they had an opportunity they chose a very elderly senator like Nerva or Pertinax. As long as hereditary heirs were forthcoming a dynasty usually endured, e.g., the descendants (by adoption) of Augustus down to Nero, Vespasian and his two sons, Septimius Severus and his family. But very unsuitable persons were liable to succeed, and dynasties usually ended by assassination or rebellion. In the latter the army (or rather its officers, who were senators for the first two centuries) played a prominent role. In the second century a happy compromise was worked out by which the emperors, who happened all to be childless, chose and adopted a suitable senator as heir. This pleased both senate and army and advanced quite able men to the throne. After the extinction of the Severi in 235, no dynasties usually ended by assassination or rebellion. In the latter Diocletian managed to reign 21 years (284–305) with a colleague whom he chose, Maximian (285–305). From this time onward there were nearly always two or more emperors, one or two in the West and one or two in the East. Diocletian also appointed junior emperors, Caesars, who succeeded when the two senior emperors abdicated. Diocletian's reign was followed by another bout of civil wars, of which Constantine was the victorious survivor. He went back to the hereditary system. On the death of the last of his family, Julian the Apostate, in 363, the generals and high officials chose Jovian, and on his death soon afterward Valentinian, who co-opted his brother Valens and founded a dynasty on whose extinction Theodosius I, co-opted by Gratian, son of Valentinian, founded another dynasty. On the extinction of his family, there was a rapid succession of fainéant emperors in the West, and orderly succession of elected emperors in the East.

Concurrently with difficulties about the succession there was periodical estrangement between the emperors and the senate, which, though powerless as a corporation, did contain all the generals and had great prestige. The senate was in general unhappy under Augustus' heirs—Tiberius, Gaius, Claudius, and Nero. It hated Domitian, Vespasian's younger son. It agreed with all the adoptive emperors from Nerva to Marcus Aurelius, but quarreled with Commodus, Marcus' young and frivolous son. It tolerated Septimius Severus, but hated Caracalla. Under Gallienus the senate ceased to be politically important, as senators were no longer appointed generals. It revived under Constantine, but never became a danger to the imperial power.

The military history is also rather dull, and mostly badly recorded. Augustus filled in the great gap left by the republic between Gaul (conquered by Julius Caesar) and the Black Sea. He or his generals—mostly members of his family—subdued the Alps and Rhaetia and Noricum (roughly Switzerland and Austria) and Pannonia and Moesia (Yugoslavia and northern Bulgaria). He thus established the Rhine-Danube frontier. He attempted to conquer Germany up to the Elbe, but failed. He advised Tiberius to keep to the bounds which he had established for the empire, and his successors in general accepted the ruling. Claudius conquered Britain in A.D. 43. Trajan conquered Dacia (roughly Roumania), but this outlying territory was abandoned by Aurelian.

The empire had no dangerous enemies on the south (the Sahara), nor on the southeast (the Arabian Desert). Its eastern neighbor was Parthia, a ramshackle empire with which Rome disputed the suzerainty of Armenia and other Caucasian kingdoms. The boundary was the Upper and Middle Euphrates, until Septimius Severus annexed Mesopotamia. In the third century the situation became more threatening owing to increasing pressure by the Germans on the Rhine and even more on the Danube, and to the revival of Persia under the strong and aggressive Sassanian dynasty. But Rome weathered the storm. With the Hunnic invasions of the later fourth century A.D. the pressure of the Germans, thrust on from behind by the Huns, became irresistible, and the western half of the empire collapsed in the early fifth century.

It is time to speak of the historians of Rome. For Augustus' reign the most valuable source is his own autobiography, or rather extended obituary, which was engraved outside his tomb at Rome, and copied in various cities of Asia Minor (in Greek and Latin). The text is given in full in this volume. It is strictly truthful, but does not tell the whole truth. Nearly contemporary are thirty-five chapters of Velleius Paterculus, who was praetor (i.e., thirty years of age) when Augustus died in A.D. 14. He is highly enthusiastic for the new régime. A contemporary geographer, Strabo of Amasia in Pontus, gives a valuable firsthand account of the provinces with much on their administration and recent history. The other chief historian of the reign, Cassius Dio, lived much later, being consul for the second time in A.D. 229. He wrote in Greek, being a native of Nicaea (in northwest Asia Minor). He was a very conscientious historian, spending ten years reading his authorities (197–207) and twelve (207–219) writing the *History*, which extended from the foundation of Rome to A.D. 229. He used not only earlier historians but public records and archives. His account of the administration is given by one who knew the whole system as it existed in the late second and early third centuries A.D.

With the accession of Tiberius in A.D. 14 begin the *Annals* of Tacitus; the surviving books cover the reign of Tiberius (A.D. 14–37) and most of Claudius and Nero (A.D. 47–66). Tacitus, a senator who wrote under Trajan, was a conscientious historian who used the *Acta senatus* as well as earlier historians, but who has a strong anti-imperial bias which distorts his presentation. For this period we have also the *History* of Cassius Dio in full, and the *Lives of the Caesars* by Suetonius, secretary of Hadrian. His lives are anecdotic, but contain much curious information, some of it drawn from the imperial archives.

After A.D. 66 our continuous sources become very meager. Tacitus' *Histories* cover only the years A.D. 69–70 in great detail; he also wrote a biography of his father-in-law Agricola, governor of Britain from A.D. 78 to 83. There are brief lives of Galba, Otho, Vitellius, Vespasian, Titus, and Domitian by Suetonius, and of Galba and Otho by Plutarch. Cassius Dio survives only in an epitome from the death of Nero, and even the epitome of the reign of Antoninus Pius is missing. There are also biographies of Hadrian, Antoninus Pius, and Marcus Aurelius in the *Historia Augusta*, a compilation professedly written under Diocletian and Constantine, but perhaps considerably later. Despite their late date, these lives are of value, being based on good sources. From the death of Marcus Aurelius (A.D. 180) the situation improves, for the epitome of Dio (who continued his *History* down to 229) becomes fuller, and is of great value as being contemporary, while Herodian, a civil servant, wrote a history covering the years A.D. 180 to 238. The lives of Commodus, Pertinax, Septimius Severus, and Caracalla in the *Historia Augusta* are also of fairly good quality.

Outside the historians and the imperial biographers, the only important literary source is the letters of Pliny the Younger, a contemporary of Tacitus, especially the official correspondence between him and Trajan when he was governor of Bithynia.

From A.D. 238 to 284 our sources become extremely poor. There are imperial biographies in the *Historia Augusta*, but the lives from this period are almost worthless; the writers of the *Historia Augusta* evidently had very little contemporary material upon which to draw, and exercised their imagination to fill the gaps. The only other narrative is that of Zosimus, who wrote in the fifth century, and he is very brief.

Jewish and Christian writers throw some light on the provincial scene. The Acts of the Apostles gives a worm's eye view of the empire from the ordinary provincial's standpoint. So does Josephus, who in the final books of his *Jewish Antiquities* and the introductory book of his *Jewish War* traces the history of the Jewish community under the Herodian dynasty and under the Roman procurators of Judaea. Christian writers are particularly valuable for the third century. Cyprian's letters and the account of his trial illustrate the Decian and Valerianic persecutions, and Eusebius, bishop of Caesarea under Constantine, in his great *Ecclesiastical History* cites valuable contemporary documents relating to the same events.

There are no secular historians of the reigns of Diocletian, Constantine, or his sons down to A.D. 350 except the sketchy and tendentious Zosimus (he was a strong pagan), who wrote a hundred years later, and the brief biographies of Aurelius Victor, who wrote in the middle of the fourth century. Religious history is on the other hand well covered by Eusebius, who records the persecution under Diocletian and his successors down to Licinius, and by Socrates, Sozomenus and Theodoret, who all wrote *Ecclesiastical Histories* in Greek in the middle of the fifth century, starting with the conversion of Constantine. Though they wrote much later than the events they describe, they are based on contemporary documents, which they often quote. Lactantius, the professor of

Latin at Diocletian's capital, Nicomedia, wrote a violent diatribe *On the Death of the Persecutors*, which contains our only account of Diocletian's administrative reforms—not that Lactantius considered them as such. Eusebius also wrote a *Life of Constantine*, which is an obituary notice rather than a biography, and Athanasius, bishop of Alexandria, wrote a series of polemical pamphlets on the Arian controversy. Optatus, who wrote a controversial work on the Donatist schism in the early fifth century, has preserved a number of very important Constantinian documents in an appendix.

In 351 begins the surviving portion of the history of Ammianus Marcellinus, an Antiochene who served as a *protector* (officer cadet) from 353 to 363, mainly on the eastern front. He is one of the greatest of Roman historians, a fair-minded pagan who could criticize his hero, Julian the Apostate. Julian has himself left valuable evidence on his own reign in his letters and in the *Misopogon*, a satirical pamphlet on his quarrel with the Christian city of Antioch.

Ammianus finished his history with the battle of Adrianople in 378. After this we have to content ourselves with Zosimus, who continued his narrative, now fuller and more interesting, down to 410. Then we have only the ecclesiastical historians, Socrates, Sozomenus, and Theodoret, the brief and partisan *Historia contra Paganos* of Orosius (which ends in 417), and fragments of secular historians, Olympiodorus (407–425) and Priscus (433–474). There is, however, for the latter half of the fourth and the first half of the fifth centuries an abundance of ancillary sources. There are the speeches of Libanius, professor of Greek literature at Antioch, which deal with many current topics of his day; the lives of saints; and the letters of many prominent laymen and ecclesiastics—Libanius; Symmachus, a senator who was prefect of the city in 383; Augustine; Theodoret, bishop of Cyrrhus in Syria in the middle of the fifth century; and Sidonius Apollinaris, a Gallic senator who became bishop of Auvergne in 469. These sources supply abundant materials, particularly on the social life of all classes, from the great senators of Rome to humble peasants.

The historians are mainly interested in the political and military history of the empire, and do not tell us much about its organization and its law, which were its great contribution to history and its chief interest to us. In this sphere we have three main sources.

The Digest is a collection of extracts from the legal writers of the first, second, and early third centuries, drawn up on the orders of Justinian in A.D. 533; the great bulk of the extracts come from the early third century. The Digest not only gives us a full conspectus of private law, but much interesting detail on imperial and municipal organization.

The inscriptions, which are abundant from the reign of Augustus to the Severi, include laws and decrees of the senate, and also imperial edicts and letters, edicts and letters of provincial governors and procurators, charters of cities, giving details of their constitutions, and decrees of cities, honorific or practical. Another interesting class is the *diplomata* or discharge certificates given to veterans. Even more important are the thousands of private inscriptions, engraved on the bases of statues or on tombstones, which set out the careers of senators, equestrian officials, soldiers, imperial slaves and freedmen, and municipal worthies. It is from these that we gain detailed information on the administrative system, the civil service, and the army and can trace the growth of the army and the gradual infusion of provincials into the equestrian order and the senate. It has even proved possible from the ages recorded on tombstones to work out the vital statistics of the Roman empire.

The papyri are the waste paper from the rubbish heaps of Egyptian villages and towns, preserved owing to the dry climate of Egypt. They are a very mixed bag, including governmental regulations, official correspondence, census returns, tax receipts, contracts, leases, wills, records of legal proceedings, private accounts, and letters. They give a far more intimate picture of the daily life of Egypt than is possible for any other province and, in particular, supply economic information on prices, rents, and wages which is not available elsewhere.

Inscriptions begin again under Diocletian, but are rarer. They include some important imperial laws, such as Diocletian's edict on prices, which fixed wages and prices in immense detail in 302. This is a very valuable document for economic history. Papyri also continue to illuminate the life of Egypt, administrative, financial, judicial, and military as well as private affairs. For the administration of the empire our most important source is the legal codes. The Theodosian Code ws compiled in 437 and was supposed to contain all imperial constitutions from 312 to that date. Many laws are missing from the earlier period, but it remains a treasure house for the administrative, fiscal, social, and economic history of the later empire. The Justinian Code, compiled in 534, is a more selective collection, including only constitutions still valid at that date, and these in an abbreviated form, but it includes laws of Diocletian and fills other lacunae in the Theodosian Code.

As this book is about institutions rather than events, I have arranged the material by topics and not chronologically; within the chapters the order is roughly chronological, though I have often preferred to group similar documents together. I have allotted, I hope, sufficient space to the major historians, but I have given the preference to firsthand contemporary documents, mostly preserved in inscription and papyri, not only laws, edicts, imperial letters, and administrative documents, but also private contracts and correspondence. This I have done partly because such documents are more difficult of access to the general reader—who can read the main literary sources in many good translations—but more because they give a more vivid and perhaps a more authentic picture of the society of the age.

I. The Foundation of the Principate

1. The acts of the deified Augustus

This long obituary notice was composed by Augustus himself and kept up to date to the year of his death (§4). He ordered it to be engraved on two bronze plaques outside his mausoleum. These have perished, but copies of the Latin original or of the official Greek translation were engraved on temples at Ancyra, Apollonia, and Antioch of Pisidia, and from these it is possible to reconstitute the entire text.

It is highly unlikely that in such a document Augustus put any false statement on record. But if he told nothing but the truth, he did not necessarily tell the whole truth. He naturally passed lightly over those aspects of his career which he wished to be forgotten, and emphasized those which he wished to be remembered. He skates very lightly over the civil wars, not mentioning by name any of his opponents; the suppression of Sextus Pompeius is covered by the sentence: "I freed the sea from pirates" (§25).

In his record of his military and diplomatic triumphs he gives no hint that the Arabian expedition (§26) was a dismal failure, or that he failed in the end to maintain client kings in Armenia (§27). Nor does he record the withdrawal from the Elbe to the Rhine after the disastrous defeat of Varus (§26).

He is also disingenuous about his constitutional prerogatives. He records at great length his titular offices and honors, but in his account of the settlement of 27 B.C. (§34) he omits to mention that he received a province comprising more than half the empire and containing the bulk of the legions (cf. Nos. 3, 4); in fact he never alludes to his lifelong tenure of this province, which was the real basis of his power. He makes no allusion to the political crisis of 23 B.C. (cf. No. 5) except very obliquely in §§4 and 10. He enlarges on the honors paid to him and the offices he refused in the following period (§§5–6, 11–12) but omits the powers conferred on him in 19 B.C. (see No. 7).

On the other hand he gives a very full account of the buildings with which he adorned Rome (§§19–21) and of the money which he spent on games and largesses to the Roman populace (§§15, 22–23), on the settlement of his veterans (§16), and on subventions to the treasury (§§17, 18). Some of these gifts came from the spoils of war (§§15, 21), which by Roman custom a commander could spend as he saw fit, but the bulk from his private fortune, which was very large; he inherited

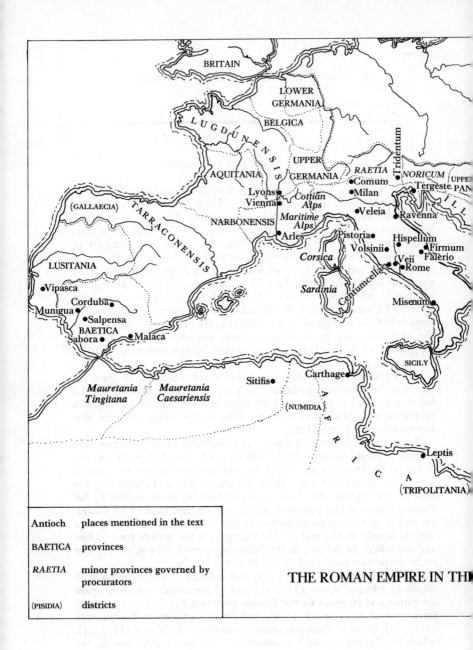

THE ROMAN EMPIRE IN TH

Antioch · places mentioned in the text

BAETICA · provinces

RAETIA · minor provinces governed by procurators

(PISIDIA) · districts

SECOND CENTURY A.D.

two estates, his father's and his adoptive father's, and received fourteen hundred million sesterces in legacies during his lifetime. The imperial patrimony, which passed from emperor to emperor and was constantly increased by legacies and later confiscations, was thus from the first an important supplement to the state's resources, and soon became virtually a public department. The standard coins of the Roman Empire from Augustus to the early third century were the *aureus* (a gold piece), equal to 25 *denarii* (silver pieces) and to 100 *sesterces* (copper pieces). The *denarius* was thus worth 4 sesterces and 16 *asses* (also copper). It is impossible to give modern monetary equivalents, but during the first century a private soldier received 225 *denarii* p.a. out of which he paid for his rations and uniform and could save nearly half (see No. 57).

1. V. Ehrenberg and A. H. M. Jones, Documents, *No. 1*

BELOW IS A copy of the acts of the deified Augustus, by which he placed the whole world under the sovereignty of the Roman people, and of the amounts which he expended upon the state and the Roman people, as engraved upon two bronze columns which have been set up in Rome.

1. AT THE AGE of nineteen, on my own initiative and at my own expense, I raised an army by means of which I restored liberty to the republic, which had been oppressed by the tyranny of a faction. For which service the senate, with complimentary resolutions, enrolled me in its order, in the consulship of Gaius Pansa and Aulus Hirtius [43 B.C.], giving me at the same time consular precedence in voting; it also gave me the *imperium*. As propraetor it ordered me, along with the consuls, to see that the republic suffered no harm. In the same year, moreover, as both consuls had fallen in war, the people elected me consul and a triumvir for settling the constitution.

2. Those who had killed my father I drove into exile, punishing their deed by due process of law, and afterward when they waged war upon the republic I twice defeated them in battle.

3. Wars, both civil and foreign, I undertook throughout the world, on sea and land, and when victorious I spared all citizens who sued for pardon. The foreign nations which could with safety be pardoned I preferred to save rather than to destroy. The number of Roman citizens who bound themselves to me by military oath was about five hundred thousand. Of these I settled in colonies or sent back to their own towns, after their term of

service, something more than three hundred thousand, and to all I assigned lands or gave money as a reward for military service. I captured six hundred ships, over and above those which were smaller than triremes.

4. Twice I triumphed with an ovation, thrice I celebrated curule triumphs, and was saluted as imperator twenty-one times. Although the senate decreed me additional triumphs I set them aside. When I had performed the vows which I had undertaken in each war I deposited upon the Capitol the laurels which adorned my *fasces*. For successful operations on land and sea, conducted either myself or by my lieutenants under my auspices, the senate on fifty-five occasions decreed that thanks should be rendered to the immortal gods. The days on which such thanks should be rendered by decree of the senate numbered 890. In my triumphs there were led before my chariot nine kings or children of kings. At the time of writing these words I had been thirteen times consul, and was in the thirty-seventh year of my tribunician power.

5. The dictatorship offered me by the people and the Roman senate, in my absence and later when present, in the consulship of Marcus Marcellus and Lucius Arruntius [22 B.C.], I did not accept. I did not decline at a time of the greatest scarcity of grain the charge of the grain supply, which I so administered that, within a few days, I freed the entire people at my own expense from the fear and danger in which they were. The consulship, either yearly or for life, then offered me I did not accept.

6. In the consulship of Marcus Vinicius and Quintus Lucretius [19 B.C.], and afterward in that of Publius and Gnaeus Lentulus [18 B.C.], and a third time in that of Paullus Fabius Maximus and Quintus Tubero [11 B.C.], when the senate and the Roman people unanimously agreed that I should be elected overseer of laws and morals, without a colleague and with the fullest power, I refused to accept any power offered me which was contrary to the traditions of our ancestors. Those things which at that time the senate wished me to administer I carried out by virtue of my tribunician power. And even in this office I five times received from the senate a colleague at my own request.

7. For ten years in succession I was one of the triumvirs for the re-establishment of the constitution. To the day of writing this I have been *princeps senatus* for forty years. I have been *pontifex maximus*, augur, a member of the fifteen commissioners for performing

sacred rites, one of the seven for sacred feasts, an Arval brother, a
sodalis Titius, a fetial priest.

8. As consul for the fifth time [29 B.C.], by order of the people
and the senate I increased the number of the patricians. Three times
I revised the roll of the senate. In my sixth consulship, with Marcus
Agrippa as my colleague [28 B.C.], I made a census of the people. I
performed the *lustrum* after an interval of forty-one years. In this
lustrum 4,063,000 Roman citizens were entered on the census roll.
A second time, in the consulship of Gaius Censorinus and Gaius
Asinius [8 B.C.], I again performed the *lustrum* alone, with the
consular *imperium*. In this *lustrum* 4,233,000 Roman citizens were
entered on the census roll. A third time, with the consular *imperium*, and with my son Tiberius Caesar as my colleague, I performed the *lustrum* in the consulship of Sextus Pompeius and
Sextus Apuleius [A.D. 14]. In this *lustrum* 4,937,000 Roman citizens were entered on the census roll. By the passage of new laws I
restored many traditions of our ancestors which were then falling
into disuse, and I myself set precedents in many things for posterity
to imitate.

9. The senate decreed that every fifth year vows should be undertaken for my health by the consuls and the priests. In fulfillment
of these vows games were often held in my lifetime, sometimes by
the four chief colleges of priests, sometimes by the consuls. In
addition the entire body of citizens with one accord, both individually and by municipalities, performed continued sacrifices for
my health at all the couches of the gods.

10. By decree of the senate my name was included in the Salian
hymn, and it was enacted by law that my person should be sacred
in perpetuity and that so long as I lived I should hold the tribunician power. I declined to be made *pontifex maximus* in succession
to a colleague still living, when the people tendered me that
priesthood which my father had held. Several years later I accepted
that sacred office when he at last was dead who, taking advantage
of a time of civil disturbance, had seized it for himself, such a
multitude from all Italy assembling for my election, in the consulship of Publius Sulpicius and Gaius Valgius [12 B.C.], as is never
recorded to have been in Rome before.

11. The senate consecrated in honor of my return an altar to
Fortuna Redux at the Porta Capena, near the temple of Honor and
Virtue, on which it ordered the pontiffs and the Vestal virgins to

perform a yearly sacrifice on the anniversary of the day on which I
returned to the city from Syria, in the consulship of Lucius Lucretius and Marcus Vinicius [19 B.C.], and named the day, after my
cognomen, the Augustalia.

12. At the same time, by decree of the senate, part of the praetors
and of the tribunes of the people, together with the consul Quintus
Lucretius and the leading men of the state, were sent to Campania
to meet me, an honor which up to the present time has been decreed to no one except myself. When I returned from Spain and
Gaul, in the consulship of Tiberius Nero and Publius Quintilius
[13 B.C.], after successful operations in those provinces, the senate
voted in honor of my return the consecration of an altar to Pax
Augusta in the Campus Martius, and on this altar it ordered the
magistrates and priests and Vestal virgins to make annual sacrifice.

13. Janus Quirinus, which our ancestors ordered to be closed
whenever there was peace, secured by victory, throughout the
whole domain of the Roman people on land and sea, and which,
before my birth is recorded to have been closed but twice in all
since the foundation of the city, the senate ordered to be closed
thrice while I was *princeps*.

14. My sons Gaius and Lucius Caesar, whom fortune snatched
away from me in their youth, the senate and the Roman people to
do me honor made consuls designate, each in his fifteenth year,
providing that each should enter upon that office after a period of
five years. The senate decreed that from the day on which they
were introduced to the forum they should take part in the councils of state. Moreover, the entire body of Roman *equites* gave
each of them the title of *princeps iuventutis* and presented them
with silver shields and spears.

15. To the Roman *plebs* I paid out three hundred sesterces per
man in accordance with the will of my father, and in my own
name in my fifth consulship [29 B.C.] I gave four hundred sesterces
apiece from the spoils of war; a second time, moreover, in my tenth
consulship [24 B.C.] I paid out of my own patrimony four hundred
sesterces per man by way of bounty, and in my eleventh consulship [23 B.C.] I made twelve distributions of food from grain
bought at my own expense, and in the twelfth year of my tribunician power [12 B.C.] I gave for the third time four hundred
sesterces to each man. These largesses of mine reached a number of
persons never less than two hundred and fifty thousand. In the

eighteenth year of my tribunician power, as consul for the twelfth time [5 B.C.], I gave to three hundred and twenty thousand of the city *plebs* sixty denarii apiece. In the colonies of my soldiers, as consul for the fifth time [29 B.C.], I gave one thousand sesterces to each man from the spoils of war; about one hundred and twenty thousand men in the colonies received this triumphal largesse. When consul for the thirteenth time [2 B.C.] I gave sixty denarii apiece to the *plebs* who were then receiving public grain; these were a little more than two hundred thousand persons.

16. To the municipal towns I paid money for the lands which I assigned to soldiers in my own fourth consulship [30 B.C.] and afterward in the consulship of Marcus Crassus and Gnaeus Lentulus the augur [14 B.C.]. The sum which I paid for estates in Italy was about six hundred million sesterces, and the amount which I paid for lands in the provinces was about two hundred and sixty million. I was the first and only one to do this of all those who up to my time settled colonies of soldiers in Italy or in the provinces. And later, in the consulship of Tiberius Nero and Gnaeus Piso [7 B.C.], likewise in the consulship of Gaius Antistius and Decimus Laelius [6 B.C.], and of Gaius Calvisius and Lucius Pasienus [4 B.C.], and of Lucius Lentulus and Marcus Messala [3 B.C.], and of Lucius Caninius and Quintus Fabricius [2 B.C.], I paid cash gratuities to the soldiers whom I settled in their own towns at the expiration of their service, and for this purpose I expended four hundred million sesterces as an act of grace.

17. Four times I aided the public treasury with my own money, paying out in this manner to those in charge of the treasury one hundred and fifty million sesterces. And in the consulship of Marcus Lepidus and Lucius Arruntius [A.D. 6] I contributed one hundred and seventy million sesterces out of my own patrimony to the military treasury, which was established on my advice that from it gratuities might be paid to soldiers who had seen twenty or more years of service.

18. Beginning with the year in which Gnaeus and Publius Lentulus were consuls [18 B.C.], whenever taxes were in arrears, I furnished from my own purse and my own patrimony tickets for grain and money, sometimes to a hundred thousand persons, sometimes to many more.

19. I built the *Curia* and the Chalcidicum adjoining it, the temple of Apollo on the Palatine with its porticoes, the temple of the

deified Julius, the Lupercal, the portico at the Circus Flaminius
which I allowed to be called Octavia after the name of him who
had constructed an earlier one on the same site, the state box at the
Circus Maximus, the temples on the Capitol of Jupiter Feretrius
and Jupiter Tonans, the temple of Quirinus, the temples of
Minerva, of Juno the Queen, and of Jupiter Libertas, on the
Aventine, the temple of the Lares at the highest point of the Sacra
Via, the Temple of the Di Penates on the Velia, the temple of
Youth, and the temple of the Great Mother on the Palatine.

20. The Capitolium and the theater of Pompey, both works in-
volving great expense, I rebuilt without any inscription of my own
name. I restored the channels of the aqueducts which in several
places were falling into disrepair through age, and doubled the
capacity of the aqueduct called the Marcia by turning a new spring
into its channel. I completed the Julian Forum and the basilica
which was between the temple of Castor and the temple of Saturn,
works begun and far advanced by my father, and when the same
basilica was destroyed by fire I began its reconstruction on an
enlarged site, to be inscribed with the names of my sons, and
ordered that in case I should not live to complete it, it should be
completed by my heirs. In my sixth consulship [28 B.C.], in accordance with a decree of the senate, I rebuilt in the city eighty-
two temples of the gods, omitting none which at that time stood in
need of repair. As consul for the seventh time [27 B.C.] I constructed the Via Flaminia from the city to Ariminum, and all the
bridges except the Mulvian and the Minucian.

21. On my own ground I built the temple of Mars Ultor and the
Augustan Forum from the spoils of war. On ground purchased for
the most part from private owners I built the theater near the
temple of Apollo which was to bear the name of my son-in-law
Marcus Marcellus. From the spoils of war I consecrated offerings
on the Capitol, and in the temple of the divine Julius, and in the
temple of Apollo, and in the temple of Vesta, and in the temple of
Mars Ultor, which cost me about one hundred million sesterces. In
my fifth consulship [29 B.C.] I remitted thirty-five thousand
pounds weight of crown gold contributed by the municipalities
and the colonies of Italy, and thereafter, whenever I was saluted as
imperator, I did not accept the crown gold, although the municipalities and colonies voted it in the same kindly spirit as before.

22. Three times in my own name I gave a show of gladiators, and

five times in the name of my sons or grandsons; in these shows there fought about ten thousand men. Twice in my own name I furnished for the people an exhibition of athletes gathered from all parts of the world, and a third time in the name of my grandsons. Four times I gave games in my own name; as representing other magistrates twenty-three times. For the college of quindecemvirs, as master of that college and with Marcus Agrippa as my colleague, I conducted the Secular Games in the consulship of Gaius Furnius and Marcus Silanus [17 B.C.]. In my thirteenth consulship [2 B.C.] I gave, for the first time, the games of Mars, which, since that time, the consuls by decree of the senate have given in successive years in conjunction with me. In my own name, or that of my sons or grandsons, on twenty-six occasions I gave to the people, in the circus, in the forum, or in the amphitheater, hunts of African wild beasts, in which about three thousand five hundred beasts were slain.

23. I gave the people the spectacle of a naval battle beyond the Tiber, at the place where now stands the grove of the Caesars, the ground having been excavated for a length of eighteen hundred and a breadth of twelve hundred feet. In this spectacle thirty beaked ships, triremes or biremes, and a large number of smaller vessels met in conflict. In these fleets there fought about three thousand men exclusive of the rowers.

24. After my victory I replaced in the temples in all the cities of the province of Asia the ornaments which my antagonist in the war, when he despoiled the temples, had appropriated to his private use. Silver statues of me, on foot, on horseback, and in chariots were erected in the city to the number of about eighty; these I myself removed, and from the money thus obtained I placed in the temple of Apollo golden offerings in my own name and in the name of those who had paid me the honor of a statue.

25. I freed the sea from pirates. About thirty thousand slaves, captured in that war, who had run away from their masters and had taken up arms against the republic, I delivered to their masters for punishment. The whole of Italy voluntarily took oath of allegiance to me and demanded me as its leader in the war in which I was victorious at Actium. The provinces of the Spains, the Gauls, Africa, Sicily, and Sardinia took the same oath of allegiance. Those who served under my standards at that time included more than seven hundred senators, and among them eighty-three who had

previously or have since been consuls up to the day on which these
words were written, and about one hundred and seventy have been
priests.

26. I extended the boundaries of all the provinces which were
bordered by races not yet subject to our empire. The provinecs of
the Gauls, the Spains, and Germany, bounded by the ocean from
Gades to the mouth of the Elbe, I reduced to a state of peace. The
Alps, from the region which lies nearest to the Adriatic as far as
the Tuscan Sea, I brought to a state of peace without waging on
any tribe an unjust war. My fleet sailed from the mouth of the
Rhine eastward as far as the lands of the Cimbri to which, up to
that time, no Roman had ever penetrated either by land or by sea,
and the Cimbri and Charydes and Semnones and other peoples of
the Germans of that same region through their envoys sought my
friendship and that of the Roman people. On my order and under
my auspices two armies were led, at almost the same time, into
Ethiopia and into Arabia which is called "The Happy," and very
large forces of the enemy of both races were cut to pieces in battle
and many towns were captured. Ethiopia was penetrated as far as
the town of Nabata, which is next to Meroe. In Arabia the army
advanced into the territories of the Sabaei to the town of Mariba.

27. Egypt I added to the empire of the Roman people. In the case
of Greater Armenia, though I might have made it a province after
the assassination of its King Artaxes, I preferred, following the
precedent of our fathers, to hand that kingdom over to Tigranes,
the son of King Artavasdes, and grandson of King Tigranes,
through Tiberius Nero, who was then my stepson. And later,
when the same people revolted and rebelled, and was subdued by
my son Gaius, I gave it over to King Ariobarzanes the son of
Artabazus, king of the Medes, to rule, and after his death to his son
Artavasdes. When he was murdered I sent into that kingdom
Tigranes, who was sprung from the royal family of the Armenians.
I recovered all the provinces extending eastward beyond the Adriatic Sea, and Cyrenae, which were then for the most part in possession of kings, and, at an earlier time, Sicily and Sardinia, which had
been seized in the servile war.

28. I settled colonies of soldiers in Africa, Sicily, Macedonia, both
Spains, Achaia, Asia, Syria, Gallia Narbonensis, Pisidia. Moreover,
Italy has twenty-eight colonies founded under my auspices which
have grown to be famous and populous during my lifetime.

29. From Spain, Gaul, and the Dalmatians, I recovered, after conquering the enemy, many military standards which had been lost by other generals. The Parthians I compelled to restore to me the spoils and standards of three Roman armies, and to seek as suppliants the friendship of the Roman people. These standards I deposited in the inner shrine which is in the temple of Mars Ultor.

30. The tribes of the Pannonians, to which no army of the Roman people had ever penetrated before my principate, having been subdued by Tiberius Nero, who was then my stepson and my legate, I brought under the sovereignty of the Roman people, and I pushed forward the frontier of Illyricum as far as the bank of the river Danube. An army of Dacians which crossed to the south of that river was, under my auspices, defeated and crushed, and afterward my own army was led across the Danube and compelled the tribes of the Dacians to submit to the orders of the Roman people.

31. Embassies were often sent to me from the kings of India, a thing never seen before in the camp of any general of the Romans. Our friendship was sought, through ambassadors, by the Bastarnae and Scythians, and by the Kings of the Sarmatians who live on either side of the river Tanais, and by the kings of the Albani and of the Hiberi and of the Medes.

32. Kings of the Parthians, Tiridates, and later Phrates, the son of King Phrates, took refuge with me as suppliants; of the Medes, Artavasdes; of the Adiabeni, Artaxares, of the Britons, Dumnobellaunus and Tim——; of the Sugambri, Maelo; of the Marcomanni and Suevi——rus. Phrates, son of Orodes, king of the Parthians, sent all his sons and grandsons to me in Italy, not because he had been conquered in war, but rather seeking our friendship by means of his own children as pledges. And a large number of other nations experienced the good faith of the Roman people during my principate who never before had had any interchange of embassies or of friendship with the Roman people.

33. From me the peoples of the Parthians and of the Medes received the kings for whom they asked through ambassadors, the chief men of those peoples; the Parthians Vonones, son of King Phrates, grandson of King Orodes; the Medes Ariobarzanes, the son of King Artavazdes, grandson of King Ariobarzanes.

34. In my sixth and seventh consulships [28–27 B.C.], when I had

extinguished the flames of civil war, after receiving by universal consent the absolute control of affairs, I transferred the republic from my own control to the will of the senate and the Roman people. For this service on my part I was given the title of Augustus by decree of the senate, and the doorposts of my house were covered with laurels by public act, and a civic crown was fixed above my door, and a golden shield was placed in the Curia Julia whose inscription testified that the senate and the Roman people gave me this in recognition of my valor, my clemency, my justice, and my piety. After that time I took precedence of all in authority, but of power I possessed no more than those who were my colleagues in any magistracy.

35. While I was administering my thirteenth consulship [2 B.C.] the senate and the equestrian order and the entire Roman people gave me the title of "Father of my Country," and decreed that this title should be inscribed upon the vestibule of my house and in the senate house and in the Forum Augustum beneath the quadriga erected in my honor by decree of the senate. At the time of writing this I was in my seventy-sixth year.

SUMMARY

1. The sum total of the money which he contributed to the treasury or to the Roman *plebs* or to discharged soldiers was six hundred million denarii.

2. The new works which he built were: the temple of Mars, of Jupiter Tonans and Feretrius, of Apollo, of the deified Julius, of Quirinus, of Minerva, of Juno the Queen, of Jupiter Libertas, of the Lares, of the Di Penates, of Youth, of the Mother of the Gods, the Lupercal, the state box at the circus, the senate house with the Chalcidicum, the Augustan Forum, the Basilica Julia, the theater of Marcellus,————the grove of the Caesars beyond the Tiber.

3. He restored the Capitol and sacred buildings to the number of eighty-two, the theater of Pompey, the aqueducts, the Flaminian Way.

4. The expenditures provided for theatrical shows, gladiatorial sports, for exhibitions of athletes, for hunts of wild beasts, and the naval combat, and his gifts to colonies in Italy, to cities in the provinces which had been destroyed by earthquake or conflagration, or to individual friends and senators whose property he raised to the required rating, are too numerous to be reckoned.

2. The restoration of the republic in 27 B.C.

This passage describes in lyrical terms the restoration of the republican form of government after the triumviral period, which is mentioned in §34 of Augustus' *Res Gestae*. Octavian, as it appears from that passage, renounced the extraordinary powers which he had hitherto exercised in virtue of the oath of allegiances (see No. 9), remaining consul, an office to which he had been elected every year since 31 B.C. In return he received a massive group of provinces, which contained most of the legions (see Nos. 3, 4), with powers of peace and war. He may also have been given some vague authority over the republic as a whole (see Nos. 3, 4). What was emphasized, however, was the restoration of the republic, and this passage shows how successful the change was as a propaganda move among the Italian upper class from which Velleius came. Velleius is mistaken in putting the two additional praetors at this date; they were added in 23 B.C. (cf. No. 4).

2. *Velleius Paterculus, II. 89*

WHEN CAESAR returned to Italy and the city, the concourse and applause whereby he was greeted by all men, ages, and ranks, and the magnificence of his triumphs and his games could not be worthily expressed in a regular historical work, much less in this brief summary. Thereafter men could hope for nothing from the gods, the gods could give nothing to men, nothing could be the object of prayer and the gift of good fortune that Augustus did not bestow upon the republic and upon the world after his return to the city. After twenty years the civil wars were ended, foreign wars buried, peace recalled, the fury of arms everywhere lulled to sleep; their force restored to the laws, authority to the courts, its majesty to the senate; the rule of the magistrates was restored to its old form—only two praetors were added to the eight. The ancient original form of the commonwealth was recalled. Tillage returned to the fields, its honor to religion, security to men, firm possession of his property to the individual. The laws were advantageously emended, and new laws passed for the good of the state. The senate was chosen without harshness, but not without severity. The leading men, who had enjoyed triumphs and the highest offices, were encouraged by the prompting of the leading man of the state (*princeps*) to adorn the city. Caesar, though he often struggled against it and resisted, was unable to prevent the consulate being continued up to an eleventh time; the dictatorship, which the people obstinately offered to him, he as firmly refused. The wars waged under his command, and the victorious pacification of the world, and his many buildings at home and outside Italy would weary a historian, who should devote a whole lifetime to that task alone. We, remembering our professed purpose, have presented to your eyes and mind a general picture of his reign.

3. The division of the provinces in 27 B.C.

Strabo's list of public provinces is slightly inaccurate in that he includes Gallia Narbonensis and Cyprus, which were added in 23 B.C. (see No. 6). And Strabo is not quite right in saying that all the public provinces were peaceful and ungarrisoned. Illyricum and Macedonia were exposed to very turbulent barbarian tribes, and Africa also required a small garrison (one legion). Illyricum was, however, transferred to the emperor c. 11 B.C. and Macedonia ceased to be a frontier province with the annexation of Moesia. Note that Augustus was given the power of peace and war (and also of making treaties, cf. No. 8, §1) in 27 B.C. Note also that Augustus received full authority over client kings—which would follow from the right of peace and war. Strabo also speaks of his receiving a vague "leadership of the empire," which is also mentioned in Dio (No. 4).

3. Strabo, XVIII. iii. 24–25, 839–40

OF ALL this territory which is subject to the Romans, some is ruled by kings, and they themselves hold the rest under the name of "provinces," sending out governors and collectors of taxes. There are also free cities, some which originally joined them in friendly relations, and others which have been freed by the Romans themselves as an honor. There are also various dynasts and tribal chiefs and priests. These live under their own ancestral laws. The provinces have been divided up in various ways at different times, but at present they are as Caesar Augustus laid down. For when his native country entrusted him with the leadership of the empire and he was given the power of war and peace for life, he divided all Roman territory into two and assigned one part to himself and the other to the people. To himself he gave whatever required a military garrison, that is the barbarian area which is near the tribes which have not yet been subdued, or is rugged and unsuited to agriculture, so that for lack of other resources and having plenty of strongholds the population is restive and disobedient; to the people the rest which is peaceful and easy to govern without military force. He divided each section into a number of provinces, some called Caesar's, the others those of the people. Caesar sends out governors and administrators to Caesar's provinces, dividing the territory up in various ways from time to time, making arrangements suitable to the occasion. The people send out ex-praetors or ex-consuls to the public provinces: they, too, are distributed in various ways as convenience dictates. But at the beginning he made two provinces consular, Africa (the part under Roman rule, excluding the area ruled first by Juba and now by his son Ptolemy) and Asia within the Halys and the Taurus, excluding the Galatians and other tribes under Amyntas and Bithynia and Propontis, and ten praetorian: in Europe and the adjacent islands, the so-called Further Spain on the rivers Baetis and Anas and Narbonensis of the Celtic area; third, Sardinia and Corsica; fourth, Sicily; fifth and sixth, the part of Illyricum next Epirus and Macedonia; seventh, Achaea, including Thessaly and Aetolia and Acarnania and the tribes of Epirus adjacent to Macedonia; eighth, Crete with Cyrenaica; ninth, Cyprus; tenth, Bithynia with Propontis and some parts of Pontus. Caesar has the other provinces and sends consuls to look after some of them, and praetors to some, and equestrians to some. And kings and dynasts and decarchies are in his portion and always were.

4. The constitution of the principate

This is Cassius Dio's account of the settlement in 27 B.C.; the circumstantial description of the senate's reception of Augustus' proposal looks as if it comes from a contemporary source. Dio, however, writing more than two centuries later, when the imperial autocracy was taken for granted, is too prone to assume that it sprang into being forthwith in 27 B.C. He is, however, supported by Strabo's nearly contemporary account (No. 3) in stating that Augustus not only took a group of provinces but some general care of the state as a whole. This is perhaps expressed in the fifth clause in the *lex de imperio* (No. 8, §5). In his account of the administrative arrangements Dio describes the practice of his own day, occasionally noting where it differed from the original scheme. It may simplify Dio's account to set out in tabular form the various classes of officials in the public and imperial provinces; for the special position of Egypt, see No. 78.

Public Provinces		Imperial Provinces
Asia and Africa	The rest	
proconsul (ex-consul)	proconsul (ex-praetor)	*legatus Augusti pro-praetore* (ex-consul or ex-praetor)
quaestor	quaestor	[*legati legionis*, ex-praetors or ex-quaestors]
three *legati* (*pro praetore*)	*legatus* (*pro praetore*)	procurator (*eques*)
procurator (*eques*)	procurator (*eques*)	legionary tribunes (future senators and other *equites*)
		tribunes and praefects of auxiliary units (*equites*)

Proconsuls were in supreme charge of their provinces; as they had no armies their duties were mainly judicial, and general supervision of the cities. The legates assisted them in these duties, their quaestors were financial officers. The procurator of a public province was concerned only with the emperor's estates. In the imperial provinces most *legati Augusti* were primarily military commanders, but were also responsible for jurisdiction and supervision. In their military capacity they were assisted by their *legati legionis* and subordinate officers (tribunes and prefects). For their judicial work some had *legati iuridici*. Some *legati Augusti* had no troops (and therefore no *legati legionis*, etc.) and only exercised jurisdiction and supervised the administration. In imperial provinces the procurator had charge both of imperial property and public finance. See No. 77.

Dio is not quite right on the early system for the allotment of provinces (see Nos. 29, 81), and his constitutional law is not very good. The governors of the imperial provinces were not called propraetors but *legati Augusti pro praetore*, "delegates of Augustus with the power of a praetor," and were so called not because they had duties which were military, but because, since they were delegates of Augustus, their *imperium* had to be of a lower grade than the consular *imperium* of their chief. It is curious that he only incidentally alludes to the provinces other than Egypt that were governed by *equites*, styled at first *praefecti*, later procurators. This type of province already existed under Augustus; it was small and unimportant.

On the imperial titulature and powers Dio reflects the constitutional thinking of his own day, but is tolerably accurate on his facts. *Imperator* was used twice, as a first name (*praenomen*) by Augustus, and from Nero onward; and with a number to mark the number of times that an emperor had been so saluted by the army (on his accession and

for subsequent victories). Neither the *praenomen* nor the title of
imperator had any constitutional significance. All emperors were proconsuls for life of their group of provinces, but did not use the title
until Trajan. They held the consulship from time to time, but this did
not increase their power. The tribunician power, first granted to
Augustus in 23 B.C. (see No. 5), was numbered annually, and was used
to date the year of the reign. All emperors were elected *pontifex
maximus* from Augustus onward (see No. 1, §10). All exercised
censorial powers, though only Domitian took the title. The title of
Father of his Country (*pater patriae*) given to Augustus (see No. 1,
§35) and to his successors was purely honorific. Caesar was a family
surname adopted by Claudius, though he was not of the Caesarian
family, and by all subsequent emperors except Vitellius. Augustus was
an honorary surname bestowed by the senate on Augustus (see No. 1,
§34) and all subsequent emperors. The emperors were originally
exempted from certain statutes only (see No. 8, §6), but this was by
Dio's day interpreted as exemption from all laws.

For examples of the imperial titulature, see Nos. 62–64, 87–88,
96–101, 141.

4. *Cassius Dio, LIII. 11–18*

WHILE CAESAR was engaged in setting his decision before them,
varied feelings filled the minds of the senators. A few of them
knew his real intention and as a result kept applauding him enthusi-
astically. Of the rest some were suspicious of what was said and
others believed in it, and were therefore both equally amazed, the
one class at his great subtlety and the other at the decision that he
had reached. One side was displeased at his involved scheming and
the other at his change of mind. For already there were some who
detested the republican constitution as a source of factional difficulties, were pleased at the change of government, and took delight
in Caesar. Consequently, though the announcement affected different persons differently, their views in regard to it were in each case
the same. As for those who believed his sentiments to be genuine,
any who wished it could not rejoice because of fear, nor the others
lament because of hope. And as many as disbelieved it did not
venture to accuse him and confute him, some because they were
afraid, and others because they did not care to do so. Hence they
all either were compelled or pretended to believe him. As for
praising him, some did not have the courage and others were
unwilling. Even in the midst of his reading there were frequent
shouts and afterward many more. The senators begged that a

monarchy be established, and directed all their remarks to that end until they forced him to assume the reins of government. At once they saw to it that twice as much pay was voted to the men who were to compose his bodyguard as to the rest of the soldiers, that this might incite the men to keep a careful watch of him. Then he began to show a real interest in setting up a monarchy.

In this way he had his headship ratified by the senate and the people. As he wished even so to appear to be republican in principle, he accepted all the care and superintendence of public business on the ground that it required expert attention, but said that he would not personally govern all the provinces and those that he did govern he would not keep in his charge perpetually. The weaker ones, because (as he said) they were peaceful and free from war, he gave over to the senate. But the more powerful he held in possession because they were unsettled and dangerous and either had enemies in adjoining territory or on their own account were able to cause a great uprising. His pretext was that the senate should fearlessly gather the fruits of the finest portion of the empire, while he himself had the labors and dangers; his real purpose was that by this plan the senators be unarmed and unprepared for battle, while he alone had arms and kept soldiers. Africa and Numidia, Asia and Greece with Epirus, the Dalmatian and Macedonian territories, Sicily, Crete, and Libya adjacent to Cyrene, Bithynia with the adjoining Pontus, Sardinia, and Baetica, were consequently held to belong to the people and the senate. Caesar's were the remainder of Spain, the neighborhood of Tarraco and Lusitania, all the Gauls (the Narbonensian and the Lugdunensian, the Aquitani and the Belgae), both themselves and the aliens settled among them. Some of the Celts whom we call Germans had occupied all the Belgic territory near the Rhine and caused it to be called Germania, the upper part extending to the sources of the river and the lower part reaching to the Ocean of Britain. These provinces, then, and the so-called Hollow Syria, Phoenicia and Cilicia, Cyprus and the Egyptians, fell at that time to Caesar's share. Later he gave Cyprus and Gaul adjacent to Narbo back to the people, and he himself took Dalmatia instead. This was also done subsequently in the case of other provinces, as the progress of my narrative will show. I have enumerated these in such detail because now each one of them is ruled separately, whereas in old times and for a long period the provinces were governed two and

three together. The others I have not mentioned because some of
them were acquired later, and the rest, even if they had been
already subdued, were not being governed by the Romans, but
either were left to enjoy their own laws or had been turned over to
some kingdom or other. All of them that after this came into the
Roman empire were attached to the possessions of the emperor
then ruling. This then was the division of the provinces.

Wishing to lead the Romans still further away from the idea that
he looked upon himself as absolute monarch, Caesar undertook the
government of the regions given him for ten years. In the course of
this time he promised to reduce them to quiet and he carried his
hypocrisy to the point of saying that if they should be sooner
pacified, he would deliver them sooner to the senate. Thereupon he
first appointed the senators themselves to govern both classes of
provinces except Egypt. This land, alone, for the reasons mentioned, he assigned to the *eques* previously named. Next he ordained that the rulers of senatorial provinces should be annual
magistrates, selected by lot, unless any one had the special privilege
accorded to a large number of children or to marriage. They were
to be sent out by the general assembly of the senate, with no sword
at their side and not wearing the military garb. The name proconsul
was to belong not only to the two ex-consuls but also to the rest
who had served as praetors or who at least held the rank of ex-
praetors. Both classes were to employ as many lictors as were usual
in the capital. He ordered further that they were to put on the
insignia of their office immediately on leaving the *pomerium** and
were to wear them continually until they should return. The heads
of imperial provinces, on the other hand, were to be chosen by
himself and be his agents, and they were to be named propraetors
even if they were from the ranks of the ex-consuls. Of these two
names which had for long been prevalent under the republic he
gave that of praetor to the class chosen by him because from very
early times war had been their care, and he called them also
propraetors: the name of consul he gave to the others, because
their duties were more peaceful, and called them in addition
proconsuls. These particular names of praetor and consul he continued in Italy, and spoke of all officials outside as governing as
their representatives. He caused the class of his own choosing to

* The ancient city wall of Rome; see No. 5.

employ the title of propraetor and to hold office for as much longer than a year as should please him, wearing the military costume and having a sword with which they are empowered to punish soldiers. No one else, proconsul or propraetor or pro-curator, who is not empowered to kill a soldier, has been given the privilege of wearing a sword. It is permitted not only to senators but also to *equites* who have this function. This is the condition of the case. All the propraetors alike employ six lictors: as many of them as do not belong to the number of ex-consuls hold a title derived from this very number. Both classes alike assume the decorations of their position of authority when they enter their appointed district and lay them aside immediately upon finishing their term.

It is thus and on these conditions that governors from among the ex-praetors and ex-consuls have customarily been sent to both kinds of provinces. The emperor would send one of them on his mission wherever and whenever he wished. Many while acting as praetors and consuls secured the presidency of provinces, as some-times happens at the present day. In the case of the senate he specially gave Africa and Asia to the ex-consuls and all the other districts to the ex-praetors. He publicly forbade senators to cast lots for a province until five years after such a candidate had held office in the city. For a short time all persons that fulfilled these requirements, even if they were more numerous than the prov-inces, drew lots for them. Later, as some of them did not govern well, this appointment too reverted to the emperor. Thus they also in a sense receive their position from him, and he ordains that only a number equal to the number of provinces shall draw lots, and that they shall be whatever men he pleases. Some emperors have sent men of their own choosing there also, and have allowed certain of them to hold office for more than a year: some have assigned certain provinces to *equites* instead of to senators.

These were the customs thus established at that time in regard to those senators that were authorized to execute the death penalty upon their subjects. Some who have not this authority are sent out to the provinces called "provinces of the senate and the people"— namely, such quaestors as the lot may designate and men who are assessors to those who hold the actual authority. This would be the correct way to speak of these associates, with reference not to their ordinary name but to their duties: others call these also *presbeutai*, using the Greek term; about this title enough has been said in the foregoing narrative. Each separate official chooses his own assessors, the ex-praetors selecting one from either their peers or their inferiors, and the ex-consuls three from among those of equal length, subject to the approval of the emperor. There were certain innovations made also in regard to these men, but since they soon lapsed this is sufficient to say here.

This is the method followed in regard to the provinces of the people. To the others, called provinces of the emperor, which have more than one citizen-legion, lieutenants are sent chosen by the ruler himself, generally from the ex-praetors but in some instances from the ex-quaestors or those who had held some office between the two. Those positions, then, appertain to the senators.

From among the *equites* the emperor himself despatches the military tribunes, both the prospective senators and the remainder, concerning whose difference in rank I have previously spoken in the narrative, the former to the legions only, the latter also to the auxiliary units according to the custom then instituted by Caesar. The procurators (a name that we give to the men who collect the public revenues and spend what is ordered) he sends to all the provinces alike, his own and the people's, and some of these officers belong to the *equites*, others to the freedmen. By way of exception, the proconsuls levy the tribute upon the people they govern. The emperor gives certain mandates to the procurators, the proconsuls, and the propraetors, in order that they may proceed to their place of office on fixed conditions. Both this practice and the giving of salaries to them and to the remaining employees of the government were made the custom at this period. In old times contractors from the public treasury furnished them with everything needed for their office. It was only in the days of Caesar that they themselves began to receive a definite sum. This salary was not assigned to all of them in equal amounts, but as need demanded. The procurators get their very titles of rank from the amount of money which they receive. The following laws were laid down for all alike, that they should not conscript troops or levy money beyond the amount appointed, unless the senate should so vote or the emperor so order: also that when their successors should arrive, they were immediately to leave the province and not to delay on their return, but be back within three months.

These matters were so ordained at that time—or at least one

might say so. In reality Caesar himself was destined to hold absolute control of all of them for all time, because he commanded the soldiers and was master of the money; nominally the public funds had been separated from his own, but in fact he spent the former also as he saw fit.

When this decade had come to an end, there was voted him another five years, then five more, after that ten, and again another ten, and a like number the fifth time, so that by a succession of ten-year periods he continued monarch for life. Consequently the subsequent emperors, though no longer appointed for a specified period but for their whole life at once, nevertheless have been wont to hold a festival every ten years as if then renewing their sovereignty once more: this is done even at the present day.

Caesar had received many honors previously, when the matter of declining the sovereignty and the division of the provinces was under discussion. For the right to fasten a laurel in front of his palace and to hang an oak-leaf crown above the doors was then voted him to symbolize the fact that he was always victorious over enemies and preserved his citizens. The palace is called Palatium, not because it was ever decreed that that should be its name, but because Caesar lived on the Palatine and had his headquarters there; and his house secured some renown from the mount as a whole because it had once been the habitation of Romulus. Hence, even if the emperor resides somewhere else, his dwelling retains the name of Palatium.

When he had really completed the details of administration, the name Augustus was finally bestowed upon him by the senate and by the people. They wanted to call him by some name of their own, and some proposed this, while others chose that. Caesar was exceedingly anxious to be called Romulus, but when he preceived that this caused him to be suspected of desiring the kingship, he no longer insisted on it but took the title of Augustus, signifying that he was more than human. All most precious and sacred objects are termed *augusta*. Therefore they saluted him also in Greek as *sebastos*, meaning an august person, from the verb *sebazesthai*.

In this way all the power of the people and the senate reverted to Augustus, and from his time there was a genuine monarchy. Monarchy would be the truest name for it, no matter how much two and three hold the power together. This name of monarch the Romans so detested that they called their emperors neither dictators

nor kings nor anything of the sort. Yet since the management of
the government devolves upon them, it cannot but be said that
they are kings. The offices that commonly enjoy some legal sanction are even now maintained, except that of censor. Still, everything is directed and carried out precisely as the emperor at the
time may wish. In order that they may appear to hold this power
not through force, but according to law, the rulers have taken
possession, names and all, of every position (save the dictatorship)
which under the republic was of great influence among the citizens
who bestowed the power. They very frequently become consuls
and are always called proconsuls whenever they are outside the
pomerium. The title of *imperator* is invariably given not only to
such as win victories but to all the rest, to indicate the complete
independence of their authority, instead of the name "king" or
"dictator." These particular names they have never assumed since
the terms first fell out of use in the state, but they are confirmed in
the prerogatives of these positions by the appellation of *imperator*.
By virtue of the titles mentioned they get the right to enroll troops,
to collect moneys, declare war, make peace, rule foreign and native
territory alike everywhere and always, even to the extent of
putting to death both *equites* and senators within the *pomerium*,
and all the other privileges once granted to the consuls and other
officials with full powers. By virtue of the office of censor they
investigate our lives and characters and take the census. Some they
list in the equestrian and senatorial class and others they erase from
the roll, as pleases them. By virtue of being consecrated in all the
priesthoods and furthermore having the right to give the majority
of them to others and from the fact that one of the emperors (if
there be two or three holding office at once) is chosen to be high
priest, they are themselves also masters of holy and sacred things.
The so-called tribunician authority which the men of very greatest
attainment used to hold gives them the right to stop any measure
brought up by someone else, in case they do not approve it, and to
be free from personal injury. Moreover, if they are thought to be
wronged in even the slightest degree not merely by action but even
by conversation, they may destroy the guilty party without a trial
as one polluted. They do not think it lawful to be tribune, because
they belong altogether to the patrician class, but they assume all
the power of the tribuneship undiminished from the period of its
greatest extent; and the years of their reign are counted by that

office on the assumption that they receive it year by year along with the others who are successively tribunes. Thus by these names they have secured these privileges in accordance with all the various usages of the republic, in order that they may appear to possess nothing that has not been given them.

They have gained also another prerogative which was given to none of the ancient Romans outright to apply to all cases, and it is through this alone that it would be possible for them to hold the above offices and any others besides. They are freed from the action of the laws, as the very words in Latin indicate. That is, they are liberated from every consideration of compulsion and are subjected to none of the written ordinances. So by virtue of these republican names they are clothed in all the strength of the government and have all that appertains to kings except the vulgar title. "Caesar" or "Augustus" as a mode of address confers upon them no distinct privilege of its own but shows in the one case the continuance of their family and in the other the brilliance and dignity of their position. The salutation "father" perhaps gives them a certain authority over us which fathers once had over their children. It was not used, however, for this purpose in the beginning, but for their honor, and to admonish them to love their subjects as they would their children, while the subjects were to respect them as they respected their fathers.

Such is the number and quality of the titles to which those in power are accustomed according to the laws and according to what has now become tradition. At present all of them are, as a rule, bestowed upon the rulers at once, except the title of censor; to the earlier emperors they were voted separately and from time to time. Some of the emperors took the censorship in accordance with ancient custom and Domitian took it for life. This is, however, no longer done at the present day. They possess its powers and are not chosen for it and do not employ its name except in the censuses.

5. The settlement of 23 B.C.

This important constitutional change is mentioned only by Dio, and is not given its full political significance by him. Early in 23 B.C. a conspiracy had been detected, led by Augustus' colleague in the consulship, Terentius Varro Murena, and another prominent noble, Fannius Caepio (this conspiracy and the trial of Primus which preceded it are wrongly put by Dio in the year 22 B.C.—see No. 6). Their discontent was apparently due to Augustus' continuous consulships from 31 B.C., and Augustus must have realized that if he was to escape his adoptive father's fate he must yield to the feelings of the nobility; he accordingly resigned the consulship half way through the year, alleging illness as his excuse, and never held the office again during the remaining thirty-six years of his reign except on two special occasions. He remained proconsul of his group of provinces, and reinforced his authority in two ways. The first point was purely technical. As a proconsul Augustus would, under the existing law, have lost his *imperium* on returning from his province to Rome. But this would be inconvenient if he was to play any part in the central direction of affairs, and he was therefore excused from this rule. Secondly, his *imperium* was made greater than that of any other proconsul, so that he could, if necessary, enforce his will against theirs (cf. No. 139).

Finally Augustus received the powers of a tribune of the plebs (cf. No. 1, §§4, 10) for life, an office which was given a high place in the imperial titulature and used to date the years of his reign.

The tribunician power had some practical uses, personal inviolability (*sacrosanctitas*), the veto, and the rights of summoning the senate and the assembly of the plebs, and proposing resolutions of the senate and plebiscites. But Augustus had had sacrosanctity since 36 B.C. and rarely used the other powers; for dealing with the senate he was accorded extra special powers (cf. Nos. 6 and 8, §2), since a tribune of the plebs had a very low priority for his motions. It seems likely that the adoption of the tribunician power was largely a propaganda move to enlist the support of the common people, who traditionally regarded the tribunes as their champions.

5. *Cassius Dio, LIII. 32*

BESIDES DOING this Augustus appointed ten praetors, feeling that he did not require any more. This number remained constant for several years. The rest were intended to fulfill the same duties as before and two of them to have charge of the administration of the finances each year. Having settled these details he resigned the consulship and went to Albanum. He himself, ever since the constitution had been arranged, had held office for the entire year, as had most of his colleagues, and he wished now to interrupt this custom again, in order that as many as possible might be consuls. His resignation took place outside the city, to prevent his being hindered in his purpose.

For this act he received praise, as also because he chose to take his place Lucius Sestius, who had always been an enthusiastic follower of Brutus, had compaigned with the latter in all his wars, and even at this time spoke of him, kept his images, and delivered eulogies upon him. So far from disliking the friendly and faithful qualities of the man, the emperor even honored him.

The senate consequently voted that Augustus be tribune for life and that he might bring forward at each meeting of the senate any business he liked concerning any one matter, even if he should not be consul at the time, and allowed him to hold the office of proconsul once for all perpetually, so that he had neither to lay it down on entering the *pomerium* nor to take it up again outside. The senate also granted him more power in subject territory than the several governors possessed. As a result both he and subsequent emperors gained a certain legal right to the use of the tribunician authority, in addition to their other powers. But the actual name of tribune neither Augustus nor any other emperor has held.

6. Troubles following the settlement of 23 B.C.

Dio here describes in more vivid language the reaction of the common people to Augustus' resignation of the consulship, which is also related by Augustus himself in No. 1, §§5, 6. He also describes in the wrong year the trial of Primus, which demonstrated the suspicion of the nobility that Augustus was exceeding his legal powers, and the conspiracy of Murena and Caepio. The transfer of Cyprus and Gallia Narbonensis and the grant of the right to summon the senate are also probably to be dated to 23 B.C.

6. *Cassius Dio, LIV. 1–4*

THE FOLLOWING year, during which Marcus Marcellus and Lucius Arruntius were the consuls [22 B.C.], the river caused another flood which submerged the city, and many objects were struck by thunderbolts, among them the statues in the Pantheon; and the spear even fell from the hand of Augustus. The pestilence raged throughout Italy so that no one tilled the land, and I think that the same was the case in foreign parts. The Romans, therefore, reduced to dire straits by disease and by famine, thought that this had happened to them for no other reason than that they did not have Augustus for consul at this time also. They accordingly wished to elect him as dictator, and shutting the senate up in its hall they forced it to vote this measure by threatening to burn down the building. Next they took the twenty-four rods and accosted Augustus, begging him both to be named dictator and to become commissioner of grain, as Pompey had once been. He accepted the latter duty under compulsion and ordered two men from among those who had served as praetors five years or more previously to be chosen annually to attend to the distribution of grain. As for the dictatorship, however, he would not hear of it and went so far as to rend his clothing when he found himself unable to restrain them in any other way, either by reasoning or by prayer. As he already had authority and honor even beyond that of dictators he did right to guard against the jealousy and hatred which the title would arouse. His course was the same when they wished to elect him censor for life. Without entering upon the office himself he immediately designated others as censors, namely Paulus Aemilius Lepidus and Lucius Munatius Plancus, the latter a brother of that Plancus who had been proscribed and the former a person who at that time had himself been under sentence of death. These were the last private citizens to hold the appointment, as was at once made manifest by the men themselves. The platform on which they were intended to perform the ceremonies pertaining to their position fell to the ground in pieces when they had ascended it on the first day of their office. After that there were no other censors appointed together, as they had been. Even at this time Augustus in spite of their having been chosen took care of many matters which properly belonged to them. Of the public banquets he abolished some altogether and reformed others so that greater temperance prevailed. He committed the charge of all the festivals to the praetors, commanding that an appropriation be given them from the public treasury. Moreover he forbade any of them to spend from their own means on these occasions more than the others, or to give gladiatorial shows unless the senate should so decree, and even then there were to be not more than two such contests in each year and they should consist of not more than one hundred and twenty men. To the curule aediles he entrusted the fire service, for which purpose he granted them six hundred slave assistants. And since *equites* and women of note had thus early appeared on the stage, he forbade not only the children of senators, to whom the prohibition had even previously extended, but also their grandchildren, who naturally found a place in the equestrian class, to do anything of the sort again.

In these ordinances he let both the substance and the name of the lawgiver and emperor be seen. In other matters he was more moderate and even came to the aid of some of his friends when their conduct was subjected to official scrutiny. But a certain Marcus Primus was accused of having made war upon the Odrysae, while he was governor of Macedonia, who said at one time that he had done it with the approval of Augustus, and again with that of Marcellus. The emperor thereupon came of his own accord into the court and, when interrogated by the praetor as to whether he had instructed the man to make war, entered a denial. The advocate of Primus, Licinius Murena, in the course of some rather disrespectful remarks that he made to him, enquired: "What are you doing here?" and "Who summoned you?" To this Augustus only replied: "The public good." For this he received praise from sensible persons and was even given the right to convene the senate as often as he pleased. Some of the others looked down upon him. Indeed, not a few voted for the acquittal of Primus and others united to form a plot against Caesar. Fannius Caepio was at the head of it, though others had a share. Murena also was said, whether truly or by way of calumny, to have been one of the conspirators, since he was insatiate and unsparing in his outspokenness to all alike. These men did not appear for trial in court but were convicted by default on the supposition that they intended to flee; shortly after, however, they were put to death. Murena found neither his brother Proculeius nor Maecenas, his sister's husband, of any avail, though they were the recipients of distinguished honors from Augustus. And as some of the jurymen actually voted to acquit these conspirators, the emperor made a law that votes should not be cast secretly in cases by default and that the persons on trial must receive a unanimous conviction. That he authorized these provisions not in anger but as really conducive to the public good he gave overwhelming evidence. Caepio's father liberated one of his slaves who had accompanied his son on his flight, because he had wished to defend the younger man when he met his death; but a second slave who had betrayed him the father led through the middle of the Forum with an inscription making known the reason why he should be killed, and after that crucified him: yet at all this the emperor showed no indignation. He would have allayed all the criticism of those not pleased with the course of events had he not allowed sacrifices, as for some victory, to be both voted and offered.

It was at this period that he restored both Cyprus and Gallia Narbonensis to the people as provinces no longer needing military protection. Thus proconsuls began to be sent to these places also.

7. The settlement of 19 B.C.

After the events described in No. 6, Augustus left Rome in 22 B.C. to visit the eastern provinces. When the consular elections came on in the same year the people insisted on electing him in absence as consul for 21 B.C., although he was not a candidate. They did the same in 20 B.C. (for 19 B.C.), riots ensued, and a state of emergency was declared. The senate, thoroughly humbled, gave Augustus a great welcome when he at last returned from the East in 19 B.C., as he proudly records in his *Res Gestae* (No. 1, §§11–12).

Both the powers said by Dio to have been granted to Augustus on this occasion have been questioned. There seems however little reason to doubt that he did accept a *censoria potestas* in order to increase his authority to revise the list of the senate in 18 B.C., as he certainly had done ten years earlier. If Augustus was to levy and command troops and exercise criminal and civil jurisdiction in Italy, as he certainly did from now on, he also required a consular *imperium*, for since 23 B.C. he had been a proconsul only, and his *imperium* was therefore confined to his own provinces. He alludes to his consular *imperium* in connection with his second and third censuses (No. 1, §8).

7. *Cassius Dio, LIV. 10*

THE CONSUL that year [19 B.C.] was Gaius Sentius. When it was found necessary that a colleague be appointed to hold office with him, for Augustus again refused to accept the place which was being saved for him, an uprising once more broke out in Rome and assassinations occurred, so that the senators voted Sentius a guard. When he expressed himself as opposed to using it, they sent envoys to Augustus, each with two lictors. As soon as the emperor learned this and felt assured that nothing but evil would come of it, he did not adopt an attitude like his former one toward them but appointed a consul from among the envoys themselves, Quintus Lucretius, though this man's name had been posted among the proscribed, and hastened to Rome himself. For this and his other actions while absent from the city many honors of all sorts were voted, none of which he would accept, save the founding of an altar to Fortuna Redux (this being the name they applied to her), and that the day on which he arrived should be numbered among the thanksgiving days and be called Augustalia. Since even then the magistrates and the rest made preparations to go out to meet him, he entered the city by night; and on the following day he gave Tiberius the rank of ex-praetor and allowed Drusus to become a candidate for offices five years earlier than custom allowed. The quarrelsome behavior of the people during his absence did not accord at all with their conduct, influenced by fear, when he was present; he was accordingly invited and elected to be commissioner of morals for five years, and to hold the authority of the censors for the same length of time and that of the consuls for life, being allowed to use the twelve rods always and everywhere and to sit in the chair of office between the consuls of each year. After voting these measures they begged him to set right all these matters and to enact what laws he liked. And whatever ordinances might be composed by him they called from that time *leges Augustae* and desired to take an oath that they would abide by them. He accepted their principal propositions, believing them to be necessary, but absolved them from the requirement of an oath.

8. The lex de imperio

This inscription, preserved throughout the middle ages on a bronze plaque in the church of the Ara Celi on the Capitol, records the grant of the imperial powers to Vespasian. The lost opening clauses presumably conferred the consular *imperium* and the tribunician *potestas*. What survive are various miscellaneous powers, for which precedents are carefully recorded when available. Caligula and Nero, whose memories were condemned, are omitted, as are the ephemeral emperors of A.D. 69—Galba, Otho, and Vitellius.

The power of making treaties presumably went with the power of peace and war (cf. No. 3). The special powers relating to the senate were voted to Augustus in 23 B.C. (cf. No. 5). There was apparently no legal precedent for the power of "commending" candidates for the republican magistracies—it had hitherto, it would seem, been a gentlemen's agreement (cf. No. 10). The fifth clause appears to establish a complete autocracy and thus to make nonsense of the whole elaborate constitutional settlement. It is probably to be interpreted rather as a vote of confidence passed by the senate, probably in 27 B.C., when, according to Strabo, Augustus did accept a general "leadership of the empire" (see No. 3). The sixth clause originally dispensed Augustus from specific statutes, but was later interpreted as putting the emperor above the law (see No. 4).

The document is a law but is drafted in the form of a resolution of the senate. Presumably the senate voted the powers first, and their resolution was put unchanged to the people.

8. *Dessau*, ILS, *244*

1. AND THAT he may make a treaty with whomsoever he wishes, as was permitted to the deified Augustus, Tiberius Julius Caesar Augustus, and Tiberius Claudius Caesar Augustus Germanicus.

2. And that he may convene the senate, make or withdraw a motion, and make a resolution of the senate by motion and division, as was permitted to the deified Augustus, Tiberius Julius Caesar Augustus, and Tiberius Claudius Caesar Augustus Germanicus, and that when the senate is convened by his wish and authority or order or command or in his presence, all the proceedings shall be deemed to be legal and maintained just as if the senate had been convened and summoned according to law.

3. And that whomsoever he has commended to the senate and Roman people as candidates for any magistracy, office, command, or administration of any matter and to whomsoever he has given or promised his support, that at the several elections the candidatures of such persons shall be given special consideration.

4. And that he may carry and move forward the boundaries of the *pomerium* when he shall think it in the interests of the republic as was permitted to Tiberius Claudius Caesar Augustus Germanicus.

5. And that whatever he shall deem to be conducive to the interests of the republic and the majesty of things divine and human, public and private, he shall have the right and power to do and act accordingly, as had the deified Augustus, Tiberius Julius Caesar Augustus, and Tiberius Claudius Caesar Augustus Germanicus.

6. And that by whatever laws or plebiscites it was written that the deified Augustus, Tiberius Julius Caesar Augustus, and Tiberius Claudius Caesar Augustus Germanicus should not be bound, Imperator Caesar Vespasianus shall be released from these laws and plebiscites and that Imperator Caesar Vespasianus Augustus may do everything that the deified Augustus, Tiberius Julius Caesar Augustus, and Tiberius Claudius Caesar Augustus Germanicus ought to have done in accordance with the several laws and plebiscites.

7. And that whatever has been done, performed, decreed or commanded by Imperator Caesar Vespasianus Augustus or by any persons on his orders or authorization before this law was proposed shall be valid and confirmed as if it had been done by command of the people or the plebs.

8. SANCTION.

If anyone shall have acted in virtue of this law contrary to laws, bills, plebiscites, or resolutions of the senate, or if he shall not have done in virtue of this law what he ought to have done in accordance with a law, bill, plebiscite, or resolution of the senate, let this not prejudice him, nor ought he to give anything to the people therefore, and let there be no action or judgment against him therefore, and let no one allow action to be taken therefore before him.

9. The oath of allegiance

This oath was taken by the inhabitants of Paphlagonia, when the district, hitherto under a client king, was annexed in 3 B.C., and they came under direct Roman rule. The form of the oath is probably similar to that taken in 32 B.C. by Italy and the western provinces before the campaign of Actium (see No. 1, §25). It may be noted that it is not a military or official oath to Augustus as commander in chief or head of state, but is a personal oath of allegiance to him and his family. Similar but not identical oaths are preserved to Tiberius in Cyprus, and to Caligula at Assos in Asia and Aritium in Spain. A similar oath was taken to Tiberius on Augustus' death (see No. 10) and to all subsequent emperors; it later became an annual ceremony.

9. Dittenberger, OGIS, 532

IN THE third year after the twelfth consulship of *Imperator* Caesar, son of the god, Augustus, on the day before the nones of March at Gangra in the market place, this oath was sworn by the inhabitants of Paphlagonia and the Romans who do business in the country.

I swear by Zeus, Hera, the Sun, and all the gods and goddesses, and Augustus himself, that I will be loyal to Caesar Augustus and his children and descendants all the time of my life by word and deed and thought, holding as friends whomsoever they so hold, and considering as enemies whomsoever they so judge, and for their interests I will spare neither body nor soul nor life nor children, but will endure every peril for their cause. If I see or hear anything being said or planned or done against them, I will lay information and I will be the enemy of such sayer or planner or doer; whomsoever they themselves judge to be their enemies, them I will pursue and resist by land and by sea, with arms and with iron. If I do anything contrary to this oath or not according as I have sworn, I invoke death and destruction upon myself and my body and soul and children and all my race and interests to the last generation of my children's children, and may neither the earth nor the sea receive the bodies of my family and my descendants, nor bear crops for them.

The same oath was sworn by all the rural population at the shrines of Augustus in the districts beside the altars of Augustus, and similarly the Phazimonites, who inhabit what is now called the New City, all swore in the shrine of Augustus beside the altar of Augustus.

10. Augustus' reforms

The judges mentioned in the first paragraph were panels from which juries in the criminal courts and individual judges in civil actions were allocated. They consisted mostly of *equites* (free-born citizens owning at least four hundred thousand sesterces) but also included senators. The imperial jurisdiction, both civil and criminal, is a new feature introduced by Augustus. It was both in the first instance and appellate. The latter was more important as it not only enabled injustices in the ordinary courts to be redressed, but, since the emperor's decisions were accepted as authoritative in similar cases, settled dubious points of law, and sometimes modified the law. Appeals were so numerous that Augustus had to delegate his jurisdiction. For later examples of imperial jurisdiction, see Nos. 136–37.

Some of the laws referred to were introduced by Augustus himself in virtue of his tribunician power, e.g., the *lex Iulia de adulteriis*, which set up a criminal court for adultery and other sexual offenses, and the *lex Iulia de maritandis ordinibus*, which penalized the unmarried and the childless and rewarded those with several children. Others were proposed on his suggestion by the consuls of the year, e.g., the *lex Fufia Caninia* and the *lex Aelia Sentia*, restricting the manumission of slaves (cf. No. 126).

Suetonius describes only the first revision of the senate in 28 B.C., which was, as he says, in two stages. There were three revisions later in the reign. The privy council, a preparatory drafting committee of the senate chosen by lot, was an innovation; it is seen in action in No. 139. Of the new offices the best documented are those of the prefect of the city (see No. 25) and of the curators of the aqueducts (see No. 91).

Augustus enforced military service on young men aspiring to become senators, and this remained the rule (see the senatorial careers in Nos. 29, 30, 32, 153). It will be noted that he confirmed the existing tendency for membership of the senate to be hereditary; but he also encouraged young commoners to stand for the tribunate and thus enter the senate. The elections to the magistracies were still made by the popular assembly under Augustus, but transferred to the senate by Tiberius (see No. 12). He purged not only the senate but the equestrian order, from which he drew his junior military officers and financial agents (procurators); see Part IV.

10. Suetonius, Augustus, 32–40

To THE three panels of judges then existing, he added a fourth, consisting of persons of inferior rank, who were called *ducenarii* and decided all litigation about trifling sums. He chose judges from the age of thirty years, which was five years sooner than had been usual before. And a great many declining the office, he was with much difficulty prevailed upon to allow each panel of judges a twelve-month's vacation in rotation; and that the courts might be exempted from attendance during the months of November and December.

He was himself assiduous in his application to the trial of cases, and would sometimes protract his sitting to a late hour, if he was indisposed, upon a couch placed upon the bench, or lying in bed at home; displaying on all these occasions not only the greatest attention, but mildness. To save a culprit who evidently appeared guilty of murdering his father from being stitched up in a sack, because none were punished in that manner but such as confessed the fact, he is said to have interrogated him thus: "Surely you did not kill your father, did you?" And when, in the trial of a case about a forged will, all those who had signed it were liable to the penalty of the Cornelian law, he ordered that all those who sat with him upon the trial should not only be furnished with the two usual tablets for condemnation or acquittal, but a third likewise, for the pardon of such as should appear to have subscribed their names through any deception or mistake. All appeals in cases betwixt inhabitants of the city, he assigned every year to the praetor; and where the provincials were concerned, to men of consular rank, who had each his province for that purpose.

Some laws he amended, and some, originally framed by himself, he introduced into the code; such as the sumptuary law, that relating to adultery and the violation of chastity, the law against bribery in elections, and likewise that for the encouragement of marriage. Having been more severe in his reform of this law than the rest, he found the people utterly averse to adopt it, without his taking off or mitigating the penalties, besides allowing a respite of

three years after the death of a wife, and increasing the advantages
of the married state. Notwithstanding all these modifications of this
obnoxious statute, the equestrian order, at a public entertainment in
the theater, were importunate for the repeal of it; insomuch that he
sent for the children of Germanicus, and showed them partly sitting upon his own lap, and partly on their father's; intimating by his
looks and gestures a request, that they would not be displeased to
imitate the example of that young man. But finding that the force
of the law was eluded, by the marrying of girls much under the age
proper for matrimony and the frequent change of wives, he limited
the time for consummation after the marriage contract, and restrained the great license which had been admitted in the practice
of divorce.

He reduced, by two revisions, to their former number and
splendor the senate, which had been filled up and overcharged with
a rabble of people, degrading the dignity of that house (for they
were now above a thousand, and some of them very mean persons,
that after the death of Caesar had been chosen by the dint of
interest and bribery, and were commonly called by the people
Orcivi). The former of these revisions was left to their own determination, each man as he was named naming another. But the
latter was managed exclusively by himself and Agrippa: at which
time, it is believed, he presided at the revision with a coat of mail
and a sword under his garment, with ten of the most able-bodied
senators his friends attending about him. Cordus Cremutius relates
that no senator was suffered to approach him but alone, and after
having been searched whether he carried about him any sword.
Some he obliged to the reluctant modesty of excusing themselves
from the acceptance of the honor; and to such he allowed the
privilege of using the senatorial tunic, of sitting at public diversions
in the seats assigned to the order, and of feasting publicly amongst
them. That such as were chosen and approved of might discharge
their duty the more religiously, and with less trouble, he ordered
that every member, before he took his seat in the house, should pay
his devotions, with an offering of frankincense and wine, at the
altar of that god, in whose temple they should assemble, and that
their stated meetings should be only twice in the month, viz., upon
the Kalends and Ides; and that in the months of September and
October, a certain number only, chosen by lot, such as the law
required to give a resolution of the house the force of a decree,

should be obliged to give their attendance. He resolved upon the choice of a new privy council every six months, to consult with them previously upon such affairs as he judged proper at any time to lay before the house. He likewise asked the opinion of the senators upon a subject of importance, not according to custom, nor in order, but as he pleased; that every one might give the same attention to the business before them, as if to deliver his sentiments at large upon it to influence the rest, rather than assent to what had been advanced by others.

He likewise introduced several other alterations in the management of public affairs; as that the acts of the senate should not be published, nor the magistrates sent into the provinces immediately after the expiration of their office: that the proconsuls should have a certain sum assigned them out of the treasury for mules and tents, which used before to be contracted for by the government with private persons: that the management of the treasury should be transferred from the city quaestors to the praetors, or those who had already served in the latter office: and that the ten commissioners should call together the centumviral court, which had formerly been used to assemble at the summons of persons who had held the office of quaestors.

That a greater number of persons might be employed in the administration of the state, he devised several new offices; such as the superintendency of the public buildings, roads, aqueducts, the channel of the Tiber; for the distribution of corn to the people; the prefecture of the city; a triumvirate for the revision of the senate; and another for taking an account of the several troops of the equestrian order, as often as necessary. He revived the office of censor, which had been a long time disused, and increased the number of praetors. He likewise desired that as often as the consulship was conferred upon him, he should have two colleagues instead of one; but in respect of this point, they did not comply with his request; all unanimously crying out upon the occasion that he stooped below his grandeur sufficiently in holding the office not alone but in conjunction with another.

He was no less attentive to the reward of military merit upon all occasions. He granted to above thirty generals the honor of a triumph; and took care to have triumphal ornaments voted by the senate for more than that number. That the sons of senators might become sooner acquainted with affairs of state, he permitted them,

at the time when they took upon them the manly habit, to assume
the senatorial tunic likewise, and to be present at the debates of the
house. When they entered the service of their country in the wars,
he invested them not only with the commission of tribune, but
likewise the command of the auxiliary horse. And that none might
want an opportunity of acquiring sufficient experience in military
affairs, he commonly joined two sons of senators in commission for
the latter appointment. He frequently reviewed the troops of
equites, reviving the ancient custom of the march past, which had
been long laid aside, but he did not suffer any one to be obliged by
his accuser to dismount, whilst he passed in review, as had formerly
been the practice. And for such as were infirm with age, or in any
way deformed, he allowed them to send their horses before them,
and when called upon, only to answer to their names; permitting,
soon after, those who had attained the age of thirty-five years and
desired not to keep their horse any longer, to have the privilege of
resigning him.

Having obtained ten assistants from the senate, he obliged every
one of the *equites* to give an account of his life: in regard to those
of whom he disapproved, upon some he set a mark of infamy, and
others he punished in different ways. The most part he only
reprimanded, but not in the same terms. The most gentle mode of
reproof was by delivering them wax tablets, which they were
obliged to read to themselves upon the spot. Some he disgraced for
borrowing money at low interest, and letting it out again upon
usurious profit.

In the election of tribunes, if there was not a sufficient number of
senatorial candidates, he nominated others from the equestrian
rank; granting them the liberty, after the expiration of their office,
to continue in whichsoever of the two orders they pleased. Because
most of the *equites* had been much reduced in their estates by the
late civil wars, and therefore durst not sit to see the public diversions in the theater in the seats allotted to their order, for fear of
the punishment provided by the law in that case, he publicly declared that none were liable to the penalty of that law who had,
either themselves, or their parents, ever had an equestrian estate.
He took the survey of the Roman people street by street: and that
the commonalty might not be too often taken from their business,
to attend the distribution of corn, he intended to deliver tickets for
four months, that they might receive a greater quantity at once; but

at their request, he continued the former regulation. He revived the ancient usage in elections, and endeavored, by various penalties, to suppress the practice of bribery. Upon the day of election, he distributed to the freemen of the Fabian and Scaptian tribes, in which he himself was enrolled, a thousand sesterces each, that they might entertain no expectations from any of the candidates. Extremely desirous of preserving the Roman people pure and untainted with a mixture of foreign or servile blood, he not only bestowed the citizenship with a sparing hand, but laid some restriction upon the practice of manumitting slaves. When Tiberius interceded with him for the Roman citizenship on behalf of a Greek client, he wrote to him for answer that he would not grant it, unless he came himself, and gave him a satisfactory reason why he made that request. He gave a denial likewise to Livia, upon her desiring the same privilege for a tributary Gaul, but offered him an immunity from taxes, adding a declaration in these words: "I shall sooner suffer the revenue of my exchequer to be diminished, than the honor of Roman citizenship to be rendered too common." Not content with debarring slaves from the benefit of complete emancipation, by various legal difficulties, relative to the number, condition, and distinction of such as should be manumitted, he likewise enacted that none who had been bound in chains or put to the rack should in any degree obtain the citizenship. He endeavored also to restore the old habit and dress of the Romans; and upon seeing once an assembly of the people in black clothes he exclaimed with indignation, "See there! *Romanos rerum dominos, gentemque togatam.*" (Rome's sons whose laws the subject world repress: Of whom the toga is the civic dress.) He gave order to the aediles not to permit in future any Roman to stand in the Forum or Circus with cloaks on without a toga.

11. The speech of Maecenas

This speech, put into the mouth of Maecenas, the friend and adviser of Augustus, is in fact Dio's own program of how the empire ought to be governed. It is naturally very largely modeled on the actual practice of the imperial government in Dio's own day, the early third century, with some bias in favor of the senate, since Dio was a senator. It includes, however, some novel ideas of Dio himself, which either were never realized or did not come about until very much later.

The following are the main headings of the speech:

A and *B*. Senators and *equites*. The senate and the equestrian order were gradually thrown open not only to Italians but to provincials, and men of provincial origin, like Trajan, even became emperors. Nomination to the equestrian order was always in the hands of the emperor. Membership of the senate was obtained by election to the quaestorship, in Augustus' time by the popular assembly, from Tiberius by the senate (see No. 12).

C. Senatorial magistracies at Rome. These offices were virtual sinecures by the third century and their holders nominated by the emperor.

D. The prefect of the city. This office was an innovation of Augustus', being at first an occasional appointment, but from Augustus' later years permanent (see No. 25).

E. The subcensor. This is an idea of Dio's which was never realized.

F. The provinces. This scheme of provincial government is an innovation of Dio's in two respects. Italy is divided into provinces; this did not come about until Diocletian. All the provinces have a uniform structure of government with one consular and two praetorian legates. The actual system of government is described by Dio in No. 4.

G. Salaries. Augustus instituted the payment of salaries to provincial governors (see No. 10).

H. The equestrian offices. The offices of the praetorian prefect, prefect of the night watch (*praefectus vigilum*), and prefect of the corn supply (*praefectus annonae*) were all instituted by Augustus and remained, with the prefecture of Egypt, the most important posts accessible to the equestrian order; see No. 42. The financial procurators were also drawn from the equestrian order.

I. Promotion of *equites* to the senate. This was quite a common practice, as the old senatorial families always tended to die out and had to be replaced by new men.

J. The education of *equites* and senators. This is an unrealized dream of Dio's.

K. The army. The standing army was a creation of Augustus'. Legions were, it is true, often kept in being for long periods under the later republic, but there was no fixed term of service for soldiers. Augustus fixed the term of service at sixteen, later twenty, years (it subsequently rose to twenty-five) and made the legions permanent formations. Similar measures were taken with the auxiliary cohorts (infantry units) and *alae* (cavalry units), raised from the provincials. Legionaries received land or a money bonus on discharge, at first from Augustus' own pocket, from A.D. 6 from the new military treasury (see No. 1, §§16, 17).

L and *M*. Finance. The emperors never took Dio's advice to sell the imperial estates, but built up an important department, the *patrimonium*, to which Marcus Aurelius added another, the *res privata*, which was greatly increased by Septimius Severus and ultimately absorbed the *patrimonium*. The rents collected by these departments were used for public purposes, but the main revenue was the provincial tribute. Dio's proposal that all the inhabitants of the empire should pay uniform taxation was not realised until Diocletian's reign. Until then Italy and a number of Roman colonies and free cities in the provinces were immune.

N. Municipal government and finance. Despite Dio, popular assemblies continued to elect the municipal magistracies after his time, but the government of the provincial cities was always in the control of the city councils. The imperial government did, as Dio suggests, endeavor to curb extravagant expenditure by the cities on their buildings and games (see No. 108).

O. The powers of the senate. As a senator Dio recommends that it should be allowed to play at any rate a formal part in foreign affairs and legislation. Many emperors followed this advice.

P. Trials for treason. Under suspicious emperors trials for treason could be a serious menace. Like every senator Dio urged that frivolous accusations should not be entertained and that trials should be held by the senate (see No. 135).

Q. Imperial jurisdiction. From the time of Augustus the emperors played an important part as judges, especially of appeal (see Nos. 10, 136–37).

R. The civil service. This paragraph begins with a brief mention of the imperial secretariats, which were originally manned by the emperor's slaves and freedmen. The power exercised by these humble persons caused great offense to the aristocracy and from the end of the first century the higher posts were filled by equites. The rest of the paragraph is general advice on law enforcement.

S. Excessive honors. Dio advises the emperor not to accept extravagant and especially divine honors. Many emperors showed reluctance to accept such honors (see Nos. 96, 166).

T. Religious policy. Dio disapproves of religious innovations and of philosophy, and recommends that atheists (i.e., Christians) should be persecuted. His reasons are, it may be noted, strictly practical, that these new cults are liable to cause sedition and disorder.

11. Cassius Dio, LII. 19–40

A. I MAINTAIN, therefore, first of all that you ought to subject the senatorial body to a sifting process, because some who are not fit have become senators on account of the civil dissentions: such of them as possess any excellence you ought to retain, but the rest you should erase from the roll. Do not, however, get rid of any man of worth because of poverty, but give him the money that he needs. In the place of those who have been dropped introduce the noblest, the best, and richest men obtainable, selecting them not only from Italy but from the allies and subject nations. In this way you will be employing many assistants and you will insure a correct attitude on the part of the chief men from all the provinces. These districts, having no renowned leader, will not be disposed to rebel, and their prominent men will entertain affection for you because they have been made sharers in your empire.

B. Take precisely these same measures in the case of the *equites*, by enrolling in the equestrian class such as hold second place everywhere in birth, excellence, and wealth. Register as many in both classes as may please you, not troubling at all about their numbers. The more men of repute you have as your associates, the more easily will you yourself settle everything in case of need and persuade your subjects that you are treating them not as slaves nor in any way as inferior to us, but are sharing with them besides all the other blessings that belong to us the chief magistracy also, that so they may be devoted to it as their own possession. I am so far from assuming this to be a mistaken policy that I say they ought all to be given a share in the government. Thus, having an equal allotment in it, they might be faithful allies of ours, believing that they inhabit one single city owned in common by all of us, regarding this as their real city, and their own as fields and villages. But about this and what ought to be done so as not to grant them absolutely everything, we shall reflect in greater detail at another time.

C. It is proper to put men on the roll of the *equites* at eighteen years of age, for at that period of life physical condition is at its best and suitability of temperament can be discerned. But for the senate they should wait till they are twenty-five years old. Is it not disgraceful and hazardous to entrust public business to men younger than this, when we will commit none of our private affairs to any one before he has reached such an age? After they have served as quaestors and aediles, or tribunes, let them be praetors, when they have attained their thirtieth birthday. These offices and that of consul are the only ones at home which I maintain you ought to recognize; and that for the remembrance of ancestral customs and in order not to seem to be changing the constitution altogether. You, however, should yourself choose all who are to hold them and no longer put any of these offices in charge of the rabble or the populace, for they will surely quarrel, nor in charge of the senate, for its members will contend for the prize. Moreover, do not keep up the ancient powers of these positions, for fear history may repeat itself, but preserve the honor attached to them while abating their influence to such an extent as will enable you to deprive each place of none of its esteem but to forestall any desire of insubordination. This can be done if you require the incumbents to stay in town, and do not permit any of them to handle arms either during their period of office or immediately afterward, but only after the lapse of some time, as much as you think sufficient in each instance. In this way none of them will rebel by becoming masters of armies while holding a grand title, and they will be matured by being private citizens for a time. Let these magistrates conduct such of the festivals as would naturally belong to their office, and let them all individually try cases, save those of homocide, during their tenure of office in Rome. Courts should also be made up of the senators and *equites*, but the final authority should lie with the aforesaid officials.

D. Let a prefect of the city be appointed from the ranks of the prominent men and from such as have previously passed through the necessary offices. His duties should not be to govern when the consuls are somewhere out of town, but to exercise at all times a general supervision of the city's interests and to decide the cases referred to him by all the other magistrates and such as may be appealed from them, together with any that involve the death penalty; and he must have authority in all of them that concern men both in the city (except such as I shall name) and those dwelling outside to the distance of seven hundred and fifty stades.

E. Still another magistrate ought to be chosen, himself also from the same class, to investigate and watch the matters of family, property, and morals of senators and *equites*, alike of men and of the children and wives belonging to them. He should also set right such behavior as properly entails no punishment, yet if neglected becomes the cause of many great evils. The more important details he must report to you. This duty ought to be assigned to some senator, and to the most distinguished one after the prefect of the city, rather than to one of the *equites*. He would naturally receive his name from your authority as censor (for you must certainly be in control of the census), so that he might be called sub-censor. Let these two hold office for life, unless either of them deteriorates in any way or becomes sick or superannuated. They would do nothing dangerous by reason of the permanence of their positions, for one would be entirely unarmed and the other would have but a few soldiers and be acting for the most part under your eye. By reason of their rank they would shrink from coming into collision with any one and would be afraid to do any act of violence, for they would foresee their retirement to ordinary citizenship and the supremacy of others in their stead. Let them also draw a certain salary, to compensate them for the time consumed and to increase their reputation. This is the opinion I have to give you in regard to these officials.

F. Let those who have been praetors hold some office among the subject nations. Before they have been praetors I do not think they should have this privilege. Let those who have not yet been praetors serve for one or two terms as lieutenants to such persons as you may have designated. Then, under these conditions, let them be consuls if they continue to govern rightly, and after that let them take the greater positions of command. The following is the way I advise you to arrange it. Divide up all of Italy which is over seven hundred and fifty stades from the city and all the rest of the territory which owns our sway, both on the continents and in the islands; divide up all the cities everywhere, according to races and nations, into groups important enough to be ruled by one man with full powers. Then establish soldiers and a governor in each one and send out one of the ex-consuls to take general charge and two of the ex-praetors. One of the latter, fresh from the city, should have the care of private cases and the supply of provisions: the other should be one of those who have already had this training, who will attend to the public interests of the cities and will govern the soldiers, except in cases that concern disenfranchisement or death. These must be referred only to the ex-consul who is governor, except in regard to the centurions in the legions and to the foremost private individuals in every place. Do not allow any other person than yourself to punish either of these classes, so that they may never be impelled by fear of anyone else to take any action against you. As for my proposition that the second of the ex-praetors should be put in charge of the soldiers, it is subject to the following limitations. If only a few are in service in auxiliary units or in one citizen legion, it is well enough for this to be so. But if two citizen legions are wintering in the same province (and more than this number I should not advise you to trust to one commander), it will be necessary for the two ex-praetors to superintend them, each having charge of one besides managing the remaining political and private interests. The ex-consul then will perform these duties and will likewise judge the cases which are appealed or referred to him from his praetors. And do not be surprised that I recommend to you to divide Italy also into such sections. It is large and populous, and so is incapable of being well managed by the magistrates at the capital. The governor of any district ought to be always present and no duties should be laid upon our city magistrates that are impossible of fulfillment.

G. Let all these men to whom affairs outside the city are committed receive pay, the greater ones more, the inferior ones less, those of medium importance a medium amount. They cannot in a foreign land live on their own resources nor, as now, stand an unlimited and uncalculated expense. Let them govern not less than three years (unless any one of them commits a crime), nor more than five. Annual and short-time appointments, after teaching persons what they need to know, send them back again before they can display any of their knowledge: and, on the other hand, longer and more lasting positions fill many with conceit and incline them to rebellion. Hence I think that the greater posts of authority ought not to be given to persons consecutively, without interval, for it makes no difference whether a man is governor in the same province or in several in succession, if he holds office longer than is proper. Appointees improve when a period of time is allowed to elapse and they return home and live as ordinary citizens.

H. Senators accordingly, I affirm, ought to discharge these duties and in the way described. Of the *equites* the two best should command the bodyguard which protects you. To entrust it to one man is hazardous, and to several is sure to breed turmoil. Let these prefects therefore be two in number, in order that, if one of them suffers any bodily harm, you may still not lack a person to guard you: and let them be appointed from those who have been on many campaigns and have been active also in many other capacities. Let them have command both of the praetorians and of all the remaining soldiers in Italy with such absolute power that they may put to death such of them as do wrong, except in the case of the centurions, and any others who have been assigned to members of the senate holding office. These should be tried by the senatorial magistrates themselves, in order that the latter may have authority both to honor and to chastise their dependents and so be able to count on their unhesitating support. Over all the other soldiers in Italy those prefects should have dominion (aided of course by lieutenants), and further over the Caesarians, both such as wait upon you and all the rest that are of any importance. These duties will be both fitting and sufficient for them to discharge. They should not have more labors laid upon them than they will be able to dispose of effectively, that they may not be weighed down by the press of work or find it impossible to see to everything. These men ought to hold office for life like the prefect of the city and the sub-censor. Let someone else be appointed commander of the night watch, and still another commissioner of grain and of the other market produce, both of these from the foremost *equites* after those mentioned and appointed to hold their posts for a definite time like the magistrates elected from the senatorial class. The disposition of the funds, also, of both the people and the empire, I mean, whether in Rome or in the rest of Italy or outside, should be entirely in the hands of the *equites*. These treasurers also, as well as all of the same class who have the management of anything, should draw pay, some more and some less, with reference to the dignity and magnitude of their employment. The reason is that it is not possible for them, since they are poorer than the senators, to spend their own means while engaged in business even in Rome. And then again, it is neither possible nor advantageous for you that the same men should be made masters of both the troops and the finances. Furthermore, it is well that all the business of the empire should be transacted through a number of agents, in order that many may receive the benefit of it and become experienced in affairs. In this way your subjects, reaping a multiform enjoyment from the public treasures, will be better disposed toward you, and you will have an abundant supply of the best men on every occasion for all necessary lines of work. One single *eques*, with as many subordinates (drawn from the *equites* and from your freedmen) as the needs of the case demand, is sufficient for every separate form of business in the city and for each province outside. You need to have these assistants along with them in order that your service may contain a prize of excellence, and that you may not lack persons from whom you may learn the truth even contrary to the wishes of their superiors, in case there is anything irregular happening.

I. If any one of the *equites* after passing through many forms of service distinguishes himself enough to become a senator, his age ought not to hinder him at all from being enrolled in the senate.

Let some even be registered of those who have held the post of
centurion in citizen forces, unless it be one who has served in the
rank and file; for it is a shame and a reproach to have on the list of
the senate any of these persons who have carried loaded panniers
and charcoal baskets. But in the case of such as were originally
centurions there is nothing to prevent the most distinguished of
them from being advanced to a better class. With regard to the
senators and the *equites*, this is my advice to you.

J. I have this to say further. While they are still children they
should attend schools, and when they come out of childhood
into youth they should turn their minds to horses and arms and
have paid public teachers in each of these two departments. In this
way from very boyhood they will both learn and practice all that
they must themselves do on becoming men, and so they will prove
far more serviceable to you for every kind of work. The best ruler,
who is of any value, must not only himself perform all his required
tasks, but also look forward to see how the rest shall become also
as excellent as possible. And this name can be yours, not if you
allow them to do whatever they please and then censure those who
err, but if before any mistakes occur you teach them everything
which, when practiced, will render them more useful both to themselves and to you. And afford nobody any excuse whatever, either
wealth or birth or any other distinction, for affecting indolence or
effeminacy or any other unworthy behavior. Many persons, fearing that on account of some such distinction they may incur
jealousy or danger, do much that is unworthy of themselves, ex-
pecting by such behavior to live in greater security. As a consequence they commiserate themselves, believing themselves wronged
in this very thing, that they are, it would seem, not allowed to live
good lives. Their ruler also suffers a loss because he is deprived of
the services of good men, and suffers ill repute for the censure imposed upon them. Therefore never permit this to be done, and have
no fears that any one brought up and educated as I propose will
ever adopt a rebellious policy. Quite the reverse; it is only the
ignorant and licentious that you need suspect. Such persons are
easily influenced to behave most disgracefully and abominably in
absolutely every way, first toward their own selves and next toward other people. Those, however, who have been well brought
up and educated are purposed not to wrong any one and least of all
him who cared for their rearing and education. If any one, accord-

ingly, shows himself wicked and ungrateful, do not entrust him with any such position as will enable him to effect any harm: if even so he rebels, let him be tried and punished. Do not be afraid that any one will blame you for this, if you carry out all my injunctions. For in taking vengeance on the wrongdoer you will be guilty of no sin, any more than the physician who burns and cuts. All will pronounce the man justly treated, because after partaking of the same rearing and education as the rest, he plotted against you. This is the course of action I advise in the case of the senators and *equites*.

K. A standing army should be maintained, drawn from the citizens and from the subject nations and allies, its numbers being varied, province by province, as the necessities of the case demand; and they ought to be always under arms and make a practice of warfare continually. They must have secure winter quarters at the most opportune points, and serve for a definite time, so that a certain period of active life may remain for them before old age. For, separated so far as we are from the frontiers of the empire, with enemies living near us on every side, we should otherwise no longer be able to count on auxiliaries in the case of emergencies. Again, if we allow all those of military age to have arms and to practice warlike pursuits, quarrels and civil wars will always be arising among them. However, if we prevent them from doing this and then need their assistance in battle, we shall always have to face danger with inexperienced and untrained soldiers at our back. For this reason I submit the proposition that most of them live without arms and away from forts; but that the hardiest and those most in need of a livelihood be registered and kept in practice. They themselves will fight better by devoting their leisure to this single business; and the rest will the more easily farm, manage ships, and attend to the other pursuits of peace, if they are not forced to be called out for service, but have others to stand as their guardians. The most active and vigorous element, which is very often obliged to live by robbery, will be supported without harming others, and all the rest of the population will lead a life free from danger.

L. From what source will the money come for these soldiers and for the other expenses that will be found necessary? I shall make this point clear, with only the short preliminary statement that even were we under a republic, we should in any case need money. We cannot survive without soldiers, and without pay none of them

will serve. Hence let us not feel downhearted in the belief that the
compulsory collection of money appertains only to monarchy, and
let us not turn away from the system for that reason, but conduct
our deliberations with a full knowledge of the fact that in any case
it is necessary for us to obtain funds, whatsoever form of government we may adopt. Consequently I maintain that you should first
of all sell the estates which belong to the public treasury—and I
notice that these have become numerous on account of the wars—
except a few which are exceedingly useful and necessary to you:
and you should loan all this money at some moderate rate of interest. In this way the land will be worked, being delivered to men
who will cultivate it themselves, and the latter will obtain capital
and so grow more prosperous, while the treasury will have a
sufficient and perpetual revenue. This amount should be computed
together with all the rest of the revenue that can be derived from
the mines and with certainty from any other source; and after that
we ought to reckon the cost not only of the army but of everything else which contributes to the successful life of a city, and
further how much it will be necessary to lay out in campaigns at
short notice and other critical occurrences which are liable to take
place. Then, to make up the deficiency in income, we ought to
levy a tribute upon everything which produces any profit for the
men who possess it, and we should exact taxes from all whom we
rule. It is both just and proper that no one of them should be
exempt from taxation, individual or people, because they are destined to enjoy the benefit of the taxes in common with the rest. We
should set over them tax collectors everywhere to manage the
business, so that they may levy from all sources of revenue everything that falls due during their term of management. The following plan will render it easier for the officers to gather the taxes and
will be of no little service to those who contribute them. I mean
that they will bring in whatever they owe in an appointed order
and little by little, instead of being left alone for a while and then
having the entire sum demanded of them in one payment.

M. I am not unaware that some of the incomes and taxes established will be disliked. But I know this, too, that if the people
secure immunity from any further abuse and really believe that
they will be contributing all of this for their own safety and for
subsidiary benefits in abundance, and that most of it will be received not by others but by themselves, some as governors, others

as managers, others by army service, they will be very grateful
to you, giving as they do a small portion out of large possessions, the profits of which they enjoy without oppression. Especially will this be true if they see that you live temperately and
spend nothing foolishly. Who, if he saw you very economical of
your own means and very lavish of the public funds, would not
willingly contribute, and deem your possession of wealth to constitute his safety and prosperity? By these means a very large amount
of money would be on hand.

N. The rest I urge you to arrange in the following way. Adorn
this city in the most expensive manner possible and add brilliance
by every form of festival. It is fitting that we who rule many
people should surpass all in everything, and such spectacles tend in
a way to promote respect on the part of our allies and alarm on the
part of our enemies. The affairs of other nations you should order
in this fashion. First, let the populace have no power in any matter
nor meet in assemblies at all. They would decide nothing good and
would always be creating more or less turmoil. Hence I say that
even our own populace ought not to gather for trials or for elections or for any other such meeting where any business is to be
transacted. Next, they should not indulge in numbers or size of
buildings beyond what is necessary, and they should not expend
money upon many and all kinds of contests: so they will neither be
worn out by vain zeal nor become hostile through unreasonable
rivalries. They ought, however, to have certain festivals and spectacles, apart from the horse races held among us, but not to such an
extent that the treasury or private estates will be injured, or any
stranger be compelled to spend anything whatever in their midst,
or maintenance for a lifetime be furnished to all who have merely
won in some contest. It is unreasonable that the well-to-do should
submit to compulsory expenditure outside their own countries; and
for the athletes the prizes for each event are sufficient. This ruling
does not apply to any of them who might come out victor in the
Olympian or Pythian games, or some contest here at Rome. Such
are the only persons who ought to receive pensions, and then the
cities will not exhaust themselves without avail nor anybody practice save those who have a chance of winning, since one can follow
some other pursuit that is more advantageous both to one's self and
to one's country.

This is my decision about these matters. Now as to the horse races which are held without gymnastic contests, I think that no other city but ours should be allowed to hold them, so that vast sums of money may not be dissipated recklessly nor men go frantic, and most of all that the soldiers may have a plentiful supply of the best horses. This therefore I would forbid altogether, that these races should take place anywhere else than here. The other amusements I have determined to moderate so that all communities should make the enjoyment of entertainments for eye and ear inexpensive, and men thereby live more temperately and free from discontent.

Let none of them employ their own coinage or weights or measures, but let them all use ours. And they should send no embassy to you, unless it involve a point for decision. Let them instead present to their governor whatever they please and through him forward to you all such requests of theirs as he may approve. In this way they will neither spend anything nor effect their object by crooked practices, but receive their answers at first hand without any expenditure.

O. Moreover, in respect to other matters, you would seem to be ordering things in the best way if you should, in the first place, introduce before the senate the embassies which come from the enemy and from those under truce, both kings and peoples. For it is awe-inspiring and impressive to let the senate appear to be master of all situations and to exhibit many adversaries prepared for petitioners who are guilty of double-dealing. Next, have all the laws enacted by the senators, and do not impose a single one upon all the people alike, except the decrees of that body. In this way the dignity of the empire would be the more confirmed and the decisions made in accordance with the laws would prove indisputable and evident to all alike. Thirdly, it would be well, in case the senators who are serving in the city, their children, or their wives, are ever charged with any serious crime, so that a person convicted would receive a penalty of disenfranchisement or exile or even death, that you should put the situation before the senate, without any previous condemnation, and commit to that body the entire decision. Thus those guilty of any crime would be tried before all their peers and punished without any ill feeling against you. The rest, seeing this, would improve in character for fear of being

themselves publicly apprehended. I am speaking here about those
offenses regarding which laws are established and judgments are
rendered according to the laws.

P. As for talk that someone has abused you or spoken in an un-
fitting way about you, do not listen to any one who brings such an
accusation nor investigate it. It is disgraceful to believe that any
one has wantonly insulted you who are doing no wrong and
benefiting all. Only those who rule badly will credit these reports.
Because of their own conscience they surmise that the matter has
been stated truthfully. It is a shame to be angry at complaints for
which, if true, one had better not have been responsible, and about
which, if false, one ought not to pretend to care. Many in times
past by angry behavior have caused more things and worse to be
said against them. This is my opinion about those accused of uttering some insult. Your personality should be too strong and too
lofty to be assailed by any insolence, and you should never allow
yourself to think nor lead others into thinking that any person can
be disrespectful toward you. Thus they will think of you as of the
gods, that you are sacrosanct. If any one should be accused of
plotting against you (such a thing might happen), do not yourself
sit as judge on a single detail of the case nor reach any decision in
advance, for it is absurd that the same man should be made both
accuser and judge, but take him to the senate and make him plead
his defense. If he be convicted, punish him, though moderating the
sentence so far as is feasible, in order that belief in his guilt may be
fostered. It is very difficult to make most men believe that any unarmed person will plot against him who is armed. And the only
way you could gain credence would be by punishing him not in
anger nor overwhelmingly, if it be possible. This is apart from the
case of one who had an army and revolted directly against you. It
is not fitting that such a one be tried, but that he be chastised as an
enemy.

In this way refer to the senate these matters and most of the
highly important affairs that concern the commonwealth. Public
interests you must administer publicly. It is also an inbred trait of
human nature for individuals to delight in marks of esteem from a
superior, which seem to raise one to equality with him, and to
approve everything which the superior has determined after consulting them, as if it were their own proposal, and to cherish it, as if
it were their own choice. Consequently I affirm that such business

ought to be brought before the senate. In regard to most cases all those senators present ought equally to state their opinions: but when one of their number is accused, not all of them should do so, unless it be someone who is not yet a senator or is not yet in the ranks of the ex-quaestors that is being tried. And, indeed, it is absurd that one who has not yet been a tribune or an aedile should cast a vote against such as have already filled these offices, or that any one of the latter should vote against the ex-praetors or they against the ex-consuls. Let the last named have authority to render a decision in all cases, but the rest only in the cases of their peers and their subordinates.

Q. You yourself must try in person the referred and the appealed cases which come to you from the higher officials, from the procurators, from the prefect of the city, from the sub-censor, and the prefects, the commissioners of grain and of the night watch. No single one of them should have such absolute powers of decision and such independence that a case can not be appealed from him. You should be the judge, therefore, in these instances, and also when *equites* are concerned and legionary centurions and the foremost private citizens, if the trial involves death or disenfranchisement. Let these be your business alone, and for the reasons mentioned let no one else on his own responsibility render a decision in them. You should always have associated with you for discussion the most honored of the senators and of the *equites*, and further certain others from the ranks of the ex-consuls and ex-praetors, some at one time and some at another. In this association you will become more accurately acquainted with their characters beforehand, and so be able to put them to the right kind of employment, and they by coming in contact with your habits and wishes will have them in mind on going out to govern the provinces. Do not, however, openly ask their opinions when a rather careful consideration is required, for fear that they, being outside their accustomed sphere, may hesitate to speak freely; but let them record their views on tablets. To these you alone should have access, that they may become known to no one else, and then order the writing to be immediately erased. In this way you may best get at each man's exact opinion, when they believe that it cannot be identified among all the rest.

R. Moreover, for lawsuits, letters, and decrees of the cities, for the consideration of the demands of individuals and everything else which belongs to the administration of the empire, you must have supporters and assistants from among the *equites*. Everything will move along more easily in this way, and you will neither err through want of fairness nor become exhausted by doing everything yourself. Grant everyone who wishes to make any suggestion whatever to you the right of speaking freely and fearlessly. If you approve what he says, it will be of great service: and if you are not persuaded, it will do no harm. Those who obtain your favorable judgment you should both praise and honor, since by their devices you will receive glory; and those who fail of it you should never dishonor or censure. It is proper to look at their intentions, and not to find fault because their plans were unavailing. Guard against this same mistake when war is concerned. Do not be enraged at any one for involuntary misfortune nor jealous of his good fortune, to the end that all may zealously and gladly run risks for you, confident that if they make a slip they will not be punished nor if successful become the objects of intrigue. There are many who, through fear of jealousy on the part of those in power, have chosen to meet reverses rather than to effect anything. As a result they retained their safety, but the loss fell upon their rulers. Be of good cheer, for you have in your own hands a great safeguard by never wronging another. And believe me when I tell you that you will never be the object of hatred or plots. Since this is so, you must quite inevitably lead a pleasant life. What is pleasanter, what is more conducive to prosperity, than to enjoy in a rightful way all blessings among men and to have the power of granting them to others?

With this in mind, together with all the rest that I have told you, heed my advice and let not that fortune slip which has chosen you out of all and set you at the head of all. If you would choose the substance of monarchy but fear the word "kingdom" as accursed, do not use the title, but rule with the name of "Caesar." If you need any further appellations, they will give you that of *Imperator*, as they gave it to your father. They will reverence you also by still another name, so that you may obtain all the advantages of a kingdom without the disfavor that attaches to the term itself.

So, since both good and bad fortune alike will redound mainly to you, do not allow yourself to envy others in appearance, but really yourself.

In everything that you wish your subjects to think or do,

instruct them and set them an example. You will educate them
more effectively in this way than by terrifying them with legal
penalties. The first course produces emulation, the second fear. A
man will imitate a better course if he sees it being actually followed, more readily than he will avoid evil courses hearing them
verbally prohibited. So you must yourself be very exact, allowing
yourself no respite, knowing full well that everything will at once
be learned about your words and actions. Therefore you will live
as if on the stage of the whole world: your slightest mistakes will
inevitably be detected. You can never do anything in solitude, you
must always act with a numerous audience. Everyone takes the
utmost pleasure in scrutinizing the actions of their rulers. So if they
find that you are ordering them to do one thing and yourself doing
the reverse, they will not be frightened by your threats, but will
imitate your actions. Keep a watch over the lives of others, but do
not examine them too strictly. Judge complaints brought by
others, but turn a blind eye where no accusation is brought, except
for offenses against the state. These require proper punishment
even if no accuser comes forward. You should know about the
private affairs of others, so that you may not make a mistake and
employ unsuitable persons for any purpose. But do not pass judgment on them. For nature causes many to offend against the laws,
and if one were to proceed rigorously against them, one would
leave no one or very few unpunished. But if one humanely mixes
equity with law, one might perhaps reform them. The law, though
necessarily making the penalties severe, cannot always master nature. And some men, who think that their vices are concealed, and
are rebuked in a moderate way, do amend their lives, some being
ashamed at being found out, others through fear of making a
second mistake. But if they were exposed to shame or punished to
an immoderate degree, they would confound and trample on all
laws and become slaves of their natural impulses. So it is not easy to
punish everybody, but on the other hand, it is unseemly to overlook openly flaunted vice. I advise you to handle offenses in this
manner except for the absolutely incorrigible characters. Whatever
your subjects do well, praise it even beyond its worth. That is the
best way to make them refrain from evil courses and strive for the
better, by humanity and liberality. Do not be afraid that you will
run short of money or anything else with which you reward those
who do good. I rather think that those who deserve to be benefited

will be too few, though your rule is so wide a stretch of land and sea. And do not be afraid that those you benefit will be ungrateful. There is nothing that makes a man your devoted servant, if he is alienated from you or even an enemy, like receiving no wrong but actually a benefit.

S. That is the way I advise you to behave to others. As for yourself, do not allow any unusual or extravagant honor to be given in word or deed, different from those common to senators. Honor from you brings glory to others. But to you, nothing greater can be given than what you have, and much suspicion of insincerity would result. For none of the others will be believed to vote such honors to the ruler of their free will, while the ruler who of his own motion takes all honors, so far from being praised, is the object of ridicule. Gain another kind of glory by your achievements and never allow golden or silver statues of yourself to be made—not only are they expensive, but they are the cause of plots and do not last long. By the benefits of your rule, carve other statues that are ageless and immortal in the hearts of men. Never allow a temple to be built to you. It is futile to spend on such purposes money that is needed for necessities. For genuine wealth is not created by large receipts, but by sparing expenditure—and no glory comes from them. It is virtue which makes man equal to gods, and no gods have been made with hands. If you are a virtuous man and rule well, all the earth will be your sanctuary, and all the cities your temples, and all men your statues. You will always be enthroned in glory in their hearts. Such things, even if displayed in every city, so far from conferring glory on bad rulers, add to their bad name, becoming trophies of their vices and memorials of their wickedness. The longer they endure, the longer their ill repute survives.

T. Therefore if you desire to become in very truth immortal, act in this way; and, further, reverence the Divine Power yourself everywhere in every way, following our fathers' belief, and compel others to honor it. Those who introduce strange ideas about it you should both hate and punish, not only for the sake of the gods (because if a man despises them he will esteem nothing else sacred) but because such persons by bringing in new divinities persuade many to adopt foreign customs. As a result conspiracies, factions, and clubs arise which are far from desirable under a monarchy. Accordingly, do not grant any atheist or charlatan the right to be at large. The art of soothsaying is a necessary one and you should by all means appoint some men to be diviners and augurs, to whom people can resort who desire to consult them on any matter; but there ought to be no workers of magic at all. Such men tell partly truth but mostly lies, and frequently inspire many of their followers to rebel. The same thing is true of many who pretend to be philosophers. Hence I urge you to be on your guard against them. Do not, because you have come in contact with such thoroughly admirable men as Areus and Athenodorus, think that all the rest who say they are philosophers are like them. Some use this profession as a screen to work untold harm to both populace and individuals.

Your spirit, then, because you have no desire for anything more than you possess, ought to be most peaceful, whereas your equipment should be most warlike, in order that no one ordinarily may either wish or try to harm you, but, if he should, may be punished easily and instantly. For these and other reasons it is requisite for some persons to keep their ears and eyes open to everything appertaining to your position of authority, in order that you may not fail to notice anything which needs guarding against or setting right. Remember however that you must not trust all they say, but investigate their words carefully. There are many who, some through hatred of certain persons, others out of desire for what they possess, or as a favor to some one, or because they ask money and do not receive it, oppress others under the pretext that the latter are rebellious or are guilty of harboring some design or uttering some statement against the supreme ruler. Therefore it is not right to pay immediate or ready attention to them, but to inquire into absolutely everything. If you are slow in believing anybody, you will suffer no great harm, but if you are hasty, you may make a mistake which cannot easily be repaired.

Now it is both right and necessary for you to honor the excellent both among the freedmen and among the rest of your associates. This will afford you great renown and security. They must however not have any extraordinary powers but all carefully moderate their conduct, that so you may not be ill spoken of through them. For everything they do, whether well or ill, will be accredited to you, and the estimate of yourself made by all men will depend upon what you permit these persons to do.

Do not then, allow the influential either to make unjust gains or to exercise blackmail: but let no one be complained of for being influential, if he is otherwise irreproachable. Defend the masses vigorously when they are wronged and do not attend too easily to accusations against them. Examine every deed on its merits, not being suspicious of everyone who is prominent nor believing everyone who is lower in the social scale. Those who are active and are the authors of any useful device you must honor, but the idle or such as busy themselves with foolish activities you must hate. Thus your subjects will be inclined to the former conduct because of the benefits attached and will refrain from the latter on account of the penalties, and will become better as individuals and more serviceable for your employment in the public service.

It is an excellent achievement also to render private disputes as few as possible and their settlement as rapid as may be. But it is best of all to cut short the impetuosity of communities and, if they appeal to your sovereignty and safety and good fortune and endeavor to use force upon anybody or to undertake exploits or expenditures that are beyond their power, not to permit it. You should abolish altogether their enmities and rivalries among themselves and not authorize them to create any empty titles or anything else which will breed differences between them. All will readily obey you both in this and in every other matter, private and public, if you never permit anyone to transgress this rule. Nonenforcement of laws makes null and void even wisely framed precepts. Consequently you should not allow persons to ask for what you are not accustomed to give. Try to compel them to avoid diligently this very practice of petitioning for something prohibited. This is what I have to say on that subject.

I advise you never to make use of your authority against all the citizens at once nor to deem it in any way curtailed if you do not do absolutely everything that is within your power. But in proportion as you are able to carry out all your wishes, you must be anxious to wish only what is proper, make always a self-examination to see whether what you are doing is right or not, in order that you may perform the one set of acts and avoid the other. Do not admit the thought that you will sufficiently escape the reputation of acting contrary to this rule, if only you hear no one censuring you; and do not look for anyone to be so mad as to reproach you openly for anything. No one would do this, not even if he should be violently wronged. Quite the reverse, many are compelled in public to praise their oppressors, and while engaged in opposition not to manifest their anger. The ruler must infer the disposition of people not from what they say but from the way it is natural for them to feel.

This and a similar policy is the one I wish you to pursue. I pass over many matters because it is not feasible to speak of them all at one time and within present limits. One suggestion therefore I will make to sum up both previous remarks and whatever is lacking. If you yourself by your own motion do whatever you would wish someone else who ruled you to do, you will make no mistakes and will be always successful, and consequently your life will be most pleasant and free from danger. How can all fail to regard you and to love you as father and preserver, when they see you are orderly, leading a good life; good at warfare, but a man of peace; when you are not wanton, do not defraud; when you meet them on a footing of equality, and do not yourself grow rich while demanding money from others; are not yourself given to luxury while imposing hardships upon others; are not yourself unbridled while reproving others; when, instead, your life in every way without exception, is precisely like theirs?

II. The Emperors

---

12. The accession of Tiberius

Since the office of emperor was an amalgam of powers voted to an individual for life, it ceased to exist when that individual died. A prudent emperor therefore made provision for the succession by having the chief powers, the proconsular *imperium* and the tribunician *potestas*, voted to a junior colleague during his own lifetime. When Augustus died, Tiberius was already in possession of these powers and lacked only the name of Augustus, the office of *pontifex maximus* and some minor powers, e.g., that of summoning the senate. He was also the adoptive son and heir of Augustus, and as such received the oath of allegiance forthwith. The senate thus had no say in determining the succession, except that, as Tiberius suggested, it could have elected a colleague for him. Eventually it did give Tiberius a junior colleague at his own request, his nephew Germanicus. He was already in command of Gaul and its legions, and received only the proconsular *imperium*, not the tribunician power.

The contrasting summaries of Augustus' reign are interesting, and may be compared with the opening chapters of the *Res Gestae*. Tacitus seems to favor the more sinister version, and it is probably fortunate for Augustus' posthumous reputation that Tacitus began his *Annals* with his death. Under Augustus, popular elections for the magistracies had been maintained. He himself had canvassed for certain candidates and commended them to the people, at first in person but later, when he became infirm, by public notice. Such candidates were always elected, and we here see the process hardening into a constitutional convention. *Commendatio* did not become a legal right until Vespasian's accession; see the *lex imperii* (No. 8, §3), where no earlier precedents are cited.

12. Tacitus, Annals, I. 7–15

MEANWHILE AT Rome people plunged into slavery—consuls, senators, *equites*. The higher a man's rank, the more eager his hypocrisy, and his looks the more carefully studied, so as neither to betray joy at the decease of one emperor nor sorrow at the rise of another, while he mingled delight and lamentations with his flattery. Sextus Pompeius and Sextus Appuleius, the consuls, were the first to swear allegiance to Tiberius Caesar, and in their presence the oath was taken by Seius Strabo and Gaius Turranius, respectively the commander of the praetorian cohorts and the superintendent of the corn supplies. Then the senate, the soldiers, and the people did the same. For Tiberius would inaugurate everything with the consuls, as though the ancient constitution remained and he hesitated about being emperor. Even the proclamation by which he summoned the senators to their chamber, he issued by right of the tribunician power, which he had received under Augustus. The wording of the proclamation was brief and in a very modest tone. "He would," it said, "provide for the honors due to his father, and not leave the lifeless body, and this was the only public duty he now claimed."

As soon however as Augustus was dead, Tiberius had given the watchword to the praetorian cohorts as commander in chief. He had the guard under arms, with all the other adjuncts of a court; soldiers attended him to the forum; soldiers went with him to the senate house. He sent letters to the different armies, as though supreme power was now his, and showed hesitation only when he spoke in the senate. His chief motive was fear that Germanicus, who had at his disposal so many legions, such vast auxiliary forces of the allies, and such wonderful popularity, might prefer the possession to the expectation of empire. He looked also at public opinion, wishing to have the credit of having been called and elected by the state rather than of having crept into power through the intrigues of a wife and a dotard's adoption. It was subsequently understood that he assumed a wavering attitude, to test likewise the temper of the nobles. For he would twist a word or a look into a crime and treasure it up in his memory.

On the first day of the senate he allowed nothing to be discussed but the funeral of Augustus, whose will, which was brought in by the Vestal Virgins, named as his heirs Tiberius and Livia. The latter was to be admitted into the Julian family with the name of Augusta; next in expectation were the grand and great-grand-children. In the third place, he had named the chief men of the state, most of whom he hated, simply out of ostentation and to win credit with posterity. His legacies were not beyond the scale of a private citizen, except a bequest of forty-three million five hundred thousand sesterces to the people and populace of Rome, of one thousand to every praetorian soldier, of five hundred to those of the urban cohorts, and of three hundred to every man in the legions and in the cohorts composed of Roman citizens.

Next followed a deliberation about funeral honors. Of these the most imposing were considered fitting. The procession was to be conducted through the gate of triumph, on the motion of Gallus Asinius; the titles of the laws passed, the names of the nations conquered by Augustus were to be borne in front, on that of Lucius Arruntius. Messala Valerius further proposed that the oath of allegiance to Tiberius should be yearly renewed, and when Tiberius asked him whether it was at his bidding that he had brought forward this motion, he replied that he had proposed it spontaneously, and that in whatever concerned the state he would use only his own discretion, even at the risk of offending. This was the only style of adulation which yet remained. The senators unanimously exclaimed that the body ought to be borne on their shoulders to the funeral pyre. The emperor left the point to them with disdainful moderation, and he then admonished the people by a proclamation not to indulge in that tumultuous enthusiasm which had distracted the funeral of the Divine Julius, or express a wish that Augustus should be burnt in the Forum instead of in his appointed resting place in the Campus Martius.

On the day of the funeral soldiers stood round as a guard, amid much ridicule from those who had either themselves witnessed or who had heard from their parents of the famous day when slavery was still something fresh, and freedom had been resought in vain, when the slaying of Caesar, the dictator, seemed to some the vilest, to others the most glorious of deeds. "Now," they said, "an aged sovereign, whose power had lasted long, who had provided his heirs with abundant means to coerce the state, requires forsooth the defense of soldiers that his burial may be undisturbed."

Then followed much talk about Augustus himself, and many expressed an idle wonder that the same day marked the beginning of his assumption of empire and the close of his life, and again that he had ended his days at Nola in the same house and room as his father Octavius. People extolled too the number of his consulships, in which he had equalled Valerius Corvus and Caius Marius combined, the continuance for thirty-seven years of the tribunician power, the title of *imperator* twenty-one times earned, and his other honors which had been either frequently repeated or were

wholly new. Sensible men however spoke variously of his life with
praise and censure. Some said that dutiful feeling towards a father,
and the necessities of the state in which laws had then no place,
drove him into civil war, which can neither be planned nor conducted on any right principles. He had often yielded to Antonius,
while he was taking vengeance on his father's murderers, often also
to Lepidus. When the latter sank into feeble dotage and the former
had been ruined by his profligacy, the only remedy for his distracted country was the rule of a single man. Yet the state had been
organized under the name neither of a kingdom nor a dictatorship,
but under that of a *princeps*. The ocean and remote rivers were the
boundaries of the empire; the legions, provinces, fleets, all things
were linked together; there was law for the citizens; there was
respect shown to the allies. The capital had been embellished on a
grand scale; only in a few instances had he resorted to force, simply
to secure tranquillity.

It was said, on the other hand, that filial duty and state necessity
were merely assumed as a mask. It was really from a lust of
sovereignty that he had excited the veterans by bribery, had,
when a young man and a subject, raised an army, tampered with
the consul's legions, and feigned an attachment to the faction of
Pompeius. Then, when by a decree of the senate he had usurped
the high functions and authority of praetor, when Hirtius and
Pansa were killed—whether they were destroyed by the enemy, or
Pansa by poison infused into a wound, Hirtius by his own soldiers
and Caesar's treacherous machinations—he at once possessed himself of both their armies, wrested the consulate from a reluctant
senate, and turned against the state the arms with which he had
been entrusted against Antonius. Citizens were proscribed, lands
divided without so much as the approval of those who executed
these deeds. Even granting that the deaths of Cassius and of the
Bruti were sacrifices to a hereditary enmity (though duty requires
us to waive private feuds for the sake of the public welfare), still
Pompeius had been deluded by the phantom of peace, and Lepidus
by the mask of friendship. Subsequently, Antonius had been lured
on by the treaties of Tarentum and Brundisium, and by his marriage with his sister, and paid by his death the penalty of a
treacherous alliance. No doubt there was peace after all this, but it
was a peace stained with blood; there were the disasters of Lollius
and Varus, the murders at Rome of the Varros, Egnatii, and Julii.

The domestic life, too, of Augustus was not spared. Nero's wife had been taken from him, and there had been the farce of consulting the pontiffs, whether, with a child conceived and not yet born, she could properly marry. There were the excesses of Quintus Tedius and Vedius Pollio; last of all, there was Livia, terrible to the state as a mother, terrible to the house of the Caesars as a stepmother. No honor was left for the gods, when Augustus chose to be himself worshiped with temples and statues, like those of the deities, and with flamens and priests. He had not even adopted Tiberius as his successor out of affection or any regard to the state, but, having thoroughly seen his arrogant and savage temper, he had sought glory for himself by a contrast of extreme wickedness. For, in fact, Augustus, a few years before, when he was a second time asking from the senate the tribunician power for Tiberius, though his speech was complimentary, had thrown out certain hints as to his manners, style, and habits of life, which he meant as reproaches, while he seemed to excuse. However, when his obsequies had been duly performed, a temple with a religious ritual was decreed him.

After all this prayers were addressed to Tiberius. He on his part urged various considerations, the greatness of the empire, his distrust of himself. Only, he said, the intellect of the Divine Augustus was equal to such a burden. Called as he had been by him to share his anxieties, he had learnt by experience how exposed to fortune's caprices was the task of universal rule. Consequently, in a state which had the support of so many great men, they should not put everything on one man, as many, by uniting their efforts, would more easily discharge public functions. There was more grand sentiment than good faith in such words. Tiberius' language, even in matters which he did not care to conceal, either from nature or habit, was always hesitating and obscure, and now that he was struggling to hide his feelings completely, it was all the more involved in uncertainty and doubt. The senators, however, whose fear was lest they might seem to understand him, burst into complaints, tears, and prayers. They raised their hands to the gods, to the statue of Augustus, and to the knees of Tiberius, when he ordered a document to be produced and read. This contained a description of the resources of the state, of the number of citizens and allies under arms, of the fleets, subject kingdoms, provinces, taxes, direct and indirect, necessary expenses, and customary bounties. All these details Augustus had written with his own hand, and had added a counsel that the empire should be confined to its present limits, either from fear or out of jealousy.

Meantime, while the senate stooped to the most abject supplication, Tiberius happened to say that although he was not equal to the whole burden of the state, yet he would undertake the charge of whatever part of it might be entrusted to him. Thereupon Asinius Gallus said, "I ask you, Caesar, what part of the state you wish to have entrusted to you?" Confounded by the sudden inquiry Tiberius was silent for a few moments; then, recovering his presence of mind, he replied that it would by no means become his modesty to choose or to avoid in a case where he would prefer to be wholly excused. Then Gallus, who had inferred anger from his looks, said that the question had not been asked with the intention of dividing what could not be separated, but to convince him by his own admission that the body of the state was one, and must be directed by a single mind. He further spoke in praise of Augustus, and reminded Tiberius himself of his victories, and of his admirable deeds for many years as a civilian. Still he did not thereby soften the emperor's resentment, for he had long been detested from an impression that, as he had married Vipsania, daughter of Marcus Agrippa, who had once been the wife of Tiberius, he aspired to be more than a citizen, and kept up the arrogant tone of his father, Asinius Pollio.

Next Lucius Arruntius, who differed but little from the speech of Gallus, gave like offense, though Tiberius had no old grudge against him, but simply mistrusted him, because he was rich and daring, had brilliant accomplishments, and corresponding popularity. For Augustus, when in his last conversations he was discussing who would refuse the highest place, though sufficiently capable, who would aspire to it without being equal to it, and who would unite both the ability and ambition, had described Marcus Lepidus as able but contemptuously indifferent, Gallus Asinius as ambitious and incapable, Lucius Arruntius as not unworthy of it, and, should the chance be given to him, sure to make the venture. About the two first there is a general agreement, but instead of Arruntius some have mentioned Gnaeus Piso, and all these men, except Lepidus, were soon afterward destroyed by various charges through the contrivance of Tiberius. Quintus Haterius, too, and Mamercus Scaurus ruffled his suspicious temper; Haterius by having said, "How long, Caesar, will you suffer the state to be without a head?" Scaurus by the remark that there was a hope that the senate's prayers would not be fruitless, seeing that he had not used his right as tribune to veto the motion of the consuls. Tiberius instantly broke into invective against Haterius; Scaurus, with whom he was far more deeply displeased, he passed over in silence. Wearied at last by the assembly's clamorous importunity and the urgent demands of individual senators, he gave way by degrees, not admitting that he undertook empire, but yet ceasing to refuse it and to be entreated. It is known that Haterius, having entered the palace to ask pardon, and thrown himself at the knees of Tiberius as he was walking, was almost killed by the soldiers, because Tiberius fell forward, accidentally or from being entangled by the suppliant's hands. Yet the peril of so great a man did not make him relent, till Haterius went with entreaties to Augusta, and was saved by her very earnest intercessions.

Great too was the senate's sycophancy to Augusta. Some would have her styled "parent," others "mother of the country," and a majority proposed that to the name of Caesar should be added "son of Julia." The emperor repreatedly asserted that there must be a limit to the honors paid to women, and that he would observe similar moderation in those bestowed on himself, but annoyed at the invidious proposal, and indeed regarding a woman's elevation as a slight to himself, he would not allow so much as a lictor to be assigned her, and forbade the erection of an altar in memory of her adoption, and any like distinction. But for Germanicus Caesar he asked proconsular powers, and envoys were despatched to confer them on him, and also to express sympathy with his grief at the death of Augustus. The same request was not made for Drusus, because he was consul-elect and present at Rome. Twelve candidates were named for the praetorship, the number which Augustus had handed down, and when the senate urged Tiberius to increase it he bound himself by an oath not to exceed it.

It was then for the first time that the elections were transferred from the Campus Martius to the senate. For up to that day, though the most important rested with the emperor's choice, some were settled by the partialities of the tribes. Nor did the people complain of having the right taken from them, except in mere idle talk, and the senate, being now released from the necessity of bribery and of degrading solicitations, gladly upheld the change, Tiberius confining himself to the commendation of only four candidates who were to be chosen without rejection or canvass. Meanwhile the tribunes of the people asked leave to exhibit at their own expense games to be named after Augustus and added to the calendar as the Augustales. Money was however voted from the exchequer, and though the use of the triumphal robe in the circus was prescribed, it was not allowed them to ride in a chariot. Soon the annual celebration was transferred to the praetor to whose lot fell the administration of justice between citizens and foreigners.

13. Claudius as a young man

These letters were written by Augustus to his wife Livia and concern the future emperor Claudius (Tiberius Claudius Nero), who was the younger son of Drusus, younger son of Livia by her previous marriage to Tiberius Claudius Nero. The emperor Tiberius was the elder son of Livia, and thus uncle of Claudius; Gaius (Caligula) was son of Claudius' elder brother, Germanicus, and thus his nephew.

Suetonius, as Hadrian's secretary, had access to these very intimate letters in the imperial archives. They reveal how the future emperor was regarded in his youth as subnormal and make his choice by the praetorians all the more remarkable. But he proved a capable and enlightened, if rather eccentric, emperor. Several letters and speeches, all in his very characteristic style are preserved (see Nos. 23, 96, 138, 141). The prefecture of the city during the Latin festival was a purely ornamental office, usually given to a young aristocrat (see No. 25).

13. *Suetonius*, Claudius, 4

"I HAVE had some conversation with Tiberius, according to your desire, my dear Livia, as to what must be done with your grandson Tiberius at the games of Mars. We are both agreed in this, that once for all we ought to determine what course to take with him. For if he be really perfect and entire, as I may say, with regard to his intellect, why should we hesitate to promote him by the same steps and degrees we did his brother? But if we find him indeed unfinished, and defective both in body and mind, we must beware of giving occasion for him and ourselves to be laughed at by the world, which is ready enough to make matters of this kind the subject of mirth and derision. For we never shall be easy, if we are always to be debating upon every occasion of this kind, without coming to a final decision, whether he be really capable of public offices or not. With regard to what you consult me about at present, I am not against his superintending at the feast of the priests, if he will suffer himself to be governed by his kinsman Silanus' son, that he may do nothing to make the people stare and laugh at him. But I do not approve of his seeing the Circensian games from the Pulvinar. He will be there exposed to view in the very front of the theater. Nor do I like he should go to the Alban mountain, or be at Rome during the Latin festival. For if he be capable of attending his brother to the mountain, why is he not made prefect of the city? Thus, my dear Livia, you have my thoughts upon the matter. I am of opinion we ought to settle this affair once for all, that we may not be always in suspense between hope and fear. You may, if you think proper, give our kinswoman Antonia this part of my letter to read."

In another letter he writes as follows: "I shall invite the youth Tiberius, every day during your absence, to supper, that he may not sup alone with his friends Sulpicius and Athenodorus. I wish he were more cautious and attentive in the choice of some person, whose motion, air, and gait, might be proper for his imitation. The poor boy is unfortunate. For in serious studies, where his mind does not run astray, he discovers a noble disposition."

In a third letter he says: "Let me die, my dear Livia, if I am not astonished that your grandson Tiberius should declaim to please me: for how he that talks so obscurely should be able to declaim so clearly and properly, I cannot imagine."

There is no doubt but Augustus, after this, came to a resolution upon the subject, and accordingly left him invested with no other honor than that of the Augural Priesthood, naming him amongst the heirs of the third degree, and such as were but distantly allied to his family, for a sixth part of his estate only, and left him a legacy of no more than eight hundred thousand sesterces.

14. The accession of Claudius

Gaius (Caligula), the successor of Tiberius, was assassinated after a short reign, and the senate hoped to restore the republican form of government. The soldiers and the people, however, would have none of this, and insisted on an emperor, and, moreover, a member of the family of Caesar (if only by adoption). This hereditary sentiment always remained strong in the Roman empire. This is the first occasion on which an emperor was acclaimed by the army (in this case the praetorian guard) in defiance of the senate, which had subsequently to

ratify its choice. The army, or rather some part of it, acclaimed
emperors on many subsequent occasions, notably in the year of the
four emperors (69 B.C.), when Galba was acclaimed by the army of
Spain, Otho by the praetorians, Vitellius by the German legions, and
Vespasian by those of the East. Once again in 193–96 the praetorians
and the armies of the East, the Danube, and Britain successively proclaimed emperors. This is also the first occasion, as Suetonius remarks,
that an emperor gave a donative to the troops on his accession. The
donative became a regular routine, but rarely influenced the issue.

14. Suetonius, Claudius, 10

HAVING SPENT the greater part of his life under these and like
circumstances, he came at last to the empire in the fiftieth year of
his age, by a very surprising turn of fortune. Being amongst others
prohibited by the conspirators from approaching the emperor,
under the pretext of his desiring to be private, he retired into an
apartment called the Hermaeum: and soon after, terrified by the
report of his being slain, he crept into an adjoining balcony, where
he hid himself behind the hangings of the door. A common soldier
that happened to pass that way, spying his feet, and desirous to
discover who he was, pulled him out; when immediately knowing
him, he threw himself in a great fright at his feet, and saluted him
by the title of emperor. He than conducted him to his fellow
soldiers, all in great rage, and irresolute what they should do. They
put him into a chair, and because the slaves of the palace had all
fled, took their turns of carrying him, and brought him into the
camp, very melancholy and in great consternation; the people that
met him lamenting his situation, as if the poor innocent man was
being carried away to execution. Being received within the ram-
parts, he continued all night with the watch, recovered somewhat
from his fright, but in no great hopes of the succession. For the
consuls, with the senate and city battalions, had possessed themselves of the Forum and the Capitol, with a resolution to assert the
public liberty: and he being sent for likewise, by a tribune of the
commons, to the house, to give his advice upon the present junc-
ture of affairs, returned answer, "I am under constraint, and cannot
possibly come." The day after, the senate being slow in the
execution of their project, on account of great divisions amongst
themselves, and the insolence of the populace, who insisted upon
being governed by one person, and Claudius by name, he suffered
the soldiers to assemble under arms, and swear to support him;

when he promised them fifteen thousand sesterces a man, he being
the first of the Caesars that purchased the fidelity of the soldiers
with money.

15. Galba's adoption of Piso

The provincials, the common people of Rome and Italy, and above all
the army, preferred a hereditary monarchy, and so long as adoptive
descendants of Julius Caesar and Augustus survived they got their
way. But many senators and upper-class Italians felt it undignified that
the empire should pass like a landed estate from father to son, and
wished that the best man should rule irrespective of his birth. Galba
had been proclaimed emperor by his troops and accepted by the
senate, and in this passage he institutes a new policy for the succession,
that the reigning emperor should choose the best man and adopt him as
his son. It was not successful on this occasion, as Galba and Piso were
both killed by the praetorians, who proclaimed Otho, but the policy
was followed later by Nerva and his successors down to Antoninus
Pius. Its success depended on the emperor having no sons, for public
feeling would not have tolerated a son being passed over in favor of an
outsider, and Marcus Aurelius left his son Commodus as his successor,
despite his complete unsuitability for the imperial office. Later Diocletian revived the adoptive policy, but it collapsed almost at once, since
Maxentius, the son of his colleague Maximian, and Constantine, the son
of Maximian's successor Constantius, were acclaimed by the armies of
Italy and Britain respectively.

15. *Tacitus*, Histories, *I. 15–16*

WE ARE told that Galba, taking hold of Piso's hand, spoke to this
effect: "If I were a private man, and were now adopting you by
the act of the *curiae* before the pontiffs, as our custom is, it would
be a high honor to me to introduce into my family a descendant of
Gnaeus Pompeius and Marcus Crassus; it would be a distinction to
you to add to the nobility of your race the honors of the Sulpician
and Lutatian houses. As it is, I, who have been called to the throne
by the unanimous consent of gods and men, am moved by your
splendid endowments and by my own patriotism to offer to you, a
man of peace, that power, for which our ancestors fought, and
which I myself obtained by war. I am following the precedent of
the Divine Augustus, who placed on an eminence next to his own,
first his nephew Marcellus, then his son-in-law Agrippa, afterwards
his grandsons, and finally Tiberius Nero, his stepson. But Augustus

looked for a successor in his own family; I look for one in the state, not because I have no relatives or companions of my campaigns, but because it was not by any private favor that I myself received the imperial power. Let the principle of my choice be shown not only by my connections which I have set aside in your favor, but by your own. You have a brother, noble as yourself, and older, who would be well worthy of this dignity, were you not worthier. Your age is such as to be now free from the passions of youth, your life such that in the past you have nothing to excuse. Hitherto you have only borne adversity; prosperity tries the heart with keener temptations; for hardships may be endured, whereas we are spoiled by success. You indeed will cling with the same constancy to honor, freedom, friendship, the best possessions of the human spirit, but others will seek to weaken them with their servility. You will be fiercely assailed by adulation, by flattery, that worst poison of the true heart, and by the selfish interests of individuals. You and I speak together today with perfect frankness, but others will be more ready to address us as emperors than as men. For to urge his duty upon a prince is indeed a hard matter; to flatter him, whatever his character, is a mere routine gone through without any heart.

"Could the vast frame of this empire have stood and preserved its balance without a directing spirit, I was not unworthy of inaugurating a republic. As it is, we have been long reduced to a position, in which my age can confer no greater boon on the Roman people than a good successor, your youth no greater than a good emperor. Under Tiberius, Caius, and Claudius, we were, so to speak, the inheritance of a single family. The choice which begins with us will be a substitute for freedom. Now that the family of the Julii and the Claudii has come to an end, adoption will discover the worthiest successor. To be begotten and born of a princely race is a mere accident, and is only valued as such. In adoption there is nothing that need bias the judgment, and if you wish to make a choice, an unanimous opinion points out the man. Let Nero be ever before your eyes, swollen with the pride of a long line of Caesars; it was not Vindex with his unarmed province, it was not myself with my single legion, that shook his yoke from our necks. It was his own profligacy, his own brutality, and that, though there had been before no precedent of an emperor condemned by his own people. We, who have been called to power by the issues of war, and by the deliberate judgment of others, shall incur unpopularity, however illustrious our character. Do not however be alarmed, if, after a movement which has shaken the world, two legions are not yet quiet. I did not myself succeed to a throne without anxiety; and when men shall hear of your adoption I shall no longer be thought old, and this is the only objection which is now made against me. Nero will always be regretted by the thoroughly depraved; it is for you and me to take care that he be not regretted also by the good. To prolong such advice suits not this occasion, and all my purpose is fulfilled if I have made a good choice in you. The most practical and the shortest method of distinguishing between good and bad measures is to think what you yourself would or would not like under another emperor. It is not here, as it is among nations despotically ruled, that there is a distinct governing family, while all the rest are slaves. You have to reign over men who cannot bear either absolute slavery or absolute freedom."

This with more to the same effect, was said by Galba; he spoke to Piso as if he were creating an emperor; the others addressed him as if he were an emperor already.

16. Diocletian

After the extinction of the Severan family in 235 no emperor succeeded in founding a dynasty, and there was a spate of military pronunciamentos and civil wars. Not only was the empire thus greatly weakened, but the German pressure on the Rhine and more particularly on the Danube became much heavier, and on the eastern frontier the Parthian Arsacids were in 227 replaced by the Persian Sassanian dynasty, which was much more efficient and aggressive. The currency was, moreover, progressively debased in order to meet mounting military expenditure, until money became almost worthless, and the money taxes had to be supplemented by levies in kind. Diocletian, who was proclaimed in 284, pulled the empire together again during his long reign of twenty-one years.

This bitterly hostile account of Diocletian's reforms was written by Lactantius, professor of Latin at Nicomedia, the emperor's favorite residence. Being a Christian he was naturally prejudiced against the author of the great persecution of the church. However the passage does mention most of Diocletian's reforms, though it distorts their objects. Diocletian did set up the system known as the tetrarchy, whereby the empire was ruled by a college of four emperors, two Augusti, one in the East and one in the West, assisted by two inferior emperors, called Caesars, who were in due course to succeed the two

Augusti. So long as the four worked together, as they did under Diocletian, the system greatly strengthened the empire, which in the troubled conditions of the late third century was more than one man could manage. In order to meet the mounting pressure of the barbarians Diocletian also greatly increased the army, though he did not as Lactantius declares, quadruple its size. He also, to cope with the administrative problems arising from increased taxation, enlarged the civil service, doubling the number of provinces and grouping them in twelve dioceses managed by deputy praetorian prefects. He reintroduced regular conscription to fill up the ranks of his enlarged army, and greatly increased taxation, which was mostly in kind. But also introduced a new system of assessment which was fairer and more efficient. He tried to stabilize the currency but failed to stem the inflationary rise in prices, and tried in 302 to fix prices by edict (see No. 154).

16. Lactantius, de mortibus persecutorum, VII

DIOCLETIAN, WHO was an inventor of crimes and an engineer of evils, when he had ruined everything, could not keep his hands even off God. He subverted the world by his avarice and timidity. For he created three partners of his realm, dividing the world into four parts, and multiplying the armies, so that each of them strove to have a far larger number than previous emperors had had, when they ruled the commonwealth alone. The number of those who received began to be so much greater than that of those who gave that the strength of the peasants was exhausted by the outrageous tax demands and the fields were deserted and cultivation turned to waste. To fill everything with terror, the provinces were chopped into bits: there were many governors, more offices in charge of individual districts and almost of individual towns, many accountants, too, and agents and deputy prefects. They all rarely dealt with civil actions, only with condemnations and frequent confiscations, and I will not say frequent but perpetual exactions of innumerable objects and intolerable wrongs in their exactions. Intolerable, too, were the measures taken for furnishing recruits. With insatiable avarice, he never allowed his treasures to be diminished, but always piled together extraordinary resources and donations, so that he could keep whole and intact what he had stored up. When he had by his various iniquities created a vast shortage, he tried to impose a legal restraint on the prices of goods for sale. Much blood was shed for a few poor articles, and nothing was offered for sale owing to the terror, and the shortage became much more acute, until, after many had died, the law was of necessity relaxed. To this was added an unbounded passion for building, with more exactions from the provinces of craftsmen and workmen and wagons and everything that is needed for building works. Here there was a basilica, there a racing track, here a mint, there an arms factory, here a house for his wife, there a house for his daughter. Suddenly a great part of a city was pulled down. Everyone fled with wives and children, as if the city had been taken by the enemy. And when they had been finished to the ruin of the provinces, "They have been wrongly done," he would say, "they must be done another way." More demolitions and alterations were required, and these again often would fall. He was always insanely striving to make Nicomedia the equal of the city of Rome. I pass over the fact that many were killed for their possessions and their wealth. That was usual and almost lawful, so accustomed to that we are. But the chief thing was that whenever he saw well-tilled land or a well-built house, a false charge was got up against the owner, and a capital penalty imposed, as though it were impossible to commit robbery without bloodshed.

17. Julian's accession

After the abdication of Diocletian and his colleague Maximian in 305, military rebellions and civil wars soon broke out again until Constantine, first proclaimed in Britain in 306, eliminated his rivals and became sole emperor in 324. He divided the empire between his three sons, but the eldest, Constantine, was killed by Constans, and Constans fell to a usurper, and in 350 Constantius became sole emperor. He in 355 appointed his nephew Julian to be Caesar in charge of Gaul and Britain.

This passage describes how Julian's army proclaimed him Augustus, that is, the equal colleague of Constantius, much against his will. The donative of five gold coins and one pound of silver was by now standardized. It may be noted that many of Julian's soldiers were Germans from east of the Rhine who had volunteered for service in the Roman army.

A Caesar was served by the same group of ministers and officials—with a few exceptions—as the Augustus himself. The following are mentioned in this passage. Lupicinus was the commander in chief (*magister militum*), an office created by Constantine. Florentius was the praetorian prefect. The prefect had since Constantine's reign lost his military functions, but remained the highest civilian minister, being supreme judge of appeal, side by side with the emperor, and also the principal financial officer, since he had charge of the levies in kind which formed the bulk of the revenue. The lesser officers mentioned are Sintula, the *tribunus stabuli*, who had charge of military remounts, and Excubitor, the *comes domesticorum;* the *domestici* were a corps of officer cadets who served on the emperor's staff. Decentius was a senior member of the corps of notaries, who recorded the proceedings of the imperial council or consistory. These confidential clerks were often used for important and difficult missions such as this.

17. Ammianus Marcellinus, XX. 4

EVEN WHILE he was hastening to lead reinforcements to the East, which, as the concurrent testimony of both spies and deserters assured him, was on the point of being invaded by the Persians, Constantius was greatly disturbed by the virtues of Julian, which were now becoming renowned among all nations, so highly did fame extol his great labors, achievements, and victories, in having conquered several kingdoms of the Alamanni, and recovered the towns in Gaul which had been plundered and destroyed by the barbarians, whom he himself made subjects and tributaries of the empire.

Influenced by these considerations, and fearing lest Julian's influence should become greater, at the instigation, as it is said, of the prefect Florentius, he sent Decentius, the tribune and notary, to bring away at once the auxiliary troops of the Heruli and the Batavi, and the Celtae with the Petulantes, and three hundred picked men from each of the other regiments, enjoining him to make all speed on the plea that their presence was required with the army which it was intended to march at the beginning of spring against the Parthians. Also, Lupicinus was directed to come as commander of these auxiliary troops with the three hundred picked men from the other regiments, and to lose no time, as it was not known that he had crossed over to Britain; and Sintula, at that time the tribune of Julian's stables, was ordered to select the best men of the Scutarii and Gentiles, and to bring them also to join the emperor.

Julian made no remonstrance, but obeyed these orders, yielding in all respects to the will of the emperor. But on one point he could not conceal his feelings nor keep silence: but entreated that those men might be spared from this hardship who had left their homes on the other side of the Rhine and had joined his army on condition of never being moved into any country beyond the Alps, urging that if this were known, it might be feared that other volunteers of the barbarian nations, who had often enlisted in our service on similar conditions, would be prevented from doing so in future. But he argued in vain. For the tribune, disregarding his complaints, carried out the commands of the emperor, and having chosen a band suited for forced marches, of pre-eminent vigor and activity, set out with them full of hope of promotion.

And as Julian, being in doubt what to do about the rest of the troops whom he was ordered to send, and revolving all kinds of plans in his mind, considered that the matter ought to be managed with great care, as there was on one side the fierceness of the barbarians, and on the other the authority of the orders he had received (his perplexity being further increased by the absence of the commander of the cavalry), he urged the prefect, who had gone some time before to Vienne under the pretense of procuring corn, but in reality to escape from military troubles, to return to him. For the prefect reflected that the withdrawal from the defense of Gaul of these troops, so renowned for their valor and already objects of dread to the barbarians, was due to a dispatch which he, it was believed, had sent some time before.

The prefect, as soon as he received Julian's letters, informing him of what had happened and entreating him to come speedily to him to aid the republic with his counsels, positively refused, being alarmed because the letters expressly declared that in any crisis of danger the prefect ought never to be absent from the emperor. And it was added that if he declined to give his aid, Julian himself would of his own accord renounce the emblems of authority, thinking it better to die, if so it was fated, than to have the ruin of the provinces attributed to him. But the obstinacy of the prefect prevailed, and he resolutely refused to comply with the wishes thus reasonably expressed and enforced.

But during the delay which arose from the absence of Lupicinus and of any military movement on the part of the alarmed prefect, Julian, deprived of all assistance in the way of advice and greatly perplexed, thought it best to hasten the departure of all his troops from the stations in which they were passing the winter, and to let them begin their march.

When this was known, some one privily threw down a bitter complaint near the standard of the Petulantes, which among other things contained these words, "We are being driven to the farthest parts of the earth like condemned criminals, and our relations will become slaves to the Alamanni after we have delivered them from their first captivity by desperate battles." When this letter was taken to headquarters and read, Julian, considering the reasonableness of the complaint, ordered that their families should go to the East with them, and allowed them the use of public wagons for the purpose of moving them. And as it was for some time doubted which road they should take, he decided, at the suggestion of the notary Decentius, that they should go by Paris, where he himself still was, not having moved.

And so it was done. And when they arrived in the suburbs, the prince, according to his custom, met them, praising those whom he recognized, and reminding individuals of their gallant deeds. He congratulated them with courteous words, encouraging them to go cheerfully to join the emperor, as they would reap the most worthy rewards of their exertions where power was the greatest and most extensive.

And to do them the more honor, as they were going to a great distance, he invited their officers to a supper, when he bade them ask whatever they desired. And they, having been treated with such liberality, departed, anxious and sorrowful on two accounts, because cruel fortune was separating them at once from so kind a ruler and from their native land. And with this sorrowful feeling they retired to their camp.

But when night came on they broke out into open discontent and their minds being excited, as his own griefs pressed upon each individual, they had recourse to force and took up arms, and with a great outcry thronged to the palace and surrounding it so as to prevent any one from escaping, they saluted Julian as Augustus with loud vociferations, insisting vehemently on his coming out to them; and though they were compelled to wait till daylight, still, as they would not depart, at last he did come out. And when he appeared, they saluted him Augustus with redoubled and unanimous cheers.

But he steadily resisted them individually and collectively, at one time showing himself indignant, at another holding out his hands and entreating and beseeching them not to sully their numerous victories with anything unbecoming, and not to let unseasonable rashness and precipitation awaken materials for discord. At last he appeased them, and having addressed them mildly, he added: "I beseech you let your anger depart for a while: without any dissen-

sion or attempt at revolution what you wish will easily be obtained.
Since you are so strongly bound by love of your country, and fear
strange lands to which you are unaccustomed, return now to your
homes, certain that you shall not cross the Alps, since you dislike it.
And I will explain the matter to the full satisfaction of the emperor,
who is a man of great wisdom and will listen to reason."

Nevertheless, after his speech was ended, the cries were repeated
with as much vigor and unanimity as ever; and so vehement was the
uproar and zeal, which did not even spare reproaches and threats,
that Julian was compelled to consent. And being lifted up on the
shield of an infantry soldier, and raised up in sight of all, he was
saluted as Augustus with one universal acclamation, and was
ordered to produce a diadem. And when he said that he had never
had one, his wife's coronet or necklace was demanded.

And when he protested that it was not fitting for him at his first
accession to be adorned with female ornaments, the frontlet of a
horse was sought for so that being crowned therewith, he might
have some badge, however obscure, of supreme power. But when
he insisted that that also would be unbecoming, a man named
Maurus, afterward a count, the same who was defeated in the defile
of the Succi, but who was then only one of the front-rank men of
the Petulantes, tore from his own neck a chain, which he wore in
his quality of standard-bearer, and placed it boldly on Julian's head,
who, being thus brought under extreme compulsion, and seeing
that he could not escape the most imminent danger to his life if he
persisted in his resistance, consented to their wishes, and promised a
largesse of five pieces of gold and a pound of silver to every man.

After this Julian felt more anxiety than ever; and keenly alive to
the future consequences, neither wore his diadem or appeared in
public, nor would he even transact the serious business which
pressed upon his attention, but sought retirement, being full of
consternation at the strangeness of the recent events. This continued till one of the decurions of the palace (which is an office of
dignity) came in great haste to the standards of the Petulantes and
of the Celtae, and in a violent manner exclaimed that it was a
monstrous thing that he who had the day before been by their will
declared emperor should have been privily assassinated.

When this was heard, the soldiers, as readily excited by what
they did not know as by what they did, began to brandish their
javelins, and draw their swords, and (as is usual at times of sudden

tumult) to flock from every quarter in haste and disorder to the palace. The sentinels were alarmed at the uproar, as were the tribunes and Excubitor, the commander of the officer cadets, and suspecting some treachery from the fickle soldiery, they fled, fearing sudden death to themselves. When all before them seemed tranquil, the soldiers stood quietly awhile; and on being asked what was the cause of their sudden and precipitate movement, they at first hesitated, and then avowing their alarm for the safety of the emperor, declared that they would not retire till they had been admitted into the council chamber, and had seen him safe in his imperial robes.

18. The death of Julian

Constantius refused to accept Julian's promotion to Augustus, and a civil war had begun when he died. Thus Julian became sole emperor without fighting. He carried through a number of reforms and promoted a pagan revival, but his main object was to bring the longstanding war with Persia to a victorious conclusion. He won brilliant initial successes, but on his withdrawal his army was greatly harassed by the Persians, and he himself killed.

According to his practice, Ammianus gives a character sketch of the dead emperor. Ammianus, who had served personally under Julian and was a pagan, obviously had a great admiration for him, but he nevertheless makes some sharp criticisms of both his religious and his secular policy; for the municipal councils, see Nos. 115-16.

On Julian's death a council was held of the generals and senior regimental officers, and also, it would seem, of the civilian ministers, since Salutius the praetorian prefect was present, to choose a new emperor. Salutius having refused, the choice fell, as so often in a hotly contested election, on a nonentity. For Jovian was about thirty years of age and was still only an officer cadet (*domesticus*). Religious feeling seems to have played little part in the choice, for Salutius was a convinced and learned pagan, and Jovian was a Christian.

18. Ammianus Marcellinus, XXV. 4-5.

JULIAN WAS a man to be classed with heroic characters, and conspicuous for the brilliancy of his exploits and his innate majesty. For since, as wise men lay it down, there are four cardinal virtues, temperance, prudence, justice, and fortitude, with corresponding external accessories, such as military skill, authority, prosperity, and liberality, he eagerly cultivated them all as if they had been but one.

In the first place, he was of a chastity so inviolate that, after the loss of his wife, he never indulged in any sexual pleasures, recollecting what is told in Plato of Sophocles the tragedian, that being asked when he was a very old man whether he still had any commerce with women, he said No, with the further addition that he was glad to say that he had at all times avoided such indulgence as a tyrannous and cruel master. To strengthen this resolution he often called to mind the words of the lyric poet Bacchylides, whom he used to read with pleasure, and who said that as a fine painter makes a handsome face, so chastity adorns a life that aims at greatness. And even when in the prime of life he so carefully avoided this taint that there was never the least suspicion of his becoming enamoured even of any of his household, as has often happened.

This kind of temperance increased in him, being strengthened by a sparing indulgence in eating and sleeping, to which he rigidly adhered whether abroad or at home. For in time of peace his frugal allowance of food was a marvel to all who knew him, as resembling that of a man always wishing to resume the philosopher's cloak. And in his various campaigns he used commonly only to take a little plain food while standing, as is the custom of soldiers. And when after being fatigued by labor he had refreshed his body with a short rest, as soon as he awoke he would go by himself round all the sentries and outposts; after which he retired to his serious studies. And if any voice could bear witness to his use of the nocturnal lamp, by which he pursued his lucubrations, it would show that there was a vast difference between some emperors and him, who did not even indulge himself in those pleasures permitted by the necessities of human nature.

Of his prudence there were also many proofs, of which it will be sufficient to recount a few. He was profoundly skilled in war, and also in the arts of peace. He was very attentive to courtesy, claiming just so much respect as he considered sufficient to mark the difference between contempt and insolence. He was older in virtue than in years, being eager to acquire all kinds of knowledge. He was a most incorruptible judge, a rigid censor of morals and manners, mild, a despiser of riches, and indeed of all mortal things. Lastly, it was a common saying of his, that it was beneath a wise man, since he had a soul, to aim at acquiring praise by his body.

Of his justice there are many conspicuous proofs; first that, with all proper regard to circumstances and persons, he inspired awe without being cruel; secondly that he repressed vice by making examples of a few, and also that he threatened severe punishment more frequently than he employed it. Lastly, to pass over many circumstances, it is certain that he treated with extreme moderation some who were openly convicted of plotting against him, and mitigated the rigor of the punishment to which they were sentenced with genuine humanity.

His many battles and constant wars displayed his fortitude, as did his endurance of extreme cold and heat. From a common soldier we require the services of the body, from an emperor those of the mind. But having boldly thrown himself into battle, he would slay a ferocious foe at a single blow; and more than once he by himself checked the retreat of our men at his own personal risk. And when he was putting down the rule of the furious Germans, and also in the scorching sands of Persia, he encouraged his men by fighting in the front ranks of his army.

Many well-known facts attest his skill in all that concerns a camp: his storming of cities and castles amid the most formidable dangers, the variety of his tactics for battles, the skill he showed in choosing healthy spots for his camps, the safe principles on which his lines of defense and outposts were managed. So great was his authority that while he was feared he was also greatly loved as his men's comrade in their perils and dangers. And in the hottest struggles he took notice of cowards for punishment. And while he was yet only Caesar, he kept his soldiers in order while confronting the barbarians, though destitute of pay as I have mentioned before. And haranguing his discontented troops, the threat which he used was that he would retire into private life if they continued mutinous. Lastly, this single instance will do as well as many, by haranguing the Gallic legions, who were accustomed to the frozen Rhine, in a simple address he persuaded them to traverse vast regions and to march through the hot plains of Assyria to the borders of Media.

His good fortune was so conspicuous that, riding as it were on the shoulders of Fortune, who was long his faithful guide, he overcame enormous difficulties in his victorious career. And after he quitted the regions of the West, they all remained quiet during his lifetime, as if under the influence of a wand powerful enough to tranquilize the world.

Of his liberality there are many and undoubted proofs. Among which are his light exactions of tribute, his remission of the crown gold, and of debts long due, his putting the rights of individuals on an equal footing with those of the treasury, his restoration of their revenues and their lands to the cities, with the exception of such as had been lawfully sold by former princes; and also the fact that he was never covetous of money, which he thought was better kept by its owners, often quoting the story that Alexander the Great, when he was asked where he kept his treasures, kindly answered, "Among my friends."

Having discussed those of his good qualities which have come within our knowledge, let us now proceed to unfold his faults, though they have been already slightly noticed. He was of an unsteady disposition; but this fault he corrected by an excellent plan, allowing people to set him right when guilty of indiscretion. He was a frequent talker, rarely silent. Too much devoted to divination, so much so as in this particular to equal the emperor Hadrian. He was rather a superstitious than a legitimate observer of sacred rites, sacrificing countless numbers of victims; so that it was reckoned that if he had returned from the Parthians there would have been a scarcity of cattle. Like the celebrated case of Marcus Caesar, about whom it was written, as it is said, "The white cattle to Marcus Caesar, greeting. If you conquer there is an end of us." He was very fond of the applause of the common people, and an immoderate seeker after praise even in the most trifling matters; often, from a desire of popularity, indulging in conversation with unworthy persons.

But in spite of all this he deserved, as he used to say himself, to have it thought that ancient Justice, whom Aratus says fled to heaven from disgust with the vices of men, had in his reign returned again to the earth; only that sometimes he acted arbitrarily and inconsistently. For he made laws which, with but few exceptions, were not offensive, though they very positively enforced or forbade certain actions. Among the exceptions was that cruel one which forbade Christian masters of rhetoric and grammar to teach unless they came over to the worship of the gods. Another ordinance was equally intolerable which allowed some persons to be unjustly enrolled in the municipal councils, though they were not citizens, or by privilege or birth wholly unconnected with them.

As to his personal appearance it was this. He was of moderate

stature, with soft hair, as if he had carefully dressed it, a rough
beard ending in a point, beautiful brilliant eyes, which displayed
the subtlety of his mind, handsome eyebrows and a straight nose, a
rather large mouth, broad shoulders. From head to foot he was
straight and well proportioned, which made him strong and a good
runner.

And since his detractors have accused him of provoking new
wars to the injury of the commonwealth, let them know the
unquestionable truth, that it was not Julian but Constantius who
occasioned the hostility of the Parthians by greedily acquiescing in
the falsehoods of Metrodorus, as we have already set forth. In
consequence of this conduct our armies were slaughtered, numbers
of our soldiers were taken prisoners, cities were razed, fortresses
were stormed and destroyed, provinces were exhausted by heavy
expenses, and in short the Persians, putting their threats into effect,
were led to seek to become masters of everything up to Bithynia
and the shores of the Propontis. The Gallic wars grew more and
more violent, the Germans overrunning our territories and being
on the point of forcing the passes of the Alps in order to invade
Italy. There was nothing to be seen but tears and consternation,
the recollection of the past being bitter, the expectation of the
future still more woeful. All these miseries, this youth, being sent
into the West with the rank of Caesar, put an end to with marvel-
lous celerity, treating the kings of those countries as base-born
slaves.

Then in order to re-establish the prosperity of the East, with
similar energy he attacked the Persians, and would have gained in
that country both a triumph and a surname, if the will of heaven
had been in accordance with his glorious plans and actions. And as
we know by experience that some men are so rash and hasty that if
conquered they return to battle, if shipwrecked, to the sea, in
short, each to the difficulties by which he has been frequently
overcome, so some find fault with this emperor for returning to
similar exploits after having been repeatedly victorious.

After these events there was no time for lamentation or weeping.
For after he had been laid out as well as the circumstances and time
permitted, that he might be buried where he himself had formerly
proposed, at daybreak the next morning, which was on the 27th of
June, while the enemy surrounded us on every side, the generals of
the army assembled, and having convened the chief officers of the

cavalry and of the legions, deliberated about the election of an emperor.

There were great and noisy divisions. Arinthaeus and Victor, and the rest of those who had been attached to the court of Constantius, sought for a fit man of their own party. On the other hand, Nevitta and Dagalaiphus, and the nobles of the Gauls, sought for a man among their own ranks. While the matter was thus in dispute, they all unanimously agreed upon Salutius. And when he pleaded ill health and old age, one of the soldiers of rank observing his real and fixed reluctance said, "And what would you do if the emperor while absent himself, as has often happened, had entrusted you with the conduct of this war? Would you not have postponed all other considerations and applied yourself to extricating the soldiers at once from the difficulties which press on them? Do so now: and then, if we are allowed to reach Mesopotamia, it will be time enough for the united vote of both armies to declare a lawful emperor."

Amid these little delays in so important a matter, before opinions were justly weighed, a few made an uproar, as often happens in critical circumstances, and Jovian was elected emperor, being the senior member of the officer cadets, and a man of fair reputation in respect of his father's services. For he was the son of Varronianus, a distinguished count, who had not long since retired from military service to lead a private life. He was immediately clothed in the imperial robes and suddenly led out of the tent and passed at a quick pace through the army as it was preparing to march. As the line extended four miles, those in the van hearing some persons salute Jovian as Augustus, raised the same cry still more loudly, for they were caught by the relationship, so to say, of the name, which differed only by one letter from that of Julian, and so they thought that Julian was recovered and was being led forth with great acclamations as had often been the case. But when the new emperor, who was both taller and less upright, was seen, they suspected what had happened, and gave vent to tears and lamentations.

If any lover of justice should find fault with what was done at this extreme crisis as imprudent, he might still more justly blame sailors who, having lost a skillful pilot when both winds and waves are agitated by a storm, commit the helm of their vessel to some one of their comrades.

19. Valentinian I

Ammianus is perhaps less than fair to Valentinian I, though he gives him credit for his military ability. Being himself of humble origin, Valentinian was hostile to the upper classes, and took a strong interest in the welfare of the poor. His most important measure in this matter, which is not recorded by Ammianus, was the establishment in each city of a *defensor plebis*, who provided cheap justice for the poor and was supposed to protect them against the exactions of officials and town councilors (see No. 117). Another remarkable feature of his policy was that almost alone among emperors he was, though a pious Catholic, neutral in religious questions, and persecuted neither heretics nor pagans.

The brilliant career of the elder Gratian is not unparalleled. We know of several private soldiers who rose even higher, Arbetio to be *magister militum*, Marcian and Justin to be emperors.

19. *Ammianus Marcellinus, XXX. 7–9*

THIS IS a seasonable opportunity to do as we have often done before, to retrace from the original appearance of the father of this emperor down to the time of his own death all his actions, just touching on them cursorily with a brief mention, not omitting to distinguish between his vices and his virtues, both of which his lofty position held up to the world, being a condition which naturally reveals the inward disposition of every man.

The elder Gratian was born at Cibalae, a town of Pannonia, of a mean family; and from his childhood he received the nickname of Roper, because, while still very young, while he was carrying about a rope for sale, he resisted the attempt of five soldiers who labored with all their might to take it from him: thus rivaling Milo of Croton, from whom no amount of strength could ever wrest an apple, whether he held it in his right or his left hand. Therefore, on account of his exceeding personal strength, and his skill in wrestling after the military fashion, he became well known to many persons, was promoted to the rank of an officer cadet, then to the post of tribune: after this he was made count, and sent to command the forces in Africa: but there he was suspected of embezzlement; and having quitted that province, he was some time afterward sent to command the army in Britain, with the same rank which he had enjoyed in Africa. At length he received an honorable discharge from military service, and returned home; and while living there quietly he suddenly had all his property confiscated by Constantius, on the ground that, when the civil discord was at its height, he was said to have received Magnentius as a guest when passing through his land to carry his designs into execution.

The merits of Gratian brought Valentinian into notice from his early youth; he was further aided by his own eminent qualities, so that he received the ornaments of the imperial majesty at Nicaea; when he also made his brother Valens his colleague, as one bound to him not only by his relationship as a brother, but also by the most perfect agreement, Valens, as we shall show at a suitable time, being made up almost equally of vices and of virtues.

Therefore Valentinian, after having experienced many dangers and much distress as a private individual, as soon as he began to reign went to visit the towns and cities on the Danube and the Rhine, and repaired to Gaul, which was exposed to the inroads of the Alamanni, who had begun to recover their courage and to reassume an imposing attitude since they had heard of the death of the emperor Julian, the only prince whom they had feared since the time of Constans. Valentinian was deservedly dreaded by them because he took care to keep up the numbers of his army by strong reinforcements, and because also he fortified both banks of the Rhine with lofty fortresses and castles, to prevent the enemy from ever passing over into our territory without being perceived.

We may pass over many circumstances, and many acts which he performed with the authority of an emperor whose power was fully established, and many of the reforms which he either effected himself, or caused to be carried out by his vigorous lieutenants. But we must record how after he had raised his son Gratian to partnership in the imperial authority, he contrived the secret murder of Vithigabius, the king of the Alamanni and the son of Vadomarius, a young man in the flower of youth, who was actively stirring up the surrounding nations to tumults and wars; doing this because he found it impossible to procure his death openly. How also he fought a battle against the Alamanni near Solicinium, where he was nearly trapped and killed by the maneuvers of the enemy; but where at last he utterly destroyed their whole army with the exception of a few who saved themselves by the aid of the darkness which assisted the rapidity of their flight.

Amid all these prudent actions he also turned his attention to the

Saxons, who had lately broken out with extreme ferocity, making attacks in every direction where they were least expected, and had now penetrated into the inland districts, from which they were returning enriched by a vast booty. He destroyed them utterly by a device which was indeed treacherous, but most advantageous; and he recovered by force all the booty which the defeated robbers were carrying off. Nor did he disregard the condition of the Britons, who were unable to make head against the vast hosts of their enemies, who were overrunning their country. He revived their hopes of better fortune, and re-established liberty and steady tranquillity among them, routing their invaders so completely that scarcely any of them returned to their own country.

With similar vigor he crushed Valentinus, the Pannonian exile (who was laboring to disturb the general tranquillity in that province), before his enterprise could become dangerous, at a time when it was thrown into confusion by an unexpected disaster, when Firmus, unable to bear the greed and arrogance of the soldiers, was exciting the people of Mauritania to every kind of discord and disturbance. He would have avenged the disasters sustained in Illyricum with similar resolution, had he not left that important duty incompleted in consequence of being cut off by a premature death.

Although these various achievements, which we have here recorded, were consummated by the assistance of his admirable generals, yet it is notorious that he himself also performed many considerable exploits; being a man fertile in resources and of long experience and great skill in military affairs: and certainly it would have been an admirable crown to his great actions if he had been able to capture King Macrianus, who at that time was a very formidable sovereign; nevertheless he exerted great energy in attempting to do so, after he heard that he had escaped from the Burgundians, whom he himself had led against the Alamanni; and the news of his escape was a cause of great sorrow and indignation to him.

Thus have I rapidly run over the different actions of this prince. Now, relying on the certainty that posterity, inasmuch as it is free both from fear and from base flattery, is usually an honest judge of all past transactions, I will rapidly run over his vices, intending afterward to relate his good qualities.

Sometimes he put on an affectation of clemency, though the

bent of his natural disposition inclined him more to cruelty; forgetful that by a man who governs a vast empire extremes of every
kind are to be avoided as rocks by a mariner. Nor indeed was he
ever found to be content with moderate punishments, but was
continually commanding cruel tortures to be multiplied; so that
many, after undergoing this murderous kind of examination, were
brought to death's door. And he was so eager to inflict injury, that
he never once saved any one who had been condemned to death by
a milder sentence, though even the most inhuman of emperors have
sometimes done so.

Besides this the aforesaid emperor was a prey in his inmost heart
to a devouring envy; and as he knew that most vices put on a
semblance of virtue, he used to be fond of repeating that severity is
the inseparable companion of lawful power. And as magistrates of
the highest rank are in the habit of thinking everything permitted
to them, and are always inclined to depress those who oppose them
and to humiliate those who are superior to them, so he hated all
who were well dressed or learned or opulent or high-born; and he
was always disparaging the brave, that he might appear to be the
only person eminent for virtue. And this is a vice which, as we
read, was very flagrant in the emperor Hadrian.

This same emperor continually abused the timid, calling them
sordid and base, and people who deserved to be depressed below
the very lowest of the low; and yet he himself often grew pale in
the most abject manner with groundless fears, and often from the
bottom of his soul was terrified at things which had no existence at
all. Remigius, the master of the offices, knowing this, and also that
Valentinian used to get into furious passions at every trifling
incident, spread a report, among other things, that some of the
barbarians were in motion; and the emperor, when he heard this,
became at once so broken-spirited through fear that he became as
gentle and merciful as Antoninus Pius.

He never intentionally appointed unjust judges, but if he learned
that those whom he had once promoted were acting cruelly, he
boasted that he had discovered new Lycurguses and Cassiuses,
those ancient pillars of justice; and he used to be continually
exhorting them by his letters severely to chastise even the slightest
errors. Nor had those who were under accusations, if any misfortune fell upon them, any refuge in the kindness of the prince;
which ought to be, as it were, a desirable haven to those tossed

about in a stormy sea. For, as wise men teach us, "The advantage and safety of the subject is the true end of just government."

It is natural for us, after discussing these topics, if we would act fairly, now to come to his virtuous and laudable actions; since if he had tempered his vices fairly with them he would have been a second Trajan or Marcus Aurelius. Toward the people of the provinces he was very considerate, lightening the burden of the tribute throughout the empire. He also exerted himself in a very beneficial manner in building towns and strengthening the frontiers. He was a strict observer of military discipline, erring only in this respect, that while he punished even slight misconduct on the part of the common soldiers, he allowed the crimes of the more important generals to proceed to greater and greater lengths, and shut his ears against every complaint that was uttered against them. And this partiality of his was the cause of the tumults in Britain, and the disasters in Africa, and the devastation of Illyricum.

He was, both at home and abroad, a strict observer of modesty and chastity, keeping his conscience wholly free from all taint of impurity or obscenity, and in consequence he bridled the wantonness of the imperial court with a strong rein; and he was the more easily able to do this because he had never shown any indulgence to his own relations, whom he either kept in obscurity, or (if he promoted them at all) raised to a very moderate rank, with the exception of his brother, whom, in deference to the necessities of the times, he made his partner in the imperial dignity.

He was very scrupulous in giving high rank to any one; nor, as long as he was emperor, did any moneyed man become ruler of a province, nor was any office sold, unless it was at the beginning of his reign, when wicked actions were sometimes committed in the hope that the new prince would be too much occupied to punish them.

In waging war and in defending himself from attacks, he was prudent and very skillful, like a veteran of great experience in military affairs. He was a very wise admirer of all that was good, and a dissuader from all that was bad; and a very accurate observer of all the details of military service. He wrote with elegance, and described everything with great neatness and skill in composition. He was an inventor of new arms. He had an excellent memory, and a fluent, easy style of speaking, which at times bordered closely upon eloquence. He was a lover of elegant simplicity, and was fond not so much of profuse banquets as of entertainments directed by good taste.

Lastly, he was especially remarkable during his reign for his moderation in this particular, that he kept a middle course between the different sects of religion; and never troubled any one nor issued any orders in favor of one kind of worship or another; nor did he promulgate any threatening edicts to submit the necks of his subjects to the form of worship to which he himself was inclined; but he left these parties just as he found them, without making any alterations.

His body was muscular and strong; the brightness of his hair, the brilliancy of his complexion, with his blue eyes, which always looked askance with a stern aspect, the beauty of his figure, his lofty stature, and the admirable harmony of all his features, filled up the dignity and beauty of an appearance which bespoke a monarch.

20. The usurpation of Silvanus

This story, which belongs to the year 354, a few years after Constantius' defeat of the usurper Magnentius in Gaul, vividly illustrates the intrigues of the imperial council, the consistory. It may be noted how many of the military officers, including Silvanus himself, were Franks, and how completely loyal they were to the empire. Silvanus only thinks of fleeing to his tribesmen as a last resort and is evidently completely out of touch with them. The other two generals mentioned, Arbetio and Ursicinus, were Romans. Ammianus had served on the latter's staff and greatly admired him. The Gentiles and the Armaturae were regiments of the *scholae*, the imperial guard; the *candidati* was the emperor's personal bodyguard. The civilian ministers mentioned included, beside Lampadius the praetorian prefect, Florentius, *magister officiorum*, who controlled imperial audiences, Eusebius, *comes rei privatae*, who managed the extensive imperial lands and their revenue, and Aedesius, the *magister memoriae*, one of the imperial secretaries who wrote letters and petitions.

20. *Ammianus Marcellinus, XV. 5*

FROM LONG neglect the Gallic provinces, having no assistance on which to rely, had borne cruel massacres, with plunder and conflagration, from barbarians who raged throughout their land with impunity. Silvanus, the commander of the infantry, being a man well suited to correct these evils, was sent there at the command of the emperor, Arbetio at the same time urging with all his power that this task should be undertaken without delay, with the object of imposing the dangerous burden of this duty on his absent rival, whom he was vexed to see still in prosperity.

There was a certain man named Dynamius, the superintendent of the emperor's beasts of burden, who had begged of Silvanus recommendatory letters to his friends as if he were admitted to his most intimate friendship. Having obtained this favor, as Silvanus, having no suspicion of any evil intention, had with great simplicity granted what he was asked, Dynamius kept the letters, in order at a future time to plan something to his injury.

Therefore when the aforesaid commander had gone to the Gauls in the service of the republic, and while he was engaged in repelling the barbarians, who already began to distrust their own power and to be filled with alarm, Dynamius, being restless, like a man of cunning and practiced deceitfulness, devised a wicked plot; and in this it is said he had for his accomplices Lampadius, the praetorian prefect, Eusebius, who had been the superintendent of the emperor's private property and was known by the nickname of Mattyocopa, and Aedesius, formerly master of the memory, whom the prefect had arranged to have invited to his consular celebrations as being his dearest friends. He then with a sponge effaced the contents of the letters, leaving nothing but the signature, and inserted a text materially differing from the original writing, as if Silvanus had by indirect hints begged and entreated his friends who were within the palace, or who had no office (among whom was Albinus of Etruria, and many others), to aid him in projects of loftier ambition, as one who would soon attain the imperial throne. This bundle of letters he thus made up, inventing at his leisure, in order to endanger the life of an innocent man.

This packet of letters the prefect received from Dynamius. And going into the private chamber of the emperor and finding him alone, he presented them to him secretly, hoping to receive a reward from the emperor as a most watchful and careful guardian of his safety. And when with subtle cunning the forged packet of letters had been read in the consistory, the tribunes were ordered to be committed to custody, and also the several private individuals were commanded to be arrested and brought up from the provinces, whose names were mentioned in those letters.

But presently Malarichus, the commander of the Gentiles, being struck with the iniquity of the business, and taking his colleagues to his counsel, spoke out loudly that men devoted to the preservation of the emperor ought not to be circumvented by factions and treachery. He accordingly demanded that he himself, his nearest relations being left as hostages, and Mallobaudes, the tribune of the Armaturae, giving bail that he would return, might be commissioned to go with speed to bring back Silvanus, who he was certain had never entertained the idea of any such attempt as these bitter plotters had imputed to him. Or, as an alternative, he entreated that he might become security for Mallobaudes, and that that officer might be permitted to go and do what he had proposed to take upon himself. For he affirmed that he knew beyond all question that, if any stranger were sent, Silvanus, who was inclined to be somewhat apprehensive of danger, even when no circumstances were really calculated to alarm him, would very likely throw matters into confusion.

But, although the advice which he gave was useful and necessary, he spoke as to the winds, to no purpose. For by the counsel of Arbetio, Apodemius, who was a persevering and bitter enemy to all good men, was sent with letters to summon Silvanus to the presence. When he had arrived in Gaul, taking no heed of the commission with which he was charged, and caring but little for anything that might happen, he remained inactive, without either seeing Silvanus or delivering the letters which commanded him to appear at court. And having taken the accountant of the province into his counsel, he began with arrogance and malevolence to harass the clients and servants of the master of the infantry, as if that officer had already been condemned and was on the point of being executed.

In the meantime, while the arrival of Silvanus was looked for, and while Apodemius was throwing everything, though quiet before, into commotion, Dynamius, that he might by still more convincing proofs establish belief in his wicked plots, had sent other forged letters (agreeing with the previous ones which he had brought under the emperor's notice by the agency of the prefect) to the tribune of the arms factory at Cremona: these were written in the names of Silvanus and Malarichus, in which the tribune, as one privy to their secrets, was warned to lose no time in having everything in readiness.

But when this tribune had read the whole of the letters, he was for some time in doubt and perplexity as to what they could mean (for he did not recollect that the persons whose letters he had thus received had ever spoken with him upon private transactions of any kind); and accordingly he sent the letters themselves, by the courier who had brought them, to Malarichus, sending a soldier also with him, and entreated Malarichus to explain in intelligible language what he wanted, and not to use such obscure terms. For he declared that he, being but a plain and somewhat simple man, had not in the least understood what was intimated so obscurely.

Malarichus, the moment he received the letters, being already in sorrow and anxiety, and alarmed for his own fate and that of his countryman Silvanus, called around him the Franks, of whom at that time there was a great number in the palace, and in resolute language laid open and proved the falsehood of the machinations by which their lives were threatened, and was loud in his complaints.

When these things became known to the emperor, he appointed the members of his consistory and the chief officers of his army to make further investigation into the matter. And when the judges appeared to make light of it Florentius, the son of Nigrinianus, who at that time was the acting master of the offices, having examined the writings carefully, and detecting beneath them some vestiges of the tops of the former words which had been effaced, perceived, as was indeed the case, that by interpolation of the original letter, matters very different from any of which Silvanus was author had been written over them, according to the fancy of the contriver of this forgery.

On this the cloud of treachery was dispersed, and the emperor, informed of the truth by a faithful report, recalled the powers granted to the prefect, and ordered him to be submitted to an examination. Nevertheless he was acquitted through the active combination of many of his friends; while Eusebius, the former treasurer of the emperor's private estates, being put to the torture, confessed that these things had been done with his privity. Aedesius, affirming with obstinate denial that he had known anything which had been done in the matter, escaped and was adjudged innocent. And thus the transaction was brought to an end, and all those who had been accused in the original information were acquitted; and Dynamius, as a man of exceeding accomplishments and prudence, was appointed to govern Etruria with the rank of corrector.

While these affairs were proceeding, Silvanus was living at Agrippina, and having learned by continual information sent to him by his friends what Apodemius was doing with the hope of effecting his ruin, and knowing also how impressible the mind of the feeble emperor was, began to fear lest, in his absence and without being convicted of any crime, he might still be treated as a criminal. And so, being placed in a situation of the greatest difficulty, he began to think of trusting himself to the good faith of the barbarians.

He was dissuaded from this by Laniogaisus, at that time a tribune, whom we have already spoken of as the only person who was present with Constans when he was dying, being then a *candidatus*. Being assured by Laniogaisus that the Franks, of whom he himself was a countryman, would put him to death, or else betray him for a bribe, Silvanus saw no safety anywhere in the present emergency, and so was driven to extreme counsels. And by degrees, having secretly conferred with the senior officers, and having excited them by the magnitude of promised rewards, he tore for use on this occasion the purple silk from the insignia of the dragons and standards, and so assumed the title of emperor.

While these events were passing in Gaul, one day a little before sunset an unexpected messenger arrived at Milan relating fully that Silvanus, being ambitious to rise above his place as commander of the infantry, had tampered with the army, and assumed the imperial dignity. Constantius, at this amazing and unexpected event, seemed as if struck by a thunderbolt of fate, and at once summoned the consistory to meet at the second watch. All the nobles hastened to the palace. No one had either mind to conceive or tongue to recommend what was best to be done; but in suppressed tones they mentioned the name of Ursicinus as a man eminent for skill in affairs of war, and one who had been undeservedly exposed to most injurious treatment. He was immediately sent for by the master of the admissions, which is the most honorable kind of summons, and as soon as he entered the consistory he was offered the purple to salute much more graciously than at any former time. Diocletian was the first who introduced the custom of offering reverence to the emperor after this foreign manner and royal pretension; whereas all former princes, as we have read, had been saluted like judges.

And so the man who a little while before, through the malevo-

lent persecution of certain of the courtiers, had been termed the
whirlpool of the East, and who had been accused of a design to aim
at the supreme power for his sons, was now recommended as one
who was a most skillful general and had been the comrade of the
great Constantine, and was the only man capable of extinguishing
the threatened conflagration. And though the reasons for which he
was sent for were honest, they were not wholly free from under-
hand motives. For while great anxiety was felt that Silvanus should
be destroyed as a most formidable rebel, yet, if that object mis-
carried, it was thought that Ursicinus, being damaged by the
failure, would himself easily be ruined; so that no scruple, which
else was to be feared, would interpose to save him from destruction.

While arrangements were being made for accelerating his journey, the general was preparing to repel the charges which had been
brought against him; but the emperor prevented him, forbidding
him in conciliatory language, saying that this was not an opportunity suitable for undertaking any controversy in defense of his
cause, when the imminent necessity of affairs rather prompted that
no delay should be interposed to the restoration of parties to their
pristine concord before the disunion got worse.

Therefore, after a long deliberation about many things, the first
and most important matter in which consultation was held was by
what means Silvanus could be led to think the emperor still
ignorant of his conduct. The most likely manner to confirm him in
his confidence appeared to be that he should be informed, in a
complimentary despatch, that Ursicinus was appointed his successor, and that he was invited to return to court with undiminished power.

After this affair was arranged he was ordered to start forthwith
with some tribunes and ten of the officer cadets, given him as an
escort at his own request, to aid him in the discharge of his public
duty. And of these I myself was one, with my colleague Verrin-
ianus; and all the rest were either friends or relation of mine. And
now all of us, fearing mainly for ourselves, accompanied him on his
long journey; and although we seemed as exposed to danger as
gladiators about to fight with wild beasts, yet considering in our
minds that evils are often the forerunners of good, we recollected
with admiration that expression of Cicero's, uttered by him in
accordance with the eternal maxims of truth, which runs in these

words: "Although it is a thing most desirable that one's fortune should always continue in a most flourishing condition, still that general level state of life brings not so much sensation of joy as we feel when, after having been surrounded by disasters or by dangers, fortune returns into a happier condition."

Accordingly we hastened onward by forced journeys, in order that the master of the horse, who was eager to acquire the honor of suppressing the revolt, might make his appearance in the suspected district before any rumor of the usurpation of Silvanus had spread among the Italians. But rapidly as we hastened, fame like the wind had outstripped us, and had revealed some part of the facts; and when we reached Agrippina we found matters quite out of the reach of our attempts.

For a vast multitude of people, assembled from all quarters, were with a mixture of haste and alarm strengthening the foundations of Silvanus's enterprise, and a numerous military force was collected; so that it seemed more advisable, in the existing emergency, for our unfortunate general to await the intentions and pleasure of the new emperor, who was assuring himself by ridiculous omens and signs that he was gaining accessions of strength. By permitting his feelings of security to increase by different pretenses of agreement and flattery, Silvanus, it was thought, might be relieved from all fear of hostility, and so be the more easily deceived.

But the accomplishment of such a design appeared difficult. For it was necessary to use great care and watchfulness to make our desires subordinate to our opportunities, and to prevent their either outrunning them or falling behind them; since if our wishes were allowed to become known unseasonably, it was plain we should all be involved in one sentence of death.

However our general was kindly received, and (the very business itself forcing us to bend our necks), having been compelled to prostrate himself with all solemnity before the newly robed prince, still aiming at higher power, was treated as a highly favored and eminent friend; having freedom of access and the honor of a seat at the royal table granted to him in preference to everyone else, in order that he might be consulted with the more secrecy about the principal affairs of state.

Silvanus expressed his indignation that, while unworthy persons had been raised to the consulship and to other high dignities, he and Ursicinus alone, after the numerous great toils which they had endured for the sake of the republic, had been so despised that he himself had been accused of treason in consequence of the examination of some slaves, and had been exposed to an ignoble trial; while Ursicinus had been brought over from the East, and placed at the mercy of his enemies; and these were the subjects of his incessant complaints both in public and in private.

While, however, he was holding this kind of language, we were alarmed at the widespread murmurs of the soldiers, who were now suffering from want, and were eager to make a rapid march through the defiles of the Cottian Alps. In this state of anxiety and agitation, we occupied ourselves in secretly deliberating on the means of arriving at our object; and at length, after our plans had been repeatedly changed out of fear, it was determined to use great industry in seeking out prudent agents, binding them to secrecy by solemn oaths, in order to tamper with the Bracati and Cornuti, who were of doubtful fidelity, and at any time open to change for a sufficient reward.

Therefore, after we had secured our success by the address of some agents among the common soldiers, men by their very obscurity fitted for the accomplishment of such a task, and now excited by the expectation of reward, at sunrise, as soon as the east began to redden, a band of armed men suddenly sallied forth, behaving, as is common in critical moments, with more than usual audacity. They killed the sentinels and penetrated into the palace, and so, having dragged Silvanus out of a little chapel in which in his terror he had taken refuge on his way to a conventicle devoted to the ceremonies of the Christian worship, they slew him with repeated strokes of their swords.

In this way did a general of no slight merit perish, through fear of false accusations heaped on him in his absence by a faction of wicked men, which drove him to the utmost extremities in order to preserve his safety. For although he had acquired strong claims on the gratitude of Constantius by his seasonable treachery with the Armaturae before the battle of Mursa, and although he could boast the valorous exploits of his father Bonitus, a Frank, who had espoused the party of Constantine, and often in the civil war had exhibited great prowess against the troops of Licinius, still he always feared him as a prince of wavering and fickle character.

III. The Senatorial Order

21. The senate in the early principate

These reflections were suggested to Tacitus by a proposal, rejected by Tiberius, to enforce the sumptuary laws of Augustus (see No. 10). Tacitus rightly ascribes the more sober way of life followed by senators in his own day to the gradual change in the membership of the senate by the admission of new members from Italy (the municipalities and colonies) and the provinces. Though membership of the senate was *de facto* hereditary, the older families tended to die out, and a large number of recruits had to be obtained from the outside. Although luxury went out of fashion, wealth increased, since the estates of the old families which died out normally passed through heiresses or by adoption or by will to other senatorial families.

21. *Tacitus*, Annals, *III. 55*

WHEN THEY had heard the emperor's letter, the aediles were excused from so anxious a task, and the luxury of the table, which from the close of the war at Actium to the armed revolution in which Servius Galba rose to empire, had been practiced with profuse expenditure, gradually went out of fashion. It is as well that I should trace the causes of this change.

Formerly rich or highly distinguished noble families often sank into ruin from a passion for splendor. Even then men were still at liberty to court and be courted by the city populace, by our allies and by foreign princes, and everyone who from his wealth, his mansion, and his establishment was conspicuously grand, gained too proportionate luster by his name and his numerous clientele. After the savage massacres in which greatness of renown was fatal, the survivors turned to wiser ways. The new men, who were often admitted into the senate from the municipalities and colonies and even from the provinces, introduced their household thrift, and though many of them by good luck or energy attained an old age of wealth, still their former tastes remained. But the chief encourager of strict manners was Vespasian, himself old-fashioned both in his dress and diet. Henceforth a respectful feeling toward the prince and a love of emulation proved more efficacious than legal penalties or terrors. Or possibly there is in all things a kind of cycle, and there may be moral revolutions just as there are changes of seasons. Nor was everything better in the past, but our own age, too, has produced many specimens of excellence and culture for posterity to imitate. May we still keep up with our ancestors a rivalry in all that is honorable!

22. Senators from the provinces

Claudius held the censorship (with a colleague) in A.D. 48, and took the opportunity to enroll in the senate some Gallic nobles who were already Roman citizens. His speech, as reported by Tacitus, is a statesmanlike vindication of the traditional Roman policy of absorbing conquered enemies into the citizen body and admitting their leaders to the aristocracy.

22. *Tacitus*, Annals, *XI. 23–25*

IN THE consulship of Aulus Vitellius and Lucius Vipstanus the question of filling up the senate was discussed, and the chief men of Gallia Comata, as it was called, who had long possessed the rights of allies and of Roman citizens, sought the privilege of obtaining public offices at Rome. There was much talk of every kind on the subject, and it was argued before the emperor with vehement opposition. "Italy," it was asserted, "is not so feeble as to be unable to furnish its own capital with a senate. Once our native-born citizens sufficed for peoples of our own kin, and we are by no means dissatisfied with the Rome of the past. To this day we cite examples, which under our old customs the Roman character exhibited as to valor and renown. Is it a small thing that the Veneti and Insubres have already burst into the senate house, unless a mob of foreigners, a troop of captives, so to say, is now forced upon us? What distinctions will be left for the remnants of our noble houses, or for any impoverished senators from Latium? Every place will be crowded with these millionaires, whose ancestors of the second and third generations at the head of hostile tribes destroyed our armies with fire and sword, and actually besieged the divine Julius at Alesia. These are recent memories. What if there were to rise up the remembrance of those who fell beneath the Capitol and Rome's citadel by the hands of these same barbarians! Let them enjoy indeed the title of citizens, but let them not vulgarize the distinctions of the senate and the honors of office."

These and like arguments failed to impress the emperor. He at once addressed himself to answer them, and thus harangued the assembled senate. "My ancestors, the most ancient of whom was made at once a Roman citizen and a patrician, encourage me to govern by the same policy of transferring to this city all conspicuous merit, wherever found. And indeed I know as facts that the Julii came from Alba, the Coruncanii from Camerium, the Porcii from Tusculum, and not to inquire too minutely into the past, that new members have been brought into the senate from Etruria and Lucania and the whole of Italy, that Italy itself was at last extended to the Alps, to the end that not only single persons but entire countries and tribes might be united under our name. We had unshaken peace at home, we prospered in all our foreign relations, in the days when Italy beyond the Po was admitted to share our citizenship, and when, enrolling in our ranks the most vigorous of the provincials, under color of settling our legions throughout the world, we recruited our exhausted empire. Are we sorry that the Balbi came to us from Spain, and other men not less illustrious from Narbonese Gaul? Their descendants are still among us, and do not yield to us in patriotism.

"What was the ruin of Sparta and Athens but this, that mighty as they were in war, they spurned from them as aliens those whom they had conquered? Our founder Romulus, on the other hand, was so wise that he fought as enemies and then hailed as fellow citizens several nations on the very same day. Strangers have reigned over us. That freedmen's sons should be entrusted with public offices is not, as many wrongly think, a sudden innovation, but was a common practice in the old commonwealth. But, it will be said, we have fought with the Senones. I suppose then that the Volsci and Aequi never stood in array against us. Our city was taken by the Gauls. Well, we also gave hostages to the Etruscans, and passed under the yoke of the Samnites. On the whole, if you review all our wars, never has one been finished in a shorter time than that with the Gauls. Thenceforth they have preserved an unbroken and loyal peace. United as they now are with us by manners, education, and intermarriage, let them bring us their gold and their wealth rather than enjoy it in isolation. Everything, senators, which we now hold to be of the highest antiquity, was once new. Plebeian magistrates came after patrician; Latin magistrates after plebeian; magistrates of other Italian peoples after Latin. This practice, too, will establish itself, and what we are this day justifying by precedents, will be itself a precedent."

The emperor's speech was followed by a decree of the senate, and the Aedui were the first to obtain the right of becoming senators at Rome. This compliment was paid to their ancient alliance, and to the fact that they alone of the Gauls cling to the name of brothers of the Roman people.

About the same time the emperor enrolled in the ranks of the patricians such senators as were of the oldest families, and such as had had distinguished ancestors. There were now but scanty relics of the Greater Houses of Romulus and of the Lesser Houses of Lucius Brutus, as they had been called, and those, too, were exhausted which the dictator Caesar by the Cassian and the emperor Augustus by the Saenian law had chosen into their place. These acts, as being welcome to the state, were undertaken with hearty gladness by the imperial censor. Anxiously considering how he was to rid the senate of men of notorious infamy, he preferred a gentle method, recently devised, to one which accorded with the sternness of antiquity, and advised each to examine his own case and seek the privilege of laying aside his rank. Permission, he said, would be readily obtained. He would publish in the same list those who had been expelled and those who had been allowed to retire, that by this confounding together of the decision of the censors and the modesty of voluntary resignation the disgrace might be softened.

For this, the consul Vipstanus moved that Claudius should be called "Father of the Senate." The title of "Father of the Country" had, he argued, been indiscriminately bestowed; new services ought to be recognized by unusual titles. The emperor, however, himself stopped the consul's flattery as extravagant. He closed the lustrum, the census for which gave a total of 5,984,072 citizens.

23. Claudius' speech on the Gallic senators

We are fortunate in possessing an engraved copy of part of Claudius' speech on the admission of the Gallic senators; it was found at Lyons, where all the communities of northern Gaul assembled to celebrate the

imperial cult. It will be seen that Tacitus has much improved Claudius'
original speech by eliminating a great deal of irrelevant antiquarian
lore.

23. Dessau, ILS, 212

I MYSELF deprecate that first thought of everyone, which I foresee
will be my chief and first obstacle—you should not be alarmed, as
if a novelty is being introduced, but rather think of all the many
novelties which this city has undergone, and of the many shapes
and forms which our commonwealth assumed right from the origin
of our city.

At one time kings ruled the city, and yet they did not hand the
kingship on to successors of their own house. Outsiders, and even
foreigners, came in; Numa, who succeeded Romulus, came from
the Sabines, a neighbor it is true, but in those days a foreigner, and
Ancus Martius was followed by Priscus Tarquinius. He, owing to
his impure blood—his father was Demaratus of Corinth and his
mother a noble lady of Tarquinii, but poor, seeing that she had to
descend to such a husband—since he was excluded from holding
office at home, migrated to Rome and obtained the kingship. He,
too, and his son or grandson—the authorities differ on this point—
was succeeded by Servius Tullius, who was, if we follow our
historians, son of a captive Ocresian woman, if we follow the
Etruscans, a former faithful companion of Caelius Vivenna and
the companion of all his fortunes, who, when after various turns of
fortune he had been expelled with all the survivors of Caelius' army
and left Etruria, occupied the Caelian hill, so called from his leader
Caelius, and changing his name (for he had been called Mastarna in
Tuscan) took the name by which I have spoken of him and obtained the kingship to the great advantage of the commonwealth.
Then, of course, after the character of Tarquinius Superbus had
begun to be hateful to our city, both his and his son's characters,
we were disgusted with the kingship and the administration of the
commonwealth was transferred to the consuls, annual magistrates.

Why should I speak now of the power of the dictatorship, which
our ancestors invented as being stronger than the consular power
itself, to use in severer wars or more difficult civil commotions? Or
the tribunes of the plebs, created to protect the plebs? Why of the
transfer of power from the consuls to the decemvirs, and of its
subsequent return to the consuls after the overthrow of the de-

cemviral tyranny? Why of the division of the consular power
among a larger number, the so-called military tribunes with consular power, of whom six or often eight were elected? Why of the
first sharing with the plebs of not only the offices of command but
of the priesthoods, too? If I should now relate the wars which our
ancestors began and what progress was made, I fear that I may
seem to be boastful, and to have sought an occasion for bragging of
the extension of our empire beyond the ocean. But I will return to
the point. The citizenship ——— by a new policy both my great
uncle, the deified Augustus, and my uncle Tiberius wished all the
cream of the colonies and the municipalities everywhere, that is
good worthy men, to be members of this house. What then? Is not
an Italian senator better than a provincial one? I will show you,
now that I am beginning to justify this part of my censorship, what
I think on the matter. I believe that not even provincials can be
rejected, if only they can adorn the senate house.

For how long a time now has the distinguished and powerful
colony of Vienna conferred senators on this house? From that
colony comes that ornament of the equestrian order, Lucius
Vestinus, whom I count among my friends and at this moment
employ upon my business. I beg that his sons may enjoy the
highest ranks of the priesthood, who increase their dignity as the
years go by. I will pass over in silence the foul name of a brigand—
I hate that athletic prodigy—who introduced the consulship into
his family before his colony had achieved the full benefit of the
Roman citizenship. I can say the same about his brother, his fate is
pitiable and undeserved, that he cannot be a useful senator for you.
It is now time, Tiberius Caesar Germanicus, that you revealed to
the conscript fathers where your speech is tending, for you have
already come to the further boundary of Gallia Narbonensis.

All these distinguished young men whom I see are no more to be
despised as senators than my noble friend Persicus is ashamed to
read the name of Allobrogicus on the portraits of his ancestors. But
if you agree that this is so, what more do you desire than that I
should point out this one fact, that senators are sent to you from
beyond the boundaries of the Narbonese province, since we are
not sorry to have men from Lugdunum in our order. I have timidly
passed, conscript fathers, the customary boundaries of provinces
familiar to you, but now the case of Gallia Comata must be
vigorously urged. If anyone regards the fact that for ten years they

engaged the deified Julius in wars, he should count against it a century of unwavering loyalty and service, time and again proved in moments of difficulty for us. They furnished my father Drusus, when he was conquering Germany, safe and secure peace in his rear by their tranquillity, and that, too, when he had been summoned to the wars from the work of the census, which was something new and strange to the Gauls. How hard that work is for us, we realize only too well now by personal experience, though nothing is required except that our work should be publicly known.

24. A recommendation for admission to the senate

Equites who had achieved distinction in war or administration, or more commonly their sons (see No. 29), might achieve senatorial rank.

This letter of Pliny to Trajan demonstrates another way in which new members were recruited to the senate—by the interest of influential senators. Pliny claims no merits for Voconius Romanus except that he is a nice young man and well off; the minimum qualification for the senate was one million sesterces.

24. Pliny, Letters, X. 4.

THE AMPLE experience, Sir, I have had of your unbounded generosity to me in my own person, encourages me to hope I may be yet further obliged to it in favor of my friends. Voconius Romanus (who lives and was bred up with me) claims the first rank in that number; in consequence of which I petitioned your sacred father to promote him to the dignity of the senatorial order. But the completion of my request is reserved to your goodness; for his mother had not then advanced, in the manner the law directs, the four million sesterces, which she engaged to give him in her letter to the emperor, your late father. This, however, by my advice she has since done, having conveyed to him a sufficient estate in land, with all the necessary formalities. The difficulties which deferred our wishes therefore being removed, it is with full confidence I venture to assure you of the merit of my friend Romanus, heightened and adorned as it is not only by the liberal and polite arts, but by his extraordinary tenderness to his parents. It is to that virtue he owes the present liberality of his mother; as well as his immediate succession to his late father's estate, and his

having been adopted by his father-in-law. To these personal qualifications the wealth and rank of his family given an increase of
luster; as I persuade myself it will be some additional recommendation to your favor, that I solicit in his behalf. Let me then
entreat you, Sir, to put it in my power to congratulate Romanus,
on an occasion so highly agreeable to me; and at the same time to
gratify an eager, and I hope a laudable, ambition of being able to
boast that your favorable regards are extended, not only to myself, but also to my friend.

25. The prefect of the city

As Tacitus explains, the prefect of the city was a very ancient office
which had become a ceremonial sinecure. Augustus revived it in a new
form, appointing senior senators, at first temporarily when he was
absent from Rome, toward the end of his reign, permanently. The
function of the city prefect was, at first, as Tacitus says, primarily to
maintain order in Rome; he had the urban cohorts at his disposal.
Gradually his jurisdiction, both civil and criminal, became important.
Maecenas, despite Tacitus, did not hold the office. Messala was appointed in 25 B.C. when Augustus went away to Spain, Taurus in 16
B.C., when he went to Gaul; Piso held office from A.D. 12 to 32. The
office was henceforth held for life.

25. *Tacitus*, Annals, *VI. 11*

IN FORMER days, when the kings and subsequently the chief
magistrates went from Rome, an official was temporarily chosen to
administer justice and provide for emergencies, so that the capital
might not be left without government. It is said that Denter
Romulius was appointed by Romulus, then Numa Marcius by
Tullus Hostilius, and Spurius Lucretius by Tarquinius Superbus.
Afterward, the consuls made the appointment. The shadow of the
old practice still survives, whenever in consequence of the Latin
festival someone is deputed to exercise the consul's functions. And
Augustus, too, during the civil wars gave Cilnius Maecenas, a
Roman knight, charge of everything in Rome and Italy. When he
rose to supreme power, in consideration of the magnitude of the
state and the slowness of legal remedies, he selected one of the ex-
consuls to overawe the slaves and that part of the population
which, unless it fears a strong hand, is disorderly and reckless.
Messala Corvinus was the first to obtain the office, which he laid

down within a few days, as not knowing how to discharge it. After
him Taurus Statilius, though in advanced years, sustained it ad-
mirably; and then Piso, after twenty years of similar credit, was, by
the senate's decree, honored with a public funeral.

26. Poppaeus Sabinus

Sabinus governed Moesia from A.D. 12 to 32, when he died in office.
Such very long terms were quite exceptional, three years being the
norm. Sabinus was of humble origin and, according to Tacitus, up to
his task but not above it, a safe man to hold a military command. The
senatorial provinces of Macedonia and Achaea were in this year (A.D.
15) attached at their own request to the imperial province of Moesia,
they were restored to the senate in A.D. 44.

The consulship, though it no longer had any practical power, continued to be the supreme honor and a great object of ambition. Tiberius
would seem from this passage to have studiously avoided exercising
any pressure on the senate in the elections. Later the consuls came to
be virtually nominated by the emperor.

26. *Tacitus*, Annals, *I. 80–81*

POPPAEUS SABINUS was continued in his government of the province of Moesia with the addition of Achaea and Macedonia. It was
part of Tiberius' character to prolong indefinitely military commands and to keep many men to the end of their life with the same
armies and in the same administrations. Various motives have been
assigned for this. Some say that, out of aversion to any fresh
anxiety, he retained what he had once approved as a permanent
arrangement; others, that he grudged to see many enjoying promotion. Some, again, think that though he had an acute intellect, his
judgment was irresolute, for he did not seek out eminent merit, and
yet he detested vice. From the best men he apprehended danger to
himself, from the worst, disgrace to the state. He went so far at last
in this irresolution, that he appointed to provinces men whom he
was never going to allow to leave Rome.

I can hardly venture on any positive statement about the consular elections, now held for the first time under this emperor, or
indeed, subsequently, so conflicting are the accounts that we find
not only in historians but in Tiberius' own speeches. Sometimes he
kept back the names of the candidates, describing their origin, their
life, and military career, so that it might be understood who they
were. Occasionally even these hints were withheld, and, after

urging them not to disturb the elections by canvassing, he would promise his own help toward the result. Generally he declared that only those had offered themselves to him as candidates whose names he had given to the consuls, and that others might offer themselves if they had confidence in their influence or merit. A plausible profession this in words, but really unmeaning and delusive, and the greater the disguise of freedom which marked it, the more cruel the enslavement into which it was soon to plunge us.

27. Plautius Silvanus

This inscription records the career of a distinguished senator of military ability. He puts first his two priesthoods, then his career in chronological order, first a minor office, then quaestor (one of the two attached to the emperor), commander of a legion, praetor at Rome, on the staff of Claudius in the invasion of Britain, consul, proconsul of Asia, governor of Moesia, governor of Spain, prefect of the city.

A senator normally began his career with a military tribunate (see No. 10). Every senator was obliged to hold a fixed sequence of magistracies, a minor magistracy, the quaestorship (which gave him access to the senate), the aedileship or tribunate of the plebs (unless he was a patrician), the praetorship, and the consulate. Five years or more after his praetorship and his consulate he could be proconsul of a province. He could become legate of a legion before his praetorship, after his praetorship govern a less important province as imperial legate, and after his consulate be legate of a major province.

27. *Dessau,* ILS, *986*

To TIBERIUS PLAUTIUS, son of Marcus, of the tribe Aniensis, Silvanus Aelianus, pontifex, Sodalis Augustalis, one of the three commissioners for smelting and striking gold, silver, and bronze, quaestor of Tiberius Caesar, legate of legion V in Germany, city praetor, legate of the emperor Claudius Caesar in Britain, consul, proconsul of Asia, *legatus propraetore* of Moesia, to which he transported more than one hundred thousand of the peoples beyond the Danube with their wives and children and chiefs or kings to pay tribute; he suppressed an incipient rising of the Sarmatians although he had sent a great part of his army to the Armenian expedition; he brought kings hitherto unknown or hostile to the Roman people to adore the Roman standards on the bank of the river which he guarded; he returned to the kings of the Bastarnae and Rhoxolani their sons, to those of the Dacians their brothers who had been captured or seized by the enemy; he received hostages from some of them; whereby he confirmed and extended the peace of the province. He also repelled the king of the Scythians from the siege of Cheronesus, which is beyond the Borysthenes. He was the first to assist the corn supply at Rome with a large quantity of wheat from that province. Having been sent as legate to Spain and then recalled to be prefect of the city, the senate honored him with triumphal decorations in his prefecture on the proposal of Imperator Caesar Vespasianus Augustus in the following words, quoted from his speech: "His command of Moesia was so distinguished that the honor of his triumphal decorations ought not to have been deferred to my reign, except that by the delay he received the higher title of prefect of the city."

28. Pedanius Secundus

This incident, which occurred in A.D. 61, illustrates the wealth and luxury of great senators. Pedanius Secundus, the prefect of the city, had no less than four hundred domestic slaves in his town house. Cassius was an aged jurist, whose views were, as he admits, highly conservative and in conflict with the growing humanitarianism of the age. It is noteworthy that the urban populace, many of whom were freedmen or of servile descent, protested violently against the execution. The majority of the senators, who were slave owners on a large scale, voted for maintaining the old Draconia rule.

28. *Tacitus*, Annals, *XIV. 42–45*

SOON AFTERWARD one of his own slaves murdered the city prefect, Pedanius Secundus, either because he had been refused his freedom, for which he had made a bargain, or in the jealousy of a love in which he could not brook his master's rivalry. Ancient custom required that the whole slave establishment which had dwelt under the same roof should be executed, when a sudden gathering of the populace, which was for saving so many innocent lives, brought matters to actual insurrection. Even in the senate there was a strong feeling on the part of those who shrank from extreme rigor, though the majority were opposed to any innovation. Of these, Gaius Cassius, in giving his vote, argued to the following effect:

"Often I have been present, senators, in this assembly when new decrees were demanded from us contrary to the customs and laws of our ancestors, and I have refrained from opposition, not because

I doubted but that in all matters the arrangements of the past were
better and fairer and that all changes were for the worse, but that I
might not seem to be exalting my own profession out of an excessive partiality for ancient precedent. At the same time I thought
that any influence I possess ought not to be destroyed by incessant
protests, wishing that it might remain unimpaired, should the state
ever need my counsels. Today this has come to pass, since an ex-
consul has been murdered in his house by the treachery of slaves,
which not one hindered or divulged, though the senate's decree,
which threatens the entire slave establishment with execution, has
been till now unshaken. Vote impunity, in heaven's name, and then
who will be protected by his rank, when the prefecture of the
capital has been of no avail to its holder? Who will be kept safe by
the number of his slaves when four hundred have not protected
Pedanius Secundus? Which of us will be rescued by his domestics,
who, even with the dread of punishment before them, regard not
our dangers? Was the murderer, as some do not blush to pretend,
avenging his wrongs because he had bargained about his father's
money or because a family slave was taken from him? Let us
actually decide that the master was justly slain.

"Is it your pleasure to search for arguments in a matter already
weighed in the deliberations of wiser men than ourselves? Even if
we had now for the first time to come to a decision do you believe
that a slave took courage to murder his master without letting fall a
threatening word or uttering a rash syllable? Granted that he
concealed his purpose, that he procured his weapon without his
fellows' knowledge. Could he pass the night guard, could he open
the doors of the chamber, carry in a light, and accomplish the
murder, while all were in ignorance? There are many preliminaries
to guilt; if these are divulged by slaves, we may live singly amid
numbers, safe among a trembling throng; lastly, if we must perish,
it will be with vengeance on the guilty. Our ancestors always
suspected the temper of their slaves, even when they were born on
the same estates, or in the same houses with themselves and thus
inherited from their birth an affection for their masters. But now
that we have in our households nations with different customs to
our own, with a foreign worship or none at all, it is only by terror
you can hold in such motley rabble. But, it will be said, the innocent will perish. Well, even in a beaten army when every tenth
man is felled by the club, the lot falls also on the brave. There is

some injustice in every great precedent, which, though injurious to individuals, has its compensation in the public advantage."

No one indeed dared singly to oppose the opinion of Cassius, but clamorous voices rose in reply from all who pitied the number, age, or sex, as well as the undoubted innocence of the great majority. Still, the party which voted for their execution prevailed. But the sentence could not be obeyed in the face of a dense and threatening mob, with stones and firebrands. Then the emperor reprimanded the people by edict, and lined with a force of soldiers the entire route by which the condemned had to be led to execution. Cingonius Varro had proposed that even all the freedmen under the same roof should be transported from Italy. This the emperor forbade, as he did not wish an ancient custom, which mercy had not relaxed, to be strained with cruel rigor.

29. Agricola

Agricola, the father-in-law of the historian Tacitus, came like many senators of the principate from a well-to-do provincial family, which rose first into the equestrian and then into the senatorial order. His career was normal, a legionary tribunate (in Britain), the quaestorship (in Asia), the tribunate of the plebs, and the praetorship, in which office he had no duties, as there were by this time more praetors than judicial posts and he drew a blank in the lottery. He then became a legate of a legion (again in Britain); *legatus pro praetore* of Aquitania, an imperial province with no legion; consul, and finally *legatus Augusti pro praetore*, of the important imperial province of Britain. He also received a priesthood and was made a patrician.

The two senior ex-consuls were entitled to draw lots for the proconsulships of Africa and Asia. As there were by this time four or six consuls per annum, there was a long interval between the consulship and proconsulship. Agricola, in response to broad hints, did not enter for the ballot, and was not offered the consolation prize of the salary, which amounted to a million sesterces.

29. *Tacitus*, Agricola, *4–9, 42*

GNAEUS JULIUS AGRICOLA, born in the ancient and illustrious colony of Forum Julii, had both his grandfathers procurators of the Caesars, which is the equestrian nobility; his father, Julius Graecinus, of the senatorial order, was famous for his study of eloquence and philosophy, and by these accomplishments he brought on himself the displeasure of Gaius Caesar: for he was ordered to prosecute Marcus Silanus and, because he refused, was put to death. His mother was Julia Procilla, a woman of singular chastity: brought up in her bosom and affection, he passed his childhood and youth in the constant cultivation of the liberal arts. In addition to his own chaste and virtuous disposition, it preserved him from the allurements of the vicious that immediately from his childhood he made Marseilles his residence and place of education, a city tempered with, and happily combining, Grecian politeness and provincial frugality. I remember he used to say that in early youth he would have pursued the study of philosophy more eagerly, beyond what was allowed a Roman and a senator, had not his mother's discretion restrained his ardent and vehement mind. His high and elevated disposition sought after the beauty and grandeur of exalted and great glory with more eagerness than caution: reason and years, soon after, mitigated this ardor; and, a thing which is very difficult, he observed a mean even in the pursuit of wisdom.

The first rudiments of a camp he passed in Britain, to the satisfaction of Suetonius Paulinus, an active and prudent commander, having been chosen as one whom he deemed worthy of being his tent companion. Nor did Agricola employ the title and inexperience of his tribuneship in licentiousness, after the manner of young men, who convert military service into lasciviousness, nor in indolence, nor pleasures and absence from duty; but he endeavored to know the province, to become known to the army, to learn from the experienced, to imitate the best, to seek nothing through ostentation, to refuse nothing through timidity, and at the same time to act with solicitude and determination. Nor indeed was Britain at any other period more disturbed or more precarious: our veterans slaughtered, our colonies destroyed by fire, our armies hemmed in: at that time they contended for safety, soon after for victory. Though all these matters were conducted by the counsels and directions of another, and though the chief command and the glory of recovering the province fell to the general, still they added skill, experience, and incentives to the youth; and a desire of military glory entered his mind, unpopular in those times, when unfavorable constructions were put on the acts of men of eminence, and there was no less danger from a great character than from a bad one.

Having departed hence into the city to take on him the magistracy, he married Domitia Decidiana, a lady of splendid birth; and this connection was an ornament and support to him when aspiring to higher objects: they lived in wonderful harmony, in mutual affection, each giving the other the preference, except that in a virtuous wife the merit is greater in proportion as there is more censure for a vicious one. The lot of the quaestorship assigned him Asia as his province, and Salvius Titianus as proconsul; by neither of which circumstances was he corrupted; though the province was rich and open for the profligate, and the proconsul, bent on all manner of avarice, would with all possible ease have stipulated for a mutual connivance in rapine. He was here blessed with a daughter, both as a support and consolation; for he lost in a short time a son, who was born before this event. Afterward, the interval between the quaestorship and the tribuneship of the people, and even the year of the tribuneship, he spent in peace and repose, well aware of the temper of the times under Nero, when indolence passed for wisdom. The tenor and silence of the praetorship were precisely the same: for no judicial duties fell to him. The games and the pageantry of the office he conducted under the restrictions of propriety and sufficiency, approaching to popularity in proportion as he was removed from extravagance. Being appointed by Galba to inspect the offerings in the temples, by a most careful investigation he brought it to pass that the state should feel the sacrilege of no other person than that of Nero.

The following year inflicted a severe blow on his feelings and his family: for the fleet of Otho, roving in a disorderly manner, whilst they were ravaging Intemelium (a part of Liguria) in a hostile manner, murdered Agricola's mother on her own estate; and pillaged the estate itself, and a considerable portion of the property, which had been the cause of the murder. Agricola, having set out to perform the last offices of filial affection, was overtaken by the account of Vespasian's having aspired to the empire, and immediately went over to his side. Mucianus took charge of the commencement of the reign and of the government of the city, Domitian being very young, and of all his father's power claiming only a license for debauchery. He appointed Agricola, who had been sent to hold the levies, and who had discharged the office with integrity and activity, to the command of the twentieth legion, as his predecessor was reported to be acting seditiously: for it had now become unmanageable, and formidable even to the consular legates, nor was the praetorian commander able to restrain it, it is uncertain whether from his own disposition or that of his soldiers. Thus being appointed at the same time his successor and avenger, by a most surprising instance of moderation he chose rather that it should appear he had found them obedient than that he had made them so.

Vettius Bolanus at that time governed Britain, in a manner more gentle than suited a turbulent province; Agricola tempered his spirit and restrained his ardor so that it should not increase, well skilled in obeying, and knowing full well how to combine what was profitable with what was honorable. In a short time Britain received, as its consular governor, Petilius Cerialis. His talents now had free scope to produce noble examples for others. At first, indeed, Cerialis shared with him only the toils and dangers; soon after, the glory also: he often appointed him over a part of the army, by way of trial, sometimes over a larger force, according to the result: nor did Agricola ever exult in his exploits to his own fame, but always, as a subordinate, he referred his success to his superior and commander; thus by industry in obeying, by modesty in speaking of himself, he kept clear of envy, nor was he still deprived of glory.

On his return from the command of the legion, the deified Vespasian raised him to patrician rank, and afterward appointed him over the province of Aquitania, a dignity particularly splendid, from the office itself, and also from the hope of the consulship for which it destined him. Most persons think that military minds are deficient in subtlety, because the jurisdiction of the camp, regardless of forms and rather blunt, employs not the nice discrimination of the forum. Agricola, by his natural good sense, acted with ease and precision even amongst civilians. But now the hours of business and of relaxation were distinct: when the counsels and the judicial bench called for it, he was dignified, strict, severe, and more frequently merciful; when his official duty was over, there was no longer an assumption of authority. Sternness, arrogance, and avarice he totally divested himself of; and, what is very rare, his affability did not impair his authority, nor his severity his popularity. To mention integrity and exemption from corruption in such a man would be an insult to his virtues. He did not even court fame, to which good men make sacrifices, by a display of virtue, or by artifice: keeping aloof from competition with his colleagues, or contention with the procurators, he considered it inglorious to conquer, and disgraceful to be put down. In this command he was detained somewhat less than three years, and was then recalled to a hope of the consulship, an opinion accompanying him that Britain was given to him as his province—not from any suggestion of his own on the matter, but because he was considered equal to it. Report does not always err—it has sometimes even directed the choice. When consul, he betrothed his daughter, a girl at that time of splendid hopes, to me, a very young man, and after the consulship gave her to me in marriage, and immediately after was appointed to the government of Britain, with the additional honor of the pontificate.

*　　　　*　　　　*

The year was now arrived in which he was to cast lots for the proconsulate of Asia and Africa; and, Civica having been lately put to death, neither Agricola wanted a lesson, nor Domitian an example. Some persons, well acquainted with the intentions of the prince, came to him and inquired, "whether he intended to proceed to his province"; and, at first somewhat disguisedly, they began to extol "quiet and a life of ease"; presently they offered "their services in supporting his excuse"; at length, no longer using disguise, advising and at the same time intimidating him, they forced him to go to Domitian, who, prepared to dissemble, assuming an air of haughtiness, listened to the petition of him excusing himself, and, when he had granted it, he suffered thanks to be returned to him; nor did he blush at the invidious nature of the favor: the salary, however, usually offered to the proconsul, and granted to some by himself, he did not give to Agricola: whether from being offended at its not being solicited, or from an apprehension lest he should appear to have purchased what he had really forbidden. It is a principle of human nature to hate the person whom you have injured: but the disposition of Domitian, naturally prone to anger, and the more difficult to be averted in proportion as it was more smothered, was notwithstanding softened by the modesty and prudence of Agricola, because he did not provoke fame and destruction by contumaciousness and a vain display of liberty. Let those whose custom it is to admire what is forbidden, know that, even under wicked princes, men may be great; and that submission and modesty, if industry and energy be combined with them, may reach that height of glory, by which men have signalized themselves through dangerous paths, but without any advantage to their country, by means of an ambitious death.

30. Pliny

This is a memorial to Pliny the Younger, the author of the letters, several of which are quoted in this book (Nos. 24, 35, 37, 54, 60, 82–84, 95, 107–11, 136, 144, 169). He was a native of Comum, to which he gave in his lifetime the endowment for a school (see No. 111) as well as the benefactions under his will here listed. Foundations for the maintenance of poor children were popular at this time; the imperial government gave large sums for the purpose (see No. 146). Pliny gives his career in reverse order. He first held a minor magistracy at Rome and a military tribunate in Syria, was appointed to the honorary post of *sevir equitum* (see No. 35), was chosen as one of the emperor's two quaestors, and elected tribune of the plebs and praetor. He then held three senior administrative posts at Rome. For the Tiber board see No. 10, for the military treasury, No. 1 (17); the treasury of Saturn was the old treasury of the Roman people, managed since Augustus' day by praetors or expraetors (see No. 10). He became consul, and received a priesthood. Finally he was appointed special imperial governor of Bithynia, which was normally a public province governed by a proconsul. His despatches from Bithynia, with Trajan's replies, form the tenth book of his letters. It may be noted that Pliny, after his tribunate, held no military posts, in contrast with Agricola, whose appointments were nearly all military.

30. *Dessau*, ILS, 2927

Gaius Plinius, son of Lucius of the tribe Oufentina Caecilius Secundus, consul, augur, *legatus propraetore* of the province of Pontus and Bithynia with consular powers, sent to the same province by resolution of the senate by Imperator Caesar Nerva Trajan Augustus Germanicus Dacicus, father of his country, curator of the bed and banks of the Tiber and of the drains of the city, prefect of the treasury of Saturn and of the military treasury, praetor, tribune of the plebs, quaestor of the emperor, commander of one of the six squadrons of Roman *equites*, military tribune of Legion III Gallica, one of the ten commissioners for deciding disputes, ordered by his will to be built baths at a cost of ———— sesterces, adding for their adornment 300,000 sesterces and 2,000 sesterces per annum for their upkeep; he also bequeathed to his city for the maintenance of his one hundred freedmen 1,865,666 sesterces, whose interest he wished to be spent thereafter on a feast for the urban populace; he also gave during his life for the maintenance of the boys and girls of the urban populace 500,000 sesterces, also a library and 100,000 sesterces for the upkeep of the library.

31. Tertullus

Cornutus Tertullus was a friend and almost exact contemporary of Pliny. His career, given in reverse order, is, like Pliny's, entirely civil. He started normally with the quaestorship and aedileship and was then advanced to praetorian rank by the emperor without holding the praetorship, served as legate to the proconsul of Crete and Cyrene, held two administrative posts in Italy, an administrative post in Aquitania, and then, like Pliny, governed Bithynia as an imperial legate. He then became proconsul of Narbonensis, as ex-praetor, consul, and finally proconsul of Asia.

31. Dessau, ILS, 1024

To GAIUS JULIUS, son of Publius of the tribe Horatia, Cornutus Tertullus consul, proconsul of the province of Asia, proconsul of the province of Narbonensis, *legatus pro praetore* of the deified Trajan Parthicus of the province of Pontus and Bithynia, *legatus pro praetore* of the province of Aquitania for receiving the census returns, curator of the Aemilian road, prefect of the treasury of Saturn, *legatus pro praetore* of the province of Crete and Cyrenae, enrolled among the ex-praetors by the deified Vespasian and Titus, censors, Cereal aedile, urban quaestor.

32. Hadrian

This is the career of the future emperor Hadrian, given in reverse order. Like Pliny he was *sevir equitum* (see No. 35), and also as a young man he held the honorary post of prefect of the city for the Latin games (see No. 25). He was military tribune of three legions before becoming one of the emperor's quaestors, held the command of a legion concurrently with his praetorship, was then consul and governor of the military province of Lower Pannonia. His career was almost entirely military. He held two priesthoods. Hadrian was a great admirer of Greek culture, and held the archonship of Athens for a year.

32. Dessau, ILS, 308

To PUBLIUS AELIUS, son of Publius of the tribe Sergia Hadrianus, consul, one of the seven commissioners for religious banquets, companion of the order of Augustus, *legatus pro praetore* of the emperor Nerva Trajan Caesar Augustus Germanicus Dacicus of

Lower Pannonia, praetor and at the same time legate of Legion I Minervia the Loyal and Faithful in the Dacian war, also tribune of the plebs, quaestor of the emperor Trajan and his companion on the Dacian expedition, twice granted military decorations by him, tribune of Legion II Adiutrix the Loyal and Faithful, also of Legion V Macedonica, also of Legion XXII Primigenia the Loyal and Faithful, commander of one of his six squadrons of *equites*, prefect of the Latin Games, one of the ten commissioners for deciding disputes.

[The foregoing is in Latin; the final portion is in Greek.] The Council of the Areopagus and the Council of the six hundred and the people of Athens to their own chief magistrate Hadrian.

33. Salvius Julianus

Salvius Julianus, who gives his career in chronological order, was a distinguished jurist to whom Hadrian entrusted the codification of the praetor's edict. His posts are all civilian, for Spain, though it had one legion, was by this time entirely pacified.

33. *Dessau*, ILS, *8973*

To LUCIUS CORNELIUS, son of Publius Salvius Julianus Aemilianus, one of the ten commissioners, quaestor of the emperor Hadrian, for whom alone the deified Hadrian doubled the salary of the quaestor in recognition of his notable learning, tribune of the plebs, praetor, prefect of the treasury of Saturn, and also of the military treasury, consul, pontifex, companion of the order of Hadrian, companion of the order of Antoninus, curator of sacred buildings, legate of the emperor Antoninus Augustus and Verus Augustus of Hither Spain, proconsul of the province of Africa, their patron, by resolution of the decurions.

34. The senate in the fourth century

The senate of Rome had in the fourth century ceased to be of any political importance. The emperors rarely, if ever, resided at Rome, and the imperial council and the ministers of state and all men of ambition followed the emperor. Rome remained, however, the residence of the old and immensely wealthy families which Ammianus here satirizes. One may suspect that he had himself been rudely snubbed in the way he describes when he visited Rome. His account is not altogether fair, for many of the wealthy senators were men of culture and even of learning.

34. *Ammianus Marcellinus, XIV. 6*

AT THIS time Orfitus was the governor of the Eternal City, with the rank of prefect; and he behaved with a degree of insolence beyond the proper limits of the dignity thus conferred upon him. A man of prudence indeed, and well skilled in all the forensic business of the city, but less accomplished in general literature and in the fine arts than was becoming in a nobleman. Under his administration some very formidable seditions broke out in consequence of the scarcity of wine, as the people, being exceedingly eager for an abundant supply of that article, were easily excited to frequent and violent disorders.

And since I think it likely that foreigners who may read this account (if, indeed, any such should meet with it) are likely to wonder how it is that, when my history has reached the point of narrating what was done at Rome, nothing is spoken of but seditions and shops and cheapness and other similarly inconsiderable matters, I will briefly touch upon the causes of this, never intentionally departing from the strict truth.

At the time when Rome first rose into mundane brilliancy—that Rome which is fated to last as long as mankind shall endure, and to be increased with a sublime progress and growth—virtue and fortune, though commonly at variance, agreed upon a treaty of eternal peace, as far as she was concerned. For if either of them had been wanting to her, she would never have reached her perfect and complete supremacy. Her people, from its very earliest infancy to the latest moment of its youth, a period which extends over about three hundred years, carried on a variety of wars with the natives around its walls. Then, when it arrived at its full-grown manhood, after many and various labors in war, it crossed the Alps and the sea, till, as youth and man, it had carried the triumphs of victory into every country in the world.

And now that it is declining into old age, and often owes its victories to its mere name, it has come to a more tranquil time of life. Therefore the venerable city, after having bowed down the haughty necks of fierce nations, and given laws to the world, to be the foundation and eternal anchor of liberty, like a thrifty parent, prudent and rich, entrusted to the Caesars, as to its own children, the right of governing its ancestral inheritance. And although the tribes are indolent, and the centuries peaceful, and although there are no contests for votes, but the tranquillity of the age of Numa has returned, nevertheless in every quarter of the world Rome is still looked up to as the mistress and the queen of the earth, and the name of the Roman people is respected and venerated.

But this magnificent splendor of the assemblies and councils of the Roman people is defaced by the inconsiderate levity of a few, who never recollect where they have been born, but who fall away into error and licentiousness, as if a perfect impunity were granted to vice. For, as the lyric poet Simonides teaches us, the man who would live happily in accordance with perfect reason ought above all things to have a glorious country.

Of these men, some, thinking that they can be handed down to immortality by means of statues, are eagerly desirous of them, as if they would obtain a higher reward from brazen figures unendowed with sense than from a consciousness of upright and honorable actions; and even are anxious to have them plated over with gold, a thing which is reported to have been first done in the instance of Acilius Glabrio, who by his wisdom and valor had subdued King Antiochus. But how really noble a thing it is to despise all these inconsiderable and trifling things, and to bend one's attention to the long and toilsome steps of true glory, as the poet of Ascrea has sung, and Cato the Censor has shown by his example. For when he was asked how it was that while many other nobles had statues he had none, he replied: "I had rather that good men should marvel how it was that I did not earn one, than (what would be a much heavier misfortune) inquire how it was that I had obtained one." Others place the height of glory in having a coach higher than usual, or splendid apparel; and so toil and sweat under a vast burden of cloaks, which are fastened to their necks by many clasps, and blow about from the excessive fineness of the material; showing a desire, by the continual wriggling of their bodies, and especially by the waving of the left hand, to make their long fringes and tunics, embroidered in multiform figures of animals with threads of various colors, more conspicuous.

Others, without anyone asking them, put on a feigned severity of countenance, and extol their patrimonial estates in a boundless degree, exaggerating the yearly produce of their fruitful fields, which they boast of possessing in numbers from east to west, being forsooth ignorant that their ancestors, by whom the greatness of Rome was so widely extended, were not eminent for riches; but through a course of dreadful wars overpowered by their valor all who were opposed to them, though differing but little from common soldiers in riches or in their mode of life or in the costliness of their garments. This is how it happened that Valerius Publicola was buried by the contributions of his friends, and that the destitute wife of Regulus was, with her children, supported by the aid of the friends of her husband, and that the daughter of Scipio had a dowry provided for her out of the public treasury, the other nobles being ashamed to see the beauty of this full-grown maiden, while her moneyless father was so long absent on the service of his country.

But now if you, as an honorable stranger, should enter the house of any one well off, and on that account full of pride, for the purpose of saluting him, at first indeed you will be hospitably received, as though your presence had been desired; and after having had many questions put to you, and having been forced to tell a number of lies, you will wonder, since the man had never seen you before, that one of high rank should pay such attention to you who are but an unimportant individual; so that in view of these eminent advantages you begin to repent of not having come to Rome ten years ago. And when relying on this affability you do the same thing the next day, you will stand waiting as one utterly unknown and unexpected, while he who yesterday encouraged you to repeat your visit, counts upon his fingers who you can be, marvelling for a long time whence you come and what you want. But whan at length you are recognized and admitted to his acquaintance, if you should devote yourself to saluting him for three years consecutively, and after this intermit your visits for an equal length of time, then if you return to repeat a similar course, you will never be questioned about your absence any more than if you had been dead, and you will waste your whole life in submitting to court the humors of this blockhead.

But when those long and unwholesome banquets, which are indulged in at certain intervals, begin to be prepared, or the distribution of the usual dole baskets takes place, then it is discussed with anxious deliberation whether, when those to whom a return is due are to be entertained, it is proper to invite also a stranger; and if, after the matter has been thoroughly sifted, it is determined that it may be done, that person is preferred who waits all night before the houses of charioteers, or who professes a skill in dice, or pretends to be acquainted with some peculiar secrets.

For they avoid all learned and sober men as unprofitable and useless; and in addition the nomenclators are accustomed to make a market of these invitations and of similar favors, selling them for bribes, and thrust in mean and obscure men at these dinners.

The whirlpools of banquets, and the various allurements of luxury, I omit, that I may not be too prolix and with the object of passing on to this fact, that some people, hastening on without fear of danger, drive their horses as if they were post horses with a regular license, as the saying is, through the wide streets of the city, over the roads paved with flint, dragging behind them large bodies of slaves like bands of robbers; not leaving at home even Sannio, as the comic poet says. And many matrons, imitating these men, gallop over every quarter of the city with their heads covered, in closed carriages. And as skillful conductors of battles place in the van their densest and strongest battalions, then their light-armed troops, behind them the darters, and in the extreme rear troops of reserve, ready to join in the attack if necessity should arise; so, according to the careful arrangements of the stewards of these city households, who are conspicuous by wands held in their right hands, as if a regular watchword had been issued from the camp, first of all, near the front of the carriage march all the slaves concerned in spinning and working; next to them come the blackened crew employed in the kitchen; then the whole body of slaves promiscuously mixed up with a gang of idle plebeians from the neighborhood; last of all, the multitude of eunuchs, beginning with the old men and ending with the boys, pale and unsightly from the distorted deformity of their features; so that whichever way anyone goes, seeing troops of mutilated men, one will detest the memory of Semiramis, that ancient queen who was the first person to castrate male youths of tender age; doing as it were a violence to nature, and forcing it back from its appointed course, which at the very first beginning and birth of the child, by a kind of secret law revealing the primitive fountains of seed, points out the way of propagating posterity.

And as this is the case, those few houses which were formerly celebrated for the serious cultivation of becoming studies are now filled with the ridiculous amusements of torpid indolence, re-echoing with the sound of vocal music and the tinkle of flutes and lyres. Lastly, instead of a philosopher, you find a singer; instead of an orator, some teacher of ridiculous arts is summoned; the libraries are closed forever, like so many tombs; organs to be played by water power are made; and lyres of so vast a size that they look like wagons; and flutes, and ponderous machines suited for the exhibitions of actors.

Last of all, they have arrived at such a depth of unworthiness, that when, no very long time ago, on account of an apprehended scarcity of food, outsiders were driven in haste from the city; those who practiced liberal accomplishments, the number of whom was exceedingly small, were expelled without a moment's breathing space; yet the followers of actresses, and all who at that time pretended to be of such a class, were allowed to remain; and three thousand dancing girls had not even a question put to them, but stayed unmolested with the members of their choruses, and a corresponding number of dancing masters. Wherever you turn your eyes, you may see a multitude of women with their hair curled, who, as far as their age goes, might, if they had married, have been by this time the mothers of three children, sweeping the pavements with their feet till they are weary, whirling round in rapid gyrations, while representing innumerable groups and figures which the theatrical plays contain.

It is a truth beyond all question that, when at one time Rome was the abode of all the virtues, many of the nobles, like the Lotophagi, celebrated in Homer, who detained men by the deliciousness of their fruit, allured foreigners of free birth by manifold attentions of courtesy and kindness. But now, in their empty arrogance, some persons look upon everything as worthless which is born outside of the walls of the city, except only the childless and the unmarried. Nor can it be conceived with what a variety of obsequious observance men without children are courted at Rome.

And since among them, as is natural in a city so great as to be the metropolis of the world, diseases attain to such an insurmountable degree of violence that all the skill of the physician is ineffectual even to mitigate them; a certain assistance and means of safety has been devised in the rule that no one should go to see a friend in such a condition, and to a few precautionary measures a further remedy of sufficient potency has been added, that men should not re-admit into their houses servants who have been sent to inquire how a man's friends who may have been seized with an illness of this kind are, until they have cleansed and purified their persons in the bath. So that a taint is feared, even when it has only been seen with the eyes of another. Nevertheless, when these rules are observed thus stringently, some persons, if they be invited to a wedding, though the vigor of their limbs be much diminished, yet, when gold is offered in the hollow palm of the right hand, will go actively as far as Spoletium. These are the customs of the nobles.

But of the lower and most indigent class of the populace some spend the whole night in the wine shops, some lie concealed in the shady arcades of the theaters, which Catulus was in his aedileship the first person to raise in imitation of the lascivious manners of Campania; or else they play at dice so eagerly as to quarrel over them, snuffing up their nostrils and making unseemly noises by drawing back their breath into their noses; or (and this is their favorite pursuit of all others) from sunrise to evening they stay gaping through sunshine or rain, examining in the most careful manner the most sterling good or bad qualities of the charioteers and horses. And it is very wonderful to see an innumerable multitude of people with great eagerness of mind intent upon the event of the contests in the chariot race. These pursuits, and others of like character, prevent anything worth mentioning or important from being done at Rome. Therefore, we must return to our original subject.

IV. The Equestrian Order

35. The financial qualification for equestrian status

The term *eques Romanus* seems to have been used in two senses. On the one hand, any Roman citizen of free birth for three generations who possessed four hundred thousand sesterces was allowed to use the title, but from these were chosen the six "squadrons"—purely ornamental formations—of *equites equo publico*. These were commanded by the *seviri equitum* (see Nos. 30, 32), young men destined for the senate, who until they obtained the quaestorship and thus entered the senate, ranked as *equites*. From the larger body were drawn the panels of jurymen (see Nos. 10, 138). From the *equites*—it is not certain in which sense—were also drawn the lower grade of military officers: the tribunes of the legions and the auxiliary cohorts and the prefects of the auxiliary *alae* (cavalry squadrons) and the procurators of the emperor, and the prefects of Egypt and of some smaller provinces, and the prefects of the praetorian guard, the corn supply of Rome, and the fire guard of Rome.

The members of the equestrian order were normally drawn, like the recipient of this letter, from the well-to-do families of the Italian and provincial towns, but also from centurions who had risen to be *primipili* (senior centurions of legions).

35. *Pliny*, Letters, *I. 19*

As YOU are my countryman, my school fellow, and the earliest companion of my youth; as there was the closest friendship between my mother and my uncle and your father; a happiness which I also enjoyed as far as the great inequality of our ages would admit; can I fail (biased as I am toward your interest by so many strong and weighty reasons) to contribute all in my power to the advancement of your dignity? The rank you bear in our native place as a town councillor is a proof that you are possessed at least of a hundred thousand sesterces; but that we may also have the pleasure of seeing you a Roman *eques*, give me leave to present you with three hundred thousand, in order to make up the sum

requisite to entitle you to that dignity. The long acquaintance we
have had leaves me no room to doubt you will ever be forgetful of
this instance of my friendship. And I need not advise you (as, if I
did not know your disposition, I should) to enjoy this honor with
the modesty that becomes one who received it from me; for the
dignity we possess by the good offices of a friend is a kind of sacred
trust, wherein we have his judgment, as well as our own character,
to maintain, and therefore to be guarded with particular attention.

36. The judicial powers of procurators

The procurators of the emperor, though they paid the troops and
collected the taxes in his provinces (see No. 77), were by origin
merely his private agents and had no magisterial powers until Claudius
gave them jurisdiction, although only in fiscal cases. The prefect of
Egypt naturally had full powers of jurisdiction from the beginning,
and so apparently had the lesser prefects (later called procurators)
who governed small provinces; Pontius Pilate and Festus certainly
administered justice in Judaea (cf. No. 143). Tacitus grossly exagger-
ates the jurisdiction of equestrian officials.

36. *Tacitus*, Annals, *XII. 60*

THAT SAME year the emperor was often heard to say that the legal
decisions of his procurators ought to have the same force as if
pronounced by himself. Lest it might be supposed that he had
stumbled inadvertently into this opinion, it was enacted by a decree
of the senate on a more complete and ample scale than before. It
had indeed already been arranged by the Divine Augustus that the
Roman *equites* who governed Egypt should hear causes, and that
their decisions were to be as binding as those of Roman magistrates,
and after a time in other provinces and in Rome most of the cases
formerly tried by the praetors were conceded. Claudius handed
over to them the whole administration of justice, about which there
had been so many struggles political and military; the Sempronian
laws vesting judicial power in the equestrian order, and those of
Servilius restoring it to the senate, while it was for this above everything else that Marius and Sulla fought of old. But those were days
of political conflict between classes, and the results of victory were
binding on the state. Gaius Oppius and Cornelius Balbus were the
first who were able, with Caesar's support, to settle conditions of

peace and terms of war. To mention after them the Matii, Vedii, and other influential names of Roman *equites* would be superfluous, when Claudius raised freedmen whom he had set over his household to equality with himself and with the laws.

37. A recommendation for promotion

This letter shows how a young man got into the equestrian service, partly by merit, partly by the interest of influential senators. His father had risen from being a centurion to equestrian officer posts. The son had started with an equestrian commission.

37. *Pliny*, Letters, X. 87

NYMPHIDIUS LUPUS, Sir, a former first centurion, and myself served in the army together; he was a prefect at the same time that I was tribune; and it was from thence my affection for him began. A long acquaintance has since mutually endeared us and strengthened our friendship. For this reason I did violence to his repose, and insisted upon his attending me into Bithynia, as my assessor in council. He most readily granted me this proof of his friendship; and without any regard to the plea of age or the ease of retirement, he shared with me the fatigue of business; and upon all occasions is still ready to give me his assistance. I look upon his relations therefore as my own; in which number Nymphidius Lupus, his son, claims my particular notice. He is a youth of great merit and indefatigable application; and in every view of his character, well worthy of so excellent a father. That he is equal to any honor you shall think proper to confer upon him, the early proof he gave of his qualifications, when he was prefect of a cohort, will easily convince you; as it gained him the full applause of those most illustrious personages, Julius Ferox and Fuscus Salinator. And I will add, Sir, that any increase of dignity which he shall receive will be an occasion of particular congratulation to myself.

38. A recommendation for appointment

Here we have another letter of recommendation. Appian was an Alexandrian lawyer who wrote a lengthy history of the wars of Rome. The normal equestrian career began with three officer posts in the army, but civilians were sometimes permitted to procuratorships, particularly lawyers who had risen to be counsel for the crown (*advocatus fisci*). It appears from this letter that procuratorships were often sought merely as honors as in the second century.

38. *Fronto*, ad Antoninum Pium, 9

MY FRIEND's modesty prevents me from making outrageous requests. At my request, you advanced to the dignity of a Roman *eques* my old friend Sextus Calpurnius by the grant of two procuratorships. I count the grants of two procuratorships as four; two when you gave the procuratorships, two again when you accepted his excuses.

I have already petitioned you for two years for my friend Appianus, with whom I have a long acquaintance and an almost daily scholarly intercourse. Moreover, I am sure and dare to assert that he, too, will show the same modesty as did my friend Calpurnius Julianus. He hopes to gain this honor to adorn his dignity and old age, not for ambition or greed for a procurator's salary. When I first spoke for Appianus you received my prayers with such kindness that I have cause for hope. Last year you made many favorable replies to my petitions, and you also said very pleasantly that as soon as, at my request, you gave a procuratorship to Appianus, there would be a flood of lawyers making the same request. You remember which Greek you named in a gracious and laughing fashion. But there are many differences, his age and his childlessness, to relieve which he needs solaces. I would venture to add that in good character and uprightness too, though both are good men, still there is some difference. I say that the more readily in that I have not mentioned the person to whom I prefer my friend. I will finally say, such is my honest and forthright character and my confidence in your affection for me, that it would be fairer that the other man, too, should gain on my account.

Remember, too, my dear emperor, when he makes his request, following my example, that I asked for it for two years. So if you please, give it to him, too, after two years. He will follow my example if he himself begs to be excused and gains his request.

39. An imperial letter of appointment

Marsianus, who gives his career in reverse order, was enrolled on the panels of jurors and served one officer post before going on to a series

of procuratorships; he came from Africa. Procurators were graded by
salary, receiving sixty thousand, then one hundred thousand, then two
hundred thousand sesterces.

39. L'Année Epigraphique, 1962, 183

To QUINTUS DOMITIUS, son of Lucius, of the tribe Quirina, Marsianus, procurator of Augustus of the patrimony of the province of
Narbonensis, procurator of Augustus for the iron mines, procurator of Augustus for receiving the census returns in Gaul in the
province of Belgica, in the districts of the Tungri and Frisiavones,
and in the province of Lower Germany and the Batavians, military
prefect, enrolled in the decuries by the emperor Marcus Aurelius
Antoninus and Lucius Aurelius Verus Caesar. When the council
resolved to set up an equestrian statue to him at public expense, his
brother Lucius Domitius Fabianus relieved the city of the expense
and put it up at his own charges.

COPY OF THE LETTER OF APPOINTMENT

Caesar Antoninus Augustus to his friend Marsianus, greeting.
Having long desired to promote you to the splendor of a procuratorship at a salary of two hundred thousand sesterces I make
use of the opportunity which has been offered. You will, therefore,
succeed Marius Pudens, with every hope of my lasting favor, if
you maintain your record of incorruptibility, industry, and ability.
Farewell, Marsianus, my dearest friend.

40. Baebius Atticus

This is a very early equestrian career of a man who started as a centurion, then became the prefect of two small provinces, commanded a
cohort of the praetorian guard, and became procurator (governor) of
a small province. This inscription shows the change from the title
prefect to procurator. Atticus was a chief magistrate (*II vir iuri
dicundo*) of his native town.

40. Dessau, ILS, 1349

To GAIUS BAEBIUS ATTICUS, son of Publius, of the Claudian tribe,
duumvir with judicial powers, first centurion of Legion V Macedonica, prefect of the tribes of Moesia and Treballia, prefect of the
tribes in the Maritime Alps, military tribune of Praetorian Cohort

VIII, first centurion for the second time, procurator of Tiberius Claudius Caesar Augustus Germanicus in Noricum, the community of the Saevates and Laeanci.

41. Julius Possessor

Possessor, who lived in the second century, follows a standard equestrian career, starting with three officer posts in Dacia and in Syria (the second and third commands were apparently held concurrently) and going on to two administrative jobs. He was also enrolled in the panels of jurors, and was appointed during his military career as *curator* of two cities, Romula in Dacia and Arca in Cappadocia. A *curator civitatis* was a commissioner appointed by the emperor to control the finances of a city.

41. Dessau, ILS, 1403

To SEXTUS JULIUS, son of Sextus, of the tribe Quirina, Possessor, prefect of Cohort III of the Gauls, commander of a *numerus* of Syrian archers, also of Ala I of the Spaniards, curator of the city of Romula Maluensis, military tribune of Legion XII Fulminata, curator of the colony of Arca, enrolled in the decuries by the best and greatest emperors Antoninus and Verus Augusti, assistant of Ulpius Saturninus, prefect of the corn supply, for valuing the African and Spanish oil, also for transferring reliefs, also for paying freight to the shippers, procurator of the Augusti for the banks of the Baetis.

The bargees of Hispalis in recognition of his preeminent honesty and justice.

42. Bassaeus Rufus

This career, recorded in reverse order, shows how a centurion could rise to what was in effect the most important post in the empire, that of praetorian prefect, and win the insignia of a consul. Ex-centurions normally held three military tribunates in the forces stationed at Rome (the *vigiles* or night watch, the urban cohorts under the city prefect, and the praetorians) before rising to procuratorships and the higher prefectures. Then followed provincial procuratorships, then a ministry at Rome (in this case that of finance), and then the four great prefectures; Bassaeus omitted either the *vigiles* or the corn supply (the word is missing in the inscription) and then held Egypt and the praetorian guard.

42. *Dessau, ILS, 1326*

To MARCUS BASSAEUS, son of Marcus, of the tribe Stellatina, Rufus, praetorian prefect of the emperors Marcus Aurelius Antoninus and Lucius Aurelius Verus and Lucius Aurelius Commodus the Augusti, decorated with consular ornaments and awarded by the same emperors a mural, rampart, and gold crowns, and four untipped spears and four siege banners on account of the German and Sarmatian victory of Antoninus and Commodus Augusti; prefect of Egypt, prefect of the *vigiles*, procurator of finance, procurator of Belgica and the two Germanies, procurator of the kingdom of Noricum, procurator of Asturia and Gallaecia, tribune of the ———— praetorian cohort, tribune of X urban Cohort, tribune of V Cohort of the *vigiles*, first centurion twice.

The senate, on the proposal of the emperors Antoninus and Commodus the Augusti, voted that a statue in uniform be erected to him in the forum of the deified Trajan and another in civilian dress in the temple of the deified Pius and a third in a breastplate in the temple of Mars Ultor.

V. The Civil Service

43. An imperial freedman of Augustus

The early emperors had to build up their civil service out of nothing. To handle their financial business they appointed, as we have seen, men of equestrian rank as private agents or procurators in the several provinces; these procurators gradually acquired official status. At Rome, to keep their accounts and to handle their correspondence, they used their slaves and freedmen. The chief freedmen clerks, who were in effect ministers of finance and secretaries of state, acquired great power and were greatly hated by the senate and senatorial nobility. Later these posts were given to men of equestrian rank (see No. 42). Imperial slaves and freedmen were also employed as assistants of the procurators in the provinces.

This inscription shows what an important personage a freedman of the emperor could be in the reign of Tiberius. It is not known what posts he held.

43. Dessau, ILS, 6579

THE COUNCIL of One Hundred of the Augustan Municipality of Veii met at Rome in the temple of Venus Genetrix and resolved unanimously that in the interim, until a decree could be drafted, permission should be given on the authority of the whole council to Gaius Julius Gelos, freedman of the deified Augustus, who has not only continually assisted the municipality of Veii with his advice and favor, but has also wished a celebration to be made at his own expense through his son, that the well-deserved honor be decreed to him that he should be counted among the Augustales, just as if he had held that office, and that he should be allowed at all spectacles at our municipality to sit in his own chair among the Augustales, and take part in all public banquets with the Council of One Hundred, and it is further resolved that no tax of the Augustan Municipality of Veii should be levied on him or on his children.

Present [thirteen names, including two *duoviri* and two quaestors].

Done in the consulship of Gaetulicus and Calvisius Sabinus [A.D. 26].

44. An imperial slave of Tiberius

This inscription again shows in what grand style a slave of the emperor Tiberius lived. He holds only a subordinate financial post in the provinces but has sixteen domestic slaves of his own.

44. *Dessau*, ILS, *1514*

To MUSICUS SCURRANUS, slave of Tiberius Caesar Augustus, cashier of the Gallic treasury, province of Lugdunum, by his slaves who were with him at Rome when he died, to their worthy master.

VENUSTUS, agent	EPAPHRA, butler	FACILIS, footman
DECIMIANUS, accountant	PRIMUS, valet	ANTHUS, butler
DICAEUS, secretary	COMMUNIS, chamberlain	HEDYLUS, chamberlain
MUTATUS, secretary	POTHUS, footman	FIRMUS, cook
CRETICUS, secretary	TIASUS, cook	SECUNDA
AGATHOPUS, doctor		

45. A recommendation for promotion for an imperial freedman

From this letter it appears that by the second century imperial freedmen followed a regular ladder of promotion, aided, like equestrian officials, by the interest of senators.

45. *Fronto*, ad Marcum Caesarem, *V. 52*

SIR, ARIDELUS, who brings you this letter, has looked after me from childhood, from my passion for partridges to more serious duties. He is your freedman. He will be a diligent procurator for you; for he is honest, sober, energetic, and hard-working. He now applies for a procuratorship in due form, in accordance with his position and at the proper time. Give him whatever favor you can, Sir. If you do not recognize the man's face, when you come to the name Aridelus, remember that Aridelus has been recommended to you by me. Farewell, dearest master. Greet my mistress.

46. A recommendation for promotion for an imperial slave

This letter shows how imperial slaves obtained promotion in the service.

46. P. Ryl., 608

To ——— SON of Titus Claudius Hermeros, procurator of Augustus.

Ulpius Celer to his friend Hermeros, greeting.

I beg you, sir, to accept my recommendation of ——— slave of our lord the emperor, my intimate and friend. He is most worthy of promotion and of your favor, and I do not conceal from you that anything that you do for his dignity will be most welcome to me. Farewell.

47. A military clerk

Imperial slaves and freedmen were employed in the financial offices in the provinces, and in the central ministries at Rome. For general clerical duties, soldiers were seconded to assist provincial governors. This soldier of the I Urban Cohort, stationed at Lyons, served three successive governors of the province, rising from ordinary clerk (*beneficiarius*) to senior clerk (*cornicularius*), before returning to his original cohort as centurion. (Cf. also Nos. 56, 58.)

47. Dessau, ILS, 2118

MARCUS CARANTIUS MACRINUS, centurion of the I Urban Cohort, enlisted in the same cohort in the second consulship of Domitian [A.D. 73], clerk of Tettienus Serenus, legate of Augustus in the tenth consulship of Vespasian,[1] chief clerk of Cornelius Gallicanus, legate of Augustus, with trooper's pay, in the ninth consulship of Domitian [A.D. 83], also under Minicius Rufus, legate of Augustus, recalled to the colors in the fourteenth consulship of Domitian [A.D. 88], centurion in the second consulship of the emperor Nerva [A.D. 90].

48. Hereditary civil servants

The civil service of the later Roman empire was derived from the military clerks of the principate; the slaves and freedmen staffs were given military status. The object of this law of Constantine seems not so much to exact hereditary service from civil servants as to forbid

1. The date is wrong as Vespasian never held a tenth consulship; the year may be any year between 74 and 77 or 79, when Vespasian was Consul V to IX.

sons of civil servants from entering other offices. The hereditary
obligation was enforced only on the lowest grade of civil servants, the
cohortales who served the provincial governors, since it was only in
the provincial offices that service was unpopular.

48. Codex Theodosianus, *VII. 22.3*

THE SAME Augustus to Evagrius.

Sons of members of any office staffs whatever, whether their
fathers are still under oath of office, or have already been discharged from service, shall succeed into the station of their fathers.

Given on the day before the nones of August in the consulship
of Bassus and Ablabius [August 4, 331].

49. The perquisites of civil servants

Civil servants were very badly paid, and supplemented their salaries by
taking tips or bribes from litigants in the courts where they served as
ushers and kept the records. Constantine in this law endeavors to
suppress tips, but they became recognized fees, and came to form the
major part of the income of civil servants.

49. Codex Theodosianus, *I.16.*7

THE SAME Augustus to the provincials.

The rapacious hands of the apparitors shall immediately cease,
they shall cease, I say; for if after due warning they do not cease,
they shall be cut off by the sword. The chamber curtain of the
judge shall not be venal; entrance shall not be gained by purchase,
the private council chamber shall not be infamous on account of
the bids. The appearance of the governor shall not be at a price;
the ears of the judge shall be open equally to the poorest as well as
to the rich. There shall be no despoiling on the occasion of escort-
ing persons inside by the one who is called chief of the office staff.
The assistants of the aforesaid chiefs of the office staff shall employ
no extortion on litigants; the intolerable onslaught of the centurions and other apparitors who demand small and great sums
shall be crushed; and the unsated greed of those who deliver the
records of a case to litigants shall be restrained. Always shall the
diligence of the governor guard lest anything be taken from a
litigant by the aforesaid classes of men. If they should suppose that
anything ought to be demanded by them from those involved in
civil cases, armed punishment will be at hand, which will cut off

the heads and necks of the scoundrels. Opportunity shall be granted to all persons who have suffered extortion to provide for an investigation by the governors. If they should dissemble, We hereby open to all persons the right to express complaints about such conduct before the counts of the provinces or before the praetorian prefects, if they are closer at hand, so that We may be informed by their references to Us and may provide punishment for such brigandage.

Given on the kalends of November at Constantinople in the consulship of Bassus and Ablabius [November 1, 331].

50. The imperial couriers

The corps of imperial couriers (*agentes in rebus*) was an important organization under the control of the master of the offices, numbering about twelve hundred men (in the eastern part of the empire in the fifth century). They ranked as cavalrymen, advancing from trooper (*eques*) through the usual noncommissioned grades of *biarchus*, *centenarius*, and *ducenarius*. Their primary function was to carry imperial despatches to the provinces, but the senior members of the corps became successively inspectors of the postal service and then chief clerks (*principes*) to the praetorian and urban prefects, proconsuls, and vicars. The main object of the system was no doubt to strengthen the control of the central government over its representatives in the provinces, but it also provided lucrative final posts for the *agentes in rebus*. As in all offices, the government tried to prevent promotion by graft rather than by seniority and merit. The assistant (*adiutor*) was the chief of staff to the master of the offices, and was to be chosen by merit.

50. Codex Theodosianus, *I.9.1*

EMPERORS Constantius Augustus and Julian Caesar to the Imperial Couriers:

All persons who are of unworthy birth and of the worst character, and who have aspired to or have been transferred to the department of the Imperial Couriers shall, upon investigation by the most noble count and master of offices, be removed from your society, in order that you may thus be able to enjoy the privileges which were formerly granted to you. Furthermore, no person shall attain to the office of *ducenarius*, of *centenarius*, or of *biarchus* through patronage, but each one shall arrive at it by his labor and by using the testimony of all. But he shall acquire the position of chief of office staff (*princeps*) by his position on the office register, so that those persons shall go out as supervisors of the public post who are called thereto by their order in the imperial service and by their labors. The assistant (*adiutor*), moreover, on whom depends the standing of the whole corps and the security of the master, shall be a person suitable by his high character and possessed of good qualities, on the testimony of the whole corps, and be presented to our inspection by the master, so he may be appointed with our approval; all are allowed to object if anyone attempts to violate this law.

Given and posted at Rome in the Forum of Trajan on the kalends of November in the consulship of Eusebius and Hypatius [November 1, 359].

51. The number of officials

In the later empire the number of officials always tended to rise, and from time to time the government fixed ceilings for the various offices. Vicars, who governed dioceses, are here limited to three hundred officials; provincial governors, by another law, were limited to one hundred. For decurions, see Nos. 115–16. They were forbidden in the early fourth century to join the civil service.

51. Codex Theodosianus, *I.15.12*

EMPERORS Valentinian, Theodosius, and Arcadius Augusti to all vicars.

Each and every vicar shall know that only three hundred men each shall be members of the imperial service in the dioceses which have been entrusted to them. It shall be provided that if any persons are obligated to the municipal councils by the bond of ancestry, they shall be returned to the functions of decurions, and no person shall defend himself from this service under the pretext of some privilege or by the excuse of old age.

Given on the sixth day before the kalends of November in the consulship of Honorius, the prince, and Evodius [October 27, 386].

52. The salaries of officials

Civil servants of the later empire, being technically soldiers, received rations in kind; indeed in most cases the rations were their sole official emoluments—apart from tips or fees taken from the public. The collection of these rations led to much extortion from the provinces, and they are here commuted into cash.

52. Codex Theodosianus, *VII.4.35*

THE SAME Augusti to Asclepiodotus, Praetorian Prefect.

We command that commutation into money shall be made of all rations which are customarily assigned to all the office staffs and ministries of the sacred palace and the sacred bureaus and to the rest of the assistants of all the high offices; which have been torn violently from the vitals of the provincials by those who have been sent to collect them, in accordance with their own greed and lust. This commutation shall be made in the same way as in the case of the soldiers to whom rations commuted into money are paid. A regulation of Your Eminence shall prescribe that the emoluments due to all persons designated above shall be issued in money at prices valued according to the public authority.

Given on the sixteenth day before the kalends of March at Constantinople in the consulship of Asclepiodotus and Marinianus [February 14, 423].

VI. The Army

53. The distribution of the forces

Tacitus in this passage gives a useful picture of the distribution of the legions and other forces in the reign of Tiberius. It will be seen that most of the army was stationed on the frontiers—the Rhine, the Danube, and the East. This tendency was accentuated as time went on. The three legions in Spain were reduced to one, Africa normally had one only, and the garrison of Egypt, originally three (see No. 78), had become one by the second century. On the other hand the eastern and Danube armies were strengthened and Britain, conquered by Claudius, required three legions; only the Rhine garrison was reduced to four legions. The total number of legions rose gradually, reaching thirty under Trajan. For the fleets, see Nos. 61 and 63; for the praetorian and urban cohorts, No. 62.

The remainder of the passage gives a general view of the working of the regime set up by Augustus. The old republican magistrates and the senate have some share in the government, though the emperor is the supreme authority. One may note that the republican system of farming the revenues still applied to certain taxes (see No. 125), though not to the tribute, and that the private property of the emperor is important (cf. No. 1); also that slaves and freedmen staff the central imperial administration (cf. Nos. 43–46).

53. *Tacitus*, Annals, *IV.* 5–7

ITALY ON both seas was guarded by fleets, at Misenum and at Ravenna, and the contiguous coast of Gaul by ships of war captured in the victory of Actium, and sent by Augustus powerfully manned to the town of Forum Julii. But our chief strength was on the Rhine, as a defense alike against Germans and Gauls, and numbered eight legions. Spain, lately subjugated, was held by three. Mauretania was King Juba's who had received it as a gift from the Roman people. The rest of Africa was garrisoned by two legions, and Egypt by the same number. Next, beginning with Syria, all within the entire tract of country stretching as far as the Euphrates, was kept in restraint by four legions, and on this frontier were the Iberian, Albanian, and other kings, to whom our greatness was a protection against any foreign power. Thrace was held by Rhoemetalces and the children of Cotys; the bank of the Danube by two legions in Pannonia, two in Moesia, and two also were stationed in Dalmatia, which, from the situation of the country, were in the rear of the other four, and, should Italy suddenly require aid, not too distant to be summoned. But the capital was garrisoned by its own special soldiery, the three city and nine praetorian cohorts, levied for the most part in Etruria and Umbria, or ancient Latium and the old Roman colonies. There were, besides, in commanding positions in the provinces, allied fleets, cavalry, and light infantry, of but little inferior strength. But any detailed account of them would be misleading, since they moved from place to place as circumstances required, and had their numbers increased and sometimes diminished.

It is, however, I think, a convenient opportunity for me to review the hitherto prevailing methods of administration in the other departments of state, inasmuch as that year brought with it the beginning of a change for the worse in Tiberius's policy. In the first place, public business and the most important private matters were managed by the senate; the leading men were allowed freedom of discussion, and when they stooped to flattery, the emperor himself checked them. He bestowed honors with regard to noble ancestry, military renown, or brilliant accomplishments as a civilian, letting it be clearly seen that there were no better men to choose. The consuls and the praetors retained their prestige; inferior magistrates exercised their authority; the laws, too, with the single exception of cases of treason, were properly enforced.

As to the levies of corn, the indirect taxes, and other branches of the public revenue, they were in the hands of companies of Roman *equites*. The emperor entrusted his own property to men of the most tried integrity or to persons known only by their general reputation, and once appointed they were retained without limitation, so that most of them grew old in the same employments. The city populace indeed suffered much from high prices, but this was no fault of the emperor, who actually endeavored to counteract barren soils and stormy seas with every resource of wealth and foresight. And he was also careful not to distress the provinces by new burdens, and to see that in bearing the old they were safe from any rapacity or oppression on the part of governors. Corporal punishments and confiscations of property were unknown.

The emperor had only a few estates in Italy, slaves on a moderate scale, and his household was confined to a few freedmen. If ever he had a dispute with a private person, it was decided in the law courts.

54. The draft under the principate

The Roman army of the principate was for the most part voluntarily recruited, largely from sons of soldiers or veterans, but conscription was from time to time applied if necessary, both to Roman citizens to fill the legions and to provincials for the auxiliary units. It appears from this passage that men who were drafted could offer substitutes. Slaves and freedmen were debarred from military service.

54. Pliny, Letters, X. 29–30

PLINY TO TRAJAN

SEMPRONIUS CAELIANUS (whose merit I must always mention with esteem) having discovered two slaves among the recruits, has sent them to me. But I deferred passing sentence till I had conferred with you, the glorious founder and firm support of military discipline, concerning the punishment proper to be inflicted upon them. My principal doubt is, that though they have taken the military oath, they are not yet entered into any particular unit. I beg therefore, Sir, you would let me know what method I shall pursue, especially as it is an affair in which example is concerned.

TRAJAN TO PLINY

Sempronius Caelianus has acted agreeably to my orders, in sending such persons to be tried before you as appear to deserve capital punishment. It is material, however, in the case in question, to enquire whether these slaves enlisted themselves voluntarily, or were chosen, or presented as proxies for others. If they were chosen, the recruiting office is guilty; if they are proxies, the blame rests with those who deputed them; but if, conscious of the legal disabilities of their station, they presented themselves voluntarily, the punishment must fall upon their own heads. That they are not yet entered into any unit makes no great difference in their case; for they ought to have given a true account of themselves immediately upon their being approved as fit for the service.

55. A letter from an Egyptian recruit

The two imperial fleets established by Augustus were recruited from provincials, that of Ravenna mainly from Dalmatia, that of Misenum from Egypt. Note that Apion is given a Roman name on joining his ship though he would not become a Roman citizen until his discharge.

55. BGU, 423

APION TO Epimachus, his father and lord, very many greetings. Before all else I pray for your health and that you may always be well and prosperous, together with my sister and her daughter and my brother. I thank the lord Serapis that when I was in danger at sea he straightway saved me. On arriving at Misenum I received from Caesar three gold pieces for traveling expenses. And it is well with me. Now I ask you, my lord and father, write me a letter, telling me first of your welfare, secondly of my brother's and sister's, and thirdly enabling me to make obeisance before your handwriting, because you educated me well and I hope thereby to have quick advancement, if the gods so will. Give many salutations to Capiton and my brother and sister and Serenilla and my friends. I have sent you by Euctemon a portrait of myself. My name is Antonius Maximus, my company the Athenonica. I pray for your health.

[POSTSCRIPT] Serenus son of Agathodaemon salutes you, and ———, and Turbo son of Gallonius, and ———

[Address] To Philadelphia, to Epimachus from Apion, his son.

[Additional address] Deliver at the camp of the first cohort of the Apamenes to Julianus, vice-secretary, this letter from Apion to be forwarded to his father Epimachus.

56. A letter from an Egyptian soldier

This letter is from a Roman citizen resident in Egypt who is serving in a legion in Arabia very shortly after the annexation of that province by Trajan in A.D. 106. The legion is probably engaged in building the great road recorded in No. 87. Apollinarius prefers clerical duties and makes a successful request to the governor of the province (cf. No. 47).

56. P. Mich., 466

JULIUS APOLLINARIUS to Julius Sabinus, his dear father, best wishes. Above all things I pray that you are well; that is my prayer, because I revere you second to the gods. I am worried because, although I have written to you several times by Saturninus, the standard bearer, and also by Julianus, the son of Longinus, and by Dius, you have not yet replied to me about your health. Still, now you have been asked, make a point of writing to me about your health above all. I often asked Longinus, who brought you the letter, to carry something to you, but he refused, saying he could not do it. I want you to know that Domitius, the storekeeper for weapons, changed the basket . . . I am all right. After Serapis had given me a good journey here, while others . . . were breaking stones all day, I had none of this, but when I asked Claudius Severus, the consular, to make me his own clerk, he said, "There is not a vacancy, but meanwhile I will make you clerk of the legion with the expectation of promotion." So I have been attached to the *cornicularius* of the legion by the consular of the legion. If you love me, take the trouble to write to me at once about your health, and if you care for me, send some linen by Sempronius; merchants come to us from Pelusium every day. I will soon take pains, if the governor starts giving leave, to come to you soon. Volusius Proculus, Longinus Paccius, Valerius Sempronius, Valerius Hermas, Julius Priscus, Apollinarius,——and all the boys send their greetings to you. Give my greetings to Julia, my sister, likewise to Serapias and her mother, and grandmother Sambathion, Thermuthis and her children, Paccius' father, and to all your colleageus by name, and to the household. Goodbye.

Year 10 of the lord Trajan, 30 Phamenoth [26 March A.D. 107].

57. The pay sheets of two legionaries in Egypt

These accounts date from the early part of Domitian's reign. Legionary pay was 225 denarii per annum, payable in three installments of 75 denarii; Domitian later added a fourth installment of 75 denarii. The sum is converted at a curious rate of exchange into the local currency, Alexandrian drachmae (the normal rate was four drachmae to the denarius). It may be noted that all expenses—rations, uniform, bedding, and tent—are deducted from pay. Arms and armor were also deducted, but these two soldiers did not draw any this year. Nevertheless, they put a substantial sum into the regimental savings bank.

57. P.Gen.Lat., *1*

IN THE consulship of ——— and Lucius Asinius.

	Quintus Julius Proculus of ———	Gaius Valerius Germanicus of Cyrenae
Received first installment of pay, year 3	248 drachmae	248 drachmae
Deductions		
bedding	10	10
rations	80	80
boots and straps	12	12
saturnalia	20	20
tent	60	—
uniform	—	100
Total expenses	182	222
Balance deposited	66	26
Carried over from last account	135	20
Total	202 drachmae	46 drachmae
Received second installment of pay, same year	248 drachmae	248 drachmae
Deductions		
bedding	10	10
rations	80	80
boots and straps	12	12
for the standards	4	4
Total expenses	106	106
Balance deposited	142	142
Carried over from last account	202	46
Total	344 drachmae	188 drachmae
Received third installment of pay, same year	248 drachmae	248 drachmae
Deductions		
bedding	10	10
boots and straps	12	12
uniform	146	146
Total expenses	248	248
Balance deposited	344 drachmae	188 drachmae

58. Hadrian reviews the troops in Numidia

Hadrian was unusual in spending most of his reign touring the provinces. In the course of these journeys he inspected the troops. The troops in Numidia included one legion which had temporarily lost two of its ten cohorts, one auxiliary infantry unit (*cohors*), two auxiliary cavalry units (*alae*), and an auxiliary infantry unit with cavalry component (*cohors equitata*). Legions contained six thousand men, infantry with a small cavalry component; cohorts and *alae* were mostly five hundred strong—a few one thousand strong.

58. *Dessau*, ILS, *2487*

IMPERATOR Caesar Trajanus Hadrianus Augustus, having inspected the maneuvers, addressed his Legion III Augusta in the following terms on the kalends of July in the consulship of Torquatus for the second time and Libo [A.D. 128]:

My legate has spoken for you and told me on your behalf all the allowances I ought to make for you—that a cohort is away, that every year postings are made in rotation for the office of the proconsul, that three years ago you gave a cohort and four men from each century to reinforce a sister third legion, that many various guard duties strain your strength, that you have twice within my memory not only changed your camp but built a new one. For these reasons I would have excused you if the legion had long abandoned maneuvers. But you have not abandoned. . . . Your senior officers and centurions were active and vigorous as they always were.

THE CAVALRY OF THE LEGION

Military maneuvers have in a way their own rules, and if anything is added or subtracted, the maneuver becomes less or more difficult. The more difficulty is added, the more elegance is subtracted. You have performed the most difficult of operations, throwing javelins while wearing breastplates. . . .

THE ——— DAY BEFORE THE KALENDS OF JULY. COHORT II SPANIARDS

You have completed in one day work of fortification which others had distributed over several days. You have built a durable wall, such as is usually made for permanent barracks, in not much longer time than one is built of turf, which being cut in uniform blocks is easily transported and handled and is erected without trouble, being naturally soft and even. You used large heavy irregular blocks of stone, which no one can carry or raise or set in such a way that no irregularity appears between them. You have driven a trench straight through hard rough gravel, and have scraped it smooth. When your work was passed you entered the camp and rapidly fed and armed yourselves and followed up the cavalry which had been sent out and greeted its return with a loud cheer. . . .

I praised my distinguished colleague Catullinus for putting you on to this maneuver, which presented the appearance of a real battle, so that I can praise you unreservedly. Your prefect Cornelianus performed his duty satisfactorily. "I do not approve of head-on charges" is the verdict of. . . . The trooper should ride across from cover and pursue with caution; if he cannot see where he is going and cannot hold in his horse when he wants, he is bound to run into hidden potholes.

ON THE DAY BEFORE THE IDES, ALA I PANNONIANS

You have done everything in order. You have filled the parade ground with your charges, you have thrown the javelin in a stylish manner, though using short hand staves, a great number of you have lately thrown lances. You have jumped with speed and agility the other day. If there had been any fault, I would have noted it, and if there had been any outstanding performance, I would call attention to it. You were uniformly good throughout the whole maneuver. Catullinus, my distinguished legate, showed equal care on his part in the work of which he is in charge. Your prefect appears to look after you carefully. You will receive a bounty and you will perform a *viatoria* on the parade ground of the Commagenians.

THE CAVALRY OF COHORT VI COMMAGENIANS

It is difficult for the cavalry of a cohort to give satisfaction in any case, more difficult for them not to cause dissatisfaction after the maneuver of an *ala*. The area of the parade ground is different and so is the number of javelineers; the quality of the horses and your arms correspond with your lower pay. But you have avoided contempt by your keenness in doing what had to be done with vigor. To this you have added throwing stones with slings and combat with missiles. You have on all occasions jumped with alacrity. The special care of my distinguished legate Catullinus is apparent in your quality under his command.

59. Soldiers' marriages

Soldiers were not allowed to marry during service, and it appears from this collection of precedents that an existing marriage was dissolved when a man joined the army. It also appears that soldiers did marry. The result of the rule was that their children were illegitimate. It also appears that they received dowries from their wives' parents in the form of interest-free loans.

59. *S. Riccobono*, Fontes Iuris Romani Ante Justiniani², *III. 19*

YEAR 20 of the deified Trajan, 10 Tybi [A.D. 117]. Lucia Macrina stated through her counsel Phaneius that she claimed a deposit from the estate of Antonius Germanus, soldier, deceased. Lupus said: "We know that these deposits are dowries. I do not give a judge in such cases. For a soldier is not allowed to marry. If you ask for a dowry and I give a judge, it will look as if I believe that the marriage is legal."

Year 19 of Trajan, 10 Pauni [A.D. 115]. Chrotis stated through her counsel Philoxenus that she, being a citizen, had married Isidore, a citizen, and subsequently he joined the army in a cohort and she had by him a son, Theodore; about whom she petitions, asking that, if she had neglected to register him, it should be rectified, and that it is plain that he is his son from the will which he made, for he left him heir of his estate. When the will of Julius Martialis, soldier of the first cohort of the Thebans, had been read, Lupus, after consulting his friends, said: "Martialis could not have a legitimate son while serving in the army. But he made him his heir lawfully."

Year 5 of our lord Antoninus, 3rd extra day [A.D. 142]. Octavius Valens and Cassia Secunda, having been adjourned from yesterday, came up. Eudaemon, having conferred with those present, said: "Yesterday, directly the memorandum of the honorable Heliodorus was read, the reason for the postponement was clear, that the mother of the child should see that she is making a petition on a prohibited topic. Today, having considered the circumstances, I confirm the opinion I gave yesterday. Whether he served in a legion or in a cohort or in an *ala* the child could not be his legitimate son, and, not being the legitimate son of his father, an Alexandrian, he cannot be an Alexandrian. This child was born to Valens when he was serving in a cohort and is alien to him; he cannot be brought into the Alexandrian citizenship." He added: "You said yesterday you had other sons. How old are they? When were they born?" Octavius Valens answered: "One just recently, the other is older." Eudaimon said: "Where were you serving when the older boy was born?" Valens replied: "In the cohort, and the little one, too." Eudaimon said: "You must know that they are in the same position as he. Some rules cannot be broken." Valens said: "Now, if I manage to go abroad, will you yourself sign my petition, so that I can get my rights through a legal representative? What crime have the children committed?" Eudaimon said: "I have been a fool in saying in many words what I could have settled in a moment. Since you have attempted the impossible, neither he nor your other sons are Alexandrian citizens."

60. The use of troops as police

It appears from these letters and others in the correspondence between Pliny and Trajan that soldiers were constantly detached from their units for administrative, clerical, and police duties. This was a consequence of the fact that neither the empire nor the cities had any regular civil service or police forces.

60. *Pliny*, Letters, X.19–20

PLINY TO TRAJAN

I BEG your determination, Sir, in a point wherein I am greatly doubtful; it is, whether I should employ public slaves of the cities to guard the prisons (as has been hitherto the practice) or employ soldiers for that purpose? On the one hand, I am afraid that public slaves will not attend to this duty with the fidelity they ought; and on the other, that it will engage too large a body of the soldiery: in the meanwhile I have joined a few of the latter with the former. I suspect, however, there may be some danger that this method will occasion a general neglect of duty, as it will afford them a mutual pretense of throwing the blame upon each other.

TRAJAN TO PLINY

There is no occasion, my dear Pliny, to draw off any soldiers in order to guard the prisons. Let us rather persevere in the ancient custom observed by this province of employing public slaves for that purpose: and the fidelity with which they shall execute their duty will depend much upon your care and strict discipline. It is greatly to be feared, as you observe, if the soldiers should be mixed with public slaves, they will mutually trust each other, and by that means grow so much the more negligent. But the principal objection I have is that as few soldiers as possible should be called off from their colors.

61. Discharge of legionary veterans

Veterans from the auxiliary cohorts and *alae* and the fleets, who were provincials when they joined up and who received Roman citizenship on discharge, received certificates (see Nos. 63–64). Legionaries, who were supposed to be citizens when they joined up, did not receive certificates. This is an exceptional case, since the men concerned had been transferred from a fleet to a legion.

61. PSI, *1026*

COPIED AND checked from a petition posted with others in the colonade of Junia Ba——, in which was written the underwritten.

To Vilius Kadus *legatus Augusti pro praetore* from twenty-two veterans of Legion X Fretensis, who began to serve in the consulship of Glabrio and Torquatus [A.D. 124] and also of Paulinus and Aquilinus [A.D. 125], whose names are subjoined. Whereas, Sir, we have served in the praetorian fleet of Misenum and having by the indulgence of the deified Hadrian been transferred to Legion Fretensis have been for over twenty years in all ways good soldiers, we have now in these happy times been released from our oath and wish to go to Egypt to our native city of Alexandria and we beg that you will deign to affirm to us that we have been discharged by you, so that from your affirmation it will appear that we have been discharged from the same legion, not from the fleet, so that your subscription may serve us in all things needful to us as a document and we may always thank your humanity. [Names and centuries of twenty-two men]

I, Lucius Petronius Saturninus, have issued this on behalf of myself and my fellow veterans. I Pomponius have written it.

Subscription. It is not customary for veterans from the legions to receive a document. However, you desire that it should be notified to the prefect of Egypt that you have been discharged by me by order of the emperor. I will give a gratuity and a document.

Done at the Colonia I Flavia of Caesarea, on the eleventh day before the kalends of February (22 January) in the consulship of Squilla Gallicanus and Carminius Vetus [A.D. 150].

62. The discharge certificate of a praetorian

The nine praetorian cohorts, the imperial bodyguard, were instituted by Augustus. They received more than three times the pay of the legionaries (cf. No. 67) and served for a shorter term (sixteen years). The urban cohorts were also instituted by Augustus; three were under the prefect of the city in Rome, and one at Lyons. They received half a praetorian's pay. The *speculatores* were a picked detachment of praetorians. These troops had the privilege that after discharge they could marry a foreign wife (or legalize an existing marriage with such a woman). Their children born after discharge were thus Roman citizens, whereas the children of legionaries who married foreign women were not; they could, however, obtain the citizenship by enlisting in a legion.

62. Dessau, ILS, 1993

I, IMPERATOR Caesar Vespasianus Augustus, pontifex maximus, of the tribunician power for the eighth time, imperator for the eighteenth time, father of my country, censor, consul for the seventh time, designate for the eighth time, have appended the names of the *speculatores* who served at my headquarters, also of the soldiers of the nine praetorian and four urban cohorts to whom, having bravely and loyally completed their service, I give the right of legal marriage with their first wives (one each only), so that even if they have married women of foreign status they may produce children as if they were born of two Roman citizens. On the fourth day before the nones of December in the consulship of Galleo Tettienus Petronianus, Marcus Fulvius Gillo [A.D. 76].

Sixth praetorian cohort, Lucius Ennius, son of Lucius, of the tribe Tromentina, Ferox, of Aquae Statellae. Copied and checked from the bronze plaque which is fixed to the wall at Rome in the Capitol on the base of Jupiter Africus.

63. The discharge certificate of a sailor

From the reign of Claudius, provincials who enlisted in the fleets and in the cohorts and *alae* received on completing twenty-five years' service the Roman citizenship for themselves and their children (who were illegitimate, see No. 59) and descendants, and also a legal marriage with a foreign wife (who might be their existing wife); so that their children born thereafter were Roman citizens.

63. Dessau, ILS, 1986

TIBERIUS CLAUDIUS Caesar Augustus Germanicus, pontifex maximus, of the tribunician power for the twelfth time, imperator for the twenty-seventh time, father of his country, censor, consul for

the fifth time, to the captains and seamen who served in the fleet
which is at Misenum under Tiberius Julius Optatus, freedman of
Augustus, and have been honorably discharged, whose names are
written below, to themselves, their children and descendants he has
given the citizenship and legal marriage with the wives whom they
had at the time when the citizenship was given to them, or if any of
them were unmarried with those whom they subsequently married,
limited to one each. The third day before the ides of December in
the consulship of Faustus Cornelius Sulla Felix and Lucius Sal-
vidienus Rufus Salvianus [A.D. 52].

To able seaman Spartico, son of Diuzenus, Dipscurtus, a Bessian.
Copied and checked from the bronze plaque which is fixed to the
wall at Rome in the Capitol on the right-hand side of the Temple
of the Faith of the Roman people. [There follow the names of
seven witnesses.]

64. The discharge certificate of a foreign cavalryman

From the reign of Antoninus Pius the privileges of veterans from the
fleets and auxiliary units were reduced. Children born to them
during their service were no longer accorded the Roman citizenship.
The intention was probably to encourage such men to enlist in the
legions, whereby they could acquire citizenship.

64. Dessau, ILS, 2005

IMPERATOR CAESAR, son of the deified Hadrian, grandson of the
deified Trajan Parthicus, great grandson of the deified Nerva,
Titus Aelius Hadrianus Antoninus Augustus Pius, pontifex maximus, of the tribunician power for the eleventh time, imperator for
the second time, consul for the fourth time, father of his country,
gave to the cavalry and infantry who served in the five *alae* and
seven cohorts which are called I Ulpia Pikemen, I Thracians, the
victorious, I Spaniards of the Arvaci, I Cannefates, Roman citizens,
III Augusta Thracian archers, I Ulpia Pannonians, I Aelia Archers,
XVIII Roman citizen volunteers, IV Roman citizen volunteers, I
Thracians, Roman citizens, V Galicians of Luca and II Alpines,
which are in Upper Pannonia under Pontius Laelianus, having
served twenty-five years and having been honorably discharged,
whose names are written below, the Roman citizenship to those
who do not possess it and legal marriage with the wives whom they
had at the time that citizenship was given to them, or with whom
they married subsequently, limited to one each. The seventh day

before the ides of October, in the consulship of Gaius Favius
Agippinus and Marcus Antonius Zeno [A.D. 148].

Cohort I Ulpia Pannonians, whose commander is Aulus Regillus
of Suessiones, infantry man, Atta son of Nivio, Azalian. Copied
and checked from the bronze plaque which is fixed to the wall at
Rome behind the temple of the deified Augustus next to Minerva.

65. A colony of veterans at Deultum

Legionaries from the time of Augustus received upon their discharge
either a piece of land, often in a colony—that is, a city specially
designated or created for the purpose—or a cash bonus. At first
Augustus provided these benefits from his own pocket (see No. 1,
§16), but in A.D. 6 he founded the Military Treasury, fed by special
taxes to perform this service (see No. 1, §17). This measure of
Augustus' solved an old problem of the republic. In the late republic
soldiers were usually poor, landless men and naturally expected what
amounted to a pension after a long service. Their commanders normally supported their claims, but the senate regularly resisted them as
they were very expensive, and grants of land were made only after
political struggles. This state of affairs enhanced the loyalty of the
troops to their commanders as against the state, and made it possible
for commanders to use their troops against the government.

Here we see time-served troops being settled in a newly created
colony in Thrace.

65. Dessau, ILS, 6105

IN THE consulship of Domitianus Augustus for the eighth time and
Titus Flavius Sabinus [A.D. 82] on the ides of June in the Flavian
colony of Pax Deultum, whereas . . . and Gaius Occeius Niger,
the *duoviri*, spoke . . . on offering the patronage of our colony to
the distinguished Avidius Quietus, legate of Augustus, what it was
their pleasure should be done in this matter, they resolved as
follows on the matter.

Since we have served in Legion VIII Augusta and having completed twenty-five years of service have been settled by the most
holy emperor in the colony of Deultum, he should be asked that in
his great humanity he would deign to assume the patronage of our
colony and would allow a plaque recording the fact to be placed in
his house, that he may himself take pleasure in his humanity and
our increased standing and his services may be known. There were
present to record the decree [names follow].

66. A colony of veterans at Cyrene

This inscription, found at Attaleia in Pamphylia, records another military colony. The man recorded rose to be the senior centurion (*primipilus*) of a legion, and then camp commandant (*praefectus castrorum*) of another legion, and was granted equestrian rank by Domitian (whose name is omitted because his memory was condemned by the senate). His son got into the senate by being elected quaestor, and his grandson inherited senatorial rank, thus wearing the broad purple stripe. L. Gavius Fronto himself gave to his native city Attaleia an endowment for the gymnasium and held the civic priesthood of the imperial cult.

66. SEG, XVII. 584

To Lucius Gavius Fronto, son of Lucius Gavius Fronto, senior centurion of Legion III Cyrenaica and camp commandant of Legion XV Apollinaris, the first and only son of his native city to achieve these ranks, father of Lucius Gavius Aelianus, quaestor *pro praetore* of the Roman people, grandfather of Lucius Gavius Clarus, both of the broad stripe, honored with a public horse and with decorations for valor by Augustus, entrusted by the deified Trajan with 3,000 legionary veterans to colonize Cyrene, the first to have promised a perpetual presidency of the gymnasium in the fourth year of his office, high priest of all the Augusti for four years and president of the dramatic and athletic games at his own expense.

Lucius Gavius Seleucus
to his patron and benefactor.

67. A mutiny

This mutiny took place shortly after the death of Augustus. The mutineers obviously exaggerate their grievances, but most of their complaints are based on fact. Pay was 225 denarii a year, which works out at roughly 10 asses a day (one denarius = 16 asses); and deductions were made for clothing, arms, tents and rations, as may be seen from No. 57. The term of service had been initially fixed at sixteen years by Augustus but was raised in A.D. 6 to twenty. Moreover, men were kept with the colors after formal discharge for several years in order to reduce the burden on the treasury of the discharge bonuses. Veterans were often assigned uncleared land conquered from the barbarians, again to save the treasury the expense of buying land. The praetorians had better terms of service (cf. No. 62). The tips which centurions exacted for granting leave or excusing men from fatigues are often complained of elsewhere.

67. *Tacitus*, Annals, *I. 16–23*

THIS WAS the state of affairs at Rome when a mutiny broke out in the legions of Pannonia, which could be traced to no fresh cause except the change of emperors and the prospect it held out of license in tumult and of profit from a civil war. In the summer camp three legions were quartered, under the command of Junius Blaesus, who on hearing of the death of Augustus and the accession of Tiberius, had allowed his men a rest from military duties, either for mourning or rejoicing. This was the beginning of demoralization among the troops, of quarreling, of listening to the talk of every pestilent fellow, in short, of craving for luxury and idleness and loathing discipline and toil. In the camp was one Percennius, who had once been a leader of one of the threatrical factions, then became a common soldier, had a saucy tongue, and had learnt from his applause of actors how to stir up a crowd. By working on ignorant minds, which doubted as to what would be the terms of military service after Augustus, this man gradually influenced them in conversations at night or at nightfall, and when the better men had dispersed, he gathered round him all the worst spirits.

At last, when there were others ready to be abettors of a mutiny, he asked, in the tone of a demagogue, why, like slaves, they submitted to a few centurions and still fewer tribunes. "When," he said, "will you dare to demand relief, if you do not go with your prayers or arms to a new and yet tottering throne? We have blundered enough by our tameness for so many years, in having to endure thirty or forty campaigns till we grow old, most of us with bodies maimed by wounds. Even dismissal is not the end of our service, but, quartered under a legion's standard, we toil through the same hardships under another title. If a soldier survives so many risks, he is still dragged into remote regions where, under the name of lands, he receives soaking swamps or mountainous wastes. Assuredly, military service itself is burdensome and unprofitable; ten asses a day is the value set on life and limb; out of this, clothing, arms, tents, as well as the mercy of centurions and exemption from fatigues have to be purchased. But indeed of floggings and wounds, of hard winters, wearisome summers, of terrible war, or barren peace, there is no end. Our only relief can come from military life being entered on under fixed conditions, from receiving each the pay of a denarius, and from the sixteenth year terminating our service. We must be retained no longer under a standard, but in the same camp a compensation in money must be paid to us. Do the praetorian cohorts, which receive their two denarii per man, and which after sixteen years are restored to their homes, encounter more perils? We do not disparage the guards of the capital; still, here amid barbarous tribes we have to face the enemy from our tents."

The throng applauded from various motives, some pointing with indignation to the marks of the lash, others to their gray hair, and most of them to their threadbare garments and naked limbs. At last, in their fury they went so far as to propose to combine the three legions into one. Driven from their purpose by the jealousy with which every one sought the chief honor for his own legion, they turned to other thoughts, and set up in one spot the three eagles, with the ensigns of the cohorts. At the same time they piled up turf and raised a mound, that they might have a more conspicuous meeting place. Amid the bustle Blaesus came up. He upbraided them and held back man after man with the exclamation, "Better imbue your hands in my blood: it will be less guilt to slay your commander than it is to be in revolt from the emperor. Either living I will uphold the loyalty of the legions, or pierced to the heart I will hasten your repentance."

Nonetheless, however, the mound was piled up, and it was quite breast high when, at last overcome by his persistency, they gave up their purpose. Blaesus, with the consummate tact of an orator, said, "It is not through mutiny and tumult that the desires of the army ought to be communicated to Caesar, nor did our soldiers of old ever ask so novel a boon of ancient commanders, nor did you yourselves ask it of the Divine Augustus. It is far from opportune that the emperor's cares, now in their first beginning, should be aggravated. If, however, you are bent upon attempting in peace what even after your victory in the civil wars you did not demand, why, contrary to the habit of obedience, contrary to the law of discipline, do you meditate violence? Decide on sending envoys, and give them instructions in your presence."

It was carried by acclamation that the son of Blaesus, one of the tribunes, should undertake the mission, and demand for the soldiers release from service after sixteen years. He was to have the rest of their message when the first part had been successful. After the young man's departure there was comparative quiet, but there was an arrogant tone among the soldiers, to whom the fact that their commander's son was pleading their common cause, clearly showed that they had wrested by compulsion what they had failed to obtain by good behavior.

Meanwhile the companies which previous to the mutiny had been sent to Nauportus to make roads and bridges and for other purposes, when they heard of the tumult in the camp, tore up the standards, and having plundered the neighboring villages and Nauportus itself, which was like a town, assailed the centurions who restrained them with jeers and insults, last of all with blows. Their chief rage was against Aufidienus Rufus, the camp commandant, whom they dragged from a wagon loaded with baggage, and drove on at the head of the column, asking him in ridicule whether he liked to bear such huge burdens and such long marches. Rufus, who had long been a common soldier, then a centurion, and subsequently camp commandant, had tried to revive the old severe discipline, inured as he was to work and toil, and all the sterner because he had endured.

On the arrival of these troops the mutiny broke out afresh, and straggling from the camp they plundered the neighborhood. Blaesus ordered a few who had conspicuously loaded themselves with spoil to be scourged and imprisoned as a terror to the rest; for, even as it then was, the commander was still obeyed by the centurions and by all the best men among the soldiers. As the men were dragged off, they struggled violently, clasped the knees of the bystanders, called to their comrades by name, or to the company, cohort, or legion to which they respectively belonged, exclaiming that all were threatened with the same fate. At the same time they heaped abuse on the commander; they appealed to heaven and to the gods, and left nothing undone by which they might excite resentment and pity, alarm, and rage. They all rushed to the spot, broke open the guardhouse, unbound the prisoners, and were in a moment fraternizing with deserters and men convicted on capital charges.

Thence arose a more furious outbreak, with more leaders of the mutiny. Vibulenus, a common soldier, was hoisted in front of the general's tribunal on the shoulders of the bystanders and addressed the excited throng, who eagerly awaited his intentions. "You have indeed," he said, "restored light and air to these innocent and most unhappy men, but who restores to my brother his life, or my brother to myself? Sent to you by the German army in our common cause, he was last night butchered by the gladiators whom the general keeps and arms for the destruction of his soldiers. Answer, Blaesus, where you have flung aside the corpse? Even an enemy grudges not burial. When, with embraces and tears, I have sated my grief, order me also to be killed, provided only that when we have been destroyed for no crime, but only because we consulted the good of the legions, we may be buried by these men around me."

He inflamed their excitement by weeping and smiting his breast and face with his hands. Then, hurling aside those who bore him on their shoulders, and impetuously flinging himself at the feet of one man after another, he roused such dismay and indignation that some of the soldiers put fetters on the gladiators who were among the number of Blaesus' slaves; others did the like to the rest of his household, while a third party hurried out to look for the corpse. And had it not quickly been known that no corpse was found, that the slaves, when tortures were applied, denied the murder, and that the man never had a brother, they would have been on the point of destroying the general. As it was, they thrust out the tribunes and the camp commandant; they plundered the baggage of the fugitives, and they killed a centurion, Lucilius, to whom, with soldiers' humor, they had given the name "Bring another," because when he had broken one vine stick on a man's back, he would call in a loud voice for another and another. The rest sheltered themselves in concealment, and one only was detained, Clemens Julius, whom the soldiers considered a fit person to carry messages, from his ready wit. Two legions, the eighth and the fifteenth, were actually drawing swords against each other, the former demanding the death of a centurion, whom they nicknamed Sirpicus, while the men of the fifteenth defended him, but the soldiers of the ninth interposed their entreaties, and when these were disregarded, their menaces.

68. Constantine's mobile army

Under the principate, as we have seen (see No. 53), nearly all the troops were stationed in permanent camps along the frontiers, in north Britain and along the Rhine, Danube, and Euphrates. For a major war, legions and other units were temporarily transferred from quiet sectors to the front, or special mobile forces were created from detachments drawn from the legions. The latter procedure became the rule in the second century. This system was satisfactory as long as the pressure on the frontier was intermittent and not very severe, but in the third and fourth centuries barbarian pressure mounted, and the enemy often broke through the frontiers. The solution adopted was to form a central mobile army which could be at once marched to the danger point. Such an army was formed by Aurelian and maintained by Diocletian, but, as Zosimus says, the latter's main effort was directed to strengthening the frontier. Constantine re-created the mobile army, making it much larger and giving the units in it higher status and better conditions of service. The mobile field army was called the *comitatus* (the troops which accompanied the emperor) and was commanded by the newly created Masters of the Soldiers. The old formations on the frontiers, under area commanders styled *duces*, were now called *limitanei* (frontier troops), or *ripenses* (river troops) since they were mostly stationed on the Rhine and Danube, and sank in status and efficiency. Zosimus, who was a pagan, gives a grossly unfair account of Constantine's measure.

68. Zosimus, II. 34

CONSTANTINE CARRIED out another measure which laid open to the barbarians access to the territory subject to the Romans. The Roman empire had everywhere along the frontier been studded with cities and fortresses and towers by the prudence of Diocletian, in the way I have already described, and all the army was stationed on the frontier, so that the barbarians could not cross it, since everywhere there was a force to meet and repulse the invaders. Constantine destroyed this security, by withdrawing the bulk of the troops from the frontiers, and posting them in cities which did not need defense, while he stripped of protection those that were harassed by the barbarians. Instead he imposed on peaceful cities the plague of the troops, whereby most have been ruined by now. He also softened the soldiers, who devoted themselves to theaters and to luxury. To speak plainly, it was he who initiated and sowed the seed of the present ruinous state of affairs.

69. The draft in the fourth century

Diocletian, in order to fill the ranks of his greatly enlarged army (cf. No. 16), instituted regular annual conscription. The draft fell only on the rural population, and the number of recruits to be levied was calculated on the same assessment as the taxes, that is, on a combined schedule of the land and its inhabitants. This is a law of Valens reforming the assessment of recruits. The abuses of the old system are obscure. Under the new, a recruit must be produced by a single landowner if his assessment is large enough, otherwise by a group of landowners. These take it in turn to produce the recruit from their tenants, but are compensated in money by the other members of the group. The recruit himself is valued at 30 solidi, and has to be given expenses of 6 solidi: these 36 solidi are apportioned over the members of the group according to their assessments. Sometimes the government exacted money instead of recruits (cf. No. 70), in which case it was paid on the same basis.

The last part of the law specifies the tax privileges given to the recruits, which vary according to whether they are assigned to the *comitatus* or the *ripenses*. The landlord, through whom the poll tax of his tenants was paid, was not allowed to profit from these exemptions, but had to fill up the number of his registered tenants.

69. Codex Theodosianus, *VII. 13*.7

EMPERORS VALENTINIAN, Valens, and Gratian Augusti to Modestus, Praetorian Prefect.

The furnishing of recruits shall be placed upon the resources of patrimonies rather than among the compulsory public services of persons. The public service of the *protostasia*, which feeds on the vitals of the provinces, shall be eradicated from its lowest roots, as the saying goes. For among other vices, these two We deem especially intolerable, namely, that a huge amount of gold is often demanded instead of men and that the purchase price of outsiders for recruits is estimated more exorbitantly than is fitting. Against such practices We have devised an easy and advantageous method of levy, in which no person can be exempted, as previously men were customarily released from service by special privilege, and no person who should be relieved can be consigned to a perpetual burden.

Similarly We enact also that only that person shall be separated from his associates whose taxable property is so great that he cannot receive an associate, since for his own part such a person himself can be solely responsible for supplying a recruit. But among those who are constrained to unite because of their small landholdings, alternation of years of service performed and of supplying a recruit shall be observed in such a way that senators and others who give a recruit the first year in their own name and that of their associate shall be considered exempt from the following turn, and they shall be succeeded in supplying a recruit by those associates who had been relieved from the demand for such recruit on the previous occasion. This procedure shall be observed when men are demanded; but when gold is to be paid instead of recruits, each person shall pay the sum due in proportion to the measure of his own tax assessment.

So that no doubt may be left, We designate also the number of solidi which must be paid to the person who furnishes the recruit. Thus if a senator, dignitary, chief decurion, decurion, or plebeian is going to furnish a recruit from his own land and house in his own name and that of his associates, he shall know that he will receive solidi from his partners and that the amount of the entire price shall total only thirty-six solidi. When the portion which is his proper share had been deducted, he shall receive the rest, but he shall supply six solidi for clothing and expenses to the recruit.

When persons are going to enter military service, their devotion is more easily stimulated by special privileges that are granted to them. All persons who take the oath of military service shall immediately be exempt from their own capitation tax from the year in which they were attached to their units, provided only that they remain steadfast in the task which they assumed. When they have completed five years of service, they shall also satisfy the capitation taxes of their fathers, their mothers, and their wives, on the basis of their services, if they have been attached to the units of the field troops. But if they were stationed in cavalry or auxiliary units in the river troops, they shall exempt only their wives, along with their own capitation tax, after a period of five years, as We have said, provided that it is proved that they are enrolled on the tax lists. Because the public welfare also must be considered, in order that the number of capitation tax payments listed may not be diminished under this indulgence, We order that other men, from those not listed in the tax registers and from the supernumeraries, shall be substituted for those who have been protected from taxes by military service.

Given on the fourth day before the nones of June at Antioch in the year after the third consulship of Gratian Augustus and the consulship of Equitius [June 2, 375].

70. Hereditary military service

As we have seen (see Nos. 62, 64) the imperial government had in the first and second centuries indirectly encouraged sons of soldiers to enlist, and from inscriptions it appears that service in the army was to a large extent hereditary. Either Diocletian or Constantine made the custom compulsory, and the rule was periodically enforced, as by this law.

70. Codex Theodosianus, *VII. i.8*

THE SAME Augusti to Equitius, Count and Master of Soldiers.

Your authority shall announce to all veterans whatsoever that if any of them should not, of his own free will, offer his son, who is entirely worthy of the honor of bearing arms, to the imperial service, for which the veteran himself has toiled, he shall be involved in the toils of Our law.

Given on the eighth day before the kalends of October at Heraclea in the consulship of Valentinian and Valens [September 24, 365].

71. Rations

From the time of Diocletian, the troops were largely paid in kind— rations, uniforms, arms, horses (if cavalry). Noncommissioned officers and officers received multiple rations. From this law we see that they often preferred not to draw the large quantities of bread, meat, wine, and oil to which they were entitled, but compelled the officials responsible to buy their rations from them for cash.

71. Codex Theodosianus, *VII. 4.1*

EMPEROR CONSTANTINE AUGUSTUS to Our Very Dear Friend Felix, Greetings.

The tribunes and officers who have charge of Our soldiers must not leave behind in the state storehouses the rations which are owed to them from day to day according to the information of the written record, so that the procurators or tax receivers or the provosts of the rural districts and of the state storehouses may purchase such provisions; for as a consequence it comes about that the said officials are demanding from the provincials not payment in kind, but money; the supplies also, since they remain unused, deteriorate and decay. For this reason We decree that if rations have been left unclaimed, the whole amount shall be vindicated to the fisc, and the undersecretary and the military paymaster shall be struck down by the sword, since it cannot be brought to pass either that the provincials be burdened by a repeated tax payment or that spoiled food supplies be distributed to the soldiers because the aforesaid persons refuse to accept, on the appointed day, rations commensurate with their rank. If any person should be apprehended as guilty of this offense, he shall not be defended by personal merit or by his very high position.

Given on the fourteenth day before the kalends of November at Aquae in the consulship of Paulinus and Julianus [October 19, 325].

72. Commutation of rations

Gradually issues in kind were commuted into money. In this law, we see the first stage of the change.

72. Codex Theodosianus, *VII. 4.14*

THE SAME Augusti to Secundus, Praetorian Prefect.

River troops shall receive rations in kind for nine months in the year, and for the other three months they shall receive the corresponding prices.

Received on the kalends of December at Chalcedon in the consulship of Valentinian and Valens, the Augusti [December 1, 365].

73. Commutation of recruits

The commutation of recruits was often favored by the government, which preferred to pay barbarians rather than levy Roman recruits of low quality. But it was also preferred by landlords, who were always short of tenants to cultivate their estates. Here the senate at a time of grave military crisis (the revolt of Gildo) successfully petitioned the emperor for commutation.

73. Codex Theodosianus, *VII. 13.13*

THE SAME Augusti to Theodorus, Praetorian Prefect.

Our Clemency assents to the petitions of the most August Order, that money may be paid instead of recruits. We grant, therefore, the option that the senate may have the power to choose the method which seems advantageous to it, that is, they may either furnish recruits suitable for military duties or they may pay twenty-five solidi for each recruit, after, of course, they have assumed the account of the expenses incurred for his clothing and food. But if senators should prefer to pay gold, it shall be delivered at once to Our treasury.

Given on the eighth day before the kalends of October at Padua in the consulship of Caesarius and Atticus [September 24, 397].

74. Tax privileges of soldiers and veterans

This complicated law sets out the tax privileges of soldiers and veterans in (1) the field army, (2) the legions and cavalry corps of the river troops—*ripenses*, (3) the old auxiliary troops, the *alae* and cohorts, who also formed part of the frontier army. It will be seen that group (2) had been slightly less well treated than group (1), but is now leveled up. Group (3) are much behind (1) and (2), as under the principate.

74. Codex Theodosianus, *VII. 20.4*

THE SAME Augustus to Maximus, Prefect of the City.

Field army troops, river troops, and officer cadets shall exempt from capitation tax their own persons, their fathers and mothers, and their wives, if they should have these kinsmen surviving and if they have been enrolled upon the tax lists. But if the soldiers should lack any one of these persons or should have none of them, they shall exempt from their own property only so much as they would have been able to exempt for the aforesaid kinsmen if such kinsmen were not lacking. They must not, however, make agreements with other persons whereby they exempt the property of others by pretending to own it, but they must exempt only their very own property.

We sanction, moreover, that veterans shall exempt from taxes their own persons as well as their wives, after they have received letters of discharge earned by service. If they should receive honorable discharges, they shall exempt only their own persons. We command that all other veterans from any army whatsoever, together with their wives, shall enjoy exemption of one person each. A veteran of the river troops, moreover, who by a previous law enjoyed the exemption of one person when he had obtained an honorable discharge after twenty-four years of service, even if he should earn his honorable discharge by the completion of twenty years of service, shall exempt one person, just as is provided in the case of the field army troops. Even if he should be discharged before the completion of twenty years of service, he shall enjoy the same special grant of imperial favor, since feeble and disabled persons are not inscribed on the tax lists.

Soldiers of the *alae* and cohorts shall exempt their own persons as long as they are on active duty. Their veterans also shall have the same compensations of exemption if they should obtain discharge at any time and in any area. If a soldier should be discharged from the field army troops because of old age or disability, regardless of the number of years of service, he shall exempt two persons, that is, himself and his wife. The river troops shall have the same privilege without distinction, if they should prove that they have been discharged because of wounds received in action. If any person should leave military service after fifteen years of service and before the completion of twenty-four years, he shall enjoy exemption only of his own person. If a member of the river troops should be discharged after twenty-four years of service, his wife must also be exempted.

Posted on the fifteenth day before the kalends of July at Antioch in the consulship of Paulinus and Julianus [June 17, 325].

75. Allotments for veterans

As under the principate, veterans received allotments of land or a cash bonus. These grants continued until the end of the fourth century.

75. Codex Theodosianus, *VII. 20.3*

THE SAME Augustus to all veterans.

In accordance with Our order veterans shall receive vacant lands, and they shall hold them tax exempt in perpetuity. To purchase necessary equipment for the land they shall on completion of service receive twenty-five *folles* of money in cash, a yoke of oxen, and a hundred measures of assorted grains.

If any veteran, moreover, should take pleasure in engaging in business, We permit him to have the sum of one hundred *folles* tax exempt.

Except those veterans, therefore, who are settled in their homes or in business, all of you who are unemployed and are engaged in no business should take advantage of this assistance so that you may not suffer from want.

Given on the third day before the ides of October at Constantinople in the six consulship of Constantine Augustus and the consulship of Constantius Caesar [October 13, 320; to be corrected to 325].

76. Federates

Since the reign of Aurelian, the frontier had been held against the Germans with fair success, but in the reign of Valens, the advance of the Huns, who had been sweeping westward from central Asia, spreading terror wherever they went, set the German tribes in motion again. The Visigoths, who occupied the land north of the Lower Danube, sought refuge within the Roman empire.

The immediate result of the incidents described in this passage was that Valens was crushingly defeated by the Goths in 378 at Adrianople.

The Roman government had hitherto freely recruited individual Germans into its army (see No. 20), and had often employed groups of Germans supplied under treaty by tribes outside the empire, and had settled Germans in scattered groups in the provinces with the hereditary obligation of military service. It was this last policy that Valens intended to pursue, but the Goths were provoked into fighting. Valens' successor, Theodosius I, was unable to expel the Visigoths and, after several years of indecisive warfare, was compelled to allocate them land in Thrace, where they lived under their tribal kings as *foederati* (allies) of Rome, obliged to provide troops on demand. This concession proved fatal to the western empire, for tribes thus settled en block retained their tribal cohesion, unlike the scattered groups hitherto settled, and their kings were able to blackmail the Roman government. It was a king of the Visigoths, Alaric, who captured Rome in 410, when his demands for money and land were refused by the emperor Honorius.

76. *Ammianus Marcellinus, XXXI. 3–4*

WHILE THIS important work was going on, the Huns kept pressing on his traces with great speed, and they would have overtaken and destroyed him if they had not been forced to abandon the pursuit from being impeded by the great quantity of their booty. In the meantime a report spread extensively through the other nations of the Goths, that a race of men, hitherto unknown, had suddenly descended like a whirlwind from the lofty mountains, as if they had risen from some secret recess of the earth, and were ravaging and destroying everything which came in their way. And then the greater part of the population, which, because of their want of necessaries, had deserted Athanaric, resolved to flee and to seek a home remote from all knowledge of the barbarians; and after a long deliberation where to fix their abode, they resolved that a retreat into Thrace was the most suitable for these two reasons: first of all, because it is a district most fertile in grass; and also because, by the great breadth of the Danube, it is wholly separated from the barbarians, who were already exposed to the thunderbolts of foreign warfare. And the whole population of the tribe adopted this resolution unanimously. Accordingly, under the command of their leader Alavivus, they occupied the banks of the Danube; and having sent ambassadors to Valens, they humbly entreated to be received by him as his subjects, promising to live quietly and to provide forces should need arise.

While these events were passing in foreign countries, a terrible rumor arose that the tribes of the north were planning new and unprecedented attacks upon us: and that over the whole region which extends from the country of the Marcomanni and Quadi to Pontus, a barbarian host composed of different distant nations, which had suddenly been driven by force from their own countries, was now, with all its families, wandering about in different directions on the banks of the river Danube.

At first this intelligence was lightly treated by our people, because they were not in the habit of hearing of any wars in those remote districts till they were terminated either by victory or by treaty. But presently, as the belief in these occurrences grew stronger, being confirmed, too, by the arrival of the foreign ambassadors, who, with prayers and earnest entreaties, begged that the people thus driven from their homes and now encamped on the other side of the river, might be kindly received by us, the affair seemed a cause of joy rather than of fear, according to the skillful flatterers who were always extolling and exaggerating the good fortune of the emperor; congratulating him that an embassy had come from the furthest corners of the earth unexpectedly offering him a large body of recruits; and that, by combining the strength of his own people with these foreign forces, he would have an army absolutely invincible; observing further that, by the yearly payment for military recruits which came in every year from the provinces, a vast treasure of gold might be accumulated in his coffers.

Full of this hope he sent forth several officers to bring this ferocious people and their wagons into our territory. And such great pains were taken to gratify this nation which was destined to overthrow the empire of Rome, that not one was left behind, not even of those who were stricken with mortal disease. Moreover, having obtained permission of the emperor to cross the Danube and to cultivate some districts in Thrace, they crossed the stream day and night without ceasing, embarking in troops on board ships and rafts and canoes made of the hollow trunks of trees, in which enterprise, as the Danube is the most difficult of all rivers to navigate, and was at that time swollen with continual rains, a great many were drowned, who, because they were too numerous for the vessels, tried to swim across, and in spite of all their exertions were swept away by the stream.

In this way, through the turbulent zeal of violent people, the ruin of the Roman empire was brought on. This, at all events, is neither obscure nor uncertain, that the unhappy officers who were entrusted with the charge of conducting the multitude of the barbarians across the river, though they repeatedly endeavored to calculate their numbers, at last abandoned the attempt as hopeless; and the man who would wish to ascertain the number might as well (as the most illustrious of poets says) attempt to count the waves in the African sea, or the grains of sand tossed about by the zephyr.

Let, however, the ancient annals be accredited which record that the Persian host which was led into Greece was, while encamped on the shores of the Hellespont, and making a new and artificial sea, numbered in battalions at Doriscus; a computation which has been unanimously regarded by all posterity as fabulous. But after the innumerable multitudes of different nations, diffused over all our provinces, and spreading themselves over the vast expanse of our plains, who filled all the champaign country and all the mountain ranges, are considered, the credibility of the ancient accounts is confirmed by this modern instance. First of all, Fritigernus was

received with Alavivus; and the emperor assigned them a temporary provision for their immediate support, and ordered lands to be
assigned them to cultivate. At that time the defenses of our provinces were much exposed, and the armies of barbarians spread over
them like the lava of Mount Etna. The imminence of our danger
manifestly called for generals already illustrious for their past
achievements in war: but nevertheless, as if some unpropitious
deity had made the selection, the men who had been picked out for
the chief military appointments were of tainted character. The
chief among them were Lupicinus and Maximus, the one being
Count of Thrace, the other the area commander—both men of
great rashness.

Their treacherous covetousness was the cause of all our disasters.
For (to pass over other matters in which the officers aforesaid, or
others with their unblushing connivance, displayed the greatest
profligacy in their injurious treatment of the foreigners dwelling in
our territory, against whom no crime would be alleged) this one
melancholy and unprecedented piece of conduct (which, even if
they were to choose their own judges, must appear wholly un-
pardonable) must be mentioned. When the barbarians who had
been conducted across the river were in great distress from want of
provisions, those detested generals conceived the idea of a most
disgraceful traffic: and having collected dogs from all quarters with
the most insatiable rapacity, they exchanged them for an equal
number of slaves, among whom were several sons of men of noble
birth.

VII. The Provinces

77. Spain under Augustus

This passage sets out in detail the administrative setup of the Spanish provinces under the early principate. It conforms closely to the general account given by Cassius Dio in No. 4, except that *legati Augusti pro praetore* of praetorian rank had later no subordinate *legati* under them, and that later legionary legates commanded one legion only. Very few consular *legati Augusti pro praetore* had subordinate *legati* with judicial duties (*legati iuridici*); they are recorded only in Spain and in Britain.

77. *Strabo, III. iv. 20, 166–67*

BUT NOW, the provinces having been allotted, some to the people and the senate, some to the leader of the Romans, Baetica belongs to the people, and a praetor is sent to it with a quaestor and a legate; they have fixed its boundary to the east near Castulo. The rest is Caesar's, and he sends out two legates, a praetorian and a consular. The praetorian, with a legate with him, administers justice to the Lusitanians, who live next to Baetica and extend to the river Durius and its mouth; that is the name they now give to this area. Here there is Augusta Emerita. The rest, the greater part of Spain, is under the consular governor, with a considerable army of three legions and three legates. One of these keeps guard with two legions over all the country beyond the Durius to the north, what used to be called Lusitania and is now dubbed Callaecia; the northern mountains with the Astures and the Cantabri join on to it. The river Melsus runs through the Astures and a little further on is the city of Noega. Nearby is the turn of the ocean which divides the Astures from the Cantabri. The adjacent coast as far as the Pyrenees is guarded by the second legate with the other legion, and the third oversees the inland area. It contains the already mentioned peaceful peoples who have adopted civilized Italian manners and wear the toga, the Celtiberians and those that live on either side of the Iberus down to the maritime area. The governor himself winters in the maritime area, especially in Carthago and Tarraco, administering justice. And in the summer he goes on circuit, inspecting anything that needs reform: and there are equestrian procurators of Caesar who pay out money for the maintenance of the troops.

78. Egypt under Augustus

Egypt, annexed by Augustus in 30 B.C. on the death of Cleopatra, the last of the Ptolemaic dynasty, was peculiar in that no senator was allowed to enter it without imperial permission, and the administrative and military posts were entrusted to *equites*. The reason, it would appear from Tacitus, was that Egypt was economically so rich and strategically so secure that it would have been dangerous to place it under a senator, who might be tempted to rebel. The powerful garrison was very soon reduced (see No. 53). For the duties of the Special Account, see No. 126.

78. Strabo, XVII. i.12, 797

It is now a province, paying considerable taxes and administered by sound men who are sent to it as prefects. The man who is sent takes the place of the king, and under him is a minister of justice, in whose hands are the bulk of trials, and there is another minister called the Special Account, who keeps a check on ownerless properties and others which should lapse to Caesar. These are accompanied by freedmen of Caesar and agents entrusted with various tasks, great or small. There are three legions of the army, one stationed in the city [Alexandria] and the others in the country. Besides these, there are nine Roman cohorts, three in the city, three on the borders of Ethiopia at Syene as a local garrison, and three in the rest of the country. There are also three *alae* of cavalry similarly distributed at suitable points. Of the local magistrates in the city, one is the exegetes, who wears a purple robe and holds ancestral honors and looks after the interests of the city, and the keeper of the records and the chief justice, and the fourth is the commander of the night watch. These offices existed under the kings.

79. The duties of a proconsul

These are extracts made by the legal advisers of Justinian from treatises written by the jurists of the principate; Ulpian, Papinian, and Paul lived in the early third century, Venuleius Saturnius in the late second. They give an interesting picture of day-to-day administration, and show what tact was required of a provincial governor to avoid offending local susceptibilities. It may be noted that in public provinces the rules of administration are based not only on resolutions of the senate, but on imperial letters and rescripts, and on imperial mandates, i.e., standing instructions to governors.

79. Digest, I. xvi. 4–13

ULPIAN, ON THE OFFICE OF PROCONSUL, BOOK I

A PROCONSUL ought to take care not to burden his province with providing hospitality, as our present emperor and his father replied to Aufidius Severianus. No proconsul has grooms of his own, but soldiers perform this service in their place in the provinces. It is better for a proconsul to go out without his wife, but he can take his wife with him, so long as he knows that the senate resolved in the consulship of Cotta and Messala [A.D. 21] that "in future if the wives of those who go out to hold posts commit any offense, they will themselves be accountable and liable to punishment." Before he crosses the boundary of a province decreed to him, a proconsul should send an edict about his arrival, containing some recommendation of himself, if he has any acquaintance with the provincials, and in particular excusing them from coming to meet him, either publicly or privately; for it is proper that everyone should receive him in their own city. He will do rightly and in order if he sends his edict to his predecessor; uncertainty and the unexpected generally disturb the provincials, and impede business. In entering, he must also take care to enter through the part of the province through which it is usual to enter it and to observe what the Greeks call ἐπιδημίας, i.e., approach to a city, or καταπλοῦν, i.e., sailing into harbor—which city he arrives or lands at first. For the provincials think it very important that such customs and rights of precedence should be preserved for them. Some provinces have the rule that the proconsul shall come to the province by sea, e.g., Asia, so much so that the emperor Antoninus Augustus replied to the requests of the Asiatics: "the proconsul is obliged to arrive in Asia by sea, καὶ τῶν μητεοπόλεων Ἔφεσον, i.e., and to reach Ephesus first among the metropolis. After having thus entered his province he should mandate jurisdiction to his legate; he ought not to do this before entering his province. For it is quite absurd that before himself acquiring jurisdiction—and it does not belong to him before he enters the province—he should mandate to another what he does not possess himself. But if he does so before, and enters the province with the same wish, it must be believed that the legate has jurisdiction, not from the time it was mandated to him, but from when the proconsul entered the province.

PAPINIAN, QUESTIONS, BOOK I

Sometimes a proconsul can mandate his jurisdiction, although he has not yet reached his province. For what if he incurs a necessary delay on his journey, but his legate is going to arrive in good time in the province?

ULPIAN, ON THE OFFICE OF PROCONSUL, BOOK I

They also usually mandate to their legates the investigation of prisons, viz., to send up prisoners to him after a preliminary hearing, so that he himself can release an innocent man. But this kind of mandate is outside the ordinary course of law. For no one can transfer to another the power of the sword or of any other corporal punishment given to him, nor therefore the right of freeing accused persons, when they cannot be accused before him. It is in the proconsul's discretion to mandate jurisdiction or not to mandate it; so the proconsul is allowed to take away mandated jurisdiction, but he ought not to do this without consulting the emperor. Legates ought not to consult the emperor but their own proconsul, and he ought to reply to his legate's requests for advice. A proconsul ought not to abstain from taking presents altogether, but to observe moderation, so as neither to refuse presents altogether in a churlish way, nor to exceed moderation in presents in a grasping way. The deified Severus and our present emperor Antoninus regulated the issue very elegantly in a letter, of which the text is as follows. "As concerns presents, hear what we feel. There is an old proverb, 'Not everything, not on every occasion, not from everyone.' For it is very bad manners to accept nothing from anybody, but very bad taste to accept indiscriminately, and very grasping to accept everything." The clause in the mandates, "The proconsul himself and those who occupy any post shall not accept any donation or gift or buy anything, except for his daily food," does not apply to little presents, but to what exceeds things to eat. But presents cannot be extended to the character of donations."

ULPIAN, ON THE OFFICE OF PROCONSUL, BOOK II

If he comes to another famous city or to the capital of the province, he must allow the city to be commended to him, and hear his own praises with good temper, since the provincials think it an honor to them. He should also give holidays according to custom and precedent. He ought to go and inspect the temples and public buildings to see whether they are in proper repair or need any restoration, and to see to it that, if they have been begun, they are finished, as the finances of each city allow, and appoint businesslike curators of works in due form. He may also, if need be, assign military personnel to assist the curators. Whereas the proconsul has the fullest jurisdiction, the functions of all who at Rome administer justice, as quasi-magistrates or outside the normal course of law, belong to him.

ULPIAN, ON THE EDICT, BOOK XXXIX

And, therefore, he has a greater *imperium* in the province than anybody except the emperor.

ULPIAN, ON THE DUTY OF PROCONSUL, BOOK I

Nor is there anything in the province which cannot be handled by him. It is true that if there is a pecuniary fiscal case, which affects the imperial procurator, he will do better not to intervene. When a decree is required, the proconsul will not be able to deal with it by correspondence. For not everything which requires decision in a case can be conducted by correspondence. With advocates the proconsul ought to be patient, but with intelligence, so that he may not appear contemptible, and he should not pretend too much innocence, if he catches anyone who cooks up cases for the sake of the fees. He should also allow to plead only those who are permitted by his edict to do so. The proconsul ought to deal informally with such questions as obedience to parents and patrons, and orders for alimony to the sons of patrons. He ought also to threaten and put the fear of God into a son presented by his father, allegedly for not behaving as he should. He can similarly informally castigate a disobedient freedman, verbally or with a beating. He ought also to see to it that there is some order in bringing cases, so that the complaints of all can be heard. Otherwise, if deference is given to the honor of plaintiffs—or yielded to their importunity—people of modest standing cannot bring forward their own complaints, since they have not produced any advocates at all or only a few, and have not had the foresight to get themselves advocates of high position. He ought to give advocates to those who ask for them, usually to women or minors, and other persons in a weak position, or insane persons, if someone asks on their behalf, or, if nobody asks, he ought to act of his own motion. If someone says that owing to the influence of his adversary, he cannot get an advocate, he ought likewise to give him an advocate. No one ought to suffer because of the influence of his adversaries. It brings odium on the governor if anyone behaves so outrageously that every advocate is afraid to plead against him. He must also perform the common duties of all governors.

ULPIAN, ON THE OFFICE OF PROCONSUL, BOOK X

A proconsul ought to remember that he must do everything up to the arrival of his successor, since the proconsulate is one and the interests of the provincials demand someone through whom they can conduct their business. So he ought to administer justice until his successor's arrival. He ought not to dismiss his legate from the province before himself, as is advised by the Julian law on extortion and a rescript of the deified Hadrian to Calpurnius Rufus, proconsul of Achaea.

VENULEIUS SATURNINUS, ON THE OFFICE OF PROCONSUL, BOOK II

If there is anything which demands severe punishment, the legate ought to refer to the proconsul, for he has no power of execution, imprisoning, or severe flogging.

PAULUS, ON THE EDICT, BOOK II

A legate, by the jurisdiction mandated to him, has the right of appointing a judge.

POMPONIUS, ON QUINTUS MUCIUS, BOOK X

Legates of a proconsul have no power of their own, unless jurisdiction is mandated to them by their proconsul.

80. Agricola in Britain

The first part of this passage shows that, despite the instructions given to them by the emperors, provincial governors under the principate were often guilty of oppression and extortion. The malpractices about corn were a long-standing abuse, dating from the republican period. Governors had the right to purchase corn for their armies at a fixed price from the provincial cities, which had to deliver it where ordered. One abuse was to buy more corn than was needed, so that the provincials had to buy it back—at a higher price—for their own use. Another was to order cities to deliver corn to the camps most distant from them. They would then ask permission to pay money instead of corn—at a higher price than that fixed for the purchases.

The second part describes Agricola's policy of Romanizing the province. It is often stated that this was a general policy of the imperial government, but there is no other evidence that it deliberately promoted Romanization. In the west the movement seems to have been spontaneous. In the Greek-speaking provinces no Romanization took place.

80. *Tacitus*, Agricola, *19–21*

BUT, BEING well acquainted with the temper of the province, and at the same time taught by the experience of others that little advance is made by arms, if injuries follow, he resolved to eradicate the causes of war. Commencing with himself and his dependents, he first of all restrained his own domestics, which to most persons is not less difficult than to manage a province. No public business did he manage through the agency of freedmen or slaves: he did not select centurions or soldiers to serve on his staff through private partiality, nor on the recommendation and solicitation of others, but he considered every most deserving man as most faithful: he wished to know every thing, not to punish every thing: small faults he pardoned, great ones he visited with severity; nor was he always inclined to punish, more frequently he was satisfied with repentance. He appointed to offices and employments those who were not likely to offend, rather than condemned them when they had offended. He mitigated the exaction of corn and of tribute by equality of assessment, abolishing those practices which, devised for private gain, were felt more severely than the tribute itself: for, by way of mockery, they were compelled to attend at the locked granaries and to purchase their own corn, and tricks were played with the price: difficult journeys and distant places were enjoined, so that cities near to military quarters had to convey their corn to stations that were remote and devious, until that which should have been a matter of convenience to all became a matter of gain to a few.

By suppressing these practices at once in his first year he established a favorable character for peace, which, through the negligence or connivance of his predecessors, was dreaded not less than war. But when the summer came, assembling his army, assiduous on the march, he applauded obedience, rebuked the stragglers, selected in person the places for encampments, was the first to explore the estuaries and woods; and in the meantime he suffered no repose among the enemy, harassing them by sudden incursions: and when he had alarmed them sufficiently, by using forbearance he again held out the allurements of peace. By which means several states, which up to that period had asserted their independence, gave hostages, and laid aside their animosity; and were surrounded with posts and castles with such skill and judgment that no previously annexed part of Britain escaped so unmolested.

The following winter was spent in the most salutary measures; for, in order that men hitherto dispersed and uncivilized, and consequently disposed to war, might become habituated by pleasure to peace and repose, he privately encouraged and publicly assisted them to build temples, courts of justice, houses, by applauding the prompt and reprimanding the dilatory: thus the emulation for honor acted as compulsion. He also had the sons of the chiefs instructed in the polite arts, and preferred the natural genius of the Britons to the studied attainments of the Gauls; so that those who lately spurned the Roman language, now became desirous of eloquence; afterward respect began to be entertained for our dress, and the toga became frequent; and they gradually moved on to the incentives to vice, porticos, baths, and the elegancies of the table; and this, among the inexperienced, was called civilization when in reality it was a part of servitude.

81. A proconsul's preparations

Fronto, as one of the two senior ex-consuls, had the right to draw lots for the proconsulship of either Africa or Asia unless the other man enjoyed precedence under the *lex Julia de maritandis ordinibus* (see No. 29). As Fronto's opposite number had more children, he took the province of his choice, Africa, and Fronto was left with Asia. A governor had the right of selecting his own prefects and other members of his staff (*comites*).

81. *Fronto*, ad Antoninum Pium, 8

THE FACTS testify that I have worked hard, most sacred emperor, and have earnestly desired to fulfill the office of proconsul. I argued about the rule of allotment, as long as it was doubtful, and when it appeared that the other man had precedence in virtue of his children, I considered the splendid province which remained for me as chosen. Then I made careful preparations for whatever concerned staffing the province, so that I could the more easily cope with the heavy business by the resources of my friends. I summoned to my home my neighbors and friends, of whose honor and integrity I was sure. I wrote to my acquaintances at Alexandria to hurry to Athens to meet me there, and I assigned to these learned men the charge of my Greek correspondence. I also urged to come distinguished men from Cilicia, as I have a great many friends in that province, since I have always defended the pleas of Cilicians, both public and private, before you. I also called to my side from Mauretania a great friend of mine who is very dear to me, Julius Senex, to give me the aid not only of his honor and energy, but also of his military experience of hunting down and repressing brigands. I did all this in the hope that I could, by a rigid diet and by drinking water, if not altogether cure my illness, at any rate reduce its attack for a longer period. It so happened that I enjoyed good health for longer than usual, and was strong and vigorous; so much so that I pleaded two causes of friends before you, which involved a great deal of work. Then the strength of my illness so quickly increased that it showed me that all my hopes were vain.

82. A corrector of free cities

This letter is addressed by Pliny to a certain Maximus, who, having reached the rank of praetor, had been given a special commission to regulate the free cities of the province of Achaea (Greece). Some cities in the provinces enjoyed by grace of the imperial government the right to manage their own affairs without interference from the provincial governor. They often became inefficient and corrupt, and their freedom was progressively whittled away by such measures as this. More generally, the internal affairs of all cities, especially their finances, were during the second century brought under closer imperial control. Pliny had such a mission in Bithynia (see No. 30), and special commissioners (*curatores*) were more and more frequently appointed to control the finances of individual cities (see No. 41).

82. *Pliny*, Letters, *VIII. 24*

THE FRIENDSHIP I profess to have for you obliges me, not indeed to direct you (for you are far above the want of a guide) but to remind you, however, of what you already know, and to admonish you carefully to observe and resolutely put it in practice; that is, to know it to all the more useful purposes of knowledge. You will consider yourself as sent to that noble province, Achaea, the real and genuine Greece, where politeness, learning, and even agriculture itself are supposed to have taken their first rise; as sent to regulate the status of free cities; that is, to men who breathe the spirit of true manhood and liberty; who maintained the rights they received from Nature, by courage, by virtue, by alliances; in a word, by civil and religious faith. You will revere the Gods and Heroes their founders; you will respect their ancient glory, and even their very age, which, as it is venerable in men, in states is sacred. You will honor them, therefore, for their antiquity, and for those famous deeds which are truly, nay for those which are fabulously, recorded of them. You will indulge them in the full exercise of their dignity, their privileges, and even their very vanity. Remember it was from this nation we derived our laws; that she did not receive ours by conquest, but gave us hers by favor. Remember it is Athens that you approach; it is Lacedaemon you govern; and to deprive such a glorious people of the declining shadow, the remaining name of liberty, would be a hardship, would be even a barbarity of the severest kind. Physicians, you see, though with respect to diseases there is no difference between freedom and slavery, yet treat persons of the former rank with more tenderness than those of the latter. Reflect on the noble figure these cities once made; but so reflect as not to despise them for what they now are. Far be pride and asperity from my friend; nor fear by a proper condescension to lay yourself open to contempt. Can he who is vested with the power and bears the ensigns of authority fail of meeting with respect, unless by pursuing base and sordid measures and first breaking through that awful reverence he owes to himself? Ill, believe me, is power experienced by injuries; ill can terror command veneration, and far more prevalent is affection in obtaining one's desires than fear. For terror operates no longer than its object is present, but love produces its effects at a distance; and as absence changes the former into hatred, it raises the other into respect. It behoves you, therefore (and I cannot but repeat it again), it behoves you thoroughly to consider the title of your office, and to represent to yourself how great and important the task is of regulating the status of free cities. For what is more becoming to human nature than regulation, or more valuable than liberty? How ignominious then must his conduct be who turns the first into confusion and the latter into slavery? To these considerations let me add that you have an established reputation to maintain: the same you acquired by the administration of the quaestorship in Bithynia, the good opinion of the emperor, the credit you obtained when you were tribune and praetor, in a word, this very government, which may be looked upon as the reward of your former services, are all so many glorious weights which are incumbent upon you to support. So much the more, therefore, ought you to endeavor that it may not be said you showed greater humanity, integrity, and ability in a province remote from Rome, than in one which lies nearer to it; in the midst of a nation of slaves, than among a free people; that it may not be said it was chance, and not judgment, appointed you to this office; that your character was unknown and unexperienced, not tried and approved. For (and it is a maxim which your reading and conversation must have often suggested to you) it is far worse to lose the fame one has acquired, than never to have attained it. I again beg you would be persuaded that I did not write this letter with a design to instruct, but to remind you. Though indeed if I had, it would have only been in consequence of my affection for you: a point which I am in no apprehension of carrying beyond its just limits: for there cannot be any danger of excess where we ought to advance as far as possible.

83. A trial for corrupt administration

In this letter Pliny describes a trial for extortion, held, as was normal under the principate, by the senate (see Nos. 84, 135). The case was brought, again as usual, by delegates chosen by the provincial house of representatives (see No. 85). Extortion was a capital charge, but under a resolution of the senate promoted by Augustus (see No. 139), provincial claimants could if they preferred bring a civil action for restitution of the money, and the decision was then referred to a jury of five senators. By this time the senate had assumed the right of deciding whether the charge should be regarded as capital or referred to a civil jury. On the vexed question of "presents," cf. No. 79.

83. *Pliny*, Letters, *IV. 9*

WE HAVE been engaged for several days past in the cause of Julius Bassus, a man grown familiar with misfortunes, and rendered con-

spicuous by a series of calamities. In the reign of Vespasian two
private persons informed against him, and the affair being referred
to the senate, it depended there a considerable time, when at last he
was honorably acquitted. During the time of Titus he was under
continual apprehensions of his resentment, as being known to favor
the interests of Domitian: yet when that emperor ascended the
throne, Bassus was exiled; but afterward recalled by Nerva. Having obtained the proconsulship of Bithynia, he was at his return
from thence accused of bribery and extortion; and as he was
prosecuted with warmth, he was defended with vigor. The sentiments of the senate were greatly divided; however the majority
were on the most favorable side. Pomponius Rufus, a person of
great spirit and vivacity, was counsel against him. He was seconded
by Theophanes, one of the deputies from the province, and,
indeed, the chief promoter and inflamer of this prosecution. I
began the reply; for Bassus insisted that the foundation of his defense should be laid by me. He desired me to represent the consideration that was due to his illustrious birth and to the dangers he
had undergone; that his accusers were informers by profession,
who reaped considerable advantage by their trade; and to display
the true reasons which rendered him odious to the seditious, and
particularly to Theophanes; but above all, to confute the principal
charge that was brought against him: for in all the rest, however
grievous the accusation might appear, he not only deserved to be
acquitted, but highly commended. The great difficulty of the case
was that in the simplicity of his heart he had incautiously received
the gifts which some of his friends in the province (for he had been
among them before as quaestor) thought proper to send him. This,
which his accusers called rapine and extortion, Bassus justified
under the notion of presents. But then the laws expressly forbid
persons in his station to receive any presents whatsoever. Now
what method of defense should I strike into upon this occasion? If
I denied the fact, I was afraid it would look like a tacit confession
that it was actually extortion: besides to disown what was so notorious would be to heighten rather than to extenuate the charge.
And, indeed, he had put that out of the power of his counsel, if
they had thought it proper; for he had acknowledged to several
persons, and particularly to the emperor, that he had received and
returned a few slight presents upon his birthday, and at the feast of
the Saturnalia. Should I apply to the clemency of the senate? That

would be ruining my client at once, by confessing the nature of his offense was such that there was no other way of saving him. Should I then justify the fact? But in so doing I should have injured my own character, without rendering any service to Bassus. Under these difficulties I thought it would be best to steer a middle course; and I flatter myself I happily hit upon it. But night coming on separated, as usual, the combatants. I had spoken for three hours and a half, so that I had still an hour and a half remaining. For the law having allowed six hours to the plaintiff and nine to the defendant, Bassus had so divided this portion of time between me and the advocate who was to speak after me that I had five hours, and he the rest. But perceiving my speech had made a favorable impression upon the senate, I thought it would be most advisable to add nothing more; for it is not prudent, you know, to push one's success too far. Besides, I was apprehensive I should not have strength to renew the defense the next day, as it is much easier to go on without intermission than to begin again after having rested. There was yet another consideration which had great weight with me: I was afriad that as the discontinuance of my speech would abate my own ardor; so the resumption of it might prove tiresome to my hearers. When a harangue is carried on in one continued course, the speaker best keeps up his own fire and the attention of the audience, both which are apt to cool and grow languid upon a remission: just as a continued motion preserves the light of a torch, which, when once it is extinct, is not easily re-inflamed. But Bassus, almost with tears in his eyes, earnestly pressed me to go on with his defense for the remainder of the time; which I accordingly complied with, preferring his interest to my own. And the event proved extremely favorable; for I found the attention of the senate as fresh and lively as if it had been rather animated than fatigued by the former part of my speech. I was seconded by Luccius Albinus, who entered so thoroughly into my reasoning that our speeches, whilst they had the variety of different and distinct orations, had the connection and uniformity of one entire harangue. Herennius Pollio replied to us with great spirit and solidity: and after him Theophanes spoke again: in this, as in everything else, discovering his uncommon assurance by presuming to take up the time of the senate after two such eloquent persons, and of consular dignity, had spoke before him. He continued haranguing till evening, and even beyond it; for they called for lights. The next day Titius Homullus and Fronto spoke gloriously in behalf of Bassus. The fourth day was employed in examining the proofs. Baebius Macer, the consul elect, declared Bassus guilty, within the express words of the law relating to bribery and extortion. Caepio Hispo was of opinion that, without affecting his dignity, judges should be nominated; and both their sentiments were founded in reason. You will wonder how that can be, since they were so extremely different. But you will observe that Macer, who considered the mere letter of the law, might very reasonably condemn him, when it appeared he had taken presents contrary to the express prohibition of that law. On the other hand, Caepio, supposing that the senate had a power (as undoubtedly it has) to moderate or extend the rigor of the laws, might upon very good grounds think this a case worthy of their clemency, as being, though indeed contrary to the express letter of the law, yet not infrequently practiced. The motion of Caepio prevailed, and when he rose up to give the reasons for his vote, the same acclamations attended him as usually follow an approved speech. You will easily judge, therefore, how great the applause was after he had spoken when he received such unusual ones before he began. I find the sentiments of those without doors, as well as in the house, are divided into two parties: they who approve of Caepio's vote, condemn Macer's as severe and hard: on the contrary the partisans of Macer's opinion, treat the other as too mild and indeed inconsistent. They assert it is highly absurd to nominate judges for a man, and yet suffer him to retain his seat in the senate. I should have told you that there was, besides those I have mentioned, a third opinion. Valerius Paulinus, who joined in sentiments with Caepio, was for adding further that the senate should proceed against Theophanes, after he had finished his commission as deputy from the province. For he insisted that Theophanes in the course of his accusation had been guilty of several things which fell within the prohibition of this very law, upon which he grounded his information against Bassus. But though this proposal was in general highly approved by the senate, yet the consuls thought proper to drop it: Paulinus, however, had the full credit of so honest and bold a motion. At the breaking up of the house, Bassus was received by great crowds of people with the highest demonstrations of joy and the loudest acclamations. This new difficulty which he had fallen into had recalled the remembrance of his former troubles; and a name which had never been mentioned but in conjunction with some misfortune, together with the appearance of a fine person broken with sorrow and age, had raised a general compassion toward him. You may look upon this letter as the forerunner of my speech, which, full and copious as it is, I shall send you at large; but you must not expect it soon; for it is a subject of too much importance to be revised in haste.

84. A trial for abuse of powers

In this trial, as in the last, the excessive leniency of the senate to the crimes of its members is very noticeable. The Cornelius Tacitus who was Pliny's fellow advocate is the historian. Once again the provincial house of representatives initiates the accusation. The venality of Marius Priscus in the administration of justice is more remarkable in that his victims were not mere provincials but Roman citizens, and indeed Roman *equites*.

84. Pliny, Letters, II. 11

YOU TAKE pleasure, I know, in hearing of anything that is trans-acted in the senate, worthy of that august assembly: for though love of ease has called you into retirement, your heart still retains its zeal for the honor of the public. Accept then the following account of what lately passed in that venerable body: a transaction forever memorable by its importance, and not only remarkable by the quality of the person concerned, but useful by the severity of the example. Marius Priscus, formerly proconsul of Africa, being impeached by that province, instead of entering upon his defense, petitioned that a commission of judges might be appointed for his trial. Cornelius Tacitus and myself, being by the senate assigned counsel for that province, thought it our duty to inform the house, that the crimes alleged against Priscus were of too atrocious a nature to fall within the cognizance of judges: for he was charged with venality in the administration of justice, and even selling the lives of the innocent. Fronto Catius stood up in his favor, and moved that the whole inquiry should be confined to the single article of extortion; displaying upon this occasion all the force of that pathetic eloquence he is master of, in order to raise the com-passion of the senate. The debates grew warm, and the members were much divided in their sentiments. Some were of opinion that the jurisdiction of the senate was limited by the law, others that its jurisdiction was free and unfettered, and that the accused ought to be punished according to the measure of his crimes. At last Julius Ferox, the consul-elect, a man of great worth and integrity, proposed that judges should be granted him provisionally, and in the meanwhile that those persons should be summoned to whom it was alleged he had sold innocent blood. Not only the majority of the senate gave into this opinion; but, after all the contention that had been raised, it was unanimously received. From whence I could not but observe that sentiments of compassion, though they at first operate with great violence, subside at length, and give way to the cool dictates of reason and judgment: thus it happens that numbers will defend, by joining in the general cry, what they would never calmly propose by themselves. The truth is, there is no discerning an object in a crowd; one must take it aside, if one would view it in its true light. Vitellius Honoratus and Flavius Martianus, the persons who were ordered to be summoned, were brought before the house. Honoratus was charged with having given three hundred thousand sesterces to procure a sentence of banishment against a Roman *eques*, as also the capital conviction of seven of his friends. Against Martianus it was alleged, that he gave seven hundred thousand that another Roman *eques* might be condemned to suffer various tortures; which was accordingly executed, and the unhappy man was first whipped, afterward sent to work in the mines, and at last strangled in prison. But the death of Honoratus prevented the justice of the senate upon him. Martianus, however, appeared, but without Priscus. Tullius Cerealis, therefore, who had been formerly consul, thought proper to move that Priscus, agreeably to his privilege as a senator, might have notice of what they were going upon; whether it was because he thought his being present would raise more compassion, or more resentment toward him; or because, as I am inclined to believe, he thought it most equitable, as the charge was against them both, so they should both join in the defense, and be acquitted or condemned together. The affair was adjourned to the next meeting of the senate, which was the most august and solemn I was ever present at. The emperor himself (for he was consul) presided. It happened likewise to be the month of January, a season remarkable upon many accounts, and particularly for the great number of senators it always brings together: moreover the importance of the cause, the noise it had made in the world, the expectation that had been raised by the several adjournments, together

with that innate disposition in mankind to acquaint themselves with
everything great and uncommon, drew the people together from
all parts. Imagine the concern and anxiety we, who were to speak
before such an awful assembly, and in the presence of the prince,
must feel. I have often pleaded in the senate; as indeed there is no
place where I am more favorably heard; yet, as if the scene had
been entirely new to me, I found myself under an unusual fear
upon this occasion. Besides, there was something in the circumstances of the person accused which added considerably to the
difficulties I labored under: a man, once of consular dignity, and a
member of a sacred college, now stood before me stripped of all
his honors. It was a painful office, I thought, to accuse one who
appeared already condemned; and for whom therefore, though his
crimes were enormous, compassion took its turn, and seemed to
plead in his behalf. However, I collected myself enough to begin
my speech; and the applause I received was equal to the fears I had
suffered. I spoke almost five hours successively (for they indulged
me above an hour beyond the time at first allotted to me) and what
at my first setting out had most contributed to raise my apprehensions, proved in the event greatly to my advantage. The goodness, the care of the emperor (I dare not say his anxiety) were so
great toward me, that he frequently spoke to my freedman, who
stood behind me, to desire me to spare myself; imagining I should
exert my strength beyond what the weakness of my constituion
would admit. Claudius Marcellinus replied in behalf of Martianus.
After which the assembly broke up till the next day; for the evening coming on, there was not time to proceed further. The next
day, Salvius Liberalis, a very clear, artful, spirited and eloquent
orator, spoke in defense of Priscus: and he exerted all his talents
upon this occasion. Cornelius Tacitus replied to him with great
eloquence and a certain dignity which distinguishes all his speeches.
Fronto Catius arose up a second time for Priscus, and in a very fine
speech endeavored, as indeed the case required, rather to soften the
judges, than defend his client. The evening coming on, the senate
proceeded no further that day, but met the next, and entered upon
the proofs. It was something very noble, and worthy of ancient
Rome, to see the senate, adjourned only by the night, thus assemble
for three days together. The excellent Cornutus Tertullus, consul-
elect, ever firm in the cause of truth, moved that Marius should pay

into the treasury that seven hundred thousand sesterces he had received, and be banished from Italy. He was for extending the sentence still further against Martianus, and banishing him from Africa,
too. He concluded with saying that Tacitus and I having faithfully
and diligently discharged the parts assigned to us, the senate declared we had executed our trust to their satisfaction. The consuls-
elect and the ex-consuls agreed with Tertullus, except Pompeius:
he proposed that Priscus should pay the seven hundred thousand
sesterces into the treasury, but to suffer no other punishment than
what had been already inflicted upon him for extortion: as for
Martianus, he was for having him banished for five years only.
There was a large party for both opinions, and perhaps the majority secretly inclined to the milder sentence; for many of those
who appeared at first to agree with Tertullus, seemed afterward to
join with Pompeius. But upon a division of the house, all those
who stood near the consuls, went over to the side of Tertullus.
Pompeius's party observing this, deserted him, and went over, too;
so that he was extremely exasperated against those who had urged
him to this vote, particularly against Regulus, whom he upbraided
for abandoning him in a step which he himself had advised. There
is, indeed, such an inconsistency in the general character of Regulus
that he is at once both bold and timorous. Thus ended this important trial; but there remains a considerable part of the business
still behind. It is concerning Hostilius Firminus, legate to Marius
Priscus, who is strongly charged with being an accomplice with
him: for it appears by the accounts of Martianus, and by a speech
which he made in an assembly of the people at Leptis, that he
had exacted fifty thousand denarii of Martianus; that he was
otherwise accessory to the wicked administration of Priscus; and
that he received ten thousand sesterces under the title of perfume
money, a term perfectly adaptd to one of his effeminate delicacy.
It was agreed, on the motion of Tertullus, to proceed against him
at the next meeting of the senate; for either by accident or design,
he was at this time absent. Thus have I given you an account of
what is doing in town. Let me know in return the news of the
country; how your groves and your vineyards, your corn and your
fine flocks of sheep flourish? In a word, if you do not send me a
long letter, you must expect to be punished in your own way, and
to receive from me, for the future, none but short ones.

85. The provincial house of representatives

Under the principate assemblies (*concilia*) were formed in each province of delegates from all the cities. Their primary and ostensible object was to conduct the worship of Rome and Augustus (see Nos. 164, 167), but they also expressed provincial opinion by promoting prosecutions of bad governors as in Nos. 83, 84, or by conveying to the emperor or senate votes of thanks to good governors. They could also petition the emperor or the senate. The debate here recorded, which took place in A.D. 62, shows how influential these provincial councils could be at Rome.

85. *Tacitus*, Annals, *XV. 20–22*

NEXT CAME the prosecution of Claudius Timarchus of Crete, on such charges as often fall on very influential provincials, whom immense wealth has emboldened to the oppression of the weak. But one speech of his had gone to the extremity of a gross insult to the senate; for he had repeatedly declared that it was in his power to decide whether the proconsuls who had governed Crete should receive the thanks of the province. Paetus Thrasea, turning the occasion to public advantage, after having stated his opinion that the accused ought to be expelled from Crete, further spoke as follows:

"It is found by experience, senators, that admirable laws and right precedents have their origin in the misdeeds of others. Thus the license of advocates resulted in the Cincian bill; the corrupt practices of candidates in the Julian laws; the rapacity of magistrates in the Calpurnian enactments. For, in point of time, guilt comes before punishment and correction follows after delinquency. And, therefore, to meet the new insolence of provincials, let us adopt a measure worthy of Roman faith and resolution, whereby our allies may lose nothing of our protection, while public opinion may cease to say of us, that the estimate of a man's character is to be found anywhere rather than in the judgment of our citizens.

"Formerly it was not only a praetor or a consul, but also private persons, who were sent to inspect the provinces and report what they thought about each man's loyalty. And nations were timidly sensitive to the opinion of individuals. But now we court foreigners and flatter them, and just as there is a vote of thanks at any one's pleasure, so even more eagerly is a prosecution decided on. Well, let it be decided on, and let the provincials retain the right of showing their power in this fashion, but as for false praise which has been extorted by entreaties, let it be as much checked as fraud or tyranny. More faults are often committed while we are trying to oblige than while we are giving offense. Nay, some virtues are actually hated; inflexible strictness, for example, and a temper proof against partiality. Consequently, our magistrates' early career is generally better than its close, which deteriorates when we are anxiously seeking votes like candidates. If such practices are stopped, our provinces will be ruled more equitably and more steadily. For as the dread of a charge of extortion has been a check to rapacity, so, by prohibiting the vote of thanks, will the pursuit of popularity be restrained."

This opinion was hailed with great unanimity, but the senate's resolution could not be finally passed, as the consuls decided that there had been no formal motion on the subject. Then, at the emperor's suggestion, they decreed that no one was to propose to any council of our allies that a vote of thanks ought to be presented in the senate to propraetors or proconsuls, and that no one was to discharge such a mission.

86. Abuse of requisition

The occasion of these edicts, preserved in an Egyptian papyrus, was the visit to Egypt in A.D. 17 of Germanicus (cf. No. 12), the nephew and adopted son of Tiberius and, therefore, the grandson by adoption of Augustus; he was also the real grandson of Livia. The right of magistrates, officials, and soldiers to commandeer means of transport and lodging was a constant grievance of the provincials (cf. No. 147).

86. V. Ehrenberg and A. H. M. Jones, Documents, 320

GERMANICUS CAESAR, son of Augustus and grandson of the deified Augustus, proconsul, says: ["Being informed that in view of my visit] requisitions of boats and animals are being made and that quarters for lodging are being occupied by force and private persons intimidated, I have thought it necessary to declare that I wish neither boat nor beast of burden to be seized by anyone except on the order of Baebius, my friend and secretary, nor quarters to be occupied. For if it be necessary, Baebius himself will allot the

quarters fairly and justly; and for boats or animals which we requisition I command that hire be paid in accordance with my
schedule. Those who disobey I desire to be brought before my
secretary, who will either himself prevent private persons from
being wronged or will report the case to me. And I forbid beasts of
burden to be forcibly appropriated by those who meet them
traversing the city; for this is nothing but an act of open robbery."

Germanicus Caesar, son of Augustus and grandson of the deified
Augustus, proconsul, says: "Your goodwill, which you display on
all occasions when you see me, I welcome, but your acclamations,
which for me are invidious and such as are addressed to gods, I
altogether deprecate. For they are appropriate only to him who is
actually the savior and benefactor of the whole human race, my
father, and to his mother, my grandmother. But our position is
. . . their divinity, so that unless you comply with my request,
you will compel me to appear in public but seldom."

87. Road building in Arabia

One of the great benefits which the Roman government conferred on
the empire was the network of stone-paved roads which it built. The
road described below, which ran from Damascus to Aela on the Gulf
of Aqaba, was built shortly after the annexation of the Nabatean
kingdom, which became the province of Arabia in A.D. 106; cf. No. 56,
which shows that it was built by military labor. The main object of the
road was military, to link the forts along the desert frontier, but it also
had commercial value, since Aela was a port for the Indian trade.

87. Dessau, ILS, 5834

IMPERATOR CAESAR, son of the deified Nerva, Nerva Trajan Augustus Germanicus Dacicus, pontifex maximus, of the tribunician
power for the fifteenth time [A.D. 111], imperator for the sixth
time, consul for the fifth time, father of his country, having reduced Arabia to the form of a province, opened and paved a new
road from the boundary of Syria to the Red Sea, through Claudius
Severus *legatus Augusti pro praetore*. Mile 54.

88. Road building in Egypt

This road connected the Nile with the Red Sea, and was important for
the sea-borne trade with Arabia Felix (Yemen) and India. The Red

Sea, especially its northern end, was considered dangerous, and most merchants preferred to take their goods up the Nile and carry them across the Eastern Desert to the Red Sea coast.

88. *Dittenberger,* OGIS, *701*

IMPERATOR CAESAR, son of the deified Trajan Parthicus, grandson of the deified Nerva, Trajan Hadrian Augustus, pontifex maximus, of the tribunician power for the twenty-first time, imperator for the second time, consul for the third time, father of his country, opened the new Hadrianic road from Berenice to Antinoopolis through secure and level places beside the Red Sea and furnished it with ample cisterns and post houses and forts. Year 21, Phamenoth 1 [February 25, 137].

89. Purchase of office

In the early fourth century it had become a common practice for aspirants to government posts, especially provincial governorships, to bribe powerful persons at the imperial court to solicit the emperor for such appointments on their behalf. Julian endeavored to check the practice by making such bribes irrecoverable by process of law, if the patron did not fulfill his side of the bargain.

89. Codex Theodosianus, *II. 29.1*

EMPEROR JULIAN AUGUSTUS to the People.

Some men have come to occupy by disgraceful trickery offices which are bestowed upon good men for their merit. When they have gained any position whatsoever in the state, they suppose that if they had paid out any money dishonorably, they should sue to recover it more dishonorably and shamelessly; and others even suppose that the property which they then gave, or rather threw away, for unworthy causes should be recovered by forcible entry and seizure. But because Roman law completely refuses to recognize such contracts, We deny to these men all right to recover that which they squandered prodigally and wickedly. If any man, therefore, should strive to recover or should be convicted of having recovered such payment, that which he paid shall remain in the possession of such patron or if extorted shall be restored, and he shall also be forced to pay an equal amount to the account of the fisc.

Given on the kalends of February at Constantinople in the consulship of Mamertinus and Nevitta [February 1, 362].

90. A province petitions the emperor

Though the worship of the emperors stopped with Constantine, the provincial assemblies continued to meet and elect high priests of the province, and to send petitions to the emperor. The principal actors in this little drama, which was enacted A.D. 363–8, are:

1. Romanus, the count or military commander of the whole diocese of Africa,
2. Crescens, the vicar or civil administrator of the diocese,
3. Ruricius, the provincial (civilian) governor of the province of Tripolis,
4. Palladius, a tribune and notary (cf. No. 17),
5. Hesperius, a later proconsul of the province of Africa,
6. Flavian, a later vicar of the diocese of Africa,
7. Remigius, master of the offices, the imperial minister who among other duties arranged for the reception of foreign ambassadors and provincial delegates by the emperor,
8. Merobaudes, one of the commanders in chief.

90. Ammianus Marcellinus, XXVIII. 6

LET us now migrate, as it were, to another quarter of the world, and proceed to relate the distresses of Tripolis, a province of Africa; distresses which, in my opinion, even Justice herself must have lamented, and which burst out rapidly like flames. I will now give an account both of them and of their causes.

The Austurians are barbarians living on the frontier of this province, a people always in readiness for rapid invasions, accustomed to live on plunder and bloodshed; and who, after having been quiet for a while, now relapsed into their natural state of unrest, alleging the following as the serious cause for their movements. One of their countrymen, by name Stachao, while freely traversing our territories, as in time of peace, did some things forbidden by the laws; the most flagrant of his illegal acts being that he endeavored by every kind of deceit and intrigue to betray the province, as was shown by the most undeniable evidence, for which crime he was burnt to death.

To avenge his death, the Austurians, claiming him as their clansman, and affirming that he had been unjustly condemned, burst forth from their own territory like so many mad wild beasts during the reign of Jovian, but fearing to approach close to Leptis, which was a city with a numerous population and fortified by strong walls, they occupied the district around it, which is very fertile, for three days, and having massacred the agricultural population on it, whom terror at their sudden inroad had deprived of all spirit or had driven to take refuge in caves, and burnt a great quantity of furniture which could not be carried off, they returned home, loaded with vast plunder, taking with them as prisoner a man named Silva, a leading member of the city council, whom they found with his family at his country house.

The people of Leptis, being terrified at this sudden disaster and not wishing to incur the further calamities with which the arrogance of the barbarians threatened them, implored the protection of Romanus, who had recently been promoted to count of Africa. But when he came at the head of an army and received their request to come to their immediate assistance in their distress, he declared that he would not move a step further unless abundant magazines and four thousand camels were provided for his troops. At this answer the wretched citizens were stupefied, and declared to him that after the devastations and conflagrations to which they had been exposed, it was impossible for them to make such exertions, even for the reparation of the cruel disasters which they had suffered; and, after waiting forty days there with vain pretenses and excuses, the count retired without attempting any enterprise.

The people of Tripolis, disappointed in their hopes and dreading the worst extremities, when the regular day for their annual provincial assembly came, appointed Severus and Flaccianus ambassadors to carry to Valentinian some golden images of victory in honor of his accession to the empire, and to state fully and boldly to him the miserable distress of the province. When this step became known, Romanus sent a swift horseman as a messenger to the master of the offices, Remigius, his own kinsman and his partner in plunder, bidding him take care that by the emperor's decision the investigation into this matter should be committed to the vicar and himself.

The ambassadors arrived at the court, and having obtained access to the emperor, laid all their distresses before him in a set speech and presented him with a decree of their assembly in which the whole affair was fully set forth. When the emperor had read it,

he neither trusted the report of the master of the offices, framed to
defend the misconduct of the count, nor, on the other hand, did he
place confidence in these men who made a contrary report; but
promised a full investigation into the affair, which however was
deferred in the manner in which high authorities are wont to let
such matters give place to their more pleasant occupations and
amusements.

While waiting in suspense and protracted anxiety for some relief
from the emperor's staff, the citizens of Tripolis were again attacked by troops of the same barbarians, now elated with additional confidence by their past successes. They ravaged the whole
territory of Leptis and also that of Oea, spreading total ruin and
desolation everywhere, and at last retired loaded with an enormous quantity of spoil, having killed many of the city councillors,
the most distinguished of whom were Rusticianus, a former high
priest of the province, and the aedile Nicasius.

This invasion was not repelled because the conduct of military affairs, which had at first at the entreaty of the ambassadors
been entrusted to Ruricius, the governor, had been subsequently
transferred to count Romanus. So now a new messenger was sent
to Gaul with an account of this fresh disaster; and this intelligence
roused the emperor to great anger. So Palladius, a tribune and
notary, was sent at once to liquidate the pay due to the soldiers
who were dispersed over Africa, and to examine into all that had
taken place in Tripolis, he being an officer whose report could be
trusted.

But while all these delays took place from the continual deliberations held on the case, and while the people of Tripolis were still
waiting for the answer, the Austurians, now still more insolent
after their double success, like birds of prey whose ferocity has
been sharpened by the taste of blood, flew once more to attack
them; and having killed every one who did not flee from the
danger, they carried off all the spoil which they had previously left
behind, cutting down all the trees and vines. Then a certain citizen
named Mychon, a man of high station and great influence, was
taken prisoner in the district outside of the city; but before they
could bind him he gave them the slip, and because an attack of gout
rendered him unable to effect his escape, he threw himself down a
dry well, from which he was drawn up by the barbarians with his
ribs broken, and was conducted near to the gates of the city, where
he was ransomed by the affection of his wife, and was drawn up to

the battlements of the wall by a rope; but two days afterward he died.

These events encouraged the pertinacity of the invaders, so that they advanced and attacked the very walls of Leptis, which resounded with the mournful wailings of the women, who were terrified in an extraordinary manner and quite bewildered because they had never before been blockaded by an enemy. But after the city had been besieged for eight days continuously, during which many of the besiegers were wounded, while they made no progress, they retired much discouraged to their own country.

In consequence of these events, the citizens, being still doubtful of their safety, and desirous of trying every possible resource, before the ambassadors who had been first sent had returned, sent Jovinus and Pancratius to lay before the emperor a faithful account of the sufferings which they had endured, and which they themselves had seen; these envoys found the former ambassadors, Severus and Flaccianus, at Carthage; and on asking them what they had done, they learnt that they had been referred for a hearing to the vicar and the count. And immediately after this Severus was attacked by a dangerous illness and died; but notwithstanding what they had heard, the new ambassadors proceeded on their journey to the court.

After this, when Palladius arrived in Africa, the count, who knew on what account he had come, and who had been warned before to take measures for his own safety, sent orders to the principal officers of the army by certain persons who were in his secrets to pay over to him, as being a person of great influence and very nearly connected with the principal nobles of the palace, the chief part of the money for the soldiers' pay which he had brought over; and they obeyed him.

So he, having been thus suddenly enriched, reached Leptis; and that he might arrive at a knowledge of the truth, he took with him to the districts that had been laid waste, Erechthius and Aristomenes, two citizens of great eloquence and reputation, who freely unfolded to him the distress which their fellow citizens and the inhabitants of the adjacent districts had suffered. They showed him everything openly; and so he returned after seeing the lamentable desolation of the province: and reproaching Romanus for his inactivity, he threatened to report to the emperor an accurate statement of everything which he had seen.

He, inflamed with anger and indignation, retorted that he also would make a report, that the man who had been sent as an incorruptible notary had converted to his own uses all the money which had been sent out as a donation to the soldiers. The consequence was that Palladius, being hampered by the consciousness of his flagitious conduct, proceeded from henceforth in harmony with Romanus, and when he returned to court, deceived Valentian with atrocious falsehoods, affirming that the citizens of Tripolis had complained without reason. Therefore he was sent back to Africa a second time with Jovinus, the last of all the ambassadors (for Pancratius had died at Treves), in order that he, in conjunction with the vicar, might inquire into everything connected with the second embassy. And besides this, the emperor ordered the tongues of Erechthius and Aristomenes to be cut out, because this same Palladius had intimated that they made some malignant and disloyal statements.

The notary, following the vicar, as had been arranged, came to Tripolis. When his arrival was known, Romanus sent his private secretary there with all speed, and Caecilius, his assessor, who was a native of the province; and by their agency (whether they employed bribery or deceit is doubtful) all the citizens were won over to accuse Jovinus, vigorously asserting that they had never passed any of the resolutions which he had reported to the emperor; carrying their inquiry to such a pitch that Jovinus himself was compelled by them to confess, to his own great danger, that he had made a false report to the emperor.

When these events were learnt from Palladius on his return, Valentinian, being always inclined to severe measures, commanded the execution of Jovinus as the author of such a report, and of Caelestinus, Concordius, and Lucius, as privy to it and partners in it. He also commanded Ruricius, the governor, to be put to death for falsehood; the charge against him being aggravated by the circumstance that his report contained some violent and intemperate expressions.

Ruricius was executed at Sitifis; the rest were condemned at Utica by the sentence of the vicar Crescens. But before the death of the ambassadors, Flaccianus, while being examined by the vicar and the count, and while resolutely defending his own safety, was assailed with abuse, and then attacked with loud outcries and violence by the angry soldiers and was nearly killed; the charge which they made against him being that the cause which had prevented the people of Tripolis from being defended was that they had refused to furnish necessaries for the use of any expedition. On this account he was thrown into prison, till the emperor could be consulted on his case, and should decide what ought to be done; but his gaolers were tampered with, as was believed, and he escaped from prison and fled to Rome, where he concealed himself for some time till his death.

In consequence of this memorable catastrophe, Tripolis, which had been often harassed by external and domestic calamities, brought forward no further accusations against those who had left it undefended, knowing that the eternal eye of justice was awake, as well as the avenging furies of the ambassadors and the governor. And a long time afterward the following event took place. Palladius, having been dismissed from military service, and stript of all that nourished his pride, retired into private life. And when Theodosius, that magnificent commander of armies, came into Africa to put down Firmus, who was entertaining some pernicious designs, and, as he was ordered, began to examine the movable effects of Romanus, he found among his papers a letter of a certain person named Meterius, containing this passage: "Meterius, to his lord and patron Romanus"; and at the end of the letter many expressions unconnected with its general subject. "Palladius, who has been cashiered, salutes you. He says he was cashiered for no other reason than that in the case of the people of Tripolis he made a false report to the sacred ears."

When this letter was sent to the court and read, Meterius was arrested by order of the Valentinian, and confessed that the letter was in his writing. Therefore Palladius also was ordered to appear. Reflecting on all the crimes he had committed, at a halting place on the road he watched an opportunity afforded him by the absence of his guards, as soon as it got dark (for, as it was a festival of the Christian religion, they passed the whole night in the church) and hanged himself.

The news of this propitious event—the death of the principal cause of their sad troubles—being known, Erechthius and Aristomenes, who when they first heard that their tongues were ordered to be cut out for sedition had escaped, now issued from their hiding places. And when the emperor Gratian was informed of the wicked deceit that had been practiced (for by this time Valentinian was dead), their fears vanished, and they were sent to have their cause heard before Hesperius the proconsul and Flavian the vicar, men whose justice was supported by the righteous authority of the emperor, and who, after putting Caecilius to the torture, learnt from his clear confession that he himself had persuaded the citizens to bring false accusations against the ambassadors. These actions were followed by a report which gave the fullest possible account of all that had taken place, to which no answer was given.

And that the whole story want nothing of tragic interest, the following occurrence also took place after the curtain had fallen. Romanus went to court, taking with him Caecilius, with the intent to accuse the judges as having been unduly biassed in favor of the province; and being received graciously by Merobaudes, he demanded that some more necessary witnesses should be summoned. And when they had come to Milan, and had shown by proofs which seemed correct, though they were false, that they had been falsely accused, they were acquitted, and returned home. Valentinian was still alive, when after these events which we have related, Remigius also retired from public life, and afterward hanged himself, as we shall relate in the proper place.

VIII. The Cities

91. The Roman Aqueducts

This is part of a technical monograph on the aqueducts of Rome, written by Frontinus, who was appointed curator in A.D. 97. It was part of the policy of Augustus to create small senatorial boards for the various departments of the administration of Rome, hitherto badly managed by the annual magistrates (cf. No. 10). Here we see Augustus and the senate co-operating to set up an aqueduct board and providing its members with a clerical and professional staff. The workmen were also partly the property of the state and partly of the emperor, and paid for by the public and imperial treasuries respectively.

91. *Frontinus*, de aquis, *II. 89–101, 116–18*

FIRST MARCUS AGRIPPA after his aedileship, which he held when ex-consul, was a kind of life curator of the result of his own work and generosity. Now that the supply permitted, he allocated what water should be given to public buildings, what to reservoirs, and what to private persons. He also had his own gang of slaves to maintain the channels, cisterns, and reservoirs of the aqueducts. He left it in his will to Augustus, who gave it to the state. After him in the consulship of Quintus Aelius Tubero and Paulus Fabius Maximus [11 B.C.], when hitherto the business had been managed by magisterial authority and had lacked a fixed legal basis, resolutions of the senate were passed and a law promulgated. Augustus also set out in an edict the rights of those enjoying a water supply according to Agrippa's records, transferring the whole thing to his grant. He also fixed the standard pipes of which I have spoken, and to carry on the business and keep it in hand he made Messala Corvinus curator, to whom were given as assistants Postumius Sulpicius, an ex-praetor, and Lucius Cominius, a junior senator. They were allowed insignia like magistrates, and a resolution of the senate was passed as follows about their office.

'Whereas Quintus Aelius Tubero and Paulus Fabius Maximus,

the consuls, spoke about regulating the position of those who had been nominated as curators of the aqueducts by Caesar Augustus with the consent of the senate, as to what they wished to be done on that matter, they resolved on that matter as follows:

It is the pleasure of the house that the persons in charge of the aqueducts, when they are outside the city on that business, shall have two lictors, three public slaves, and one architect each, and as many clerks, secretaries, and criers as do those by whom corn is distributed to the plebs. When they do anything in the city on that business, they may employ their other attendants except for the lictors. They must enter at the treasury within ten days of the resolution of the senate being passed the attendants whom the curators of the aqueducts are allowed to employ under this resolution of the senate, and the praetors of the treasury shall pay and allocate annual salaries and rations to those who are so entered on the same scale as the prefects for the distribution of corn pay and enter. Whatever paper, stationery, etcetera these curators need to have provided for their official functions, Quintus Tubero and Paulus Fabius, the consuls, shall, both or one of them, if they think fit, having summoned the praetors in charge of the treasury, set a contract for their provision. Also seeing that the curators of the roads and of corn perform their public duties for a quarter of the year, that the curators of the aqueducts shall be immune from jury service in public or private cases.'

The officials and attendants, although the treasury still continues to pay for them, seem nevertheless to have ceased to exist owing to the slackness and inertia of the curators, who have not done their duty. The senate had ordered that when they went out of the city on official business they should have lictors with them. When I went around the aqueducts, my own good faith and the authority given to me by the emperor served instead of lictors. . . .

There remains the maintenance of the aqueducts, but before I begin to speak about this I must say a few words about the gang which is provided for the purpose. There are two gangs, one public, the other belonging to Caesar. The public is the older; it was, as I have said, left to Augustus by Agrippa and given to the people. It comprises about two hundred and forty men. Caesar's gang comprises about four hundred and sixty men; it was established by Claudius when he brought his aqueducts into the city. Both gangs are divided into various categories of service, managers, cistern men, inspectors, paviors, plasterers, and other craftsmen. Some of them ought to be outside the city for minor repairs which nevertheless need prompt attention. The men in the city are posted to the cisterns and public buildings to carry out emergency work, especially in case of sudden accident, so that protection against overflow of aqueducts can be concentrated from several regions in that for which need has arisen. The ample numbers of both gangs used, owing to the corruption or negligence of those in charge, to be diverted to private work, but I made it my policy to recall them to some discipline and to public service, ordering the day before what was to be done and keeping a record of what had been done on each day. The emoluments of the public gang are paid by the public treasury, the expense being balanced by the revenue from rents belonging to the aqueducts. These arise from sites of buildings around aqueducts, cisterns, public buildings, and reservoirs. This revenue of nearly two hundred fifty thousand sesterces was alienated and went astray, and recently found its way into Domitian's coffers, but was restored to the people by the justice of the deified Nerva. I have carefully regularized it so that it is clear which are the sites liable to this rent. Caesar's gang gets its emoluments from the imperial treasury, which also provides all the lead and all expenses on the channels and cisterns and reservoirs.

92. Rome in the fourth century

Symmachus, Lampadius, and Viventius were prefects of the city between 364 and 367; the office had now become a short-term one, held during the emperor's pleasure. The main problem of Rome was, as always, the food supply. A bread ration was provided free of charge, and wine at reduced prices; a small ration of pork was also provided free for five months of the year.

The account of the disputed papal election is interesting as showing how wealthy the Roman See had already become, largely as a result of Constantine's vast benefactions.

92. *Ammianus Marcellinus, XXVII. 3*

At this time or a little before a new kind of prodigy appeared in the province of Tuscany; those who were skillful in interpreting such things being wholly ignorant of what was portended. For in the town of Pistoria, at about the third hour of the day, in the sight

of many persons, an ass mounted the tribunal, where he was heard
to bray loudly. All the bystanders were amazed, as were all those
who heard of the occurrence from the report of others, as no one
could conjecture what was to happen. But soon afterward the
events showed what was portended, for a man of the name of
Terentius, a person of low birth and a baker by trade, as a reward
for having given information against Orfitus, who had formerly
been prefect, which led to his being convicted of peculation, was
intrusted with the government of this same province. And becoming elated and confident, he threw affairs into great disorder,
till he was convicted of fraud on transactions relating to some
shipmasters, as was reported, and was executed while Claudius was
prefect of Rome.

But some time before this happened Symmachus succeeded Apronianus; a man deserving to be named among the most eminent
examples of learning and moderation; under whose government the
most sacred city enjoyed peace and plenty in an unusual degree;
being also adorned with a magnificent and solid bridge which he
constructed and opened amid the great joy of his ungrateful fellow
citizens, as the result very plainly showed. For they some years
afterward burnt his beautiful house on the other side of the Tiber,
being enraged because some worthless plebian had invented a story,
which there was no evidence or witness to support, that he had said
that he would prefer putting out the lime kilns with his own wine,
to selling it at the price expected of him.

After him the prefect of the city was Lampadius, who had been
praetorian prefect, a man of such boundless arrogance, that he
grew very indignant if he were not praised even when he spat, as if
he did that with more grace than any one else; but still a man of
severity and frugality. When as praetor he was celebrating some
splendid games and giving abundant largesses, being unable to bear
the tumult of the populace, which was often urgent to have gifts
distributed to those who were unworthy, in order to show his
liberality and his contempt for the multitude, he sent for a crowd
of beggars from the Vatican, and enriched them with great presents. But, not to digress too much, it will be sufficient to record
one instance of his vanity, which, though of no great importance,
may serve as a warning to judges. In every quarter of the city
which had been adorned at the expense of different emperors, he
inscribed his own name, and that not as if he were the restorer of

old works but their founder. This same fault is said to have char-
acterized the emperor Trajan, from which the people in jest named
him "the ivy plant."

While he was prefect he was disturbed by frequent commotions,
the most formidable being when a vast mob of the lowest of the
people collected with firebrands and torches and would have burnt
his house near the baths of Constantine if they had not been driven
away by the prompt assistance of his friends and neighbors, who
pelted them with stones and tiles from the tops of the houses. He
himself, being alarmed at a sedition which on this occasion had
become so violent, retired to the Mulvian bridge (which the elder
Scaurus is said to have built), and waited there till the discontent
subsided, which indeed had been excited by a substantial grievance.

For when he began to construct some new buildings, he ordered
the cost to be defrayed, not from the customary sources of revenue, but if iron, or lead, or copper, or anything of that kind was
required, he sent officers who, pretending to try the different
articles, did in fact seize them without paying any price for them.
This so enraged the poor, since they suffered repeated losses from
such a practice, that it was all he could do to escape from them by
a rapid retreat.

His successor had formerly been a quaestor of the palace, his
name was Viventius, a man of integrity and prudence, a Pannonian
by birth. His administration was tranquil and undisturbed, and the
people enjoyed plenty under it. Yet he also was alarmed by fierce
seditions raised by the discontented populace, which arose from the
following occurrence.

Damasus and Ursinus, being both immoderately eager to obtain
the bishopric, formed parties and carried on the conflict with great
asperity, the partisans of each carrying their violence to actual
battle, in which men were wounded and killed. And as Viventius
was unable to put an end to or even to allay these disorders, he was
at last by their violence compelled to withdraw to the suburbs.
Ultimately Damasus got the best of the strife by the strenuous
efforts of his partisans. It is well known that on one day one hundred and thirty-seven dead bodies were found in the Basilica of
Sicininus, which is a meeting place of the Christian rite. And the
populace who had been thus roused to a state of ferocity were with
great difficulty restored to order.

I do not deny, when I consider the ostentation that reigns at

Rome, that those who desire the position may be justified in laboring with all possible exertion and vehemence to obtain their wishes;
since after they have succeeded, they will be secure for the future,
being enriched by offerings from matrons, riding in carriages,
dressing splendidly, and feasting luxuriously, so that their entertainments surpass even royal banquets. They might be really happy
if, despising the vastness of the city, which they excite against
themselves by their vices, they were to live in imitation of some of
the bishops in the provinces, whom the most rigid abstinence in
eating and drinking, plainness of apparel, and eyes always cast on
the ground, recommend to the everlasting Deity and his true wor-
shippers as pure and sober-minded men. This is sufficient digression
on this subject: let us now return to our narrative.

93. The charter of Malaca

This inscription is the surviving part of the charter granted to the
Spanish city of Malaca, when, with all the other cities of Spain, it
received Latin status from Vespasian. *Latinitas* meant that the citizens
of the town used Roman law, and their annual magistrates obtained
Roman citizenship (see No. 94). The constitutions of Latin towns
were closely modeled on those of republican Rome.

The popular assembly has no function except to elect the magistrates, and the council (*ordo*) is the real governing body. Here clauses
51–59 lay down the procedure for the election of the magistrates, the
two *duoviri*, who correspond to the Roman consuls and exercise civil
jurisdiction (cf. No. 94, §§28–29), the two aediles, who manage public
works and control the market, and the two quaestors or treasurers. It is
interesting to note that the law makes provision for the possibility that
there may be insufficient candidates. This is the first mention of a
difficulty which became acute in the third century. The main reason
was that magistrates had either by law or custom to contribute considerable sums to public purposes. The voting is, according to the
Roman rule, by groups, in this case the wards of the town (*curiae*).
Clause 61 deals with the choice of patrons, who are honorary protectors of the town. Clause 62 is interesting as showing the pride taken
in the architectural appearance of the town. Clauses 63–67 deal with
public finance, including the farming of the local taxes.

93. S. Riccobono, Fontes Iuris Romani Ante Justiniani², *I. 24*

51. CONCERNING THE NOMINATION OF CANDIDATES

IF UP to the day on which declarations of candidature ought to
be made, declarations have been made in the name of no one, or of

fewer persons than the number of magistrates to be created, or if among those in whose names declarations have been made there are fewer than the number which ought to be created who are eligible for election under this law; then the person whose duty it is to hold the election shall post up so that it can be read from the ground as many names of persons who are allowed by this law to be candidates for the magistracy as are sufficient to make up the number which ought to be created under this law. Those whose names are thus posted shall, if they wish, each nominate one person of the same condition before the person who shall hold the elections, and the persons so nominated by them shall, if they so wish, also each nominate one person of the same condition before him. And the person before whom the nominations are made shall put up all the names so that they can be read from the ground, and shall also hold the elections for them all, just as if a declaration of candidature for the magistracy had been made under this law in their names also within the prescribed date, and they had begun of their own wish to be candidates for the magistracy and had not abandoned their purpose.

52. CONCERNING HOLDING THE ELECTIONS

Whoever is the older of the present *duoviri* and of those who shall hereafter be *duoviri* in the municipality, or, if he for any reason cannot hold the elections, then the other of them, shall hold elections and by-elections under this law for choosing *duoviri*, also aediles, also quaestors, and shall cause ballots to be cast as votes should be cast under the distribution of the *curiae* which is enacted above. Those who are so created shall hold the magistracy which they have obtained by the vote for one year, or if they are created in place of another, for the remainder of that year.

53. IN WHICH CURIA NONCITIZEN RESIDENTS ARE TO VOTE

Whosoever shall hold the elections in the municipality for choosing the *duoviri*, also the aediles, also the quaestors, shall select by lot among the *curiae* one in which residents who are Roman citizens or Latin citizens shall vote, and they shall have the right of voting in that *curia*.

54. WHOSE CANDIDATURES SHOULD NOT BE RECEIVED AT THE ELECTIONS

The persons whose duty it is to hold the elections shall first cause to be created *duoviri* with judicial authority from that class of freeborn persons which is specified and enacted by this law, next aediles and also quaestors from that class of freeborn persons which is specified and enacted by this law, provided that no one shall receive at the elections the candidature for the office of *duumvir* of anyone who is under twenty-five years of age or has held the office within five years, also the candidature for the office of aedile and quaestor of any one who is under twenty-five years of age, or is subject to any of the disqualifications which would, if he were a Roman citizen, disqualify him from being in the number of the decurions or councillors.

55. CONCERNING VOTING

The person who holds the elections under this law shall call the citizens by their *curiae* to vote, so that he shall call all the *curiae* to vote by one summons, and they shall severally vote by ballot in their several enclosures. He shall also cause three citizens of the municipality who do not belong to that *curia* to attend at the ballot box of each *curia* to guard and count the votes, and before they do so to swear severally that he will count and return the votes in good faith. He shall not prevent each of the candidates from placing one guard at each ballot box. These guards placed by the person who holds the elections and also by the candidates shall severally vote in the *curia* to whose ballot box he is placed as guard, and their votes shall be valid and legal just as if each had voted in his own *curia*.

56. WHAT MUST BE DONE ABOUT THOSE WHO ARE EQUAL IN THE NUMBER OF VOTES

The person who shall hold the elections, as each candidate obtains more than another in any *curia*, shall declare him made and elected in respect of that *curia* before the others, until the number of those who should be created is completed. If in any *curia* two or more candidates shall obtain the same number of votes, he shall prefer a married man, or a person deemed to be a married man, to a bachelor having no children, who is not deemed to be a married man, or one with children to one without children, one having more children to one having less children, and he shall proclaim him first, provided that two children lost after naming, or one lost after puberty, male or female, shall count as one surviving. If two or more candidates shall have the same number of votes and be of the same condition, he shall put their names to the lot and as the name of each is drawn by lot shall declare him before the others.

57. CONCERNING THE DRAW OF THE CURIAE AND THOSE WHO ARE EQUAL IN THE NUMBER OF CURIAE

The person who shall hold the elections under this law, when the votes for all the *curiae* have been returned, shall put the names of the *curiae* to the lot and shall draw the names of the several *curiae* by lot, and as the name of each *curia* is drawn shall cause to be proclaimed those whom that *curia* has chosen; and as each candidate first completes a majority of the *curiae*, shall, when he has sworn according to the law and given security for the common funds, declare him made and elected, until there are the number of magistrates which should be created under this law. If two or more candidates have the same number of *curiae*, he shall take the same action in respect of those who have the same number of *curiae* as is enacted above in respect of those who are equal in the number of votes, and shall declare each created first in the same manner.

58. THAT NOTHING BE DONE TO PREVENT THE ELECTIONS BEING HELD

No one shall exercise his veto or do anything else to prevent the elections being held and completed in the municipality under this law. Whoever acts to the contrary knowingly and of malice shall be liable to pay for each offense ten thousand sesterces to the citizens of the Flavian municipality of Malaca; and of and concerning that money any citizen of the municipality who wishes and is permitted under this law shall have right of action, claim, and prosecution.

59. CONCERNING THE OATH OF THOSE WHO GAIN A MAJORITY OF THE CURIAE

The person who holds the elections, as each of the candidates for the offices of *duumvir* or aedile or quaestor completes a majority of the *curiae*, before he declares him made and created, shall exact from him openly at a public meeting an oath by Jupiter and the deified Augustus and the deified Claudius and the deified Vespasianus Augustus and the deified Titus Augustus and the genius of Imperator Caesar Domitianus Augustus and the gods Penates that he will do what he ought to do under this law, and that he has not acted and will not act contrary to the law of malice.

60. THAT SECURITY BE GIVEN ABOUT THE COMMON FUNDS OF THE CITIZENS

Those who shall be candidates in the municipality for the office of *duumvir* or quaestor and those who, because declarations of candidature have been made in the names of fewer than is required, have been by nomination placed in the position that votes should be cast respecting them under this law, shall severally on the day on which the elections are held, before the voting begins, at the discretion of the person who shall hold the elections, give sureties to the citizens in common that their common funds, which he shall handle in his magistracy, shall be safe. If he shall appear to be insufficiently guaranteed by sureties in this matter, he shall place properties under seal at the discretion of the same person. And he shall accept sureties and securities from them without malice until a proper guarantee is made with due regard to equity. The person who holds the election shall not receive the candidature of any of the persons respecting whom votes should be cast at the election of the *duoviri* and quaestors who is responsible for insufficient guarantees being made.

61. CONCERNING THE CHOICE OF A PATRON

No one shall publicly choose a patron for the citizens of the Flavian municipality of Malaca, nor confer on anyone the position of patron, except by a decree of the majority of the decurions, made when not less than two thirds were present, and they voted by ballot. If any publicly chooses a patron for the citizens of the Flavian municipality of Malaca, or confers on anyone the position of patron contrary to this, he shall be liable to pay ten thousand sesterces publicly to the citizens of the Flavian municipality of Malaca, and he who has been so chosen patron, or upon whom the position of patron has been conferred contrary to this law, shall not therefore be a patron of the Flavian municipality of Malaca.

62. THAT NO ONE SHALL DESTROY BUILDINGS WHICH HE IS NOT GOING TO RESTORE

No one shall remove the roof of a building or destroy it or cause it to be demolished in the town of the Flavian municipality of Malaca or the built-up area adjacent to the town, except with the approval of the decurions or councillors, when a majority are present, unless he is going to rebuild it in the following year. Whoever acts to the contrary shall be liable to pay the value of the property to the citizens of the Flavian municipality of Malaca; and of and concerning that money, any citizen of the Flavian municipality of Malaca who wishes and is permitted under this law shall have right of action, claim, and prosecution.

63. CONCERNING THE PUBLICATION OF LEASES AND THE TERMS OF LEASES
AND ENTERING THEM IN THE MUNICIPAL RECORDS

A *duumvir* with judicial authority shall lease the revenue and expenditure and whatever else ought to be leased in the common
name of the citizens of the municipality. He shall cause to be entered in the common records of the citizens of the municipality and
shall keep posted up for the remainder of his term of office, so that
it can be read from the ground, in the place where the decurions or
councillors have voted that it should be posted, what leases he has
made, and what terms he has laid down, the amount for which the
lease has been set, and what securities have been submitted and
placed under seal or obligated, and who have been accepted as
vouchers for the securities.

64. CONCERNING THE OBLIGATION OF SURETIES, SECURITIES AND VOUCHERS

Whosoever are or shall be made sureties in the Flavian municipality
of Malaca to the citizens of the municipality in common and whatsoever securities are or shall be accepted, and whosoever are or
shall become vouchers for the securities, they all and all the
property which each of them owned when he became a surety or
voucher and which accrued to them after they began to be obligated, such of them as shall not or shall not have been released or
liberated or have or shall have been so not without fraud; and all
their property which has not or shall not have been released and
liberated or has or shall have been so not without fraud; shall be
obligated to the citizens of the municipality in common just as they
would be obligated to the Roman people, if they had become
sureties or vouchers or the securities had been submitted, put under
seal and obligated to those in charge of the Roman treasury. If any
such sureties or securities or vouchers (if any of the securities for
which they became vouchers are not as stated) shall not be released
or liberated or shall be released and liberated not without fraud, the
duoviri with judicial authority, both or one of them, in accordance with a decree of the decurions or councillors made when not
less than two thirds of them were present, shall have the right and
power to sell and fix terms for selling them, provided that in selling
property he shall fix the terms which those in charge of the Roman
treasury should fix in selling sureties and securities under the law of
sureties, or, if he shall not find a buyer under the law of sureties,
what terms he should fix in selling on the open market, and pro-

vided that they fix such terms that the money be produced, paid or made over in the market of the Flavian municipality of Malaca. And whatsoever terms are so fixed shall be valid and legal.

65. THAT JUSTICE BE ADMINISTERED ACCORDING TO THE TERMS FIXED FOR SELLING SURETIES AND SECURITIES

As regards the sureties, securities, and vouchers which the *duoviri* of the Flavian municipality of Malaca have sold under this law, whosoever has judicial authority, if application is made to him on this matter, shall administer justice and appoint courts so that those who have bought the said sureties, vouchers, and securities, and their sureties, partners, and heirs and all concerned may be able lawfully to sue on these matters and claim and prosecute.

66. CONCERNING IMPOSITION OF FINES

A *duumvir* with judicial authority shall order to be entered in the common records of the citizens of the municipality fines imposed in the municipality by the *duoviri* or a prefect, also by the aediles, provided that the aediles, both or either of them, have declared before the *duoviri* that they have imposed them. If the person on whom the fine was imposed or another in his name shall request that the matter be referred to the decurions or councillors, the judgment shall belong to the decurions or councillors. The *duoviri* shall pay into the treasury of the citizens of the municipality whatever fines are not judged by the decurions or councillors to be unjust.

67. CONCERNING THE COMMON MONIES OF THE CITIZENS AND THEIR ACCOUNTS

Any person into whose hands the common monies of the citizens of the municipality shall come and his heir and all concerned shall within thirty days of the said monies coming into his hands place them in the treasury of the citizens of the municipality. Any person who has handled or dealt with the common accounts or any common business of the citizens of the municipality, he, his heir, and all concerned shall, within thirty days of his ceasing to handle and deal with such business or accounts, on a day on which the decurions and councillors are convened, produce and render accounts to the decurions or councillors, or to the person to whom the business shall be given of receiving and checking them by a decree of the decurions or councillors, passed when not less than

two thirds of them were present. Any person by whose actions
money was not so collected and paid or accounts were not so
rendered, or it was proposed that accounts should not be rendered
or money should not be collected and paid, and his heir and the
person to whom the matter in question shall belong, shall be liable
to pay to the citizens of the municipality double the amount; and
of and concerning that money any citizen of the municipality who
wishes and is permitted under this law shall have right of action,
claim, and prosecution.

68. ON APPOINTING ADVOCATES WHEN THE ACCOUNTS ARE RENDERED

When accounts are so rendered, the *duumvir* who convenes the
decurions or councillors shall refer to the decurions or councillors
as to whom they wish to plead the public cause, and the decurions
or councillors shall decree on oath by ballot, when not less than
two thirds of them are present, and the three persons who have
received most votes in the ballot shall plead the public cause, and
those who are chosen shall request time from the decurions and
councillors to prepare their case and consider their pleas and, when
the time so granted has elapsed, shall plead the cause with due
regard to equity.

94. The charter of Salpensa

This inscription is the surviving part of a similar charter given to
another Spanish town, Salpensa. Clauses 21–23 deal with the grant of
Roman citizenship to ex-magistrates with their families and its legal
consequences. Clause 24 enables the town to elect the emperor as sole
duumvir; he naturally performed his function through a delegate.
Clause 25 is concerned with the duties and powers of the magistrates.

94. S. Riccobono, Fontes Iuris Romani Ante Justiniani[2], *I. 23*

21. THAT MAGISTRATES SHALL OBTAIN THE ROMAN CITIZENSHIP

WHOEVER IS made *duumvir*, aedile, or quaestor under this law shall
be Roman citizens one year after they have ceased to be magistrates, with their parents, wives, and children who were born of a
lawful marriage and are in the legal control of their parents, also
their grandsons and granddaughters born to a son who is in the
legal control of his parents; provided that there shall not be more
Roman citizens than magistrates created under this law.

22. THAT THOSE WHO OBTAIN THE ROMAN CITIZENSHIP SHALL REMAIN IN THE LEGAL POWER OF THE SAME PERSONS

If anyone under this law or by edict of Imperator Caesar Augustus Vespasianus or Imperator Titus Caesar Augustus or Imperator Caesar Augustus Domitianus, father of his country, shall obtain Roman citizenship, he or she shall be in the legal control of him who has been made a Roman citizen under this law, and in whose legal control he or she ought to have been if he or she had not been changed by the Roman citizenship, and shall have the same right of choosing a guardian which he or she would have had if he or she had been born of a Roman citizen and had not been changed in citizenship.

23. THAT THOSE WHO OBTAIN THE ROMAN CITIZENSHIP SHALL KEEP THEIR RIGHTS OVER THEIR FREEDMEN

If anyone under this law or by edict of Imperator Caesar Vespasianus Augustus or Imperator Titus Caesar Vespasianus Augustus or Imperator Caesar Domitianus Augustus shall obtain Roman citizenship, he shall have the same right and the same condition in regard to his or her and his or her father's freedmen and freedwomen who have not received the Roman citizenship, and in respect of their goods and the duties imposed on them in return for their freedom, as he or she would have had if he or she had not been changed in citizenship.

24. CONCERNING THE PREFECT OF IMPERATOR CAESAR DOMITIANUS AUGUSTUS

If the decurions or councillors or citizens of the municipality shall in the common name of the citizens of the municipality offer the office of *duumvir* to Imperator Caesar Domitianus Augustus, father of his country, and if Imperator Domitianus Caesar Augustus, father of his country, shall accept that office and shall appoint whomsoever he wishes as prefect in his place, the prefect shall have the same rights as if he should have been created *duumvir* with judicial powers without colleague under this law, and he had been created sole *duumvir* with judicial powers under this law.

25. CONCERNING THE RIGHTS OF A PREFECT LEFT BY A DUUMVIR

If both the *duoviri* who shall be in charge of jurisdiction in the municipality shall leave the municipality and the one to leave later shall think that he will not return to the municipality on that day, he shall cause whomsoever of the decurions or councillors, being

thirty five years of age, he shall wish to leave as prefect to swear
by Jupiter and the deified Augustus and the deified Claudius and
the deified Vespasianus Augustus and the deified Titus Augustus
and the genius of Imperator Caesar Domitianus Augustus and the
gods Penates, that while he is prefect he will do what a *duumvir*
with judicial powers ought to do under this law, provided that it
can be done at that time, and will not act to the contrary knowingly and of malice; and when he has so sworn, he shall leave him as
prefect of the municipality. He who is left as prefect, until one of
the *duoviri* shall arrive in the municipality, shall in all things have
the same rights and powers, except that of leaving a prefect and of
obtaining the Roman citizenship, as are given by this law to a
duoviri with judicial authority. While he shall be prefect, whenever he leaves the municipality, he shall not be absent more than
one day.

26. CONCERNING THE OATH OF THE DUOVIRI, AEDILES, AND QUAESTORS

The *duoviri* who have judicial authority in the municipality and the
aediles who are in the municipality and the quaestors who are in
the municipality shall each of them within five days after the grant
of this law; and those who shall be created *duoviri*, aediles, and
quaestors hereafter under this law, shall within five days of becoming *duoviri*, aediles, or quaestors; before the decurions or councillors are convened, swear at a public meeting by Jupiter and the
deified Augustus and the deified Claudius and the deified Vespasianus Augustus and the deified Titus Augustus and the genius of
Domitian Augustus and the gods Penates, that he will rightly do
whatever he considers to be in accordance with this law and the
common weal of the citizens of the Flavian municipality of Salpensa, and that he will not act contrary to this law or the common
weal of the citizens of the municipality knowingly and of malice,
and that he will prevent those whom he can from so doing, and
that he will not hold or give counsel or state his opinion otherwise
than he considers to be according to this law and the common weal
of the citizens of the municipality. Whosoever does not so swear
shall be liable to pay ten thousand sesterces to the citizens of the
municipality; and of or concerning that money whoever of the
citizens of the municipality shall wish, to whom it shall be permitted by this law, shall have the right of action, claim, and
prosecution.

27. CONCERNING THE VETO OF THE DUOVIRI AND AEDILES AND QUAESTORS

Whosoever shall be *duumvir* or aedile or quaestor of the municipality shall have the right and power of veto, the *duoviri* against
each other, and whenever anyone appeals to either or both of them
from an aedile or aediles, or a quaestor or quaestors; also the aediles
against one another; and the quaestors against one another; within
three days after the appeal is made and the veto shall be possible,
provided that nothing is done contrary to this law and that appeal
shall not be made to any of them more than once in the same
matter; and that no one shall act to the contrary when a veto has
been declared.

28. CONCERNING MANUMITTING SLAVES BEFORE A DUUMVIR

If any citizen of the Flavian municipality of Salpensa who is a Latin
shall manumit his slave, male or female, from slavery to freedom
before the *duumvir* with judicial authority, and shall order him or
her to be free; provided that no ward or married or unmarried
woman may manumit anyone without the approval of his or her
guardian or order him or her to be freed; whoever is so manumitted or ordered to be freed, shall be free, whether male or female,
with the full rights of Latin freedom, provided that anyone who is
under twenty years of age shall so manumit only if the number of
decurions which is required under this law for valid decrees shall
approve the reason for the manumission.

29. CONCERNING THE APPOINTMENT OF GUARDIANS

If anyone has not a guardian or his guardian is not known, if he or
she is a citizen of the Flavian municipality of Salpensa, and is not a
ward, and shall request of the *duoviri* with judicial authority to give
him or her a guardian and shall name the person whom he or she
wishes to be given, then the magistrate of whom the request is
made, whether he has one or more colleagues, shall, with the consent of all his colleages who shall be at the time in the municipality
or within the boundaries of the municipality, having considered the
case, if he thinks fit give as guardian the person who has been
named. If the person in whose name the request is made is a ward,
male or female, or if the magistrate to whom the request is made
has no colleague, or no colleague is in the town or within the
boundaries, then the magistrate to whom the request is made shall
consider the case and within ten days, by decree of the decurions
passed when not less than two thirds of the decurions are present,

give him as guardian the person who has been named, provided that the guardianship shall not pass from the proper guardian. Any guardian given under this law shall be as proper a guardian to him to whom he is so given, provided that the guardianship does not pass from the proper guardian, as if he were a Roman citizen and his nearest agnate being a Roman citizen were his guardian.

95. A federate city

Some provincial cities enjoyed the privileges of being free, that is, running their own internal affairs without interference from the governors. Some, like Amisus in Bithynia Pontus, had the additional privilege of having their rights guaranteed by a treaty with Rome (federate). It will be noted that Trajan interprets freedom very strictly—the Amisenes are only allowed to do what their existing law permits. As will be seen from No. 110 the Roman government had a deep distrust of societies or clubs.

95. Pliny, Letters, X, 92–93

PLINY TO TRAJAN

THE FREE and federate city of Amisus enjoys by your indulgence the privilege of its own laws. A memorial being presented to me there concerning a charitable society, I have enclosed it in this letter that you may consider, Sir, whether and how far these meetings are to be permitted or prohibited.

TRAJAN TO PLINY

If a charitable society be agreeable to the laws of the Amisenes, which by the articles of alliance it is stipulated they shall enjoy, I shall not oppose it; especially if these contributions are employed not for the purposes of riot and faction but for the support of the indigent. In other cities, however, which are subject to our laws, I would have all assemblies of this nature prohibited.

96. Claudius' letter to Alexandria

In this letter, preserved in a papyrus, Claudius follows the line of Augustus and Tiberius in deprecating divine honors for himself (cf. No. 166). It is amusing that the prefect of Egypt in his edict publishing the letter calls Claudius a god without scruple. In the second paragraph Claudius deals with the internal government of Alexandria. The ephebate was an institution common among Greek cities, whereby young citizens underwent originally military, later athletic, training for a year or two, It would appear from Claudius' words that noncitizens had illicitly gone through the training and had thereby got themselves on the citizen roll. Civic magistracies were normally annual, and the long term held by those of Alexandria is unparalleled. Alexandria appears to have been deprived of its city council by one of the later Ptolemies, and despite much agitation, it did not recover it until Septimius Severus' reign. The Roman government was evidently averse to granting self-government to this turbulent and cosmopolitan city, where there was much anti-Roman sentiment. The third paragraph deals with one of the major problems of Alexandria, hostility between citizens (who were Greek) and the very large Jewish community, which enjoyed considerable communal autonomy. There had very recently been a great pogrom, encouraged by Caligula's hostile attitude to the Jews, who refused to worship him.

96. P. Lond., *1912*

Lucius Aemilius Rectus says: Seeing that all the populace, owing to its numbers, was unable to be present at the reading of the most sacred and most beneficent letter to the city, I have deemed it necessary to display the letter publicly in order that reading it one by one you may admire the majesty of our god Caesar and feel gratitude for his good will toward the city. Year 2 of Tiberius Claudius Caesar Augustus Germanicus Imperator, the 14th of Neus Sebastus [Nov. 10, A.D. 41].

Tiberius Claudius Caesar Augustus Germanicus Imperator, pontifex maximus, holder of the tribunician power, consul designate, to the city of Alexandria, greeting. Tiberius Claudius Barbillus, Apollonius son of Artemidorus, Chaeremon son of Leonidas, Marcus Julius Asclepiades, Gaius Julius Dionysius son of Sabbion, Tiberius Claudius Archibius, Apollonius son of Ariston, Gaius Julius Apollonius, Hermaiscus son of Apollonius, your ambassadors, having delivered to me the decree, discoursed at length concerning the city, directing my attention to your good will toward us, which from long ago, you may be sure, had been stored up to your advantage in my memory; for you are by nature reverent toward the Augusti, as I know from many proofs, and in particular have taken a warm interest in my house, warmly reciprocated, of which fact (to mention the last instance, passing over the others) the supreme witness is my brother Germanicus addressing you in words more clearly stamped as his own. Wherefore I gladly accepted the honors given to me by you, though I have no weakness

for such things. And first I permit you to keep my birthday as a
dies Augustus as you have yourselves proposed, and I agree to the
erection in their several places of the statues of myself and my
family; for I see that you were anxious to establish on every side
memorials of your reverence for my house. Of the two golden
statues the one made to represent the Pax Augusta Claudiana, as
my most honored Barbillus suggested and entreated when I wished
to refuse for fear of being thought too offensive, shall be erected at
Rome, and the other according to your request shall be carried in
procession on name days in your city; and it shall be accompanied
by a throne, adorned with whatever trappings you choose. It
would perhaps be foolish, while accepting such great honors, to
refuse the institution of a Claudian tribe and the establishment of
groves after the manner of Egypt; wherefore I grant you these
requests as well, and if you wish you may also erect the equestrian
statues given by Vitrasius Pollio, my procurator. As for the erection of those in four-horse chariots which you wish to set up to me
at the entrances into the country, I consent to let one be placed at
Taposiris, the Libyan town of that name, another at Pharos in
Alexandria, and a third at Pelusium in Egypt. But I deprecate the
appointment of a high priest to me and the building of temples, for
I do not wish to be offensive to my contemporaries, and my
opinion is that temples and such forms of honor have by all ages
been granted as a prerogative to the gods alone.

Concerning the requests which you have been anxious to obtain
from me, I decide as follows. All those who have become *ephebi* up
to the time of my principate I confirm and maintain in possession of
the Alexandrian citizenship with all the privileges and indulgences
enjoyed by the city, excepting such as by beguiling you have contrived to become *ephebi* though born of servile mothers; and it is
equally my will that all the other favors shall be confirmed which
were granted to you by former princes and kings and prefects, as
the deified Augustus also confirmed them. It is my will that the
wardens of the temple of the deified Augustus in Alexandria shall
be chosen by lot in the same way as those of the said deified Augustus in Canopus are chosen by lot. With regard to the civic magistracies being made triennial, your proposal seems to me to be very
good; for through fear of being called to account for any abuse of
power, your magistrates will behave with greater circumspection
during their term of office. Concerning the council, what your
custom may have been under the ancient kings I have no means of

saying, but that you had no council under the former Augusti you
are well aware. As this is the first broaching of a novel project,
whose utility to the city and to my government is not evident, I
have written to Aemilius Rectus to hold an inquiry and inform me
whether in the first place it is right that a council should be constituted and, if it should be right to create one, in what manner this
is to be done.

As for the question which party was responsible for the riots and
feud (or rather, if the truth must be told, the war) with the Jews,
although in confrontation with their opponents your ambassadors,
and particularly Dionysius son of Theon, contended with great
zeal, nevertheless I was unwilling to make a strict inquiry, though
guarding within me a store of immutable indignation against whichever party renews the conflict; and I tell you once for all that
unless you put a stop to this ruinous and obstinate enmity against
each other, I shall be driven to show what a benevolent prince can
be when turned to righteous indignation. Wherefore once again I
conjure you that on the one hand the Alexandrians show themselves forbearing and kindly toward the Jews who for many years
have dwelt in the same city, and dishonor none of the rites observed by them in the worship of their god, but allow them to
observe their customs as in the time of the deified Augustus, which
customs I also, after hearing both sides, have sanctioned; and on the
other hand I explicitly order the Jews not to agitate for more
privileges than they formerly possessed, and not in future to send
out a separate embassy as if they lived in a separate city, a thing
unprecedented, and not to force their way into the gymnasiarches
or the games given by the cosmets, while enjoying their own privileges and sharing a great abundance of advantages in a city not
their own, and not to bring in or admit Jews who sail in from Syria
or Egypt, a proceeding which will compel me to conceive serious
suspicions; otherwise I will by all means take vengeance on them as
fomenters of what is a general plague infecting the whole world. If
desisting from these courses you consent to live with mutual forbearance and kindliness, I on my side will exercise a solicitude of
very long standing for the city, as one which is bound to us by
traditional friendship. I bear witness to my friend Barbillus of the
solicitude which he has always shown for you in my presence and
of the extreme zeal with which he has now advocated your cause,
and likewise to my friend Tiberius Claudius Archibius. Farewell.

97. Vespasian's letter to Sabora

Sabora was a city in Baetica (southern Spain). Like many Spanish cities it was built on a hilltop, and wished to rebuild itself on a more convenient site, and to be allowed to adopt an imperial title. Provincial cities were not allowed to institute new local taxes without imperial permission, granted through the provincial governor, who stated the pros and cons.

97. *Dessau*, ILS, *6092*

IMPERATOR CAESAR VESPASIANUS AUGUSTUS, pontifex maximus, of the tribunicial power for the ninth time, imperator for the eighteenth time, consul for the eighth time, father of his country, to the four chief magistrates and decurions of the Saborenses [A.D. 78].

Since you indicate that your weakness is oppressed by many difficulties, I allow you to build your city under my name, as you wish, on the plain. I maintain the revenues which you say you received from the deified Augustus. If you wish to add more revenues you must approach the proconsul about them, for I cannot make any decision if no one replies. I received your decree on the sixth day before the kalends of August: I received your envoys on the fourth day before the kalends.

The *duoviri* Gaius Cornelius Severus and Marcus Septimius Severus engraved the above on bronze at the public expense.

98. Titus' letter to Munigua

Munigua was another city of Baetica. It would appear that the city had borrowed money from the contractor to whom it had farmed its local taxes and failed to repay him, and, having been sued and lost its case, had appealed to the emperor. It is not clear why this appeal was irregular, but the city had thereby incurred a penalty of fifty thousand sesterces.

98. AE, *1964, 288*

IMPERATOR TITUS CAESAR VESPASIANUS AUGUSTUS, pontifex maximus, of the tribunician power for the ninth time, imperator for the fourteenth time, consul for the seventh time, father of his country, to the four chief magistrates and decurions of Munigua [A.D. 79].

Since you have appealed with the object of not paying the

money which you owe to Servilius Pollio in accordance with the judgment of Sempronius Fuscus, the penalty of an irregular appeal ought to have been exacted from you. But I have preferred to pay regard to my indulgence rather than your rashness and have excused the fifty thousand sesterces to the public poverty which you plead. I have written to my friend Gallicanus, the proconsul, that if you pay the money which was adjudged to Pollio, he should release you from the calculation of interest from the day of the sentence being given. It is equitable that the revenue arising from your taxes, for which you state Pollio had contracted, should come into account, so that your city may not lose anything on this score.

Given on the seventh day before the ides of September.

99. Domitian's letter to Falerio

The dispute between the two cities is obscure. *Subseciva* were pieces of land which were left over when a colony was founded and most of the land allotted to the colonists. They technically belonged to the state, but had generally been occupied by squatters. Vespasian tried to reclaim them for the state, but Domitian generally, as here, confirmed the squatters' rights. Falerio was apparently one of the twenty-eight colonies of veterans founded by Augustus (cf. No. 1, §28).

99. S. Riccobono, Fontes Iuris Romani Ante Justiniani², *I.* 75

IMPERATOR CAESAR son of the deified Vespasianus [Domitianus erased] Augustus, pontifex maximus, of the tribunician power, imperator for the second time, consul for the eighth time, designate for the ninth time, father of his country, to the four chief magistrates and decurions of Falerio in Picenum [A.D. 82].

That you may know the decision that I made, having examined the case, between you and the people of Firmum, I have ordered it to be appended to this letter.

In the consulship of Publius Valerius Patruinus and [name erased] on the fourteenth day before the kalends of August Imperator Caesar son of the deified Vespasianus [Domitianus erased] Augustus having examined the case between the peoples of Falerio and Firmum in the presence of distinguished men of both orders pronounced as follows.

The ambiguity of the dispute which is being renewed by the people of Firmum against the people of Falerio strongly moves me, as even a smaller number of years can be sufficient for the security of occupiers; as does the letter of the deified Augustus, a most careful emperor and most indulgent to the soldiers of the fourth legion, in which he advised them to collect and sell all their *subseciva*—and I do not doubt that they obeyed such salutary advice. I therefore confirm the rights of the occupiers.

Given on the eleventh day before the kalends of August in Albanum. Supervisor Titus Bovius Verus. Envoys Publius Bovius Sabinus and Publius Petronius Achilius. By decree of the decurions at public expense.

100. Antoninus Pius' letter to Ephesus

This letter well illustrates the embittered rivalry between provincial cities for titles and honors; compare the claim of Ephesus to be the place where the proconsul must arrive in Asia (No. 79). The cities also competed in the magnificence of their buildings and the splendor of their games, with disastrous financial results, as remarked by Cassius Dio in No. 11.

100. *Dittenberger*, Sylloge³, *849*

IMPERATOR CAESAR, son of the deified Hadrian, grandson of the deified Trajan Parthicus, great grandson of the deified Nerva, Titus Aelius Hadrianus Antoninus Augustus, pontifex maximus, of the tribunician power for the ———— time, imperator for the second time, consul for the third time, father of his country, to the magistrates, council and people of Ephesus [A.D. 140–44].

I am informed that the Pergamenes in their letter to you use the titles which I declared your city should use. But I think that the Smyrnans have inadvertently omitted them in the decree about the common sacrifice, but will for the future willingly conform, if you also, in your letters to them, allude to their city in the terms which are proper and have been decided. Sulpicius Julianus, my procurator, despatched the decree. Farewell.

Publius Vedius Antoninus, secretary, made the decree.

101. Another letter from Pius to Ephesus

Wealthy citizens were expected to give generously to public buildings and games, and thereby gained popularity and election to office. The Ephesians evidently preferred games to buildings.

101. Dittenberger, Sylloge³, *850*

IMPERATOR CAESAR, son of the deified Hadrian, grandson of the deified Trajan Parthicus, great grandson of the deified Nerva, Titus Aelius Hadrianus Antoninus Augustus, pontifex maximus, of the tribunician power for the eighth time, imperator for the second time, consul for the fourth time, father of his country, to the magistrates, council, and people of Ephesus [A.D. 145].

I learned of the generosity which Vedius Antoninus displays toward you not so much from your letter as from his. For wishing to obtain assistance from me for the decoration of the public buildings which he had promised to you, he revealed how many large buildings he is adding to the city. But you do not appreciate him properly. I have granted his requests, and have noted that he prefers not to act in the usual way of politicians, who, to gain immediate applause, spend their benefactions on shows and distributions and prizes for games, but in a way in which he hopes to enhance the dignity of your city for the future. Claudius Julianus, the honorable proconsul, despatched the letter. Farewell.

102. The election of a civil magistrate

These proceedings took place at Hermopolis in Egypt in A.D. 192. They illustrate the growing reluctance of citizens to be candidates for magistracies, owing to the heavy expenses involved (cf. No. 93). Despite strong moral pressure Achilles obstinately refuses to take the more expensive office of cosmete and only offers himself, on terms, for that of exegete. Eventually a citizen nominates him "on my personal responsibility," that is, guarantees to be responsible for any financial deficit that he may incur, and having been thus formally nominated, Achilles has to accept and is forthwith inaugurated. No election is required as he is the only candidate. The cities of Egypt had no councils at this date, and the proceedings take place before the *strategus*, the governor of the nome or district of Hermopolis. In a normal city these proceedings would have taken place in the city council. In Alexandria and the Egyptian cities the chief magistrate was the exegete (cf. No. 78) and the cosmete controlled the training of the ephebes (see No. 96).

102. P. Ryl., 77

COPY OF minutes . . ., there being present at the tribunal from the magistrates in office Dius, gymnasiarch, and Dionysius also

called . . . , exegete, Olympiodorus, advocate, Apollonius son of
Heraclapollon, ex-gymnasiarch, and Achilles son of Cornelius, the
townsmen standing by cried out, "Let Achilles be crowned as
cosmete; imitate your father, the man of public spirit, the old
champion," whereupon Achilles said: "In compliance with the
wish of my native city I offer to undertake the office of a crowned
exegete on the condition that I contribute an annual sum of two
talents and am freed from the superintendence of land under
lease." Olympiodorus said: "The fortune of our lord the Emperor
provides offices abundantly and augments of prosperity of the city;
how could it be otherwise under the auspicious prefecture of
Larcius Memor? If then Achilles wishes to be crowned as exegete,
let him forthwith pay the initial contribution; if he does not, he has
nonetheless nominated himself for the office immediately required,
that of cosmete." Achilles said: "I engaged to undertake the office
of exegete on the condition that I should contribute two talents
yearly; for I am not able to support the office of cosmete." Olympiodorus said: "After engaging to undertake the greater office he
ought not to evade the lesser." Ammonion son of Dioscorus, inter-
rupting, said: "All through this day Achilles struck me, and I will
certify these very facts by means of your minutes, because I am
petitioning the most illustrious prefect concerning the insult."
Achilles said: "I neither struck him nor insulted him." Sarapion also
called Apollonius, *strategus*, said: "What you have said has been
recorded, but the cosmetes shall also be summoned in order that
you may repeat the same statements in their presence." After a
while Diogenes and Dioscorus and their fellow cosmetes came
forward at the Caesareum in the presence of Achilles, making one
of them their spokesman; and he, Diogenes, said: "We have learned
that in our absence Achilles proposed himself for the office of
exegete. But this was not permissible; for the most divine Antoninus ordained by edict that no one may become an exegete
without three designated successors; so, as there are many designated successors, he ought to pass on to the office immediately
required; in proof of which I will read you the edict." When he
had read a copy of the edict of Marcus Aurelius Antoninus Caesar,
Aspidas father of Hermas ex-cosmete, being present, said: "On my
personal responsibility I crown Achilles for the office of cosmete."
Olympiodorus said: "We have now the declaration of Aspidas that
he crowns him on his own responsibility; and he ought to be

crowned, for the office is now safeguarded for the city." The
strategus ordered the statements to be entered on the minutes.

103. Summons of a city council

Septimius Severus established councils not only at Alexandria but in
the other Egyptian towns. Here we see the president (*prytanis*) of the
council of Oxyrhynchus summoning a meeting in A.D. 284. The city
councils not only managed the internal administration but had to elect
officers to perform many services for the imperial government, including the collection of the tribute. Here they have to elect officers for
transporting army supplies. The *dioecetes* was the finance minister of
Egypt.

103. P. Oxy., 1412

AURELIUS EUDAEMON also called Helladius, formerly eutheniarch,
cosmete, exegete, hypomnematographus, councillor of the most
illustrious city of Alexandria, ex-gymnasiarch, councillor, prytanis
in office of the illustrious and most illustrious city of Oxyrhynchus.
The question of the transport of provisions for the most noble
soldiers does not admit even a brief delay, and for this reason, and
since letters from his excellency the *dioecetes* Aurelius Proteas, as
well as from his excellency Ammonius, are urging us to see to this,
and the boats to receive the supplies are already at the quay, it has
become necessary to call an extraordinary general meeting of the
council at a suitable place, in order that a discussion may be held on
this single subject and the obligatory services performed as quickly
as possible. Accordingly in order that all, being informed of this,
may willingly do their duty as councillors today, which is the 15th,
the letters are publicly exhibited. I have thought it right that you
should know by this proclamation that I have instructed you, on
being informed of the facts, to assemble promptly in view of the
orders, there being no other subject to deal with at the present
meeting, and elect by vote those who are to serve. The 2nd [?]
year, [month] 15.

104. Minutes of a city council

This debate, held in A.D. 370, is again about nomination to offices. The
most responsible are those of pagarch (*praepositus pagi*) and con-

tractor (*conductor*). The former were the governors of the districts into which the city territory was divided, the latter the managers of state services such as the public post. Breeding horses (for the city horse races) was also an office. The councillors insist strongly that the prefect of Egypt (Tatianus) and the praetorian prefect and emperor have approved the choice, but it was certainly made by the council. The ten councillors who speak are perhaps the ten *principales*, an inner committee of the council. They have all held important city offices. The *curator* was the manager of the internal finances of the city (cf. No. 41), the *exactor* the manager of imperial taxation, the gymnasiarch the president of the town sports club (see No. 66), the *prytanis* the president of the council (see No. 103), the *riparius* the chief of police.

104. P. Oxy., 2110

IN THE 3rd counsulship of our masters Valentinian and Valens, eternal Augusti [A.D. 370] Phaophi 9, t a meeting of the council, in the prytany of Claudius Hermeia son of Gelasius, ex-gymnasiarch and councilor, after the plaudits Theon son of Ammonius, councilor, represented by his son Macrobius, came forward and made the following statement: "Fellow councillors, you know as well as I that my name is on the list about to come into force and that I am one of the twenty-four ordained by our lord the most illustrious Tatianus for the pagarchies and contractorships. Perhaps in ignorance the president has appointed me to the administration of the soldiers' woolen clothing for the fourteenth indiction, at the very time when I have horses to keep; wherefore I put it to you that the ordinances ought not to be infringed." The councillors cried: "What is on the list is valid; what has been rightly ordained must not be infringed." Ptoleminus, ex-curator, said: "What has been ordained by our lord the most illustrious Tatianus with the approval of the whole council must stand fast and unshaken, whence it follows that the twenty-four are not to serve in any other service whatever but keep to the heavier offices, not only in this but in future prytanies. If, however, anyone wishes to serve in another service, he does not do so on the responsibility of the council, and Macrobius ought not to be burdened." Gerontius, ex-exactor, said: "What has been rightly ordained and legally done by my lord Tatianus and referred to our sovereigns and to my lords the most illustrious prefects of the sacred praetorium has its validity from them, and hence it is not proper for Macrobius to be burdened by either the prytanis or the future prytanis with other

administrations." Sarmates, ex-curator, said "Perhaps it was in
ignorance that our brother Hermeias the president impressed Macrobius who is one of the twenty-four ordained by my lord
Tatianus, and he ought not to be burdened on the score of an
administration. But if anyone of the twenty-four should wish to be
ostentatious, he knows his own responsibility." ———— said: "One
of the twenty-four ordained by the rectitude of my lord Tatianus
ought not to [suffer through the fault of?] presidents, and Macrobius ought not now to be burdened with the administration of the
soldiers' woolen clothing nor anything else, but should confine
himself to the heavy offices." Ammonianus, ex-exactor, said:
"What has been rightly and . . . ordained and approved by the
masters of the world and by my lords the most illustrious prefects
should not be infringed either by the present prytanis or by future
prytaneis, hence Macrobius ought not to be burdened with other
offices." Valerius son of Eudaemon, ex-gymnasiarch, said: "It is
not seemly for us to do anything beyond what has been ordained
by my lord Tatianus, hence neither Macrobius nor any other of
the twenty-four ought to be subject to intrigue in any way, but
they ought to be protected by the disposition which has been
rightly made." Macrobius, *riparius*, said: "Being one of the twenty-
four, Macrobius ought not to be burdened with another service."
Achilles son of Posi, *riparius*, said: "We all returned thanks at the
time for the disposition rightly made by my lord the most illustrious Tatianus; Macrobius accordingly ought not to be burdened
with the administration of the soldiers' woolen clothing, nor any
other service, because he is one of the twenty-four." Zoilus son of
Dionysius, ex-gymnasiarch, said: "I, too, am in agreement with the
view which has been generally expressed that these twenty-four
should not be burdened either by (the present prytanis or by)
future prytaneis; Macrobius therefore ought not to be burdened,
especially as he is one of the twenty-four." Theon son of Eusebius,
ex-prytanis, said: "Perhaps in ignorance our brother the president,
being unaware that Theon represented by his son Macrobius is one
of the twenty-four persons ordained for the heavier offices, imposed upon him the clothing; we, therefore, object that it is not
right that he should be burdened on the score of the administration
of the said woolen clothing." Eulogius son of Ptolemaeus, ex-
gymnasiarch, said: "Theon son of Ammonius, represented by his
son Macrobius, being one of the twenty-four ordained for the

heaviest offices, ought not to suffer any burden on the score of other offices." The prytanis said: "The opinions which you have advanced collectively and individually are in the safekeeping of the minutes, and Macrobius shall not be burdened with the administration of the soldiers' woolen clothing for the fourteenth indiction." [Signed] I, Aurelius Isidorus, scribe, drew up the minutes.

105. Duties of city councilors

The first passage lays down the rule that a man belongs to the city to which his father belongs—except for freed slaves, who belong to their former master's city—and is consequently obliged to hold offices in that city. If he lives elsewhere he is also liable in his city of residence. The second passage illustrates the difficulty in filling magistracies and the council early in the third century: Callistratus lived under Severus and Caracalla. Arcadius Charisius, who probably lived under Diocletian, gives a formidable list of civic offices. Most personal offices tended to become "mixed" as the city revenues diminished and their holders ceased to receive grants but had to pay out of their own pockets for the department which they supervised.

105. Digest, L, i. 6, ii. 6, iv. 18

ULPIAN, OPINIONS, BOOK II

THE ASSUMPTION of a nonexistent origin does not alter the natural truth. For one's true origin is not lost by error, nor laid aside by a lying statement that one comes from a place from which one does not come. Nor can anyone change the truth by renouncing the city from which he draws his origin, or lying about an origin which he does not possess. A son follows the city from which his father draws his natural origin, not his domicile. The learned are agreed that a man can have a domicile in two places, if he has made such arrangements in both places that he does not, therefore, appear to have put himself among the others. Freedmen follow the origin or domicile of their patrons, and so do the children of freedmen.

CALLISTRATUS, TRIALS, BOOK VI

Those who sell articles of daily use as their business ought not to be neglected as vile persons, even if they are beaten by the aediles. In fact such men are not forbidden from aspiring to the decurionate or any other office in their city. They are not infamous and are not debarred from offices even if they are flogged by the aediles,

though the aediles are properly exercising their functions. I nevertheless think it unseemly that persons of this sort, who are subject
to flogging, should be received into the council, especially in those
cities where there is an abundance of honorable citizens. For the
scarcity of men to fill public offices may necessarily call on these, if
they have the requisite property, to a municipal dignity.

ARCADIUS CHARISIUS, ON CIVIC OFFICES

There are three kinds of civic offices: for some are personal offices,
others are patrimonial, others mixed. Personal offices are those
which are carried out by the mental effort and bodily labor of the
holders without any financial loss, like guardianship of a minor or
of a woman. The care of the civic loan fund and the quaestorship
in some cities is reckoned not as a magistracy but as a personal
office. The production of recruits and of horses, or of any other
animals that have to be produced, or things that have to be
transported or escorted, fiscal monies or foodstuffs or clothing,
are personal offices. So, too, is the care of the wagon post and the
provision of teams. Also the task of buying corn or oil—for it is
customary to elect persons to look after these things, whom they
call οιτῶναι, that is, *frumentarii*, and ἐλαιῶναι, that is, *olearii*—is
reckoned among personal offices in some cities, and so is the heating
of the public baths, if money is provided from civic revenues for
the curator. The charge of maintaining an aqueduct is also reckoned among personal offices. So, too, are the chief constables, who
are in charge of public order and suppressing crime. So, too, those
who are elected to build roads, since they spend nothing out of
their own pocket for this charge. Also inspectors, who look after
the sale of bread or other wares which are needed by the population of the city for their daily diet, perform a personal office. Any
person who receives or exacts foodstuffs or distributes them, and
collectors of the toll tax, bear the burden of a personal charge. So,
too, the curators who are elected to collect the public revenues of
cities are subject to a personal charge. Those, too, who are curators
of temples or keepers of archives or accountants or billeting
officers, in some cities harbormasters, curators for erecting or repairing public buildings or palaces or docks or posting stations, if
they spend public money on building works, and those who are
put in charge of building and repairing ships where needful are
bound by personal offices. The production of camels is similarly a

personal office, for the calculation is made of the fodder and of the camels and a fixed sum of money ought to be given to the collector of camels, so that they are bound only by a personal charge. It is usual to nominate these from the register of the council in turn, and no excuses are accepted, except physical incapacity or illness. Envoys, too, who are sent to the emperor's court, because they generally receive journey money, what is called *legativum*, and commanders of the night watch and curators of bakeries perform a personal service. Legal representatives, what the Greeks called syndics, and those who are elected to plead or defend a special cause perform a personal charge. The duty of being a judge is also considered a personal office. If a man is elected to compel those who own property abutting on a public highway to repair the road, that is a personal office. Similarly those appointed to accept or receive census declarations apply their minds to the care of a personal office. The whipbearers who attend the stewards at the games, and the secretaries of magistrates, perform a personal charge.

Patrimonial charges are those which are performed at the expense and to the loss of the holders. The purchase of oil and of beans is considered to be a patrimonial charge at Alexandria. The collectors of wine in the province of Africa hold patrimonial office. There are two kinds of patrimonial charges, for some of the charges are imposed on estates or possessions, like post horses or mules and oxen for the post, or riding horses. Such services must be undertaken even by those who are not citizens of the city or domiciled in it. The emperors order that even moneylenders, although they are veterans, must undertake such charges. Neither a senior centurion nor a veteran nor a soldier nor anyone who enjoys any kind of privilege, nor a priest, is excused from this kind of charge. Moreover, some cities have the privilege that those who own land in their territories must annually provide a quantity of corn calculated on the area of their holding: this form of tax is a charge on the land.

Mixed offices are the decaprotia and icosaprotia, as Herennius Modestinus rightly and correctly ruled in his decisions and in argument: for the decaproti and icosaproti in collecting the tribute perform a bodily task, and make good to the treasury losses from the names of persons deceased. This charge should rightly be reckoned among mixed offices. But those offices which are said to be personal, if those who undertake them by the law or custom of the city also spend money out of their own pockets, or collectors of foodstuffs who suffer loss in respect of deserted farms, will be included among mixed offices. All these offices which have been divided into three categories are included by one term, for personal, patrimonial, and mixed offices are called civic or public offices. If anyone is given immunity from personal or even civic charges he is not excused from providing foodstuffs, or ox teams or horses, or from furnishing lodging or for providing a ship or for the poll tax—except soldiers and veterans.

106. The tariff of Palmyra

This huge inscription, only parts of which have been reproduced, sets out the regulations and rates for the civic revenues of Palmyra, which were farmed to a contractor. The principal tax was customs dues on caravans which passed through the city, but there were also charges for their use of the water supplies. There were also license taxes on prostitutes and shopkeepers, and a salt tax, a slaughter tax, and pasture dues. With these revenues Palmyra was a very wealthy city, as its magnificent ruins amply demonstrate. It may be noted that from the time of Germanicus, who probably annexed Palmyra in A.D. 17, the Roman authorities occasionally intervened, but that in general the management of the local revenues was left to the city council.

106. Dittenberger, OGIS, 629

[In Greek and Aramaic]

YEAR 448 [A.D. 137], 19th of the month Xandicus, resolution of the council. In the presidency of Bonees son of Bonees, grandson of Haeranus, Alexander son of Alexander, grandson of Philopator, being secretary to the council and people, Malichus son of Olaees and Zeibeidus son of Nesas being magistrates, at a lawful session of the council the following decree was voted. Whereas in old times most of the articles subject to tax where not specified in the law of the tax contract, but payments were demanded according to custom and it was written in the lease that the tax contractor should demand payment according to the law and custom, but it often resulted that disputes arose on the question between merchants and the tax contractors; be it resolved that the magistrates in office and the Committee of Ten shall examine the articles which are not specified in the law and write them into the next lease, and record the customary tax for each category, and when it has been approved by the lessee, that it shall be inscribed with the first law on the stone pillar opposite the temple called of Rabaseires, and that the magistrates and Committee of Ten and the syndics for the time being shall see to it that the lessees demand no payment contrary to it.

A wagonload of any kind pays the tax of four camel loads.

[In Aramaic only]

The customs law of Hadriana Palmyra and the wells of Aelius Caesar.

[In Greek and Aramaic]

From those who import slaves into Palmyra or the territory of Palmyra, he shall exact 22 denarii from each person. . . .

For each fleece of purple wool he shall exact 8 asses on import and 8 asses on export. For a donkey load of myrrh in alabaster jars he shall exact 13 denarii on import and on export seven denarii. For a donkey load of myrrh in goatskins he shall exact 7 denarii on import and 4 on export. For a load of oil in four goatskins on a camel he shall exact 13 denarii on import and 13 denarii on export. For a load of oil in two goatskins on a camel he shall exact 7 denarii on import and 7 denarii on export. . . .

The same contractor shall exact 1 denarius from prostitutes who charge 1 denarius or more, and 8 asses from those that charge 8 asses, and 6 asses from those that charge 6 asses. The same contractor shall according to custom exact 1 denarius per month, from shops, general stores, cobblers. . . .

From those who import or sell hides, for each hide 2 asses. Similarly retail clothiers who make sales in the city shall furnish guarantees to the tax contractor. For the use of the two springs each year, 800 denarii. The same man shall exact for a load of wheat, wine, chaff, or similar goods, for each camel load on either journey 1 denarius. For a camel brought in unloaded he shall exact 1 denarius as Cilix the freedman of Caesar did.

[In Aramaic only]

The customs law of Palmyra and the wells and the salt within the city and its territory according to the regulations made in the presence of the governor Marinus.

Whoever has salt in Palmyra or the territory of Palmyra shall pay 1 as to the tax contractor for each peck. . . .

The slaughter tax must be reckoned in denarii, Germanicus Caesar having made it plain by his letter to Statilius that the taxes must be reckoned in Italian asses. The tax contractor shall exact tax under a denarius in small change according to custom. The tax is not payable on animals abandoned because they are dead. On eatables I rule that the denarius per load laid down by the law shall be exacted when they are imported or exported outside the territory. But persons who bring them to the district or from the district shall be immune, as he agreed with them. It was decided for pine kernels and similar goods which are transported for sale that the tax shall be calculated on the dry weight, as is done in other cities. For camels which are brought in from outside the territory, whether loaded or unloaded, a denarius each is payable, as his excellency Corbulo indicated in his letter to Barbarus. . . .

It was agreed that pasture dues should not be exated from the inhabitants but that 1 denarius should be payable for animals brought in from outside to graze. The animals may be branded if the tax contractor so wishes.

107. Admission fees of city councilors

Most cities had revenues inadequate for their ambitious programs of building and entertainment and relied on gifts from their rich citizens and especially from magistrates and councillors. A common custom was that these had to pay some considerable sum on being elected. In Bithynia this custom was not yet firmly established in Pliny's day, and he wishes to standardize it. As may be seen, some cities incurring heavy expenditure sometimes asked to have their councils increased, in order to harvest a larger crop of entrance fees (cf. No. 108).

107. Pliny, Letters, X. 112–13

PLINY TO TRAJAN

THE POMPEIAN law, Sir, which is observed in Pontus and Bithynia, does not direct that any money should be given by those who are elected into the city council by the censors. It has, however, been usual for such members as have been admitted, in pursuance of the privilege which you were pleased to grant to some particular cities, above their legal number, to pay one or two thousand denarii. Subsequent to this, the proconsul Anicius Maximus ordained (though indeed his edict extended to some few cities only) that those who were elected by the censors should also pay into the treasury a certain sum, which varied in different places. It remains, therefore, for your consideration, whether it would not be proper to settle a certain fixed sum for each member who is elected into the councils to pay upon his entrance; for it well becomes you, whose every word and action deserved immortality, to give laws that shall for ever be permanent.

TRAJAN TO PLINY

I can give no general directions applicable to all the cities of Bithynia, whether those who are made members of their respective councils shall pay an honorary fee upon their admittance or not. It seems best, therefore, in this case (what indeed upon all occasions is the safest way) to leave each city to its respective laws. But I rather think that those who become decurions by invitation will see to it that they stand out from the rest by their generosity.

108. Public buildings

This letter illustrates the ambitious building schemes of the cities, and the ways in which they financed them. When a building was projected, citizens were asked to promise to supply some part of it such as a column or a whole colonnade, and such promises were made legally binding by the Roman government. Other cities asked leave of the emperor to increase the size of their councils (cf. No. 107).

108. Pliny, Letters, X. *39–40*

PLINY TO TRAJAN

THE CITIZENS of Nicaea, Sir, are building a theater, which, though it is not yet finished, has already exhausted, as I am informed (for I have not examined the account myself) above ten millions of sesterces; and, what is worse, I fear to no purpose. For either from the foundation being laid in marshy ground, or that the stones themselves were decayed, the walls are cracked from top to bottom. It deserves your consideration, therefore, whether it be best to carry on this work, or entirely discontinue it; or rather, perhaps, whether it would not be most prudent absolutely to destroy it: for the foundations upon which this building is immediately supported, appear to me more expensive than solid. Several private persons have undertaken to build parts of this theater at their own expense, some engaging to erect the porticos around it, others the galleries over the pit: but this design cannot be executed, as the principal fabric is now at a standstill. This city is also rebuilding upon a more enlarged plan the gymnasium, which was burnt down before my arrival in the province. They have already been at some (and, I doubt, a fruitless) expense. The structure is not only ir-regular and ill-disposed, but the present architect (who it must be owned is a rival to the person who was first employed) asserts that the walls, though they are twenty-two feet thick, are not strong enough to support the superstructure, as they are not encrusted without, nor the intermediate space properly cemented within. The inhabitants of Claudiopolis are sinking (for I cannot call it erecting) a large public bath, upon a low spot of ground which lies at the foot of a mountain. The fund appropriated for the carrying on this work arises from the money which those additional mem-bers you were pleased to add to their senate paid (or at least are ready to pay whenever I call upon them) for their admission. As I am afraid therefore the public money in one place, and (what is infinitely more valuable than any pecuniary consideration) your benefaction in the other should be ill applied, I am obliged to desire you would send hither an architect to inspect, not only the theater, but the bath; in order to consider whether after all the expense which has already been laid out it will be better to finish them upon the present plan, or reform the one and remove the other: for otherwise we may possibly throw away our future cost, by en-deavoring not to lose what we have already expended.

TRAJAN TO PLINY

You, who are upon the spot, will best be able to consider and determine what is proper to be done concerning the theater, which the inhabitants of Nicaea are building; as for myself, it will be suffi-cient if you let me know your resolution. With respect to the particular parts of this theater which are to be raised at a private charge, you will see those engagements fulfilled, when the body of the building, to which they are to be annexed, shall be finished. These paltry Greeks are, I know, immoderately fond of gymnastic diversions, and, therefore, perhaps, the citizens of Nicaea have en-larged their fabric for this purpose beyond its due proportion: however, they must be contented with such a one as will be suffi-cient to answer their occasions.

I entirely leave it to you to persuade the Claudiopolitans as you shall think proper with relation to their bath, which they have placed, it seems, in a very improper situation. As there is no province that is not furnished with men of skill and ingenuity, you cannot possibly want architects; unless you think it the shortest way to get them from Rome, when it is generally from Greece that they come hither.

109. Slave civil servants

Municipal workers were mostly public slaves of the cities. They were employed not only for such menial tasks as are here mentioned, but as clerks and accountants and as wardens of the city jail (cf. No. 60). The higher grade slaves, at any rate, received regular salaries.

109. Pliny, Letters, X. 31–32

PLINY TO TRAJAN

As I have your permission, Sir, to address myself to you in all my doubts, you will not esteem it below your dignity to descend to those affairs which concern the administration of my post. I find there are in several cities, particularly those of Nicomedia and Nicaea, certain persons who take upon themselves to act as public slaves, and receive an annual stipend accordingly, notwithstanding they have been condemned either to the mines, the public games, or other punishments of the like nature. Having received information of this abuse, I have been long debating with myself how I should act. On the one hand, to send them back again to their respective punishments (many of them being now grown old, and behaving, as I am assured, with sobriety and modesty) would, I thought, be proceeding against them too severely; on the other, to retain convicted criminals in the public service seemed not altogether decent. I considered at the same time that to support these people in idleness would be a useless expense to the public; and to leave them to starve would be dangerous. I was obliged therefore to suspend the determination of this matter, till I could consult with you. You will be desirous, perhaps, to be informed, how it happened that these persons escaped the punishments to which they were condemned. This inquiry I have also made myself, but cannot return you any satisfactory answer. The decrees against them were indeed produced; but no record appears of their having ever been reversed. It was asserted, however, that these people were pardoned upon their petition to the proconsuls, or their legates; which seems likely enough to be the truth, as it is improbable any person should have dared to set them at liberty without authority.

You will remember you were sent into Bithynia for the particular purpose of correcting those many abuses with which it appeared to be overrun. Now none stands more in need of reformation than that criminals who have been sentenced to punishment should not only be set at liberty (as your letter informs me) without authority, but even appointed to employments, which ought alone to be exercised by persons whose characters are irreproachable. Those therefore among them who have been convicted within these ten years, and whose sentence has not been reversed by proper authority, must be sent back again to their respective punishments: but where more than ten years have elapsed since their conviction, and they are grown old and infirm, let them be disposed of in such employments as are but few degrees removed from the punishments to which they were sentenced; that is, either to attend upon the public baths, cleanse the common sewers, or repair the streets and highways, the usual offices to which such persons are assigned.

110. A city fire brigade

In western cities fire brigades were normal, but Trajan refuses to sanction one in so important a city as Nicomedia in Bithynia, owing to his fear of its becoming a focus of political agitation (cf. No. 95).

110. Pliny, Letters, X. 33–34

WHILE I was making a progress in a different part of the province, a prodigious fire broke out at Nicomedia, which not only consumed several private houses, but also two public buildings, the Hall of the Elders and the temple of Isis, though they stood on contrary sides of the street. The occasion of its spreading thus far was partly owing to the violence of the wind, and partly to the indolence of the people, who, I am well assured, stood fixed and idle spectators of this terrible calamity. The truth is, the city was not provided either with pumps, hooks, or any one single instrument proper to extinguish fires; which I have now, however, given directions to have prepared. You will consider, Sir, whether it may not be advisable to institute a company of firemen, consisting only of one hundred and fifty members. I will take care none but those of that business shall be admitted into it; and that privileges granted them shall not be extended to any other purpose. As this incorporated body will consist of so small a number, it will be easy enough to keep them under proper regulation.

TRAJAN TO PLINY

You are of opinion it would be proper to constitute a company of firemen in Nicomedia, agreeably to what has been practiced in several other cities. But it is to be remembered, that this sort of societies has greatly disturbed the peace of that province in general, and of those cities in particular. Whatever name we give them, and for whatever purposes they may be founded, they will not fail to form themselves into dangerous assemblies. It will, therefore, be safer, to provide such machines as are of service in extinguishing fires, enjoining the owners of houses to assist upon such occasions; and if it shall be necessary, to call in the help of the populace.

111. A civic school

Cities, particularly in the eastern provinces, normally maintained salaried professors of rhetoric and literature, who gave instruction to young men of university age. Civic schools were, however, rare, secondary education being usually left to private enterprise. Here Pliny promises an endowment to help pay for a school in his native city of Comum.

111. Pliny, Letters, IV. 13

I REJOICE that you are safely arrived in Rome; for though I am always desirous to see you, I am more particularly so now. I purpose to continue a few days longer at my house at Tusculum, in order to finish a work which I have upon my hands. For I am afraid, should I put a stop to this design now that it is so nearly completed, I shall find it difficult to resume it. In the meanwhile, that I may lose no time, I send this letter before me to request a favor of you, which I hope shortly to ask in person. But before I inform you what my request is, I must let you into the occasion of it. Being lately at Comum, the place of my nativity, a young lad, son to one of my neighbors, made me a visit. I asked him whether he was at school, and where? He told me he was, and at Mediolanum. And why not here? Because (said his father, who came with him) we have no teachers. "No!" said I, "Surely it nearly concerns you who are fathers (and very opportunely several of the company were so) that your sons should receive their education here rather than anywhere else. For where can they be placed more agreeably than in their own country, or instructed with more safety and less expense than at home and under the eye of their parents? Upon what very easy terms might you, by a general contribution, procure proper masters, if you would only apply toward the raising a salary for them the extraordinary expense it costs you for your sons' journeys, lodgings, and whatever else you pay for upon account of their being abroad; as pay indeed you must in such a case for everything. Though I have no children myself, yet I shall willingly contribute to a design so beneficial to (what I look upon as a child, or a parent) my country; and, therefore, I will advance a third part of any sum you shall think proper to raise for this purpose. I would take upon myself the whole expense, were I not apprehensive that my benefaction might hereafter be abused and perverted to private ends; as I have observed to be the case in several places where public foundations of this nature have been established. The single means to prevent this mischief is to leave the choice of the teachers entirely in the breast of the parents, who will be so much the more careful to determine properly, as they shall be obliged to share the expense of maintaining them. For though they may be careless in disposing of another's bounty, they will certainly be cautious how they apply their own; and will see that none but those who deserve it shall receive my money, when they must at the same time receive theirs too. Let my example then encourage you to unite heartily in this useful design; and be assured the greater the sum my share shall amount to, the more agreeable it will be to me. You can undertake nothing that will be more advantageous to your children, nor more acceptable to your country. They will by this means receive their education where they receive their birth, and be accustomed from their infancy to inhabit and affect their native soil. May you be able to procure teachers of such distinguished abilities that the neighboring towns shall be glad to draw their learning from hence; and as you now send your children to foreigners for education, may foreigners in their turn flock hither for their instruction!"

I thought proper thus to lay open to you the rise of this affair, that you might be the more sensible how agreeable it will be to me, if you undertake the office I request. I entreat you, therefore, with all the earnestness a matter of so much importance deserves, to look out, amongst the great numbers of men of letters which the reputation of your genius brings you, proper persons to whom we may apply for this purpose; but without entering into any agreement with them on my part. For I would leave it entirely free to the parents to judge and choose as they shall see proper: all the share I pretend to claim is that of contributing my care and my money. If, therefore, any one shall be found who thinks himself qualified for the undertaking, he may repair thither; but without relying upon anything but his merit.

112. A civic theater

All cities provided entertainments, horse races, athletic competitions, and, particularly in the eastern provinces, competitions in drama and music; gladiatorial shows were common in the west, less so in the east. Both athletes and musical and dramatic performers formed empire-wide guilds or congresses to maintain their privileges. The cities provided the prizes at the games, but the office of president of a competition might involve heavy expenses in hospitality. From the last sentence of the inscription it appears that companies of actors not only competed at the games but also gave other performances as they toured from city to city.

112. SEG, VII. 825

To Titus Flavius, son of Flavius, Flaccus, of the tribe Quirina, Gerrenus, who by the choice of the city became the first president of the new annual games. Decree of the sacred world congress of the artists, crowned as victors in the sacred games and their competitors, who worship Dionysus and our lord the emperor Nerva Trajan Caesar Augustus Germanicus Dacicus.

Whereas the city of Antioch upon the Chrysorrhoas elected Titus Flavius Gerrenus, a distinguished man, like his ancestors, a lover of Caesar and of his native city, known to all governors and procurators for his generous and magnificent conduct toward all, to be the president of the first annual games which the city had

voted to be held for the preservation of our lord the emperor
Nerva Trajan Caesar Augustus Germanicus Dacicus, judging the
man worthy of the purple because of his excellent character; and
he owing to his outstanding loyalty to the house of Augustus and
his affectionate benevolence to his native city, accepted the crown
with all eagerness and not only exceeded the generosity of his
ancestors by his services to the city and his generosity to the congress both corporately and individually, but also rivaled the enthusiasm of many presidents of the games who have conducted themselves most liberally toward us; for he presided with greater judgment than those who had often held the presidency, so that we felt
that this was not the first occasion on which he was presiding but
that he had been bred to the purple for many years, so skillfully
did he make proper provision for the games. For besides his impar-
tiality in awarding prizes he often received the congress publicly
with royal entertainments and never ceased continually entertaining individuals, both the defeated and the victors, and throughout
the games he served as president of the gymnasium. It was resolved
to set up his statue in the theater in which he first presided, with
the customary inscription of congress, and to enact that all competitors in games and performers at other times shall be obliged to
place wreaths on the statue and anyone that does not place a
wreath shall pay a fine of 25 denarii, at games to the congress, at
other performances to the city. It was also resolved to proclaim his
name in all cities.

113. A civic benefactor

Unlike most civic benefactors, Lucius Fabius Severus, a young senator
at Rome (the quaestorship was normally held at twenty-five), did not
give money but his services, as an advocate in his city's litigation in
the emperor's court and in support of the city's petitions to the
emperor. The privileges that he obtained again show the difficulty that
cities had in filling their magistracies and council. Tergeste (Trieste)
was a Roman colony, and ruled as subjects two tribes in the adjacent
mountains. Members of these tribes were to be allowed to hold the
magistracies and become decurions of the colony, and were to be
encouraged to do so by the grant of Roman citizenship.

113. Dessau, ILS, 6679

To LUCIUS FABIUS, son of Lucius of the tribe Pupinia Severus,
urban quaestor, the decurions and plebs of Tergeste.

On the kalends of November.

Whereas ——— Spanius Lentulus and ——— Nepos, the *duoviri* with judicial authority, spoke to the effect that the distinguished Lucius Fabius Severus had for a long time past conferred many benefits on our city, seeing that from his early youth up he has so acted that he increased in rank and eloquence by helping his native place: for he has taken and pled and won so many magnificent public cases before the best of emperors, Antoninus Pius Augustus, without any expense to our treasury, that, though he is quite young, he has rendered his country and us all, too, his debtors by the mature deeds and achievement of an old man: but now he has bestowed upon our state so great a benefit, so salutary a design and so lasting an advantage, that he has easily surpassed all his previous actions, innumerable and distinguished though they are. For the wonder of his character lies in the fact that he every day surpasses himself in his good deeds and in the protection of his country. And, therefore, although we cannot in our gratitude vie with the measure of his benefits, nonetheless, in the meanwhile as time and occasion offers—and he will often help us by his future actions—his benevolence ought to be rewarded, not to make him more eager, for a man with such a natural disposition cannot act otherwise, but that we may prove ourselves grateful to our judge, and worthy of such honors and such assistance.

As to what action they wished to be taken, they resolved as follows on the matter, Calpurnius Certus delivering the first opinion.

Whereas the eminent and distinguished Fabius Severus has embraced the cause of our city with such loyalty and affection and so watched over its interests, great and small, and exerts all his powers, that it is plain that his object is that it should be manifested not only to us but to the neighboring cities that he was born for his country only, and that his pursuit of legal studies, in which young though he is he is already a past master, and his ambition for senatorial rank, are principally for the object of making his native city both splendid and safe and secure from all injuries, by giving his advocacy sometimes before judges appointed by Caesar, sometimes before the emperor himself, to public causes, which, both by the justice of our divine emperor and by his sublime and learned speeches, he has always returned to us confirmed by victory, and recently, as is made plain in the letter of Antoninus Augustus Pius, he has successfully urged our public desire with him by obtaining the concession that the Carni and Catali, attributed to our city by the deified Augustus, in so far as they deserve it by their life and property, should be admitted through the rank of aedile to our council and thereby acquire the Roman citizenship, and has enriched our treasury and filled up our council and enlarged our whole city by this alleviation, admitting to participate in our offices and the enjoyment of the Roman citizenship all the best and richest of them, so that those who before only contributed a money revenue now perform double service in that respect by payment of the fees for office, and are available honorably to share in full with us the burdens of the decurionate, which are now heavy for a small number. To render thanks for this, seeing that such a benefit will endure for all ages, we ought if it were possible and if the modesty of our distinguished friend allowes it, all to have gone and thanked him before our best of emperors. But since we are sure that such a display of our gratitude would be burdensome to him, this certainly ought next to be done. A gilded equestrian statue should forthwith be placed in the most frequented part of our forum and this unanimous desire of ours and this decree should be engraved on its base, so that both the fame and the actions of a distinguished man may abide among our posterity. And the excellent Fabius Verus, father of Severus, should be asked, since this project is due to his own forethought, whereby he guides our city with unwearying care, and it is a greater public benefaction to have produced and nurtured such a citizen, for us and for the empire, by whose zeal we daily find ourselves more splendid and more secure, to allow himself to be sent as our envoy, to present this matter to his son, and to be instructed to present our thanks publicly to the distinguished man by our command and to bring to his notice, as the teacher of such things, the joy and good will of each and every one of us.

114. The foundation of a city

It was the regular policy of the emperors to encourage urbanization, and here we see Constantine granting the status of a city to the village of Orcistus, which was subject to the city of Nacoleia. The process begins in 324–25 with section C, the petition of the Orcistenes to the emperor, setting out their claim; in the missing part they obviously told Constantine that they were Christians. Then in section B Constantine writes to Ablabius, his praetorian prefect, granting the petition, and in section A, Ablabius notifies the Orcistenes of the emperor's decision. Section D is a letter written some five years later, confirming that Orcistus is now, despite the claim of Nacoleia, fiscally an independent unit.

114. S. Riccobono, Fontes Iuris Romani Ante Justiniani², *I. 95*

A. YOU RIGHTLY ask to obtain what you have put in your petition, the restoration of your name and dignity. Accordingly, by the intercession of the vicar, the most pious of all emperors has restored what had been mutilated to its full ancient honor, so that you and your town, protected by your diligence, may enjoy the splendor of the legal status and title for which you ask in virtue of the appended decrees.

B. My dearest Ablabius: The inhabitants of Orcistus, now a town and city, have supplied pleasing matter for our munificence, my dearest friend Ablabius. For to those whose ambition it is to found new cities or to repair the old or to restore the moribund, this petition was most welcome. For they have declared that in times past their village possessed all the splendor of a town, and was adorned with the insignia of annual magistrates, thronged with decurions and filled with people and citizens. For the place is so convenient by its situation and nature that from all directions many public roads converge on it, for all of which it is said to be a convenient intermediate station. There is there an adequate supply of water, public and private baths also, adorned with the statues of ancient emperors, and so great a population of residents. . . . Since the aforesaid place abounds with all these blessings, they declared, the people of Nacoleia had asked for it to be joined to them in times past. It is unworthy of our age that so eminent a place should lose the title of city, and contrary to the interests of the inhabitants to lose all their advantages and conveniences by the depredations of more powerful neighbours. It is the coping stone, as it were, of this edifice that all the inhabitants are said to be followers of the most sacred religion. Since they beg that our clemency should concede to them the ancient right and title of a city, as the subjoined copy of our rescript with the petition testifies, we propose as follows. They rightly ask to obtain what they have put in their petition, the restoration of their name and dignity. Accordingly, by the intercession of your gravity, we command that what had been mutilated be restored to its full ancient honor, so that they and their town, protected by their diligence, may enjoy the splendor of the legal status and title for which they ask. It is, therefore, proper that your sincerity should hasten to fulfill for the petitioners what we have promptly granted for the dignity of our age. Farewell, my dearest friend Ablabius.

C. COPY OF THE PETITION.

We seek refuge in the assistance of your piety, lords emperors Constantine Maximus Victor, forever Augustus, and Crispus, Constantine, and Constantius, noble Caesars.

Our native place Orcistus was a most ancient town from remote antiquity and originally held also the dignity of a city. It is well situated on the boundary of Galatia. For it is the meeting place of four roads, from the city of Pessinus, which is about thirty miles from our home, also from the city of Midaeum, which is likewise thirty miles from our home, and from the city of Amorium, which. . . .

Done on the day before the kalends of July at Constantinople.

D. Imperator Caesar Constantinus Maximus Gothicus victor et triumphator Augustus, and Flavius Claudius Constantinus Alamannicus and Flavius Julius Constantius the noble Caesars, to the council of the city of Orcistus, greetings.

By the grant of our indulgence the status of a city was accorded to you not only as an honor, but the privilege of your liberty is also granted. Accordingly by our present rescript we abrogate the injury of the Nacoleians which has continued beyond the benefit of our indulgence and we accede to your prayer and petition, that you shall henceforth no longer pay the money which you formerly used to contribute in respect of cultivated land. Our clemency has, therefore, written to his honor the financial officer of the diocese of Asia, who, observing the tenor of the indulgence conceded to you, will forbid the money under the aforesaid schedule to be henceforth required or demanded from you.

We wish you good health.

In the consulship of Bassus and Ablabius [A.D. 331].

115. Decurions and government posts

In the fourth century the difficulty of filling the city councils became more acute. One of the most serious drains was due to richer decurions obtaining imperial offices (which conferred immunity for life from civic offices), and, what was worse, titular sinecure imperial offices, often by corrupt means. The last abuse is now forbidden, but persons who have served as envoys of the provincial assembly to the emperor or who have otherwise deserved promotion are allowed to obtain titular offices.

115. Codex Theodosianus, XII.1.25

THE SAME AUGUSTUS.

Since there is no doubt that municipal councils have been emptied of decurions who offer as defense titles that they have bought, it is Our pleasure that all persons who have obtained the insignia of rank through patronage shall be deprived of the splendor of the undeserved honor and shall perform the customary compulsory municipal services. It is Our will, however, that the honors shall remain inviolate and undisturbed in the case of those persons who have been chosen to the office of delegate by the judgment of the provinces or who have relied upon the support of an honorable testimonial and have thus obtained the privileges and insignia of such rank.

Given on the fifth day before the kalends of November at Emesa in the consulship of Ursus and Polemius [October 28, 338].

116. Decurions and the Roman senate

An even more serious drain was due to the richer decurions becoming members of the imperial senate, for senatorial rank was hereditary and thus gave immunity to the whole family forever. By this law decurions were permitted to enter the senate, but had to remain, with their descendants, liable to hold office in their native cities.

116. Codex Theodosianus, XII. i. 122

THE SAME Augusti to Tatianus, Praetorian Prefect.

Those persons on whom We have conferred splendid magistracies and whom We have adorned with the insignia of high rank, if they do not have a municipal council to which they are bound by the tie of kinship or the bond of blood, shall be coopted into the Most Glorious Senatorial Order and that Most Noble Senate house. But the arrangement shall be different in the case of those persons who began to be decurions immediately when they were born. For such persons, indeed, shall enjoy the prerogative of the rank which has been bestowed, and they shall be adorned with the splendor of the honor that is granted to them, but they shall remain in the bosom of their municipalities, and as if dedicated to their sacred fillets, they shall guard the perennial mystery; it shall be an inexpiable sin for them to depart. In regard to their sons, moreover, adequate provision has been made that they shall remain in their ancestral municipal councils, since the license to depart has been taken from their fathers.

Given on the fourth day before the nones of September at Verona in the fourth consulship of Valentinian Augustus and the consulship of Neoterius [September 2, 390].

117. The *defensor civitatis*

By this measure Valentinian and Valens (cf. No. 19) established the office of *defensor plebis* in each city. The *defensor* possessed judicial powers in minor civil actions, and could provide cheap and prompt justice for the poor. The praetorian prefect is to select the *defensores*, subject to the emperor's approval, from former provincial governors, lawyers, and retired high civil servants (for the imperial couriers, see No. 50). Decurions and lower civil servants are excluded as they were the chief oppressors of the poor.

117. Codex Theodosianus, *I. 29. 1*

EMPERORS VALENTINIAN and Valens Augusti to Probus, Praetorian Prefect.

We have decreed very beneficially that all the plebeians of Illyricum shall be defended by the offices of patrons against the outrages of the powerful. For each and every municipality of the aforesaid diocese Your Sincerity shall provide for the selection to this office of men of suitable character, whose past lives have been praiseworthy and who have either administered provinces or have practiced as advocates, or who have completed their service among the imperial couriers or the palatines. You shall not entrust such duties to decurions; likewise, you shall not assign this service to those persons who at any time have served the office of Your Eminence or of any governors ordinary whatever. Certainly, the appointments made in each town shall be referred to Our Wisdom.

Given on the fifth day before the kalends of May in the consulship of the late Jovian and of Varronianus [April 27, 364].

118. Civic finances in the fourth century

Constantine and his son, Constantius II, confiscated the revenues of the cities, which consisted partly of local taxes, partly of rents from civic estates. The result was that the cities could not afford even to maintain their walls. Here Honorius (following the precedent of Valens and Valentinian) gives back one third of the rents, while retaining for the imperial treasury all the taxes. The loss of their internal revenues must have thrown a heavy financial burden on the decurions, since their personal charges must have become mixed (see No. 105), and must have made them even more anxious to escape from their position.

118. Codex Theodosianus, V. 14. 35

EMPERORS ARCADIUS and Honorius Augusti to Hadrianus, Count of the Sacred Largesses.

It has been determined that one third of the rent which is paid annually from parcels of land and estates of a municipality is sufficient for the restoration of the public walls. Therefore We permit nothing at all to be taken in the name of the municipalities from the public taxes, which always used to furnish entirely the expenses of Our treasury.

Given on the eighth day before the ides of August in the consulship of Olybrius and Probinus [August 6, 395].

IX. Taxation

119. The census in Syria

Augustus, following the lead given by Caesar in the province of Asia, abolished the tithe system wherever it prevailed and substituted for it fixed direct taxes, a poll tax (*tributum capitis*) and a tax on land and other property (*tributum soli*). The assessment of these taxes involved censuses to count the population and to assess their property, and we have records of many censuses held in various parts of the empire under Augustus. These provincial censuses, it may be noted, have no connection with the Roman censuses recorded in No. 1, §8, which affected Roman citizens only, who were mostly tax free. The Quirinius here mentioned is the same governor of Syria who held the census in Judaea in A.D. 6, during which Jesus is said to have been born. Quintus Aemilius held all the magistracies in his native city before going on to hold two equestrian commissions. Chief of engineers was by now a sinecure equestrian post.

119. Dessau, ILS, 2,683

QUINTUS AEMILIUS, son of Quintus, Secundus, of the Palatine tribe. I received decorations in the camp of the deified Augustus under Publius Sulpicius Quirinius, legate of Caesar of Syria, and was prefect of the First Augustan Cohort and the Second Naval Cohort. I also by order of Quirinius held the census of the city of Apamea, 117,000 citizens. I also was sent by Quirinius against the Ituraeans of Mount Lebanon and took one of their forts. And before my military service I was entered at the treasury as chief of engineers by two consuls, and was quaestor, twice aedile, and twice *duumvir*, and *pontifex* in my colony. My son Quintus Aemilius, son of Quintus, Secundus, of the Palatine tribe, and my freedwoman Aemilia Chia are buried here. This tomb does not go to my further heirs.

120. The census in Egypt

This edict dates from A.D. 104. It is interesting that in Egypt, as in Judaea in A.D. 6, taxpayers who were resident elsewhere had to return to their original homes for registration.

120. W. Wilcken, Chrestomathie, I. 202

Gaius Vibius Maximus, prefect of Egypt, says: The house-to-house census having started, it is essential that all persons who for any reason whatsoever are absent from their homes be summoned to return to their own hearths, in order that they may perform the customary business of registration and apply themselves to the cultivation which concerns them. Knowing, however, that some of the people from the country are needed by our city [Alexandria], I desire all those who think they have a satisfactory reason for remaining here to register themselves before . . . Festus, *praefectus alae*, whom I have appointed for this purpose, from whom those who have shown their presence to be necessary shall receive signed permits in accordance with this edict up to the 30th of the present month Epeiph. . . .

121. The census returns

These extracts from early-third-century lawyers give details of the assessment for poll tax and land tax, which included other forms of property such as slaves. The third extract deals with the varying privileges of Roman colonies. The soil of Italy was tax free, and some colonies in the provinces enjoyed this "Italian right." Others, like Antioch, had no privileges. Others, like Caesarea, might receive partial immunity. A *iugerum* is ⅝ acres.

121. Digest, L.xv. 4, 8 §5–7

ULPIAN, ON THE CENSUS, BOOK II

It is necessary to state one's age in the census, as age sometimes relieves certain persons of the burden of tribute, e.g., in Syria males are liable to poll tax from fourteen years of age, females from twelve, up to sixty-five; age is reckoned as at the date of the census. Immunity granted to things does not lapse, as was correctly declared in a rescript of our present emperor to Paelignianus, since immunity granted to persons is extinguished with the person, but that granted to things is never extinguished.

ULPIAN, ON THE CENSUS, BOOK III

In the schedule of the census it is laid down that land shall be entered in the census as follows: the name of each farm, in what city it is and in what district, and the two nearest neighbors; arable, how many *iugera*, which have been sown in the last ten years;

vineyards, how many vines; olive yards, how many *iugera* and how many trees; meadow, how many *iugera*, which were mown in the last ten years; pasture, how many *iugera* approximately; also woods. The person who makes the declaration must estimate everything. The census officer, in accordance with his duty, should admit equitable claims for remission in so far as the owner was unable for certain reasons to enjoy the quantity entered in the public records. Accordingly, if part of the land has been destroyed by a landslide, he should receive a remission from the census officer. If vines have died or trees withered, it is inequitable that the original figure should be entered in the census. But if he has felled trees or vines, he is ordered to declare the number which existed at the time of the census, unless he satisfies the census officer of his reason for felling them. A man who has land in another city must make a declaration in the city in which the land is, since the tribute for land must be raised in that city in whose territory it is occupied.

Although in certain cases benefits of immunity granted to persons are extinguished with the person, nevertheless when it is granted to places or cities generally, it appears that immunity so granted is translated to later generations. If when I occupy a farm, I make a declaration, but another fails to make a declaration, it is agreed that he has a right of action.

In declaring slaves, it is to be observed that their race, age, function, and craft must be declared. The owner ought also to declare in the census fish ponds and harbors. If there are any salt pans on the estate, they, too, must be declared on the census. If anyone fails to declare the tenant of a house or of land, he commits an offense under the census. What was born after the assessment of the census or subsequently acquired can be entered on the returns before the census is completed. If anyone asks to be allowed to correct his census, and then after obtaining leave discovers that he need not have asked for it, because no correction was required, he suffers no prejudice for having asked to correct his census; this has been frequently laid down by rescript.

PAULUS, ON THE CENSUS, BOOK II

The deified Antoninus made Antioch a colony, reserving the tribute. Our present emperor Antoninus made the city of Emisa a colony of Italian right. The deified Vespasian made Caesarea a colony, not adding that it should be of the Italian right, but remitted the poll tax; but the deified Titus ruled that this meant that the soil was immune, too.

122. An Egyptian census return

In this Egyptian papyrus we have a full census return, made in A.D. 189, of a poor man with all his family and lodgers; the only property which he registers is the tenth part of a house. As children began to be liable to tax at the age of fourteen in Egypt, censuses were held every fourteen years and everyone was registered from birth. Births and deaths in the interim were supposed to be reported, but as appears from this document, this rule was often neglected. Note that two of his marriages are between brother and sister.

122. W. Wilcken, Chrestomathie, *I. 203*

To HARPOCRATION also called Hierax, royal scribe of the Arsinoite nome, section of Heraclides, from Herodes, son of Heron, grandson of Heraclides, mother Eirene from the capital, registered in the Ward of the Treasuries.

I own in the Ward of the Bithynians and Other Places the tenth part of a house, in which I reside and register myself and my household for the house-to-house registration of the past twentyeighth year of Aurelius Commodus Antoninus Caesar. I am the aforesaid Herodes, weaver, liable to poll tax, aged fifty, and my wife Eirene, who is also my sister, aged fifty-four, and the children of both, Heron, aged twenty-nine, and another, Nilus, goldsmith, aged twenty-five, and Serapion registered in the subsequent births, aged ———, and Heraclides, aged nine, and Euporas, aged seven, both not registered in the subsequent births, and ——— aged twenty-three, and Neiliaena, wife of Heron, aged ———, and Thaisarion, aged seventeen, and the children of Heron and Neiliaena, Herodes and Tryphon, twins aged one, not registered in the subsequent births, and Nilus' wife Thermutharion, daughter of Castor, granddaughter of Heron, mother Isidora from the capital, aged twenty-nine, and children of both ———, aged thirteen, and Heron aged ———, both not registered in subsequent births, and the children of my deceased brother, Heraclides, Heron, mother Eirene, beater, aged thirty-four, and Apion of the same mother, workman, aged twenty-four, and Heraclides, goldsmith, aged nineteen, and Thaisarion, wife of Heron, aged seventeen, and the daughter of both, Syra, aged one. And lodgers Nilus, son of

Demetrius, grandson of ——, mother Thaisarion, liable to poll tax, donkey driver, aged forty-four, and his wife who is also his sister, Eirene, aged fifty-two, and the son of both, Castor, not registered in subsequent births, áged eight, and the brothers by the same father and mother of the aforesaid Thermutharion, Heron, beater, liable to poll tax, aged thirty-four, and Melas, gardener, aged thirty-two, and Heron, son of Heraclides, grandson of Heron, mother Didyme, liable to poll tax, workman, aged twenty-six, and his sister by the same father and mother ——, aged thirteen, all [deleted] most of them registered with me in the register of the fourteenth year of Marcus Aurelius Antoninus in the aforesaid Ward of the Treasuries. I have made the return. [In another hand] I Herodes make the return. Year twenty-nine of Aurelius Commodus Antoninus Caesar.

123. The poll tax

Popillius Python was high priest of the provincial imperial cult, and held the games, which were an important part of this cult, in a very grand style, and showed lavish hospitality to the members of the provincial assembly (cf. No. 85). Among his other benefactions to the province, he paid the whole poll tax due from its inhabitants.

123. SEG, XVII. 315

THE HIGH priest of the Augusti for life and president of the games of the common council of Macedonia, Quintus Popillius Python, who went as envoy for his native city Beroea to the deified Nerva to urge that it alone should be the guardian of the temple of the Augusti, and have the rank of metropolis, and succeeded in his mission; and in the period of his high priesthood gave the poll tax on behalf of the province and repaired roads at his private expense and promised and performed games, both dramatic and athletic, equal to the Actian Games, with prizes of a talent, and gave fights of wild beasts of all kinds local and foreign, and fights of gladiators, and also made sales of corn at a reduced price and brought down the price in times of stress, and received the province at every congress with general distributions of gifts throughout the whole period of his high priesthood, and in the management of the gymnasium proved himself a useful citizen to everybody in general, and obliging to individuals.

The tribe Peucastice to its benefactor.

124. The land tax

This deed of sale of a house in Dacia shows that the census of property was held at regular and short intervals; otherwise the vendor would not have agreed to pay the tax on the house until the next census.

124. S. Riccobono, Fontes Iuris Romani Ante Justiniani², *III. 90*

ANDUEIA, SON of Bato, bought and received in ownership half a house, on the right hand as you go in, which is in Albernum Maius, village of Pirustae, neighbors Plator Acceptianus and Ingenuus son of Callistus, for three hundred denarii from Veturius Valens.

Andueia, son of Bato, shall lawfully hold that half of a house which is in question with its walls, fences, boundaries, entries, doors, and windows, as it is secured with nails and in the best condition.

If anyone shall evict Andueia, the son of Bato, from that house or part of it, so that he and those whom it concerns are not allowed properly to hold, possess, or occupy it, then Veturius Valens promises in good faith to give to Andueia, son of Bato, such sum as he in good faith claims to be properly given, in as much as he is not allowed so to do. And for the half of the said house Veturius Valens has received from Andueia, son of Bato, and acknowledges that he holds the price of three hundred denarii.

It was agreed between them that Veturius Valens should pay the tribute for the said house until the next census. Done at Albernum Maius, the day before the nones of May, in the consulship of Quintillus and Priscus [A.D. 159.]

[Signatures of six witnesses and the vendor]

125. Customs

Although under the principate the direct taxes, whose amount was calculable in advance, were collected by officials appointed by the cities, the indirect taxes, whose yield was unpredictable, were still farmed to companies of contractors. The principal indirect tax was the customs dues, levied at 25 per cent at the imperial frontiers, and at 2½ per cent or 2 per cent at ports and inland barriers within the empire. The last sentence shows that ships were assessed for direct tax, presumably under *tributum soli*.

125. *Tacitus*, Annals, *XIII. 50–51*

THAT SAME year, repeated demands on the part of the people, who
denounced the excessive greed of the revenue contractors, made
Nero doubt whether he should not order the repeal of all indirect
taxes, and so confer a most splendid boon on the human race. But
this sudden impulse was checked by the senators, who, having first
heartily praised the grandeur of his conception, pointed out that
the dissolution of the empire must ensue if the revenues which supported the state were to be diminished; for as soon as the customs
were swept away, there would follow a demand for the abolition
of the direct taxes. Many companies for the collection of the indirect taxes had been formed by consuls and tribunes, when the
freedom of the Roman people was still in its vigor, and arrangements were subsequently made to insure an exact correspondence
between the amount of income and the necessary disbursements.
Certainly some restraint, they admitted, must be put on the cupid-
ity of the revenue contractors, that they might not by new
oppressions bring into odium what for so many years had been
endured without complaint.

Accordingly the emperor issued an edict that the regulations
about every tax, which had hitherto been kept secret, should be
published; that claims which had been dropped should not be
revived after a year; that the praetor at Rome, the propraetor or
proconsul in the provinces, should give judicial precedence to all
cases against the contractors; that soldiers should retain their immunities except when they traded for profit, with other very
equitable arrangements, which for a short time were maintained
and were subsequently disregarded. However, the abolition of the
two per cent and two-and-a-half per cent surcharges, as well as
others bearing names invented by the contractors to cover their
illegal exactions remains in force. In our transmarine provinces the
conveyance of corn was rendered less costly, and it was decided
that merchant ships should not be assessed with their owner's
property, and that no tax should be paid on them.

126. Fines and confiscations

The Special Account was the name given in Egypt to a tax department
(and its chief) which dealt with confiscations and fines (see No. 78).

Below are some of the clauses of a schedule of rules and precedents made to guide the Special Account. It appears from the document that the Roman government systematically exploited not only the census and passport regulations but all the complicated legal rules governing wills, inheritances, dowries, and personal status in order to confiscate the property involved in any illegal transaction. It is noteworthy that Egyptians were allowed to marry their sisters (like Herodes in No. 122) and were only forbidden to do so if they became Roman citizens (§23). The Latins mentioned in §§22, 26 are irregularly manumitted freedman; the class was created by the Augustan legislation restricting manumission. The rules laid down in §§24-32 are derived from the Augustan legislation to encourage marriage and families (see No. 10).

126. BGU, V. 1210

OF THE list of directions which the deified Augustus delivered to the administration of the Special Account, with the additions made to it from time to time either by the emperors or the senate or the prefects or the Special Accounts of the day, I have appended for you a summary of the articles in common use, in order that applying your memory to the simplified form of exposition you may easily master the questions.

5. Property bequeathed by Alexandrians to persons not qualified is given to those who can legally inherit from them, if such there be and if they claim it at law.

6. An Alexandrian may not bequeath to his wife, if he has no offspring by her, more than a fourth part of his estate; and if he has children by her, he may not allot to his wife a larger share than what he bequeaths to each of his sons.

7. All wills which are not in the form of public instruments are invalid.

8. If to a Roman will is added a clause saying, "Whatever bequests I make in Greek codicils shall be valid," it is not admissible, for a Roman is not permitted to write a Greek will.

16. All property which is bequeathed to freedmen of Romans with the stipulation that it is to descend to their offspring is confiscated on the decease of the recipients if it be proved that no offspring had yet been born when the bequest was written.

17. Property left to provide sacrifices to the departed is confiscated when there are no longer any persons to take charge of them.

18. Inheritances left in trust by Greeks to Romans or by Romans to Greeks were confiscated by the deified Vespasian; nevertheless those acknowledging their trust have received half.

19. Bequests made to freedmen who have not yet acquired legal emancipation are confiscated. It is legal emancipation if the person freed is over thirty years old.

20. Bequests made to one who as a slave was put in chains and was afterwards freed or who was freed when not yet thirty years old are confiscated.

21. One who was freed under thirty years of age by receiving manumission through the prefect counts as one who was freed when over thirty.

22. The property of deceased Latins is given to their patrons and to the sons and daughters and heirs of these; and bequests made by those who have not yet acquired legal Roman freedom are confiscated.

23. Romans are not permitted to marry their sisters or their aunts, but marriage with their brother's daughters has been conceded. Pardalas indeed, when a brother married a sister, confiscated the property.

24. The dowry brought by a Roman woman over fifty years of age to a Roman husband under sixty years of age is after death confiscated by the Treasury.

25. That likewise is confiscated which is brought by a woman under fifty years of age to a husband over sixty.

26. And if a Latin woman over fifty brings any property to a husband over sixty, it is likewise confiscated.

27. Whatever property a Roman sixty years old, who has neither child nor wife, inherits, is confiscated. If he has a wife but no children and declares his position, he is allowed to take half.

28. If a woman is fifty years old, she does not inherit; if she is less and has three children, she inherits, but in the case of a freed-woman, if she has four children.

29. A freeborn Roman woman having property of 20,000 sestertii pays one-hundreth yearly so long as she is unmarried, and a freedwoman possessing 20,000 sestertii pays the same until she marries.

30. Inheritances left to Romman women possessing 50,000 sestertii, if unmarried and childless, are confiscated.

31. A Roman woman is permitted to leave to her husband the tenth part of what she possesses; anything more is confiscated.

32. Romans possessing more than 100,000 sestertii, if unmarried and childless, do not inherit, but those who have less inherit.

33. A Roman woman is not permitted to bequeath outside of the so-called *coemptio*. A legacy left by a Roman woman to a Roman girl who was a minor was confiscated.

34. Soldiers in service and after leaving service have been allowed to dispose of their property both by Roman and Greek wills and to use what words they choose; but in every case they must leave it to fellow nationals and to those to whom it is permissable.

35. Children and kinsmen of soldiers who die intestate are permitted to inherit from them, if the claimants are of the same nationality.

53. Egyptian women married to discharged soldiers are, if they formally style themselves Romans, subject to the article on nonconformity to status.

54. A discharged soldier's daughter who became a Roman was not allowed by Ursus to inherit from her mother who was an Egyptian.

55. If an Egyptian serves in a legion without being detected, he returns after his discharge to the Egyptian status. Discharged oarsmen return likewise, except only those belonging to the fleet of Misenum.

56. Soldiers who have not received a legal discharge, if they style themselves Romans, are fined a quarter of their property.

58. Persons who in the household censuses have not registered themselves and those whom they ought are fined a quarter of their property, and if they are reported not to have registered on two occasions, they are sentenced to the same fine doubled.

59. Romans and Alexandrians who have not registered those whom they ought, whether one person or more, are sentenced to a fine of one quarter.

60. Those who have failed to register slaves suffer confiscation of the slaves only.

61. The offspring [?] of unregistered slaves is given to the masters, if they have no means of support except only the slaves.

62. Soldiers on active service are not held responsible if unregistered, but their wives and children are called to account.

63. Persons called to account for not having registered at the last census are excused if the additional subject for registration was under three years old.

64. Cases of persons departing by sea without a pass are now under the jurisdiction of the prefect.

65. Slaves exported owing to their master's ignorance were sold.
66. Persons permitted to depart by sea who sail without a pass are fined a third of their property, and if they export slaves of their own without a pass they suffer confiscation of the whole.
67. Persons who by registration or sale alter the status of house-born slaves of Egyptian origin with a view to their departing by sea have suffered confiscation sometimes of their whole property, sometimes of the half, sometimes of the quarter, and penalties have been ordained against those accessory. But the house-born slaves' maternal descent is not investigated, even if their mothers are not Egyptian.
68. A Roman who departed by sea without having received his departure papers in full was sentenced to a fine of ———— talents.
69. An Egyptian woman who sent out slaves by way of Pelusium along with her sons and . . . was sentenced to a fine of one talent, 3,000 drachmae.

127. Galerius' census

This is a highly colored account by Lactantius of the census carried out by Galerius, the Caesar of Diocletian (293–305), who later succeeded him as Augustus in the East (305–311). The census had apparently been allowed to lapse in the troubled period of the third century, and Diocletian and his colleagues carried out systematic new censuses. Normally the urban population was not subject to poll tax under the later empire and, therefore, not counted in the census. Galerius' attempt to tax them was short-lived.

127. *Lactantius*, de mortibus persecutorum, *XXIII*

THE GREATEST public calamity and general sorrow was the census imposed on the provinces and cities. Census officers were posted everywhere and under their activity everything was like a hostile invasion or grim captivity. The fields were measured sod by sod, vines and trees were numbered, animals of every kind were written down, the heads of men were counted, the urban and the rural poor were contained in the cities, all the squares were filled with crowds of families, everyone was there with his children and slaves. Torture and blows reverberated, sons were hanged in their parents' presence, the most faithful slaves were tortured to inform against their masters, wives against husbands. If they reported everything they were tortured to incriminate themselves, and when fear had won the day, things which they did not possess were entered in their names. No excuse was accepted for old age or ill health. The sick and feeble were noted down, their ages were recorded, years were added to children, taken away from the aged. Everything was full of misery and lamentation. What the ancients did to the conquered by right of war, he dared to do to Romans and to Roman subjects because his parents had been subject to the census, which the victorious Trajan imposed as a penalty on the constantly rebellious Dacians. After this, money was paid for heads and a price was given for life. But he did not trust the same census officials, but others were sent to succeed them, as though they could find more, and the returns were always being doubled, not that they found anything, but that they added what they wished, to justify their appointment. Meanwhile, animals were perishing and men were dying, but tribute was paid for the dead nonetheless, so that no one could either live or die gratis. There only remained beggars from whom nothing could be exacted: their misery and misfortune made them safe from all kind of injury.

128. Diocletian's indiction

By this edict, issued in A.D. 297, the prefect of Egypt announces Diocletian's new system of taxation. There was a poll tax in money on the adult rural population and a land tax in kind. For the former the population was assessed in heads (*capita*). In some provinces each person was a *caput*, in others a woman was half a *caput* or did not count (as in Egypt). For the land tax every farm was assessed as so many tax units, usually called *iuga*, according to its area and the agricultural use and quality of the land. In Egypt the traditional land unit, the *arura* (two thirds of an acre) was used, and there were separate rates for vineyard, olive yard and arable. Later *capita* (persons) were equated with *iuga* (land) and the total of *capita* plus *iuga* formed the assessed value of a farm. The working of this system is illustrated in No. 74, where soldiers entitled to immunity on four *capita*, if not paying tax on four persons, may deduct the tax due on the lacking persons from their land tax.

The rate of tax on each *iugum* and *caput* varied from year to year and was announced in the annual indiction (cf. No. 130), the first budget in the history of finance.

128. A. E. R. Boak and H. C. Youtie, The Archive of Aurelius Isidorus, No. 1

ARISTIUS OPTATUS, prefect of Egypt, says:

Our most providential emperors, Diocletian and Maximian Augusti and Constantius and Maximian [Galerius], most noble Caesars, having seen that the levies of the public taxes take place in such a way that some people get off lightly and some are overburdened, have determined to root out this most evil and pernicious practice in the interest of their provincials and to lay down a salutary rule whereby the levies shall be made. I have therefore publicly given notice how much has been assessed for each *arura* according to the quality of the land and how much on each head of the peasants, and from what age and to what age, according to their published divine edict and the schedule annexed thereto, and I have issued copies of them in my edict. So the provincials, seeing that they have received great benefits, must take care that they make their payment with all speed according to the divine regulations and do not wait to be compelled. All must fulfill their obligations with the greatest zeal, and if anyone be found doing otherwise after such great benefits he will be punished.

129. The indiction under Julian

It was a vice of the taxation system that supplementary budgets (often called *superindictiones*) were often levied when the original indiction had been underestimated, or when there were arrears in collection. Another vice was that imperial officials, instead of merely supervising the collection of the taxes by the city magistrates, as the law laid down, themselves took over the work and used their superior authority to extort more than was due from the taxpayer.

129. Ammianus Marcellinus, XVII. 3

It was now expected that a number of tribes would unite in greater force, and therefore the prudent Julian, bearing in mind the uncertainties of war, became very anxious and full of care. And as he thought that the truce lately made, though not free from trouble and not of long duration, still gave him opportunity to remedy the grievous losses of the landowners, he began to remodel the arrangements about tribute.

When Florentius, the praetorian prefect, having taken an estimate of everything, affirmed that whatever deficiency there might be in the regular tax he would be able to make good by a supplementary levy, Julian, deprecating this practice, determined to lose his own life rather than permit it. For he knew that the wounds inflicted by such extortions, or, as I should rather call them, confiscations, are incurable, and have often reduced provinces to extreme destitution. Indeed such conduct, as will be related here-after, utterly lost us Illyricum.

When, owing to this resolution of his, the praetorian prefect exclaimed that it could not be endured that he, to whom the emperor had entrusted the chief authority in this matter, should be thus distrusted, Julian attempted to appease him, showing by exact and accurate calculations that the regular tax was not only enough, but more than enough to provide all the necessary supplies. And when some time afterward an edict for a supplementary tax was, nevertheless, presented to him by Florentius, he refused to sign or even read it; and threw it on the ground; and when warned by letters from the emperor (written on receiving the prefect's report) not to act in so embarrassing a manner, lest he should seem to be diminishing the authority of Florentius, Julian wrote in answer that it was a matter to be thankful for, if a province that had been devastated in every direction could still pay its regular taxes, without demanding from it any extraordinary contributions, which indeed no punishments could extort from men in a state of destitution: and then, and from that time forward, owing to the firmness of one man, no one ever attempted to extort anything in Gaul beyond the regular taxes.

The Caesar had also in another affair set an example wholly unprecedented, entreating the prefect to entrust to him the government of the second Belgic province, which was oppressed by manifold evils; on the special and single condition that no official either belonging to the prefect or to the provincial governor should force anyone to pay anything. And the whole people whom he thus took under his care, comforted and relieved by this mildness, paid all the taxes due from them before the appointed day, without any demand being made upon them.

130. The indiction in the fifth century

This law shows that the rate of tax varied from year to year, and orders the publication in advance of a preliminary notice to the indiction.

130. Codex Theodosianus, *XI. 5. 3*

EMPERORS THEODOSIUS and Valentinian Augusti to Isidorus, Praetorian Prefect.

Since it appears to be advantageous to the landholders of all the district of Egypt, a preliminary tax rate announcement shall be published before the kalends of May in appropriate places. This shall be done so that before the regular tax rate is sent, the taxpayers may not be compelled through ignorance to pay on the scale of the previous year amounts which later perhaps the event may challenge as undue, after the regular tax rate announcement is issued. In all particulars the finance clerks of your exalted office shall fulfill Our salutary orders, so that at the risk of the office staff of the augustal prefect and of the office staff of the governor and of the *defensor* this ordinance shall come to the knowledge of all, by being posted for a period of two months in the most frequented places.

Given on the day before the nones of June at Constantinople in the consulship of Isidorus and Senator [June 4, 436].

131. The clothing levy

In addition to the tax in food stuffs (wheat, barley, meat, wine, and oil) for army rations, there was a tax in clothing for military uniforms. Being an expensive item, one garment was assessed on a large number of taxable units of land or persons (or sometimes land only). In the oriental diocese it appears that a gold tax was levied to pay for compulsory purchase of garments and that uniforms could be set off against this tax.

131. Codex Theodosianus, *VII. 6. 3*

EMPERORS VALENS, Gratian and Valentinian Augusti to Modestus, Praetorian Prefect.

The provinces of Thrace shall contribute one unit of clothing for each twenty land tax units or personal tax units. Scythia and Moesia, meanwhile, shall make an annual payment of one unit of clothing for each thirty land tax units or personal tax units. Throughout Egypt and the districts of the Orient one unit of clothing shall be furnished for each thirty land tax units; throughout the dioceses of Asia and Pontus the annual clothing tax shall be paid according to the same number of personal or land tax units, in such a way that in the Orient the provinces, except Osroena and Isauria, shall enjoy the privilege of compensation under the title of gold for purchase, which is paid for each land tax unit. For it is established that the latter provinces do not pay gold for purchase.

Given on the fifth day before the ides of August at Hierapolis in the fourth consulship of Gratian Augustus and the consulship of Merobaudes [August 9, 377].

132. Commutation of taxes in kind

Taxes in kind were gradually commuted into gold during the late fourth and early fifth century, and similarly the payments in kind to the troops were changed into gold. In this law the tax of uniforms has been entirely converted into gold, and the issue of uniform likewise, but a small part of the tax is paid to the state weaving factories to produce uniforms for recruits and private soldiers.

132. Codex Theodosianus, *VII. 6. 5*

EMPERORS HONORIUS and Theodosius Augusti to Asclepiodotus, Praetorian Prefect.

The tax payable in military clothing commuted into money shall be exacted from the taxpayers, and, of course, paid into the sacred largesses. Five sixths of it shall be issued to our gallant soldiers in money, but the sixth portion shall be received by the weavers of Our Clemency for the aforesaid weaving, without any burden either on them or on the state, and this part shall be issued to the recruits and common soldiers in clothing which it is evident that they greatly need.

Given on the seventh day before the ides of March at Constantinople in the consulship of Asclepiodotus and Marinianus [March 9, 423].

133. Liability to the *collatio lustralis*

Constantine instituted a tax in gold and silver to be levied on merchants and craftsmen. It is here laid down that peasants who sell their own produce and rural craftsmen are exempt. This tax, though it produced little revenue, proved very oppressive to those who paid it, who were mostly very poor. It also offended Christian sentiment because it was levied on the earnings of prostitutes. It was finally abolished by the emperor Anastasius in 497.

133. Codex Theodosianus, *XIII. 1. 10*

EMPERORS VALENTINIAN, Valens, and Gratian Augusti to Italicus, Vicar of Italy.

Neither the tenants of the estates of Our privy purse nor any other rustics shall be disquieted on account of the produce which grows customarily in their fields. We decree that also those persons who seek and maintain their livelihood by manual labor, such as potters and carpenters, shall be free from the burden of such tax payment. In this way only those of the rustic common people who in view of their merchandise and assets of business are counted among the merchants shall assume the lot of a tradesman, since they are not held to the cultivation of their fields by a zeal previously engendered in them, but are involved by their acquired mode of life and by their preference in the buying and selling of goods.

Given on the nones of February at Milan in the third consulship of Gratian and the consulship of Equitius [February 5, 374].

134. The collection of the *collatio lustralis*

The *collatio lustralis* was levied at intervals of five years because the gold and silver was required for the donatives made to the army every five years. This law is of interest as showing that merchants and craftsmen were organized in their own guilds and separate from the decurions or city councilors who were normally landowners.

134. Codex Theodosianus, *XIII. 1. 17*

THE SAME Augusti to Januarinus, consular of Numidia.

We are not ignorant of the fact that the five yearly tax payment in gold is paid by merchants, and since the responsibility for tax assessment customarily reverts to those persons who are constrained by the necessity of the tax payment, decurions shall not be subject to this burden. Merchants shall know, therefore, that they must select supervisors from their own guilds, as is done in almost all municipalities, without any diminution of the resources of Our treasury; and the assessment of this alien tax shall be removed from the decurions.

Given on the day before the nones of June at Milan in the consulship of Theodorus [June 4, 399].

X. *Justice*

135. The senate as a high court

Under the republic, criminal charges were tried by jury courts under
the presidency of praetors; these are alluded to in the last sentence of
Tiberius' speech, and continued to function down into the second
century. Here we see two alternative criminal courts, the emperor,
sitting according to Roman usage with assessors (cf. Nos. 136–37),
and the senate under the presidency of the consuls (cf. Nos. 83–84).
The latter court is firmly attested under Augustus, the former is
assumed in this passage to exist early in Tiberius' reign (A.D. 20). The
accuser had, it will be seen, the choice of court, but the emperor (or
the senate) could refuse jurisdiction. The senatorial court was usually
used for crimes of senators and political crimes.

135. Tacitus, Annals, *III. 10–12*

NEXT DAY, Fulcinius Trio asked the consuls' leave to prosecute
Piso. It was contended against him by Vitellius and Veranius and
the others who had been the companions of Germanicus, that this
was not Trio's proper part, and that they themselves meant to
report their instructions from Germanicus, not as accusers, but as
deponents and witnesses to facts. Trio, abandoning the prosecution
on this count, obtained leave to accuse Piso's previous career, and
the emperor was requested to undertake the trial. To this even the
accused did not object, fearing as he did the bias of the people and
of the senate; while Tiberius, he knew, was resolute enough to
despise report, and was also entangled in his mother's complicity.
Truth, too, would be more easily distinguished from perverse mis-
representation by a single judge, while a number would be swayed
by hatred and ill will.

Tiberius was not unaware of the formidable difficulty of the
inquiry and of the rumors by which he was himself assailed.
Having, therefore, summoned a few intimate friends, he listened to
the threatening speeches of the prosecutors and to the pleadings of
the accused, and finally referred the whole case to the senate.

Drusus, meanwhile, on his return from Illyricum, though the senate had voted him an ovation for the submission of Maroboduus and the successes of the previous summer, postponed the honor and entered Rome. Then the defendant sought the advocacy of Lucius Arruntius, Marcus Vinicius, Asinius Gallus, Aeserninus Marcellus, and Sextus Pompeius, and on their declining for different reasons, Marcus Lepidus, Lucius Piso, and Livineius Regulus became his counsel, amid the excitement of the whole country, which wondered how much fidelity would be shown by the friends of Germanicus, on what the accused rested his hopes, and how far Tiberius would repress and hide his feelings. Never were the people more keenly interested; never did they indulge themselves more freely in secret whispers against the emperor or in the silence of suspicion.

On the day the senate met, Tiberius delivered a speech of studied moderation. "Piso," he said, "was my father's legate and friend, and was appointed by myself, on the advice of the senate, to assist Germanicus in the administration of the East. Whether he there had provoked the young prince by wilful opposition and rivalry, and had rejoiced at his death or wickedly destroyed him, is for you to determine with minds unbiased. Certainly if a subordinate oversteps the bounds of duty and of obedience to his commander, and has exulted in his death and in my affliction, I shall hate him and exclude him from my house, and I shall avenge a personal quarrel without resorting to my power as emperor. If, however, a crime is discovered which ought to be punished, whoever the murdered man may be, it is for you to give just reparation both to the children of Germanicus and to us, his parents.

"Consider this, too, whether Piso dealt with the armies in a revolutionary and seditious spirit; whether he sought by intrigue popularity with the soldiers; whether he attempted to repossess himself of the province by arms, or whether these are falsehoods which his accusers have published with exaggeration. For to what purpose did they strip the corpse and expose it to the pollution of the vulgar gaze, and circulate a story among foreigners that he was destroyed by poison, if all this is still doubtful and requires investigation? For my part, I sorrow for my son and shall always sorrow for him; still I would not hinder the accused from producing all the evidence which can relieve his innocence or convict Germanicus of any unfairness, if such there was. And I implore you not to take as proven charges alleged, merely because the case is intimately bound up with my affliction. Do you, whom ties of blood or your own true-heartedness have made his advocates, help him in his peril, every one of you, as far as each man's eloquence and diligence can do so. To like exertions and like persistency I would urge the prosecutors. In this, and in this only, will we place Germanicus above the laws, by conducting the inquiry into his death in this house instead of in the forum, and before the senate instead of before a court of jurors. In all else let the case be tried as simply as others. Let no one heed the tears of Drusus or my own sorrow, or any stories invented to our discredit."

136. The imperial high court under Trajan

Here we see Trajan trying three criminal cases. The emperor makes it plain that he would not normally take ordinary adultery cases, only those where military officers were concerned. He is willing to take the forgery case similarly, because one of the accused is an imperial procurator.

136. Pliny, Letters, VI. 31

I RECEIVED lately the greatest pleasure in being summoned to Centumcellae (as it is now called) by Caesar to attend him as one of his assessors. Could anything indeed afford a higher pleasure than to see the emperor exercising his justice, his wisdom, and his affability, even in retirement, where those virtues are most observable? Various were the points brought in judgment before him, which proved, in so many different instances, the great abilities of the judge. The cause of Claudius Ariston came on first. He is an Ephesian nobleman, of great munificence and unambitious popularity, whose virtues having rendered him obnoxious to a set of people of far different characters, they had spirited up an informer against him, of the same infamous stamp with themselves; but he was honorably acquitted.

The next day, the cause of Gallita, accused of adultery, was determined. Her husband, who is a military tribune, was upon the point of offering himself as a candidate for office at Rome, but she had disgraced both him and herself by an intrigue with a centurion. The husband informed the consular legate, who wrote to the emperor concerning it. Caesar, having examined the proofs, cashiered the centurion, and sentenced him to banishment. It remained that some punishment should be inflicted likewise upon the other party, as it is a crime of which both must necessarily be equally guilty. But the husband's affection for his wife inclined him to drop that part of the prosecution, not without some suspicion of connivance; for he continued to live with her even after he had commenced this prosecution, contenting himself, it would seem, with having removed his rival. But he was ordered to proceed in the suit; which though he did with great reluctance, it was necessary, however, she should be condemned. And she accordingly was, being given up to the punishment directed by the Julian law. The emperor thought proper to specify, in his sentence, the name and office of the centurion, that it might appear he passed it in virtue of military discipline; lest it should be imagined he claimed a particular cognizance in every cause of the same nature.

The third day was employed in examining into an affair which had occasioned much and various speculation; it was concerning the will of Julius Tiro, part of which was plainly genuine, the other part, it was said, was forged. The persons accused of this fraud were Sempronius Senecio, a Roman *eques*, and Eurythmus, Caesar's freedman and procurator. The heirs jointly petitioned the emperor, when he was in Dacia, that he would reserve to himself the trial of this cause, to which he accordingly consented. At his return from that expedition, he appointed a day for the hearing; and when some of the heirs, as in respect to Eurythmus, offered to withdraw the suit, the emperor nobly replied, "He is not Polycletus, nor am I Nero." However, he indulged the petitioners with an adjournment, and the time being expired, he now sat to hear the cause. Two of the heirs appeared, and desired that either their whole number might be compelled to plead, as they had all joined in the information, or that they also might have leave to desist. Carsar spoke with great wisdom and moderation; and when the counsel on the part of Senecio and Eurythmus said that unless their clients were heard, they would remain under the suspicion of guilt, "I am not concerned," said the emperor, "what suspicions they may lie under, 'tis I that am suspected"; and then turning to us, "Advise me," said he, "how to act in this affair, for you see they complain that I do not give them leave to withdraw their suit." At length, by the advice of his assessors, he ordered notice to be given to the heirs, that they should either go on with the cause, or each of them justify their reasons for not doing so; otherwise that he would pass sentence upon them as calumniators. Thus you see how usefully and seriously we spent our time, which, however, was intermixed with diversions of the most agreeable kind. We were every day invited to Caesar's table, which, for so great a prince, was spread with much plainness and simplicity. There we were either entertained with interludes, or passed the night in the most pleasing conversation. When we took our leave of him the last day, he made each of us presents; so studious is he to exert the benevolence of his temper upon all occasions! As for myself, I was not only charmed with the dignity and wisdom of the judge, the honor done to the assessors, the ease and unreserved freedom of the conversation, but with the agreeable situation of the place. This delightful villa is surrounded by the most verdant meadows, and commands a fine view of the sea, which forms itself here into a spacious harbor, in the figure of an amphitheater. The left hand of this port is defended by exceeding strong works, and they are now actually employed in carrying on the same on the opposite side. An artificial island, which is rising in the mouth of the harbor, will break the force of the waves, and afford a safe passage to ships on each side. In order for the construction of this wonderful instance of art, stones of a most enormous size are transported hither in a sort of pontoons, and being thrown one upon the other, are fixed by their own weight, gradually accumulating in the manner, as it were, of a sand bank. It already lifts its rocky back above the ocean, while the waves which beat upon it, being tossed to an immense height, foam with a prodigious noise, and whiten all the sea around. To these stones are added large piles, which in time will give it the appearance of a natural island. This haven is to be called by the name of its great author, and will prove of infinite benefit, by affording a very secure retreat to ships on that extensive and dangerous coast.

137. The imperial high court under Marcus Aurelius

This record of a trial shows how the emperors could by their judgments make changes in the existing law, usually in an equitable direction. Imperial judgments were binding precedents, and this one is quoted in a legal handbook as defining the law. In Roman law it was essential that there be a properly appointed heir (or heirs), who also acted as executor(s). The heirs might receive individual legacies, as well as sharing the residue of the estate. If the appointment of the heir(s) was in any way faulty, the whole will lapsed, including the legacies, and the estate passed by intestacy, in this case apparently, as the testator had no natural heir, to the treasury.

The last decision of the emperor illustrates the maxim of Roman law that whenever it was doubtful whether a person was free or a slave, he should have the benefit of the doubt.

137. Digest, XXVIII. iv. 3

MARCELLUS, DIGEST, BOOK 29

RECENTLY, AT a trial before the emperor, when someone had erased the names of the heirs and his estate was claimed by the Treasury as an escheat, there was a long discussion about the legacies, and especially the legacies ascribed to the persons whose appointment as heirs had been erased. Most thought that the beneficiaries of the legacies were excluded. I said that this rule should be followed if he had canceled the whole document of the will. Some thought that in strict law only the part which had been erased was canceled and everything else should stand. What follows? Can it not sometimes be believed that the man who had erased the names of his heirs had thought that he had taken sufficient steps to make himself die intestate? But in doubtful cases it is no less juster than safer to follow a more humane interpretation.

Judgment of the emperor Antoninus Augustus, in the consulship of Pedanius and Pollio [A.D. 167]: "Since Valerius Nepos changed his mind and opened his own will and erased the names of the heirs, his inheritance, according to the constitution of my deified father, does not appear to belong to those who are written in it." Counsel for the Treasury said: "You have your judges." Vivius Zeno said: "I beg you, my lord emperor, to hear me patiently. What ruling will you give about the legacies?" Antoninus Caesar said: "Do you think that a man who erased the names of his heirs wished his will to be valid?" Cornelius Priscianus, counsel of Leo, said: "He only erased the names of the heirs." Calpurnius Longinus, counsel for the Treasury, said: "No will can be valid which has no heir." Priscianus said: "He manumitted various slaves and left legacies." Antoninus Caesar ordered everyone to withdraw and, having deliberated and ordered the same persons to be recalled, said: "The present age can admit a more humane interpretation, that we should think that Nepos wished to be invalid only what he erased." He had erased the name of a slave he had ordered to be free.

Antoninus ruled that he would be free nevertheless; this ruling he clearly made to favor freedom.

138. Civil cases at Rome

This verbatim record of a speech of the emperor Claudius in the senate ("conscript fathers") is an amusing specimen of his forthright style, especially in the last paragraph. Civil cases at Rome were tried before judges nominated from the panels (*decuriae*) consisting of senators, *equites*, and others mentioned in No. 10. In the first paragraph Claudius has apparently been proposing to lower the age limit for judges from thirty (cf. No. 10) to twenty-five: the lex Laetoria provided that persons under twenty-five must have guardians. In the rest of the speech he proposes measures to prevent prosecutors from prolonging proceedings indefinitely.

138. BGU, *611*

IT SEEMS a heavy burden to put on the five decuries. At any rate be sure that you provide that no one under twenty-four years of age be appointed a judge. For it is not inequitable, I think, that those who do not need the aid of the Laetorian law for their own affairs should judge cases of freedom and slavery.

I have often, I think, conscript fathers, on other occasions brought to your notice, as I do now with emphasis, the extraordinary tricks of rogues who having initiated a case . . . that it would not pay a plaintiff to have persisted in his case. To prevent these tricks profiting evildoers, let us, if you approve, conscript fathers, decree that even when a case has been adjourned the duty of giving a decision shall be imposed on the same judges who have not, within the period of judicial business, completed cases begun. I am well aware that rascals will invent other frauds, but I hope that we will think out remedies against them. Meanwhile, it is enough to have closed this door, which is too wide open to everyone who had a bad case. I simply cannot endure the tyranny of prosecutors, who, having charged their enemies before a diligent council, leave them hanging in the case lists and themselves go abroad as if they had not done anything, whereas in the nature of things the laws hold both the prosecutor and the defendant united and bound. This scheme of prosecutors is assisted and their action is made less invidious by the frivolity of defendants, who now disdain to assume a squalid appearance and let their beards and hair grow to make their situation appear more pitiable. But they themselves should see how they would profit from these means of exciting pity granted them by nature. Let us deprive prosecutors of this tyrannical license by giving the praetor power, when the day for trial has passed, to summon the prosecutor, and, if he does not appear or excuses himself, to announce that he appears to have brought proceedings fraudulently with malicious intent.

If you approve of this, conscript fathers, signify so at once forthrightly, and in accordance with your real convictions. If you do not approve, find other remedies, but do so within the walls of this chamber, or if you wish to take more time perhaps, take it, providing that you remember that you will have to state your opinions whenever you are convened. It is unseemly and inconsistent with the dignity of this house, conscript fathers, that only one consul designate should deliver an opinion, copied word by word from the speech of the consuls, and the rest should say the word "agreed," and then when they have left the chamber: "We did speak."

139. Jurisdiction in the provinces

The first of these edicts reveals that in some provinces, at any rate, there were criminal jury courts modeled on those of Rome, which apparently tried both local Roman citizens and provincials. From edict D, it appears that the governor had the option of trying criminal cases himself without a jury.

Provincial jury courts are otherwise unknown and seem to have soon died out (cf. No. 84, where the proconsul of Africa can hardly have used a jury). The story behind edict B is obscure; probably the two men had been accused on some criminal charge and alleged that they possessed information in order to avoid trial by being sent to Rome. Edict C lays down an important principle—that citizens of provincial cities who obtain Roman citizenship remain liable to the charges of their native city (cf. No. 105). Edict D shows that in the provinces, as at Rome, civil cases were decided by private persons nominated as judges by the governor.

Edict E sets up a new procedure for trying cases of extortion in the provinces, when the prosecutors do not wish to make a criminal charge but merely recover the money. The procedure whereby the panel of judges is constituted, by drawing a number of names by lot and allowing either party to reject a fixed number, is typical of Roman practice. The distinction between criminal trials for extortion taken before the senate and civil trials taken before a small group of senatorial judges is observed in Nos. 83–84.

In edict E we see the drafting committee of the senate mentioned in

No. 10 in operation. It may be noted that Augustus makes use of his *maius imperium* (see No. 5) over the proconsuls of Crete and Cyrene, which was a public province, in edicts C and D, but uses his *auctoritas* in edict A, merely giving advice to the proconsuls.

139. SEG, IX. 8

A. IMPERATOR CAESAR AUGUSTUS, pontifex, of the tribunician power for the seventeenth time [7–6 B.C.], imperator for the fourteenth time, says:

Whereas I find that the total number of Romans in the province of Cyrene of all ages with an assessment of 2,500 denarii or more, from whom the jurors are drawn, is 215, and the embassies of the cities of the province have complained that there are conspiracies among them which oppress the Greeks in capital cases, the same persons making accusations and giving evidence for one another in turn; and I myself know that some innocent persons have been oppressed in this way and have incurred the supreme penalty:

Until the senate considers the matter, or I myself find a better solution, the future governors of Crete and Cyrenaica will in my opinion act properly and appropriately by empaneling an equal number of Greek judges as of Romans, of the highest assessment, none younger than twenty-five years of age, either Roman or Greek, or having an assessment of property, if there is a sufficient number of such persons, of less than 7,500 denarii, or if the number that ought to be empaneled as judges cannot be filled up in this way, they should empanel as judges in capital trials of Greeks those having half, and not less, of this assessment. And if a Greek accused, one day before the accuser begins to speak, on being given the choice whether he wishes all his judges to be Romans, or half Greeks, shall choose half Greeks, then when the balls have been weighed and the names written on them, the names of Romans shall be drawn from one box and those of Greeks from the other, until the total of twenty-five has been reached for each race, and of them the accuser may reject one of each race if he wishes, and the accused three out of the whole number, provided that he does not reject all Romans or all Greeks. Then all the rest shall be released for the voting, and the Romans shall place their votes in one box separately and the Greeks in another; then, when the count of the votes of either class has been made separately, the praetor shall publicly declare whatever the majority of the whole number has decided. And since the relatives of the deceased do not usually leave murders unpunished, and it is probable that the guilty parties will find Greek accusers to exact justice on behalf of dead relatives or fellow citizens, future governors of Crete and Cyrene will, in my opinion, act appropriately, if in the province of Cyrene they do not accept a Roman as accuser of a Greek in the case of the murder of a Greek man or woman, except when a person who has been honored with the citizenship prosecutes on behalf of one of his relations or fellow citizens.

B. Imperator Caesar Augustus, pontifex, of the tribunician power for the seventeenth time, says:

Publius Sextius Scaeva should not incur odium or blame, because, when Aulus Stlaccius, son of Lucius, Maximus, and Lucius Stlaccius, son of Lucius, Macedo, and Publius Lacutanius, freedman of Publius, Phileros declared that they knew and wished to report matters bearing on my safety and affairs of state, he arranged for them to be sent up to me from the province of Cyrenaica in chains; for Sextius acted with propriety and diligence in this matter. But since they know nothing affecting me or affairs of state, but admitted to me that they had made up this false story in the province, I free them and release them from prison. But I forbid Aulus Stlaccius Maximus, whom the ambassador of Cyrene accuses of having removed statues from public places, amongst them one on which the city inscribed my name, to leave without my order, until I have decided on this matter.

C. Imperator Caesar Augustus, pontifex, of the tribunician power for the seventeenth time, says:

If any persons in the province of Cyrenaica are honored with the citizenship, I order that they shall nonetheless perform public services in turn in the body of the Greeks, apart from those to whom immunity together with citizenship has been granted by law or by resolution of the senate or my father's or my own decree: and it is my pleasure that even these persons, to whom immunity has been granted, shall be exempt for the property which they had at that date, and shall pay what is due for all subsequent acquisitions.

D. Imperator Caesar Augustus, pontifex, of the tribunician power for the seventeenth time, says:

If there are any suits between Greeks in the province of Cyrenaica, except for capital cases, on which the governor of the province ought to decide and give sentence himself or provide a court of jurors, for all other matters it is my pleasure that Greek judges be appointed, unless any plaintiff or defendant wishes to have Roman citizens as judges; and whatever Greek judges shall be appointed according to my decree, it is my pleasure that no judge shall be appointed from the city to which the prosecutor or plaintiff or the accused or defendant belongs.

E. Imperator Caesar Augustus, pontifex maximus, of the tribunician power for the nineteenth time [4 B.C.], says:

I have decided to send to the provinces and to append to my edict the resolution of the senate passed in the consulship of Gaius Calvisius and Lucius Passienus, I being present and signing it, which bears on the security of the allies of the Roman people, that it may be known that we are solicitous for their interests. For it will be plain to all the inhabitants of the provinces what care I and the senate take to prevent any of our subjects suffering any improper treatment or extortion.

RESOLUTION OF THE SENATE

Whereas Gaius Calvisius Sabinus and Lucius Passienus Rufus, the consuls, spoke on the matters which Imperator Caesar Augustus, our leading citizen (*princeps*), wished to be brought by us before the senate, on the advice of the council which he has drawn by lot from the senate, matters which bear on the security of the allies of the Roman people.

It was resolved by the senate: whereas our ancestors provided by law for courts for the recovery of money, in order that the allies may more easily be able to obtain redress for their injuries and to recover moneys of which they have been deprived, since this type of court is sometimes very oppressive and disagreeable to the very persons for whom the law was enacted, seeing that the provinces are distant, and poor men or persons in bad health or of infirm age are dragged here as witnesses, it is the pleasure of the senate that if, after the passing of this resolution of the senate, any of the allies from whom money has been extorted publicly or privately shall wish to reclaim it, apart from bringing a capital charge against the person who received the money, and presenting themselves for this purpose shall lay information to any of the magistrates who are allowed to convene the senate, the magistrate shall forthwith intro-

duce them to the senate, and give them whomsoever they themselves choose as an advocate to speak on their behalf before the
senate; but no one shall be an advocate against his will who is
excused by law from this duty. And in order that those who bring
charges in the senate may be heard, the magistrate who gives them
access to the senate shall on the same day before the senate, not less
than two hundred being present, draw by lot four of all the con-
sulars in Rome itself or within twenty miles of the city, and similarly three of all the praetorians in Rome itself or within twenty
miles of the city, and similarly two of all the other senators and
those entitled to speak in the senate who are in Rome itself or
within twenty miles of the city, and he shall draw no one who is
over seventy years of age, or who holds a magistracy or post of
authority, or is president of a court or superintendent of the distribution of corn, or is prevented by illness from performing this
duty, making an affidavit before the senate and causing to swear on
his behalf three members of the senate who are not so related to
him by blood or marriage that they would not be compelled under
the Julian judiciary law to give evidence in a public court against
their will, nor anyone whom the accused swears before the senate
is his enemy; but he may not make an affidavit against more than
three. Of the nine who are selected in this way, the magistrate who
carries out the allotment shall see to it that within two days those
who are claiming the money and the man from whom they are
claiming it shall reject in turn until five are left. If any of these
judges shall die before the question is judged, or shall be prevented
by any other reason from judging, provided that his excuse is approved by the oath of five members of the senate, then the magistrate, in the presence of the judges and those who are claiming the
money and the man from whom they are claiming it, shall draw
substitutes from those persons who are of the same rank and hold
the same offices as the man in whose place the allotment of a substitute is being made has held, provided that he shall not allot a man
whom it is unlawful for the senate to allot against the accused
according to this resolution. The above judges shall hear and
decide only about those things which the accused has appropriated
publicly or privately and shall order him to restore whatever sum
of money the accusers prove that he has taken from them publicly
or privately, provided that the judges shall decide within thirty
days. The persons whose duty it is to decide and give judgment on

this matter shall until they have decided and given judgment be exempt from all public duties except public sacrifices.

It is the pleasure of the senate that the magistrate who has conducted the allotment of the judges, or if he is unable to act, the consul who has precedence for this period, shall preside, and give authority to summon witnesses who are in Italy, provided that he shall not allow a private claimant to summon more than five, or a public claimant more than ten. It is likewise the senate's pleasure that the judges who are allotted in accordance with this resolution shall severally declare their opinion openly, and that a majority vote shall prevail.

140. A dispute between two cities

In this inscription from Sardinia the proconsul, sitting with assessors, gives final judgment on a long-standing boundary dispute between the two communities. Sardinia and Corsica, originally a public province (cf. Nos. 3 and 4), were taken over by the emperor in A.D. 6 owing to local disorders but restored to the senate in A.D. 67. Rixa is one of the procurators who governed the province between A.D. 6 and 67, Simplex (a senator by his title) the proconsul who preceded Agrippa.

140. Dessau, ILS, 5947

IN THE consulship of Otho Caesar Augustus [A.D. 69], the fifteenth day before the kalends of April, copied and checked from a bound ledger of Lucius Helvius Agrippa, proconsul, produced by Gnaeus Egnatius Fuscus, quaestorian secretary, in which is written what is written below, on page 5, chapters 8, 9, and 10.

On the third day before the ides of March Lucius Helvius Agrippa, proconsul, having examined the case, gave judgment:

As it is in the public interest to stand by judicial decisions, and in the case of the Patulcenses Marcus Juventius Rixa, the distinguished procurator of Augustus, more than once gave judgment that the boundaries of the Patulcenses should be maintained as they were fixed on a bronze plaque by Marcus Marcellus, and finally gave judgment that he had wished to punish the Galillenses who constantly renewed the controversy and disobeyed his decision, but for respect to the clemency of our excellent and mighty emperor had been content to admonish them by edict, that they must keep quiet and abide by judicial decisions, and must before the 1st October next withdraw from the lands of Patulcenses and give them vacant possession; but that if they persisted in their contumacy he would severely punish those responsible for the disorders; and later his excellency Caecilius Simplex, being approached on the same matter by the Galillenses, who said that they would bring the plaque referring to the matter from the imperial record office, gave judgment that it was humane to grant a delay for proof and gave them a delay of three months to 1st December and declared that unless the plan were produced before that date he would follow the copy which was in the province.

I, too, was approached by the Galillenses, who made excuses for the map not yet being produced, and granted a delay up to 1st February last, and I understood that the delay was gratifying to the occupiers.

Let the Galillenses withdraw before the 1st April next from the territory of the Patulcenses which they have forcibly occupied. If they do not obey this pronouncement, they must know that they will be liable for their long contumacy and punishment now often threatened.

In the council were: Marcus Julius Romulus, *legatus pro praetore,* Titus Atilius Sabinus, *quaestor pro praetore,* Marcus Stertinius Rufus junior, Sextus Aelius Modestus, Publius Lucretius Clemens, Marcus Domitius Vitalis, Marcus Lusius Fidus, Marcus Stertinius Rufus.

Signatories [eleven names]

XI. Status

141. Claudius' edict on the Anauni

In the early principate, Roman citizens were a small elite among the inhabitants of the empire, comprising the Italians and the citizens of the relatively few Roman colonies and municipalities in the provinces, apart from individual provincials who had been enfranchised. There was a general tendency to expand the citizenship by converting provincial cities into municipalities, or by giving them Latin status, whereby their annual magistrates became Roman citizens (cf. Nos. 93 and 94). Claudius, who was unusually progressive in this matter, also gave citizenship to veterans in the auxiliary units and fleets (cf. Nos. 63–64).

In this edict, written in his typical style, Claudius gives the benefit of the doubt to the members of three Alpine tribes subject to the municipality of Tridentum (cf. No. 113).

141. Dessau, ILS, 206

IN THE consulship of Marcus Julius Silanus and Quintus Sulpicius Camerinus [A.D.] on the ides of March, at Veii in the military headquarters, the subjoined edict of Tiberius Claudius Caesar Augustus Germanicus was posted. Tiberius Claudius Caesar Augustus Germanicus, pontifex maximus, of the tribunician power for the sixth time, imperator for the eleventh time, father of his country, consul designate for the fourth time, says:

Whereas as a result of old controversies pending for some time even in the time of my uncle Tiberius, to settle which he had sent Pinarius Apollinarius—which were, so far as I can remember, only between the people of Comum and the Bergalei—and he first because of my uncle's persistent absence and then, too, in the reign of Gaius, because he was not asked for a report, not unwisely neglected to do so; and afterward Camurius Statutus reported to me that most of the land and the estates are my property; I have now sent my friend and companion Julius Planta, who, when he has with the assistance of my procurators, both those in the district and those in the neighborhood, carried out a most careful investigation and inquiry, I allow to decide and pass judgment himself on the other matters, as communicated to me in his own report.

As to the status of the Anauni and Tulliasses and Sinduni, some of whom an informer is said to have proved are attributed to the people of Tridentum and some not even attributed, though I observe that these people have no very solid claim to the Roman citizenship, still since they are said to have come into possession of it by long prescription, and to be so mixed with the Tridentines that they could not be separated from them without grave injury to that splendid municipality, I allow them by my grace to remain in that status to which they thought that they belonged, all the more willingly because a number of these people, I am told, are serving in my praetorian guard, in which some have become centurions, and others have been nominated to the judicial decuries at Rome.

In making this gracious concession, I order that whatever transactions they have done as Roman citizens with each other or with the Tridentines, or any others, shall be valid and I allow them to keep the names which they previously had as if Roman citizens.

142. A Roman citizen's rights

The main privilege of a Roman citizen, besides being eligible as a recruit for the legions, the praetorian guard (cf. No. 141), the equestrian order, the senate, and for the military commissions and civilian posts recruited from these orders, was that he was not, like a provincial, liable to arbitrary scourging and could appeal to the emperor against sentences of scourging or death.

It may be noted that the military tribune in command of the auxiliary cohort at Jerusalem—an equestrian commission—had obtained his citizenship by corrupt means. Judging by his name, Claudius Lysias, he was a Greek and had been enfranchised by Claudius.

142. The Acts of the Apostles, XXII. 24-29

THE MILITARY tribune commanded him to be brought into the castle and bade that he should be examined by scourging; that he might know wherefore they cried so against him. And as they bound him with thongs, Paul said unto the centurion that stood by, Is it lawful for you to scourge a man that is a Roman, and uncondemned? When the centurion heard that, he went and told the tribune, saying, Take heed what thou doest: for this man is a Roman. Then the tribune came, and said unto him, Tell me, art thou a Roman? He said, Yea. And the tribune answered, With a great sum obtained I this freedom. And Paul said, But I was free born. Then straightway they departed from him which should have examined him: and the tribune also was afraid, after he knew that he was a Roman, and because he had bound him.

143. Appeal to Caesar

In this famous case, Paul, a Roman citizen, without waiting to be condemned, objects to what he anticipates will be an unfair trial, since Festus, the procurator of Judaea, will be subject to pressure from the Jews. He accordingly appeals to the emperor. The appeal, which was irregular in being premature, is allowed by Festus, who as usual is advised by his assessors.

143. The Acts of the Apostles, XXV. 6-12

AND WHEN he had tarried among them more than ten days, he went down unto Caesarea; and the next day sitting on the judgment seat commanded Paul to be brought. And when he was come, the Jews which came down from Jerusalem stood round about, and laid many and grievous complaints against Paul, which they could not prove. While he answered, for himself, Neither against the law of the Jews, neither against the temple, nor yet against Caesar, have I offended anything at all. But Festus, willing to do the Jews a pleasure, answered Paul, and said, Wilt thou go up to Jerusalem, and there be judged of these things before me? Then said Paul, I stand at Caesar's judgment seat, where I ought to be judged: to the Jews have I done no wrong, as thou very well knowest. For if I be an offender, or have committed anything worthy of death, I refuse not to die: but if there be none of these things whereof these accuse me, no man may deliver me unto them. I appeal unto Caesar. Then Festus, when he had conferred with the council, answered, Hast thou appealed unto Caesar? Unto Caesar shalt thou go.

144. A recommendation for the citizenship

This correspondence shows how quite humble persons could acquire the Roman citizenship by the interest of senators. The difference between Egyptians and other provincials is obscure, but it is clear that Egyptians were legally ineligible for the Roman citizenship and could only get it by first being made citizens of Alexandria (which was technically not a part of Egypt). It may be observed in No. 126, §55 that Egyptians could not obtain citizenship by enlisting in the legions or by service in the fleets (except by an anomalous privilege, that of Misenum). It has been argued that Egyptians were the mysterious *dediticii* of No. 145.

A legally manumitted slave of a Roman became a Roman citizen. Hedia and Marmeris were irregularly manumitted slaves, the so-called Junian Latins (cf. No. 126, §22).

144. Pliny, Letters, X. 5–7

PLINY TO TRAJAN

HAVING BEEN attacked last year by a severe and dangerous illness, I employed a masseur, whose care and diligence, Sir, I cannot sufficiently reward, but by your gracious assistance. I entreat you, therefore, to make him a Roman citizen; for as he is the freedman of a foreigner, he is, consequently, himself also a foreigner. His name is Harpocras; his patroness (who has been dead a considerable time) was Thermuthis the daughter of Theon. I further entreat you to bestow the full privileges of a Roman citizen upon Hedia and Antonia Harmeris the freedwomen of Antonia Maximilla, a lady of great merit. It is at her desire I make this request.

PLINY TO TRAJAN

I return you thanks, Sir, for your ready compliance with my desire, in granting the complete privileges of a Roman to the freedwomen of a lady to whom I am allied, and making Harpocras my masseur a Roman citizen. But when, agreeable to your directions, I gave in an account of his age and status, I was informed by those who are better skilled in these affairs than I pretend to be, that as he is an Egyptian, I ought first to have obtained for him the citizenship of Alexandria, and then that of Rome. I confess, indeed, as I was ignorant of any difference in this case between Egyptians and other foreigners, I contented myself with only acquainting you, that he had been manumitted by a foreign lady, since deceased. However, it is an ignorance I cannot regret, since it affords me an opportunity of receiving from you a double obligation in favor of the same person. That I may legally therefore enjoy the benefits of your goodness, I beg you would be pleased to grant him the citizenship of Alexandria also. And that your gracious intentions may not meet with any further obstacles, I have taken care, as you directed, to send an account to your freedman of his age and fortunes.

TRAJAN TO PLINY

It is my resolution, in pursuance of the maxims observed by the princes my predecessors, to be extremely cautious in granting the citizenship of Alexandria: however, since you have obtained of me the Roman citizenship for your masseur Harpocras, I cannot refuse you this other request. You must let me know to what district he belongs, that I may give you a letter to my good friend Pompeius Planta, prefect of Egypt.

PLINY TO TRAJAN

I cannot express, Sir, the pleasure your letter gave me, by which I am informed that you have made my masseur Harpocras a citizen of Alexandria; notwithstanding your resolution to follow the maxims of your predecessors in this point, by being extremely cautious in granting that privilege. Agreeably to your directions, I acquaint you that Harpocras belongs to the district of Memphis. I intreat you then, most gracious Emperor, to send me as you promised, a letter to your good friend Pompeius Planta, prefect of Egypt.

As I purpose (in order to have the earliest enjoyment of your presence, so ardently wished for here) to come to meet you; I beg, Sir, you would permit me to extend my journey as far as possible.

145. The *Constitutio Antoniniana*

These texts contain practically all the information that we have on the famous edict of the emperor Caracalla, issued in A.D. 212–13. It is tolerably certain that by it all free inhabitants of the empire (including Egyptians) became Roman citizens. The papyrus text of the edict is unfortunately very fragmentary, and the clause about the *dediticii* very uncertain and obscure. Caracalla's motives are probably correctly assessed by Dio, but the edict had the effect of unifying the empire, not only in law but in sentiment.

145(a). P. Giessen, *40*

IMPERATOR Caesar Marcus Aurelius Severus Antoninus Augustus says:

. . . I must put aside accusations and petitions and seek how I may give thanks to the immortal gods for preserving me by such a . . . Accordingly, I think that I can thus magnificently and piously recompense their majesty, if I bring to the worship of the gods all foreigners [?] who are among my subjects. I, therefore, grant the Roman citizenship to all foreigners [?] throughout the world, all kinds of municipal rights [?] remaining unchanged except for the *dediticii*. For the multitude ought not only to share all our toils [?], but now also be included in our victory. Moreover, this edict will increase [?] the majesty of the Roman people because . . .

145(b). Digest, *I. v. 17*

ULPIAN, ON THE EDICT, BOOK XXII

All persons in the Roman world were made Roman citizens by the constitution of the emperor Antoninus.

145(C). CASSIUS DIO, LXXVII. 9

He invented new taxes and increased to 10 per cent the 5 per cent tax on manumissions and on inheritances, and made it applicable to all donations, abolishing successions by intestacy and the immunities granted on that score to the nearest relatives. It was for this reason that he declared all under his rule Romans, nominally honoring them, but really so that he could get more revenue from this source, because foreigners did not pay most of these taxes.

XII. Economic Affairs

146. The *Alimenta*

This is part of a very long inscription found at Veleia, recording the financial arrangements made by Trajan for the maintenance of poor children in Italy. This was a policy extensively followed by the emperors of the second century and was probably due not only to philanthropy but to a desire to maintain a shrinking population, and in particular to keep up the supply of recruits for the army. A similar private foundation by Pliny for his native town of Comum is recorded in No. 30.

Instead of paying direct annual grants from the treasury, which might be canceled by later emperors short of money, Trajan and his successors preferred to lend money on mortgage to the larger landowners and earmark the interest for their charitable purposes. The interest is that normal for the period, and the loans are very heavily secured, being under ten per cent of the assessed value of the estates; there is, therefore, no reason to think that the scheme had as a second purpose the assistance of agriculture.

146. Dessau, ILS, *6675*

MORTGAGES ON estates for 1,044,000 sesterces, in order that by the generosity of the best and greatest chief of state, imperator Caesar Nerva Trajan Augustus Germanicus Dacicus, boys and girls may receive maintenance: 245 legitimate boys at 16 sesterces each [per month], total 47,040 sesterces: 34 legitimate girls at 12 sesterces each, total 4,896 sesterces: one illegitimate boy, 144 sesterces [per year]: one illegitimate girl, 120 sesterces: grand total 52,200, which is interest at 5 per cent on the above mentioned capital.

1. Gaius Volumnius and Volumnia Alce through their freedman Volumnius Diadumenianus declared the farms Quintiacus and Aurelianus and the hill Muletas, together with its woodlands, which are in the territory of Veleia in the parish Ambitrebius, neighbors Marcus Mummius Persicus, Papius Severus, and the people, for 108,000 sesterces. They are required to accept 8,692 sesterces and to mortgage the aforesaid estate.

2. Marcus Verius Nepos declared rural estates to the value of 340,095 sesterces after deduction of rent charge. He is required to accept 25,353 sesterces and to mortgage the farm Planianus which is in the territory of Veleia in the parish of Junonius, neighbors Priscus Palamenus and Velleius Severus and the people, which he declared at 14,000 sesterces, and the farm Suigianus with three cottages in the aforesaid parish, neighbors Gaius Calidius and Velleius Proculus and the people, which he declared at 20,000 sesterces, and the farm Petronianus, parish and neighbors as aforesaid, which he declared at 4,000 sesterces.

147. A village of freeholders

While much of the land consisted of large estates owned by wealthy landlords (including the government), there were many villages of peasant proprietors like Scaptopara in Thrace. Their grievance is the compulsory provision of hospitality to government employees on tour (cf. No. 86). They present their petition through one of their number who is a soldier in the praetorian guard, who, they hoped, might receive special attention from the emperor; but Gordian in his rescript tells them to apply through the usual channels (cf. No. 97).

147. Dittenberger, Sylloge³, *888*

[In Latin]

GOOD FORTUNE! In the consulship of Fulvius Pius and Pontius Proculus, on the seventeenth day before the kalends of January, copy made and checked from the book of petitions answered by our Lord the Emperor Marcus Antonius Gordianus, the pious, the fortunate, Augustus, and posted up at Rome in the colonnade of the Baths of Trajan, in the following words, given by Aurelius Purrus, soldier of the ——— praetorian cohort, the loyal and devoted to Gordian, of the century of Proculus, a fellow villager and fellow landowner.

[In Greek]

To Imperator Caesar Marcus Antonius Gordianus, the pious, the fortunate, Augustus, a petition from the villagers of Scaptopara also called Gresa.

You have often replied that in your most fortunate and eternal times the villages should be settled and improved, rather than the inhabitants uprooted. Such a policy is for the salvation of mankind and the profit of your most sacred treasury. Accordingly, we, too, bring to your divinity a just petition, praying you graciously to accede to our request as follows. We live and own land in the aforesaid village, which is very pleasant owing to its possessing hot springs and lying between two military camps in your Thrace; and as long as the inhabitants in the old days remained free from disturbance and extortion, they used to pay the tribute and the other requirements without fail. But since in our time some people have begun to advance to injury and violence, the village, too, began to decline. Two miles from our village a celebrated fair is held and those who go there for the fair and stay for fifteen days do not stop at the site of the fair, but leave it and come to our village and force us to give them lodging and provide much else for their entertainment without payment. And, in addition to this, soldiers sent to various places leave their own routes and come to us, and similarly force us to furnish them with lodgings and provisions without paying any price. And the governors of the province, and your procurators, too, stay here a great deal to enjoy the waters. We receive the authorities constantly, because we must, but we cannot endure the others, and we have often petitioned the governors of Thrace, who in accordance with the divine mandates ordered us to be unmolested; for we demonstrated that we could not stand it any longer, but were even intending to abandon our ancestral foundations because of the violence of our visitors. For we have in fact been reduced from a large number of householders to very few. For a time the orders of the governors prevailed, and no one molested us by demands for lodging or the provision of supplies, but as time went on large numbers of people again ventured to harass us, despising our private station. So since we can no longer bear the burden and we are also really in danger, like the others, of abandoning our ancestral foundations, we therefore beg you, invincible Augustus, to order by your divine rescript that everyone should go his own way, and not leave the other villages and come to us and compel us to furnish them with provisions free, or even to provide them with lodging except in case of necessity— since the governors have often ordered us not to provide lodgings for anyone except those sent on official business by the governors and procurators, and if we are oppressed we shall flee from our homes and the treasury will suffer a great loss—so that we may be benefited by your divine providence and stay in our own homes and be able to pay the sacred tribute and the other dues. This will happen to us in your most fortunate times, if you order your divine letter to be engraved on a pillar and publicly displayed. So that, having received this boon, we may be able to give thanks to your fortune, as we now do in our devotion to you.

Diogenes of Tyre the . . . has taken up this request by divine compassion. It seems to me that one of the gods has providentially assisted the present petition. For that the divine emperor should have sent his own judgment on the matter to you, whom he knows had already decided on the matter by public notices and edicts, is to my mind the work of Good Fortune. This was the petition. The village of the soldier who seeks redress lies in the best part of our city of Pautalia, well sited among the mountains and plains, and in addition there are warm baths, suited not only for enjoyment but for health and the cure of ailments; and nearby a fair, which is held several times a year, and about 1st October enjoys immunity for fifteen days. So it has come about that the seeming advantages of this village have in the course of time been converted into disadvantages. So for these aforesaid reasons many soldiers often stay there and oppress the village by burdens and demands for hospitality. For these reasons, whereas it was formerly richer and more populous, it is now reduced to the utmost poverty. Since they have often petitioned the governors, but, while their orders prevailed for a time, they were afterward neglected owing to the prevailing habit of oppression, they have therefore of necessity had recourse to the divine. . . .

[In Latin]

Imperator Caesar Marcus Antonius Gordianus, the pious, the fortunate, Augustus, to the villagers through the soldier Pyrrhus, their fellow landowner. You should ventilate this kind of complaint put forward by the petitioner rather by informing the justice of the governor on the alleged abuses before presenting a definite ruling for the emperor's rescript.

I have replied.

I have checked.

[Seals]

148. Tenants of imperial estates

This is a petition from the tenants of an imperial estate in Africa. They are free men, some even Roman citizens; their description of themselves at the end of the petition is figurative, and meant to stress that they have lived for generations on the estate. These estates were under the management of imperial agents (procurators) who leased them in large blocks to lessees (*conductores*), who sublet the bulk of the land to small tenants. These tenants, it will be seen, were sharecroppers, and also owed labor services on the land directly cultivated by the lessees. After the petition comes the emperor's reply (*subscriptio*), written in A.D. 180–83, and the letter of the procurators sending it on.

148. S. Riccobono, Fontes Iuris Romani Ante Justiniani², *I. 103*

. . . not only with Allius Maximus our opponent, but with practically all the lessees, contrary to right and to the detriment of your finances; so that not only has he for all these years past neglected to give a decision, though we pressed him and begged him, and produced your divine subscription, but also finally was indulgent to the tricks of the highly influential lessee, the same Allius Maximus, sending soldiers into the same estate of Burunum and ordering some of us to be arrested and maltreated, others to be imprisoned, and some, even Roman citizens, to be flogged and cudgeled, our only offense being that in respect of so heavy a charge, in proportion to our modest means, and to so manifest a wrong, we had written a rather bold letter to implore your majesty's aid. . . .

This compelled our miserable selves again to supplicate your divine providence, and we, therefore, ask you, most sacred emperor, to aid us, so that the right, which is removed under the chapter of the Hadrianic law quoted above, should be removed from the procurators, too, still more from the lessee, of increasing the shares of the crops or the provision of work or of teams to the detriment of the tenants, and that as is stated in the letters of the procurators, which are in your record offices of the district of Carthage, we should not be liable for more than two days' plowing, two hoeing, and two harvesting a year, and that there may be no more dispute about it, as it is on the inscribed bronze plaque and is to this day regularly observed by all our neighbors in every direction, and is confirmed by the letters of the procurators of which we wrote above. Please help us, and since we are poor peasants who scrape a living by the toil of our hands and are not a match for a lessee who makes himself agreeable by profuse gifts in the eyes of your procurators with whom, as one succeeds the other, he is acquainted in virtue of his lease; take pity on us and by your sacred rescript deign to order that we should not furnish more than is due under the Hadrianic law and according to the

letters of your procurators, that is three times two days work, so
that by the kindness of your majesty, we, your rustic home-born
slaves and foster sons of your estates, born in your service, may no
longer be troubled by the lessees of the fiscal lands.

Imperator Caesar Marcus Aurelius Commodus Antoninus Augustus Sarmaticus Germanicus Maximus to Lurius Lucullus, in the
name of others also. My procurators in view of my discipline and
settled policy will see to it that no exactions are wrongfully made
from you contrary to the standing order [inserted by the peasants
"not more than three times two days of work."] In another hand. I
have written it. I have checked it.

Copy of the letter of his honor the procurator: Tussanius Aristo
and Chrysanthus to their friend Andronicus. According to the
sacred subscription of our lord the most sacred emperor, which was
given to his petition, and reported by Lurius Lucullus. . . .
    In another hand. We send you all good wishes. Farewell.
    Given on the day before the ides of September, at Carthage.
Happily completed and dedicated on the ides of May in the consulship of Aurelianus and Cornelianus, under the supervision of
Gaius Julius Pelops son of Salaputus, head man.

149. Emphyteutic tenures of imperial estates

In order to encourage the productivity of their estates, the emperors
gave perpetual leases to persons who brought waste patches under
cultivation, subject to the usual share of the crop, but temporary
remission was granted for vines and olives, which took some time to
come into full bearing. Leases of this type passed to the original
holder's heirs and could be left by will or sold. They were still in
existence in the fifth century A.D.

149. S. Riccobono, Fontes Iuris Romani Ante Justiniani[2], I. 102

FOR THE safety and preservation of Imperator Caesar Lucius Septi-
mius Severus Pius Pertinax Augustus and Imperator Caesar Marcus
Aurelius Antoninus Pius Augustus and Imperator Lucius Septimius
Severus Geta Caesar and Julia Domna mother of the camps,
Patroclus freedman of the Augusti, procurator, set up the altar of
the law of the deified Hadrian, and engraved on it the following

law. Copy of the Hadrianic law published on the altar. Speech of
the procurators. Whereas our Caesar in the unwearying care with
which he watches continually for the welfare of mankind, orders
that all parts of fields which are suitable both for olives and vines
and for corn be cultivated, therefore by permission of his providence anyone is allowed also to occupy those parts which are in the
leased centuries of the Blandian estate and that of Udae and in
those parts which have been joined to the estate of Thusdris from
the Laemian and Domitian estates, and are not cultivated by the
lessees. And the person who occupies the land shall have the right
of possessing it and enjoying it and leaving it to his heir, as laid
down in the Hadrianic law on virgin land and land which has not
been cultivated for ten years continuously; they shall not pay
larger shares of the crops from the Blandian estate and that of
Udae. . . .

Anyone who occupies places neglected by the lessees shall pay a
third of the crop according to custom. He shall also pay the same
for those regions which have been joined to the estate of Thusdris
from the Laemian and Domitian estates. For olives which anyone
has planted in trenches or grafted onto wild olives, no share of the
crop taken shall be demanded for the first ten years; nor from fruit
trees for the first seven years; no fruit shall be liable for division
except what is sold by the occupiers. Whatever share of cereals
anyone shall have to pay, he shall pay for the first five years to the
person within whose leasehold he has occupied the land, and thereafter to the account of the Imperial treasury.

150. Imperial silver mines

Mines under the republic and early years of the principate were
worked by companies of contractors, who employed slave labor. Slaves
grew much more expensive in the second century, and it may have
been because of this that a new system of exploitation was introduced,
which is depicted in this inscription. Shafts were leased to individual
free miners or small groups of miners; some owned a few slaves or
employed indentured labor (see No. 151). Miners could apparently
stake a claim, which was forfeited if they failed to work it; if they
struck ore they had to pay a fixed fee and the purchase price of the
government's mineral rights, thereby extinguishing the royalty of 50
per cent.

The mining town was, it will be seen, controlled by the imperial
procurator of the mine, who sold concessions for various service trades

to the highest bidder and closely specified the duties of the concession-
aires. The date of the inscription is the early second century.

150. S. Riccobono, Fontes Iuris Romani Ante Justiniani², *I. 104*

. . . TO HIS friend Ulpius Aelianus.

. . . shall personally pay to the procurator of Augustus. . . . If
he has not done so and is convicted of smelting ore before having
paid the price as stated above, the share of the occupier shall be
forfeited and the procurator of the mines shall sell the whole shaft.
Anyone who proves that a tenant has smelted ore before paying
the price of the half share belonging to the treasury, shall receive a
quarter. Silver shafts must be worked according to the specification
contained in this law. Their prices will be observed according to
the liberal offer of our most sacred emperor Hadrian Augustus,
viz., that the ownership of the share that belongs to the treasury
shall belong to the person who first pays the price for the shaft and
pays into the treasury four thousand sesterces. Anyone who has
struck ore in one of five pits shall maintain work uninterruptedly
in the others, as above stated: if he fails to do so, anyone shall have
the right of occupation. If anyone, after the twenty-five days
allowed for the preparation of expenses, at once begins to do the
work, then stops work for ten days on end, anyone else shall have
the right of occupation. If a shaft sold by the treasury shall be
abandoned for six months on end, anyone else shall have the right
of occupation, provided that when ore is produced, a half share
shall be reserved for the treasury according to custom. An occupier of shafts may have what partners he wishes, provided that
each partner contributes to the expenses for his share. If anyone
fails to do so, the person who has paid the expenses shall post up an
account of the expenses paid by him for three days continuously in
the most frequented part of the forum, and shall declare to his
partners through the public crier that each must contribute to the
expenses in proportion to his share. If anyone does not make such
contribution or does anything of malice to avoid such contribution, or to cheat his partner or partners, he shall have no share in
the shaft, and his share shall belong to the partner or partners who
have paid the expenses. The partners who have paid the expenses of
a shaft in which there are several partners shall have the right of
recovering from their partners whatever shall be proved to have
been spent in good faith. Tenants are allowed to sell to each other

for whatever price they can get those shares of shafts which they have bought from the treasury and paid the price. Anyone who wishes to sell his share or to buy one, shall make a declaration before the procurator in charge of the mines: otherwise he shall not be allowed to buy or sell. A person who is a debtor to the treasury is not allowed to give away his share. The owners of ore which has been extracted and is lying near the shafts must remove it to their workshops between sunrise and sunset. Anyone convicted of removing ore from the shafts after sunset or by night shall be obliged to pay one thousand sesterces to the treasury. If a thief of ore is a slave, the procurator shall flog him and sell him on condition that he remains always shackled and does not reside in any mine or mining territory; the price of the slave shall belong to his master. If he is a free man, the procurator shall confiscate his property and exclude him for ever from the boundaries of the mines. All shafts must be carefully propped and secured and the tenant of each shaft must replace rotten timber with good sound timber. It is illegal to touch pillars or buttresses left for reinforcement or damage them of malice or do anything whereby these pillars or buttresses are not solid and passable. Anyone who is convicted of having injured a shaft or weakened it or blocked its mouth or done anything else of malice to make it insecure, shall, if a slave, be flogged at the discretion of the procurator and sold by his owner on condition that he shall not reside in any mine. The procurator shall confiscate the property of free persons and exclude them forever from the boundaries of the mines. Anyone who works copper shafts shall keep away from the tunnel which drains water from the mines, and shall leave not less than fifteen feet on either side. No one may damage the tunnel. The procurator shall allow a passage to be driven from the tunnel in order to explore a new mine, provided that the passage does not exceed four feet in height and in breadth. It is illegal to look for new ore within fifteen feet on either side of the tunnel. Anyone who is convicted of acting otherwise with regard to passages shall, if a slave, be flogged at the discretion of the procurator and sold by his owner on condition that he shall not reside in any mine. The procurator shall confiscate the property of free persons and exclude them for ever from the boundaries of the mines. Anyone who drives silver shafts shall keep away from the tunnel which drains water from the mines and shall leave not less than sixty feet on either side, and shall operate those shafts which he has occupied or which have been assigned to him, as their boundaries are determined, and shall not advance farther or pile up spoil or drive passages outside the boundaries of the shafts assigned to him. . . .

THE 1 PER CENT TAX ON MONEY SALES

The contractor shall receive 1 per cent from the vendor for all auction sales within the boundary of the mine of Vipasca, except those held by the procurator of the mine on the emperor's orders. The contractor shall not exact 1 per cent for the price of shafts sold by the procurator of the mines. If, when the auction is held, all the goods are sold en bloc, the vendor shall be nonetheless liable to pay 1 per cent to the contractor, his partner, or agent. If the contractor, his partner, or agent shall desire a stipulation from the vendor, he shall give it. The contractor, his partner, or agent, shall exact 1 per cent also of any sum which is withdrawn in the auction. Anyone who submits goods to auction and fails to sell them, but within ten days of the auction sells them by private treaty, shall nonetheless be liable to pay 1 per cent to the contractor, his partner, or agent. Whatever shall be owed under this paragraph of the law to the contractor, his partner, or agent, shall be paid double if payment and satisfaction is not made within three days after the debt was incurred.

AUCTION DUES

The person who contracts for the office of auctioneer shall provide an auctioneer within the boundaries. As pay he shall exact 2 per cent from anyone who makes a sale of fifty denarii or less, 1 per cent from anyone who makes a sale of more than a hundred denarii. Anyone who sells slaves by auction, if he sells five or less, shall be liable to pay to the contractor, his partner, or agent ———— denarii per head as capitation due; if he sells a greater number, three denarii per head. If the procurator of the mines shall sell or lease any goods in the name of the treasury, the contractor, his partner, or agent shall be liable to furnish an auctioneer for these goods. Anyone who posts up an inventory of goods for sale shall be liable to pay one denarius to the contractor, his partner, or agent. The purchaser shall be liable to pay 1 per cent for shafts sold by the procurator of the mines. If he does not pay in three days, the contractor, his partner, or agent may seize a pledge of double the value. Anyone who sells mules, donkeys, or horses, male or female, by auction, shall be liable to pay three denarii per head. Anyone who submits slaves or other objects for auction and sells them by private treaty within thirty days, shall be liable to pay the same dues to the contractor, his partner, or agent.

THE BATHS

The contractor for the baths, or his partner, shall be obliged at his entire expense, to heat and provide the baths, for which he shall hold the contract, every day until the day before the kalends of July, from dawn to the seventh hour for women, and from the eighth hour until the second hour of the night for men, at the discretion of the procurator in charge of the mines. He shall be obliged to provide properly running water for the bath both for women and for men, up to the top in the hypocausts and up to the rim in the tank. The contractor shall exact half an as from each man and one as from each woman. Excused are freedmen and slaves of Caesar who are in the service of the procurator, or receive salaries, also children and soldiers. The contractor, his partner, or agent, shall be obliged, on the completion of the contract, to return in good condition, except for fair wear and tear, the equipment of the baths and everything which was assigned to him. He shall be obliged every thirty days properly to wash, scour, and grease with fresh grease all bronze utensils which he uses . . . to prevent proper bathing facilities; the contractor is entitled to make a proportional deduction from his payment for that period. Apart from this case, and if he does anything else in order to operate the same bath, he shall not be entitled to make any reduction. The contractor shall not be allowed to sell wood, except for the loppings of branches which are unsuitable for burning. If he acts otherwise, he shall be liable to pay a hundred sesterces to the treasury for each sale. If the baths are not properly provided, the procurator of the mines may impose a fine on the contractor of up to two hundred sesterces for each occasion on which they are not properly provided. The contractor shall hold wood in store at all times sufficient for ———— days.

COBBLING

Anyone who shall make any shoe or strap such as cobblers usually deal in or shall fix or sell any hobnail or shall be convicted of selling within the boundaries anything else that cobblers usually sell, shall be liable to pay double to the contractor, his partner, or agent. The contractor shall sell nails under the law of iron goods. The contractor, his partner, or agent, is entitled to seize pledges. No one shall be allowed to repair shoes, unless he looks after or mends his own or his owners'. The contractor is obliged to provide all kinds of shoes. If he fails to do so, everyone is entitled to buy wherever he likes.

SHAVING

The contractor is entitled to the privilege that no one shall do shaving for profit in the village of the mine of Vipasca or its territory. Anyone who so does shaving shall be liable to pay to the contractor, his partner, or agent ———— denarii for each shave, and his implements shall be forfeited to the contractor. Excepted are slaves who look after their owners or fellow slaves. Traveling barbers not despatched by the contractor shall have no right to shave. The contractor, his partner, or agent, shall have the right to seize pledges. Anyone who prevents his taking a pledge shall be liable to pay five denarii on each occasion. The contractor shall take one or more suitable executants into partnership.

LAUNDRIES

No one shall be allowed to launder new or used clothes for payment, except those to whom the contractor, his partner, or agent, have sublet the contract or given permission. Anyone convicted of breaking the rule shall be liable to pay three denarii per garment to the contractor, his partner, or agent. The contractor, his partner, or agent, shall be allowed to seize pledges.

DUES ON SLAG AND DUMPS

Whoever within the boundaries of the mine of Vipasca wishes to clean . . . sort, break up, riddle, or wash silver or bronze slag, or dust from slag or spoil, or who shall undertake any operation in the stone quarries, shall within three days declare what slaves or hired laborers they are sending for the work and shall pay to the contractor ———— denarii per month up to the day before the kalends of the next month: if they fail to do so they shall be liable to pay double. Whoever brings into the boundaries of the mines spoil containing bronze or silver from other mineral workings shall be liable to pay to the contractor, his partner, or agent, one denarius per hundredweight. Whatever is owed to the contractor, his partner, or agent, under this paragraph of the law, and is not paid, or satisfaction given, on the day when the debt is incurred, he shall be liable to pay double. The contractor, his partner, or agent, is entitled to seize pledges, and whatever such slag has been cleaned . . . sorted, broken up, riddled, or washed, and whatsoever stones or blocks have been cut in the stone quarries, shall be forfeit to him, unless what is owing to the contractor, his partner, or agent shall have been paid. Excepted are slaves and freedmen of the silver and bronze smelters, who look after the smelting operations of their owners or patrons.

SCHOOLMASTERS

It is decided that schoolmasters shall be immune from the procurator of the mines.

TAKING POSSESSION OF SHAFTS OR STAKES

Whoever within the boundaries of the mine of Vipasca shall take possession of or occupy a shaft or the site of a shaft in order to maintain his claim, according to the law laid down for the mines, shall within two days of taking possession of or occupying it make a declaration before the contractor of this tax, his partner, or agent.

151. A gold miner

By this contract Memmius, a free provincial, binds himself as an indentured laborer in the Dacian gold mines. Aurelius Adiutor, his employer, is probably the tenant of a mining shaft, and Titus and Senecio his partners.

151. S. Riccobono, Fontes Iuris Romani Ante Justiniani[2], *III. 150*

IN THE consulship of Macrinus and Celsus [A.D. 164] on the 13th day before the kalends of June, I, Flavius Secundinus, have written this at the request of Memmius son of Asclepius, because he said he did not know his letters: viz., that he said that he has leased, and he has actually leased, his labor at gold mining to Aurelius Adiutor from today until the ides of November next, for seventy denarii and his food. He will be entitled to receive his pay at intervals. He will be obliged to provide the work of a healthy and strong man to his hirer above said. If he wishes to withdraw or stop against the will of his hirer, he shall be obliged to pay five sesterces per day, reckoned from the total pay. But if he shall be hindered by flooding, he shall be obliged to reckon in proportion. If when the time is up the hirer delays to pay the wage, he shall be liable to the same penalty, apart from three days of grace. Done at Immenosus Major.

[signatures]   TITUS son of Beusans   SOCRATIO son   MEMMIUS son
                     also called Bradua   of Socratio   of Asclepius

152. An imperial quarry

This quarry is run, under the imperial procurator of quarries, by a single contractor, who is a slave of the emperor (as appears from another inscription). The quarry was probably worked by convict labor, hence the military guard. Condemnation to the mines or quarries was a common penalty for crime (cf. No. 84).

152. Dittenberger, OGIS, 678

FOR THE salvation and eternal victory of Imperator Caesar Trajanus Hadrianus Augustus and all his house and the success of the works ordered by him, this temple and all its precinct was built to Zeus, the Sun, the Great Serapis, and the associated gods by Epaphroditus, former slave of Sigerius, contractor for the quarries, under Rammius Martialis, prefect of Egypt, Chresimus, freedman of Augustus, being procurator of the quarries, Avitus being centurion of Cohort I Flavia of the Cilicians with cavalry element. Year 2 of Imperator Caesar Trajanus Hadrianus Augustus, 29 Pharmuthi [April 23, 118].

153. Price regulation

The Mediterranean countries are very liable to crop failures owing to the low and variable rainfall, and in ancient times local shortages were difficult to remedy in inland towns owing to the very high cost of land transport. The governor's only response to a famine in Antioch of Pisidia, in the heart of Asia Minor, is to prevent the aggravation of the crisis by landowners hoarding corn and thus forcing up the price. Corn is to be sold to the local authority at about double the normal price (1 denarius = 16 asses).

The first part of the inscription gives the governor's previous career in reverse order. Having started a senatorial career by a minor magistracy and a military tribunate, he was specially promoted for his military distinction by Vespasian and omitted the offices of quaestor, tribune of the plebs and praetor, proceeding at once to hold posts reserved for ex-praetors, curator of roads in Italy, legate of a legion, proconsul of Baetica, prefect of the treasury, and, finally, governor of a large imperial province and consul.

153. JRS, *XIV* (1924). 179–84

To Lucius Antistius son of Lucius of the tribe Galeria Rusticus, consul, *legatus pro praetore* of Imperator Caesar Domitianus Augustus Germanicus of the provinces of Cappadocia Galatia Pontus Pisidia Paphlagonia Armenia Minor Lycaonia, prefect of the treasury of Saturn, proconsul of the province of Further Spain, *legatus* of the deified Vespasian and the deified Trajan and of Imperator Caesar Domitian Augustus Germanicus of Legion VIII Augusta, curator of the Aurelian and Cornelian roads, enrolled in the senate with praetorian rank by the deified Vespasian and the deified Titus, decorated by the same with military prizes, a mural crown, a rampart crown, a golden crown, three banners, three plain lances, military tribune of Legion II Augusta, one of the ten commissioners for judging disputes, patron of the colony, in view of his diligent provision for the corn supply. Lucius Antistius Rusticus *legatus pro praetore* of Imperator Caesar Domitianus Augustus says:

Whereas the *duoviri* and decurions of the splendid colony of Antioch have written to me that owing to the severity of the winter the price of corn has shot up, and have asked that the common people should have the possibility of buying it; that all who are citizens or residents of the colony of Antioch shall declare before the decurions of the colony of Antioch within thirty days of this edict being posted, how much corn each has and where and how much he reserves for seed and a year's food for his household, and shall allow the buyers of the colony of Antioch to buy all the rest of his corn. I fix the time of the sale on 1st August next. If anyone disobeys, he must know that I shall confiscate whatever corn is retained contrary to my edict, an eighth being fixed as a reward for the informer. As I have been informed that before the persistent severity of this winter a modius of corn stood at 8 or 9 asses in the colony and it is inequitable that the hunger of his fellow citizens should be a source of profit to anyone, I forbid the price to exceed 1 denarius per modius.

154. Diocletian's edict on prices

During the mid-third century the denarius was seriously debased owing to the financial difficulties of the short-lived emperors of the time, and a great inflation was the result. Diocletian tried to reform the currency, but continued to mint vast quantities of silver-washed copper coins, so that prices continued to go up. Having no knowledge of economics the emperor attributed the price rise to the greed of shopkeepers and fixed maximum prices by edict. This preamble is followed by an immense and detailed schedule of maximum prices ranging from gold bullion to peas and beans, and maximum wages for occupations ranging from professors to agricultural laborers.

154. Dessau, ILS, 642

IMPERATOR Caesar Gaius Aurelius Valerius Diocletianus, the pious, the fortunate, the invincible, Augustus, pontifex maximus, Germanicus maximus for the sixth time, Sarmaticus maximus for the fourth time, Persicus maximus for the second time, Brittanicus maximus, Carpicus maximus, Armeniacus maximus, Medicus maximus, Adiabenicus maximus, of the tribunician power for the eighteenth time, consul for the seventh time, imperator for the eighteenth time, father of his country, proconsul, and Imperator Caesar Marcus Aurelius Valerius Maximianus, the pious, the fortunate, the invincible, Augustus, pontifex maximus, Germanicus maximus for the fifth time, Sarmaticus maximus for the fourth time, Persicus maximus for the second time, Brittanicus maximus, Carpicus maximus, Armeniacus maximus, Medicus maximus, Adiabenicus maximus, of the tribunician power for the seventeenth time, consul for the sixth time, imperator for the seventeenth time, father of his country, proconsul; and Flavius Valerius Constantius, Germanicus maximus for the second time, Sarmaticus maximus for the second time, Persicus maximus for the second time, Brittanicus maximus, Carpicus maximus, Armeniacus maximus, Medicus maximus, Adiabenicus maximus, of the tribunician power for the ninth time, consul for the third time, the most noble Caesar; and Galerius Valerius Maximianus, Germanicus maximus for the second time, Sarmaticus maximus for the second time, Persicus maximus for the second time, Brittanicus maximus, Carpicus maximus, Armeniacus maximus, Medicus maximus, Adiabenicus maximus, of the tribunician power for the ninth time, consul for the third time, the most noble Caesars, say:

That the fortune of our state, to which, after the immortal gods, we must be grateful for a world that is quiet and resting in the embrace of the most profound calm, as we recall the wars which we have successfully carried on, and for the blessings of a peace that was won with great effort, may be faithfully disposed and suitably adorned, is the demand of the public welfare and of the dignity and majesty of Rome. We, therefore, who by the gracious favor of the gods have repelled the former tide of barbarian ravages by destroying them, must by due defense of justice guard a peace which was established for eternity. If any self-restraint could check the excesses with which boundless and furious avarice rages, avarice which with no thought for the good of mankind hastens only to its own gain and profit, not by years or months or days but by hours and even minutes, or if the general welfare could endure the riotous license by which it, in its misfortune, is from day to day grievously injured, there would be left perhaps some room for excuse and for silence, since human forbearance might diminish the destestable cruelty of this pitiable situation. Since, however, it is the only desire of unrestrained madness to care nothing for the common need, and since it is considered among the unscrupulous and intemperate almost the creed of avarice, swelling and rising with fiery passions, to desist from ravaging the wealth of all through necessity rather than of its own wish, and since we whom the extremity of need has brought to understand their most unfortunate situation can no longer close our eyes to it, we the protectors of the human race viewing the situation have agreed that justice must intervene as arbiter, so that the long-hoped-for solution which mankind itself could not supply might through the remedy of our foresight be applied for the good of all. Common knowledge recognizes, and the facts themselves proclaim, how our provision for the situation is nearly too late, while we were laying down plans or reserving remedies already devised in the hope that, as was to be expected by the laws of nature, mankind, apprehended in the most serious offenses, might reform itself, for we think it far better that the lot of intolerable depredation should be removed from men's minds by the feeling decision of the same men, whom, as they daily plunged into more serious offenses, and turned in

their blindness to crimes against the state, their grievous iniquity
had charged with the most cruel inhumanity as the enemies of the
individual and the commonwealth. We, therefore, hasten to apply
the remedies long demanded by the situation, satisfied that there
can be no complaints that the intervention of our remedy may be
considered untimely or unnecessary, or trivial and unimportant
among the unscrupulous, who, in spite of perceiving our silence of
so many years, as a lesson in restraint, have been unwilling to copy
it. For who is so hard and so devoid of human feeling that he
cannot, or rather has not perceived, that in the commerce carried
on in the markets or involved in the daily life of cities immoderate
prices are so widespread that the unbridled passion for gain is
lessened neither by abundant supplies nor by fruitful years; so that
without a doubt men who are busied in these affairs constantly
plan to control the very winds and weather from the movements of
the stars, and, evil that they are, they cannot endure the watering
of the fertile fields by the rains from above which bring the hope
of future harvests, since they reckon it their own loss if abundance
comes through the moderation of the weather. As for the men whose
aim it is always to seek profit even from the generosity of the gods,
to restrain general prosperity, and furthermore to use a poor year
to traffic in losses and commission fees, men who, individually
abounding in great riches which could completely satisfy whole
nations, try to seize smaller fortunes and pursue ruinous percent-
ages, concern for humanity in general persuades us to set a limit,
our subjects, to the avarice of such men. But even now we must
detail the facts whose urgency after long delay has finally driven
our tolerance to action, so that, although it is difficult for the
avarice which rages throughout the whole world to be described
by a specific illustration, or rather fact, nevertheless, the establishment of a remedy may be considered more just when utterly
unrestrained men are forced by some sign and token to recognize
the untamed desires of their own minds. Everyone knows that
insolence, covertly attacking the commonwealth, wherever the
public safety demands that our armies be directed, not in villages or
towns only, but on every road, comes to the mind of the profiteer
to extort prices for merchandise, not fourfold or eightfold, but
such that human speech is incapable of describing either the price
or the act; and that sometimes the single purchase of a soldier
deprives him of his bonus and salary, so that the contributions of

the whole world to support the armies fall to the abominable profits of thieves, so that our soldiers seem with their own hands to offer the hopes of their service and their completed labors to profiteers, with the result that the pillagers of the nation constantly seize more than they know how to hold. Aroused justly and righteously by all the facts which we have detailed above, and with mankind itself now appearing to be praying for a release, we have decreed that there be established, not prices of articles for sale, for such an act would be unjust when many provinces occasionally rejoice in the good fortune of wished-for low prices and, so to speak, the privilege of prosperity, but a maximum, so that when the violence of high prices appears anywhere—and may the gods avert such an evil—avarice which over an immense area could not be restrained, might be checked by the limits of our statute or by the boundaries of our regulatory law. It is, therefore, our pleasure, that the prices listed in the subjoined summary be observed in the whole of our empire in such fashion that every man may know that while permission to exceed them has been forbidden to him, the blessing of low prices has in no case been restricted in those places where supplies are seen to abound, since special provision is made for these and avarice is definitely quieted. Moreover, among buyers and sellers who customarily visit ports and foreign provinces this universal decree should be a check so that since they, too, will know that in the time of high prices there is no possibility of exceeding the determined prices for commodities, such a reckoning of places, transportation, and the whole business may be made at the time of sale that the justice of our decree forbidding those who transport merchandise to sell anything at higher prices may be evident. Since then it is agreed that even in the time of our ancestors it was customary in passing laws to restrain insolence by prescribing a penalty and since it is rare for a situation tending to the good of humanity to be embraced spontaneously, and since, as a guide, fear is always found the most influential teacher in the performance of duty, it is our pleasure that anyone who shall have resisted this statute shall, for his daring, be subject to the capital penalty. And let no one consider this penalty harsh, since there is at hand the means of avoiding the danger—the observation of moderation. To the same penalty, moreover, those who in the desire to buy shall conspire against the statute with the greed of the seller, shall be subject; nor is he exempt from the same penalty who, though possessing the necessities of life and business, believes that subsequent to this regulation he may withdraw them from the market, since a penalty should be even more severe for him who introduces poverty than for him who harasses it against the law. We, therefore, urge upon the loyalty of all our people that a law constituted for the public good may be observed with willing obedience and due care; especially since in such a law provision has been made, not for single states and peoples and provinces, but for the whole world, to whose ruin very few are known to have been hostile, whose avarice neither the fullness of time nor the riches for which they strive can lessen or sate.

155. The origins of the colonate

This law of Constantine is the first imperial edict to record the conversion of free agricultural tenants into quasi-serfs, hereditarily tied to the soil and subject to various legal disabilities. The process probably began under Diocletian, who appears to have enacted that all agricultural workers must remain (with their children) in the places where they were registered in the census. A much earlier instance of such a rule being applied in Egypt is No. 120.

Despite the language of this law, tenants remained technically free men and not slaves; Constantine means that they may be chained like slaves.

155. Codex Theodosianus, *V. 17. 1*

EMPEROR CONSTANTINE AUGUSTUS to the provincials.

Any person in whose possession a tenant that belongs to another is found not only shall restore the aforesaid tenant to his place of origin but also shall assume the capitation tax for this man for the time that he was with him. Tenants also who meditate flight may be bound with chains and reduced to a servile condition, so that by virtue of a servile condemnation they shall be compelled to fulfill the duties that befit free men.

Given on the third day before the kalends of November in the consulship of Pacatianus and Hilarianus [October 30, 332].

156. The colonate in Palestine

It appears from this law that landlords welcomed the new rule, since agricultural labor was very scarce. It is not certain why tenants had

hitherto been free to move in Palestine, but probably the rural population was, as in Egypt, registered in their villages, and therefore free to
move from one farm to another in the village. Elsewhere, e.g., in Asia
Minor, they were registered on their farms under their landlords.

156. Codex Justinianus, XI. 51. 1

THE EMPERORS Valentinian, Theodosius, and Arcadius, Augusti,
to Cynegius, praetorian prefect.

Whereas in other provinces which are subject to the rule of our
serenity a law instituted by our ancestors holds tenants down by a
kind of eternal right, so that they are not allowed to leave the places
by whose crops they are nurtured or desert the fields which they
have once undertaken to cultivate, but the landlords of Palestine
do not enjoy this advantage: we ordain that in Palestine also no
tenant whatever be free to wander at his own choice, but as in
other provinces be tied to the owner of the farm.

157. The colonate in Thrace

This law and another in similar terms about Illyricum shows that the
original object of the rule tying agricultural workers to the land was to
facilitate the collection of the poll tax, but that tenants continued to be
bound to the soil even in areas where this tax was abolished, to benefit
their landlords.

157. Codex Justinianus, XI. 52. 1

EMPERORS Theodosius Arcadius, and Honorius, Augusti, to Ruf-
inus, praetorian prefect.

Throughout the whole diocese of Thrace the *capitatio* of persons
is abolished and only the *iugatio* of land is to be paid, and lest it may
appear that license has been given to tenants, freed from the tie of
taxation, to wander and go off where they wish, they shall be
bound by the rule of origin, and though they appear to be free-born
by condition, shall nevertheless be considered as slaves of the land
itself to which they are born, and shall have no right of going off
where they like or of changing their place, but the landowner shall
enjoy his right over them with the care of a patron and the power
of a master.

158. Legal disabilities of the colonate

Tied tenants were not allowed to alienate their own property without
the consent of their landlords, who were responsible for paying their
taxes, and are by this law denied the right of prosecuting landlords in
civil actions, except for excessive rents.

158. Codex Justinianus, *XI. 50. 2*

EMPERORS Arcadius and Honorius, Augusti, to Nebridius, proconsul of Asia.

Tenants who are inscribed on the census lists, as they are free
from those persons to whom the tribute does not make them
subject, seem nevertheless to be almost delivered over in a kind of
servitude to those to whom they are subject by their annual
payments and by the obligation of their condition. It is all the less
to be tolerated that they should dare to prosecute those by whom,
as by owners, they can indubitably be sold together with their
possessions. We, therefore, remove this power, so that no one may
dare to prosecute his owner in the courts, and they may realize that
all their property belongs to him to whom they themselves belong.
For whereas it has been frequently enacted, that no tenant is
allowed to sell or otherwise alienate any part of his belongings
without the knowledge of the owner of the estate, how can he
litigate on equal terms against his person, when the law is laid down
that his own belongings are not in his legal power, and have
allowed him the power of acquiring but not also of transferring,
and have laid down that he acquires and holds for his master? In
civil cases we forbid such persons to appear and speak against their
owners and patrons, except in the case of excessive rents, in which
previous emperors granted them the right to sue. In public accusations for crimes, their right of bringing charges on account of their
own wrongs or those of their dependents is not removed.

159. Leases of state land

One of the major economic problems of the later empire was the
progressive abandonment of land which its owners or lessees found it
unprofitable to cultivate, probably because of the high rate of land tax,
which swallowed up the low profit obtainable from marginal land.
This meant not only loss of production but loss of tax. This law deals

with imperial land, let on perpetual leases. The lessees sometimes had a loss on such lands, and had to pay the rent and taxes on them from the profits of their own private land. The government enacts that any purchaser of such private land must take responsibility for the payments due from the leased imperial land.

159. Codex Theodosianus, *XI. i. 4*

EMPEROR CONSTANTIUS AUGUSTUS

IF ANY person should purchase anything under the private ownership of an emphyteuticary or patrimonial landholder, by the substance of which property the emphyteuticary or patrimonial landholder had been accustomed to support other landholdings, and if by such a sale the rest of the property should collapse as though the sinews of its strength had been cut out, so to speak, the purchaser must assume the burdens of the landholdings which remain as useless in the possession of the seller.

Given on the eighth day before the ides of December at Thessalonica in the consulship of Felicianus and Titianus [December 6, 337].

160. Miners in the fourth century

Miners were in the late empire, like agricultural tenants, free persons tied hereditarily to their occupation. Here the emperor Valentinian tries to attract volunteers by offering liberal terms.

160. Codex Theodosianus, *X. 19. 3*

EMPERORS Valentinian and Valens Augusti to Cresconius Count of Mines.

With long-pondered deliberation We consider that a sanction must be issued to the effect that if any person should wish to enter the industry of mining, by his own labor he may acquire advantages both for himself and for the state. Therefore, if any persons should voluntarily enter the industry, Your Laudability shall require such persons to pay eight scruples each of gold dust. Moreover, if they should be able to collect more, they shall sell the same to the treasury by preference, from which they shall receive an appropriate price from Our largesses.

Given on the fourth day before the ides of December at Paris in the consulship of Valentinian and Valens [December 10, 365].

161. The state arms factories

Diocletian built a number of state arms factories and manned them with military personnel. These two factories were engaged in inlaying officers' armor with bronze, silver, and gold. Most manufactured workaday weapons.

161. Codex Theodosianus, X. 22. 1

EMPERORS Valentinian, Valens, and Gratian Augusti to Tatianus, Count of the Sacred Largesses.

Since six helmets and cheek guards for each period of thirty days are covered with bronze by each metalworker, both at Antioch and at Constantinople, but eight helmets and the same number of cheek guards are covered with silver or are gilded each thirty days at Antioch, and only three at Constantinople, We decree that at Constantinople also each metalworker shall decorate with gold and silver, not three(?) helmets for each thirty days but six each, with an equal number of cheek guards.

Given on the fifth day before the ides of March at Antioch in the third consulship of Gratian Augustus and the consulship of Equitius [March 11, 374].

162. State armorers

The workers in the arms factories became a hereditary group like agricultural tenants and miners and were not allowed, themselves or their children, to take up other occupations, being branded for identification.

162. Codex Theodosianus, X. 22.4

EMPERORS Arcadius and Honorius Augusti to Hosius, Master of Offices.

Brands, that is, the official state mark, shall be stamped upon the arms of armorers, in imitation of the practice of branding army recruits, so that in this manner at least it may be possible to recognize runaways in hiding. If any man should harbor such armorers or their children, he shall be claimed without doubt for an arms factory, just as those who for the purpose of avoiding their labor have surreptitiously passed over to the enlistment oaths of any form of the public imperial service.

Given on the eighteenth day before the kalends of January at Constantinople in the fourth consulship of Honorius and the consulship of Eutychianus [December 15, 398].

163. The mint workers

The workers in the imperial mints had always been imperial slaves, but had become a hereditary group, since their children, if they cohabited with the slave women of the group, were born slaves of the emperor. Difficulties arose when male slaves cohabited with free women, since the children by the ordinary rule of Roman law were free. Under the emperor Claudius a resolution of the senate had been passed in the terms set out in the text below. The workers in the weaving mills and dyeing establishment established by Diocletian were also hereditary state slaves.

163. Codex Theodosianus, X. 20. 10

THE SAME Augusti to Hesperius, praetorian prefect.

We decree that no woman of more splendid rank cohabiting with a mint worker shall lose the glory of her native freedom. But if the ordinance of our eternal majesty shall not remove any woman from this presumption, she shall according to the authority of the Claudian resolution of the senate either, having been warned by a legal summons, leave him, or if she thinks fit to cling to the embraces of a mint worker, shall be in no doubt that she will both degrade her children and herself to be bound to his condition. Similarly those also who appear to have been united with mint workers before our law, shall be summoned under the same head, knowing that they have changed their status unless they have abandoned the prohibited union. Again, if any woman of the tied tenant class, belonging to someone else's estate, shall, with or without her landlord's knowledge, cohabit with a mint worker, the landlords shall, on being summoned, forthwith hasten to recover the persons who are legally tied to their lands, or shall know that they have lost the right of reclaiming them for the future by the connivance of their silence. Just as we wish no alien woman to be united with a mint worker, so also we forbid a daughter of a mint worker to cohabit with outsiders.

Given the day before the ides of March at Aquileia in the year after the consulate of Auxonius and Olybrius [March 14, 380].

XIII. Religion

164. Divine honors for Augustus in Asia

This is a decree of the provincial assembly of the cities of Asia, which had immediately after the battle of Actium obtained Augustus' consent to build a temple to Rome and Augustus and to institute a cult. It may be suspected that the proconsul entered the competition—and naturally won it—in order to forestall more extravagant and expensive honors for the emperor, and to substitute for them a useful calendar reform. The highly colored messianic language of the preamble is noteworthy.

164. Dittenberger, OGIS, 458

It was resolved by the Greeks of Asia on the proposal of the high priest Apollonios son of Menophilos of Aezani:

Whereas the providence that divinely orders our life, showing zeal and emulation, ordained the perfect good for our life by producing Augustus, whom it filled with virtue for the benefit of mankind, granting as a savior for us and those that shall come after us him who has ended war and will adorn peace; and Caesar, having appeared on earth, has exceeded the hopes of all who anticipated good things, not only surpassing previous benefactors, but leaving no hope of surpassing him to those that are to come; and the birth of the god was the beginning for the world of the good tidings that he has brought about; and whereas Asia decreed at Smyrna in the proconsulship of Lucius Vulcacius Tullus, when Papion of Dioshieron was secretary, that there should be a crown given to him who invented the greatest honors for the god; Paullus Fabius Maximus, the proconsul of the province, sent as a benefactor by his right hand and by his will, in addition to the other benefactions which he bestowed upon the province, benefactions whose greatness no words can express, also devised for the honor of Augustus something hitherto unknown by the Greeks, to begin the period of our life from his birth:

Wherefore with good fortune and for salvation be it resolved by the Greeks of Asia that the New Year begin for all the cities from the ninth day before the kalends of October [23 September], which is the birthday of Augustus, and in order that the day may match in every city to co-ordinate the Roman and Greek calendars. And that the first month be called Caesar, as was previously resolved, beginning on the ninth day before the kalends of October, Caesar's birthday. And that the crown voted for him who devised the greatest honors for Caesar be given to Maximus the proconsul, and that it be proclaimed forever at the athletic competitions of the Roman Augustan Games at Pergamum that Asia crowns Paullus Fabius Maximus for piously devising honors for Caesar. And a similar proclamation shall be made at the Games of the Caesarea in the several cities. And that the memorandum of the proconsul and the decree of Asia be engraved on a white marble pillar and placed in the sanctuary of Rome and Augustus. And that the delegates of the year see to it that the memorandum of Maximus and the degree of Asia be engraved on white marble pillars in the chief cities of assize districts, and that the pillars be placed in the Caesarea. The months shall be kept as follows: Caesar thirty-one days, Appellaeus thirty days, Audnaeus thirty-one days, Peritius thirty-one days, Dystrus twenty-eight days, Xandicus thirty-one days, Artemision thirty days, Daesius thirty-one days, Panemus thirty days, Loius thirty-one days, Gorpiaeus thirty-one days, Hyperberetaeus thirty days. Total three hundred and sixty-five days. And this year, owing to the intercalary day, Xandicus will have thirty-one days. And that the months and days may proceed from now, the current month Peritius will proceed to the fourteenth, and on the ninth day before the kalends of February [14 January] we will have the first of the month Dystrus and in each month the first of the month will be the ninth day before the kalends, and the extra day shall always be the intercalary kalends of the month Xandicus, two years intervening.

It was resolved by the Greeks of Asia, on the motion of the high priest Apollonius son of Menophilos of Aezani:

Whereas New Year's day must always stand the same for everyone for entry on magistracy according to the order of Paullus Fabius Maximus the proconsul and the decrees of Asia, and there are difficulties about the date because of the appeals at the elections, that the business of the elections shall be in the tenth month, as laid down in the Cornelian law, before the tenth day.

165. Roman citizens and the imperial cult

The provincials were allowed, and sometimes encouraged, to worship the living emperor. In the Roman state religion, emperors were only deified on death. This passage shows how under his successor the divinity of Augustus began to be exploited by informers to form the basis of treason charges. Most sensible emperors, like Tiberius, discouraged this sort of thing.

165. *Tacitus*, Annals, *I. 72–73*

THAT YEAR triumphal honors were decreed to Aulus Caecina, Lucius Apronius, and Gaius Silius for their achievements under Germanicus. The title of father of his country, which the people had so often thrust on him, Tiberius refused, nor would he allow obedience to be sworn to his enactments, though the senate voted it, for he said repeatedly that all human things were uncertain, and that the more he had obtained, the more precarious was his position. But he did not thereby create a belief in his unassuming spirit, for he had revived the law of treason, the name of which indeed was known in ancient times, though other matters came under its jurisdiction, such as the betrayal of an army, or seditious stirring up of the people, or, in short, any wrongful act by which a man had impaired the majesty of the people of Rome. Deeds only were liable to accusation; words went unpunished. It was Augustus who first, under color of this law, applied legal inquiry to libelous writings, provoked as he had been by the licentious freedom with which Cassius Severus had defamed men and women of distinction in his insulting satires. Soon afterward, Tiberius, when consulted by Pompeius Macer as to whether prosecutions for treason should be received, replied that the laws must be enforced. He, too, had been exasperated by the publication of verses of uncertain authorship, pointed at his cruelty and arrogance and his dissensions with his mother.

It will not be uninteresting if I relate in the cases of Falanius and Rubrius, Roman *equites* of moderate fortune, the first experiments at such accusations, in order to explain the origin of a most terrible scourge, how by Tiberius's cunning it crept in among us, how subsequently it was checked, finally how it burst into flame and consumed everything. Against Falanius it was alleged by his accuser that he had admitted among the votaries of Augustus, who in every great house were associated into a kind of brotherhood, one Cassius, a buffoon of infamous life, and that he had also in selling his gardens included in the sale a statue of Augustus. Against Rubrius the charge was that he had violated by perjury the divinity of Augustus. When this was known to Tiberius, he wrote to the consuls that his father had not had a place in heaven decreed to him, that the honor might be turned to the destruction of the citizens. Cassius, the actor, with men of the same profession, used to take part in the games which had been consecrated by his mother to the memory of Augustus. Nor was it contrary to the religion of the state for the emperor's image, like those of other deities, to be added to a sale of gardens and houses. As to the oath, the thing ought to be considered, as if the man had deceived Jupiter. Wrongs done to the gods were the gods' concern.

166. Letter of Tiberius Gytheum

Tiberius seems to have felt a genuine distaste for divine honors, even from provincial cities, as is shown by this letter to the Greek city of Gytheum. Claudius expressed similar sentiments in his letter to the Alexandrians (No. 96).

166. SEG, XI. 923

LETTER OF TIBERIUS

TIBERIUS CAESAR, son of the god Augustus, Augustus, pontifex, of the tribunician power for the sixteenth time, to the ephors and city of Gytheum. The envoy sent by you to me and to my mother, Decimus Tyrranius Nicanor, delivered to me your letter, in which were recorded the laws voted by you in piety toward my father and in our own honor. I approve your action and consider it the duty of all men in general, and particularly of your city, to maintain special honors appropriate to the gods in view of the greatness of the benefits conferred by my father on the whole world. But for myself, I confine myself to more moderate honors suitable for a man. My mother will answer you when she learns from you what decisions you have made about honors to her.

167. A new imperial temple in Asia

This debate, held in A.D. 26, was about the building of another temple of the imperial cult in the province of Asia to the senate, Tiberius, and

Livia. There was, it may be seen, keen rivalry between the cities of the province for the expensive honor of building and maintaining the new temple.

167. Tacitus, Annals, IV. 55–56

TIBERIUS, TO divert people's talk, continually attended the senate, and gave an audience of several days to embassies from Asia on a disputed question as to the city in which the temple before mentioned should be erected. Eleven cities were rivals for the honor, of which they were all equally ambitious, though they differed widely in resources. With little variation they dwelt on antiquity of race and loyalty to Rome throughout her wars with Perseus, Aristonicus, and other kings. But the people of Hypaepa, Tralles, Laodicaea, and Magnesia were passed over as too insignificant; even Ilium, though it boasted that Troy was the cradle of Rome, was strong only in the glory of its antiquity. There was a little hesitation about Halicarnassus, as its inhabitants affirmed that for twelve hundred years their homes had not been shaken by an earthquake and that the foundations of their temple were on the living rock. Pergamum, it was thought, had been sufficiently honored by having a temple of Augustus in the city, on which very fact they relied. The Ephesians and Milesians had, it seemed, wholly devoted their respective towns to the worships of Apollo and Diana. And so the question lay between Sardis and Smyrna. The envoys from Sardis read a decree of the Etrurians, with whom they claimed kindred. Tyrrhenus and Lydus, it was said, the sons of King Atys, divided the nation between them because of its multitude; Lydus remained in the country of his fathers; Tyrrhenus had the work assigned him of establishing new settlements, and names, taken from the two leaders, were given to the one people in Asia and to the other in Italy. The resources of the Lydians were yet further augmented by the immigration of nations into that part of Greece which afterwards took its name from Pelops. They spoke, too, of letters from Roman generals, of treaties concluded with us during the Macedonian war, and of their copious rivers, of their climate, and the rich lands round them.

The envoys from Smyrna, after tracing their city's antiquity back to such founders as either Tantalus, the son of Jupiter, or Theseus, also of divine origin, or one of the Amazons, passed on to the point on which they chiefly relied, their services to the Roman people, whom they had helped with naval armaments, not

only in wars abroad, but in those under which we struggled in
Italy. They had also been the first, they said, to build a temple in
honor of Rome, during the consulship of Marcus Porcius Cato,
when Rome's power indeed was great, but not yet raised to the
highest point, inasmuch as the Punic capital was still standing and
there were mighty kings in Asia. They appealed, too, to the testimony of Lucius Sulla, whose army was once in terrible jeopardy
from a severe winter and want of clothing, and this having been
announced at Smyrna in a public assembly, all who were present
stript their clothes off their backs and sent them to our legions. And
so the senate, when the question was put, gave the preference to
Smyrna. Vibius Marsus moved that Marcius Lepidus, to whom the
province of Asia had been assigned, should have under him a
special commissioner to undertake the charge of the temple; as
Lepidus himself, out of modesty, declined to appoint, Valerius
Naso, one of the ex-praetors, was chosen by lot and sent out.

168. Nero's persecution of the Christians

This is the first recorded persecution of Christians by the imperial
government. Nero, who was suspected of having himself started the
great fire of Rome in A.D. 64, wished to find a scapegoat and found a
good one in the unpopular sect of Christians. Tertullian suggests that it
was from this time that the profession of Christianity was made a
capital offense, as it clearly was in Trajan's reign (see No. 169).

168. Tacitus, Annals, XV. 44

SUCH INDEED were the precautions of human wisdom. The next
thing was to seek means of propitiating the gods, and recourse was
had to the Sibylline books, by the direction of which prayers were
offered to Vulcanus, Ceres, and Proserpina. Juno, too, was entreated by the matrons, first, in the Capitol, then on the nearest
part of the coast, whence water was procured to sprinkle the temple
and image of the goddess. And there were sacred banquets and
nightly vigils celebrated by married women. But all human efforts,
all the lavish gifts of the emperor, and the propitiations of the gods,
did not vanish the sinister belief that the conflagration was the
result of an order. Consequently, to get rid of the report, Nero
fastened the guilt and inflicted the most exquisite tortures on a class
hated for their abominations, called Christians by the populace.
Christus, from whom the name had its origin, suffered the extreme

penalty during the reign of Tiberius at the hands of the procurator
Pontius Pilatus, and a most mischievous superstition, thus checked
for the moment, again broke out not only in Judaea, the first
source of the evil, but even in Rome, where all things hideous and
shameful from every part of the world find their center and
become popular. Accordingly, an arrest was first made of all who
pleaded guilty; then, upon their information, an immense multitude
was convicted, not so much of the crime of firing the city, as of
hatred against mankind. Mockery of every sort was added to their
deaths. Covered with the skins of beasts, they were torn by dogs
and perished, or were nailed to crosses, or were doomed to the
flames and burnt, to serve as a nightly illumination, when daylight
had expired.

Nero offered his gardens for the spectacle, and was exhibiting a
show in the circus, while he mingled with the people in the dress of
a charioteer or stood aloft on a car. Hence, even for criminals who
deserved extreme and exemplary punishment, there arose a feeling
of compassion; for it was not, as it seemed, for the public good, but
to glut one man's cruelty, that they were being destroyed.

169. Pliny and the Christians

It is clear from these two letters that the mere profession of Christianity was an offense punishable by death, quite apart from any of the
crimes of which Christians were suspected, such as ritual infanticide
and incest, and that the charge was not based on their forming illegal
clubs; nor are they accused of refusing to worship the emperor.
Sacrifice to the gods (including the emperor) is only one of the tests
whereby accused persons can clear themselves.

Trajan is not very consistent. If Christianity was a serious crime,
why were the criminals not to be searched for and why were past
offenses to be pardoned? It looks as if Trajan, like Pliny, while regarding Christians as perverse enthusiasts, had some qualms about the
drastic rule which prevailed. It was never rescinded, but until A.D. 250
(see No. 170) no systematic attempt was made to enforce it, and
persecutions were sporadic and local, usually the result of popular
clamor.

169. *Pliny*, Letters, X. 96

It is a rule, Sir, which I inviolably observe, to refer myself to you
in all my doubts; for who is more capable of removing my

scruples, or informing my ignorance? Having never been present at any trials concerning those who profess Christianity, I am unacquainted not only with the nature of their crimes, or the measure of their punishment, but how far it is proper to enter into an examination concerning them. Whether, therefore, any difference is usually made with respect to the ages of the guilty, or no distinction is to be observed between the young and the adult; whether repentance entitles them to a pardon; or if a man has been once a Christian, it avails nothing to desist from his error; whether the very profession of Christianity, unattended with any criminal act, or only the crimes themselves inherent in the profession are punishable; in all these points I am greatly doubtful. In the meanwhile the method I have observed toward those who have been brought before me as Christians is this: I interrogated them whther they were Christians; if they confessed, I repeated the question twice again, adding threats at the same time; when, if they still persevered, I ordered them to be immediately executed: for I was persuaded, whatever the nature of their opinions might be, a contumacious and inflexible obstinacy certainly deserved correction. There were others also brought before me possessed with the same infatuation, but being citizens of Rome, I directed them to be carried thither. But this accusation spreading (as is usually the case) while it was actually under prosecution, several instances of the same nature occurred. An information was presented to me without any name subscribed, containing a charge against numerous persons. Those who denied they were Christians, or had ever been so, when they had repeated after me an invocation to the gods, and offered religious rites with wine and frankincense before your statue (which for the purpose I had ordered to be brought together with those of the gods) and also reviled the name of Christ (there is no forcing, it is said, those who are really Christians, into a compliance with any of these articles), I thought proper to discharge. Some among those who were accused by the informer at first confessed themselves Christians, but immediately after denied it; whilst the rest owned indeed that they had been of that number formerly, but had now (some above three, others more, and a few above twenty years ago) forsaken that error. They all worshipped your statue and the images of the Gods, throwing out imprecations at the same time against the name of Christ. They affirmed the whole of their guilt, or their error, was that they met on a certain stated day before it was light, and addressed themselves in a form of prayer to Christ, as to some God, binding themselves by a solemn oath, not for the purposes of any wicked design, but never to commit any fraud, theft, or adultery, never to falsify their word, nor deny a trust when they should be called upon to deliver it up; after which, it was their custom to separate, and then reassemble, to eat in common a harmless meal. From this custom, however, they desisted after the publication of my edict, by which, according to your orders, I forbade the meeting of any assemblies. After receiving this account, I judged it so much the more necessary to endeavor to extort the real truth, by putting two female slaves to the torture, who were said to administer in their religious functions: but I could discover nothing more than an absurd and excessive superstition. I thought proper, therefore, to adjourn all further proceedings in this affair in order to consult with you. For it appears to be a matter highly deserving your consideration; more especially as great numbers must be involved in the danger of these prosecutions, this inquiry having already extended, and being still likely to extend, to persons of all ranks and ages, and even of both sexes. For this contagious superstition is not confined to the cities only, but has spread its infection among the country villages. Nevertheless, it still seems possible to remedy this evil and restrain its progress. The temples, at least, which were once almost deserted, begin now to be frequented; and the sacred solemnities, after a long intermission, are again revived; while there is a general demand for the victims, which for some time past have met with but few purchasers. From hence it is easy to imagine what numbers might be reclaimed from this error if a pardon were granted to those who shall repent.

TRAJAN TO PLINY

The method you have pursued, my dear Pliny, in the proceedings against those Christians which were brought before you is extremely proper, as it is not possible to lay down any fixed plan by which to act in all cases of this nature. They are not to be searched out. If they should be brought before you, and the crime is proved, they must be punished; with the restriction, however, that where the party denies himself to be a Christian, and shall make it evident that he is not, by invoking our Gods, let him (notwithstanding any former suspicion) be pardoned upon his repentance. Information without the accuser's name subscribed ought not to be received in prosecutions of any sort, as it is introducing a very dangerous precedent, and by no means agreeable to the equity of my government.

170. A certificate of sacrifice under Decius

In A.D. 250 the emperor Decius ordered that all citizens should sacrifice to the gods and obtain a certificate (*libellus*) that they had done so. The measure was evidently intended to destroy Christianity. Many Christians gave in, and many compromised, by obtaining certificates by bribing the officials, or by similar evasions. Some were executed. Decius was killed by the Goths shortly afterward, and the persecution lapsed.

170. W. Wilcken, Chrestomathie, I. 144

[First hand] To THE elected commissioners for sacrifices for the village of Alexander's Island, from Aurelius Diogenes, son of Sarabus, from the village of Alexander's Island, about sixty-two years of age, with a scar on his right eyebrow. I have always sacrificed to the gods, and now in your presence, according to the order, have made sacrifice and libation and tasted the victim's flesh, and I beg you to make a certificate.

[Second hand] I, Aurelius Syrus, saw you sacrificing with your son.

[Third hand: similar affidavit lost]

[First hand again] Year 1 of the emperor Caesar Gaius Messius Quintus Trajanus Decius, the pious, the fortunate, Augustus. 2 Epeiph.

171. Valerian's persecution in Egypt

In A.D. 257 the emperor Valerian opened a fresh persecution by forbidding Christian assemblies and banishing the clergy if they refused to accept the order. The dialogue between Dionysius, bishop of Alexandria, and the prefect of Egypt reveals one of the strongest objections to the Christians—that they were "atheists," denying the gods. The Roman government was in general tolerant of the established religions of the subject peoples, but was suspicious of propagandist religions, which were liable to cause disturbances. It did, however, tolerate such sects as Isis worship and Mithraism, which were propagandist, for their members worshiped the other gods as well. The atheism of the Christians was believed to offend the gods, who therefore punished the empire with plagues, famines, and earthquakes, and wars. This was the popular view, and seems to have been shared by some of the third-century emperors, in view of the continuous disasters which afflicted the empire at that period.

171. *Eusebius*, Ecclesiastical History, *VII. 11*

BUT AS regards the persecution which prevailed so fiercely in his reign, and the sufferings which Dionysius with others endured on account of piety toward the God of the universe, his own words shall show, which he wrote in answer to Germanus, a contemporary bishop who was endeavoring to slander him. His statement is as follows:

"Truly I am in danger of falling into great folly and stupidity through being forced to relate the wonderful providence of God toward us. But since it is said that it is good to keep close the secret of a king, but it is honorable to reveal the works of God, I will join issue with the violence of Germanus. I went not alone to Aemilianus; but my fellow presbyter Maximus, and the deacons Faustus, Eusebius, and Chaeremon, and a brother who was present from Rome went with me. But Aemilianus did not at first say to me: 'Hold no assemblies'; for this was superfluous to him, and the last thing to one who was seeking to accomplish the first. For he was not concerned about our assembling, but that we ourselves should not be Christians. And he commanded me to give this up; supposing if I turned from it, the others also would follow me. But I answered him, neither unsuitably nor in many words: 'We must obey God rather than men.' And I testified openly that I worshiped the one and only God, and no other; and that I would not turn from this nor would I ever cease to be a Christian. Thereupon he commanded us to go to a village near the desert, called Cephro. But listen to the very words which were spoken on both sides, as they were recorded:

"Dionysius, Faustus, Maximus, Marcellus, and Chaeremon being arraigned, Aemilianus the prefect said: 'I have reasoned verbally with you concerning the clemency which our rulers have shown to you; for they have given you the opportunity to save yourselves, if you will turn to that which is according to nature, and worship the gods that preserve their empire, and forget those that are contrary to nature. What then do you say to this? For I do not think that you will be ungrateful for their kindness, since they would turn you to a better course.' Dionysius replied: 'Not all people worship all gods; but each one those whom he approves. We, therefore, reverence and worship the one God, the Maker of all; who hath given the empire to the divinely favored Augusti Valerian and Gallienus; and we pray to him continually for their empire, that it may remain unshaken.' Aemilianus, the prefect, said to them: 'But who forbids you to worship him, if he is a god, together with those who are gods by nature? For you have been commanded to reverence the gods, and the gods whom all know.' Dionysius answered: 'We worship no other.' Aemilianus, the prefect, said to them: 'I see that you are at once ungrateful, and insensible to the kindness of our sovereigns. Therefore you shall not remain in this city. But you shall be sent into the regions of Libya, to a place called Cephro. For I have chosen this place at the command of our sovereigns, and it shall by no means be permitted you or any others, either to hold assemblies or to enter into the so-called cemeteries. But if anyone shall be seen outside the place which I have commanded, or be found in any assembly, he will bring peril on himself. For suitable punishment shall not fail. Go, therefore, where you have been ordered.'

"And he hastened me away, though I was sick, not granting even a day's respite. What opportunity then did I have, either to hold assemblies, or not to hold them?"

Farther on he says: "But through the help of the Lord we did not give up the open assembly. But I called together the more diligently those who were in the city, as if I were with them; being, so to speak, 'absent in body but present in spirit.' But in Cephro a large congregation gathered with us both of the brethren that followed us from the city, and those that joined us from Egypt; and there 'God opened unto us a door for the Word.' At first we were persecuted and stoned; but afterward not a few of the heathen forsook their idols and turned to God. For until this time they had not heard the Word, since it was then first sown by us. And as if God had brought us to them for this purpose, when we had performed this ministry, he transferred us to another place. For Aemilianus, as it appeared, desired to transport us to rougher and more Libyan-like places; so he commanded them to assemble from all quarters in Mareotis, and assigned to them different villages throughout the country. But he ordered us to be placed nearer the highway that we might be seized first. For evidently he arranged and prepared matters so that whenever he wished to seize us he could take all of us without difficulty. When I was first ordered to go to Cephro I did not know where the place was, and had scarcely ever heard the name; yet I went readily and cheerfully. But when I was told that I was to remove to the district of Colluthion, those who were present know how I was affected. For here I will accuse myself. At first I was grieved and greatly disturbed; for though these places were better known and more familiar to us, yet the country was said to be destitute of brethren and of men of character, and to be exposed to attacks on travelers and incursions of robbers. But I was comforted when the brethren reminded me that it was nearer the city, and that while Cephro afforded us much intercourse with the brethren from Egypt, so that we were able to extend the Church more widely, as this place was nearer the city we should enjoy more frequently the sight of those who were truly beloved and most closely related and dearest to us. For they would come and remain, and special meetings could be held, as in the more remote suburbs. And so it turned out."

172. Valerian's persecution in Africa

Valerian next year intensified the persecution by the methods here recorded, by which he hoped to destroy the leadership of the churches. Cyprian, bishop of Carthage, was himself executed under this edict. Valerian was shortly afterward captured by the Persians, and his son Gallienus revoked the persecution. Christianity was tolerated until the great persecution under Diocletian.

172. Cyprian, Letters, 82

CYPRIAN TO his brother Successus.

The reason why I did not write to you at once, dearest brother, is that all the clergy who were subjected to the blow of the ordeal were quite unable to withdraw from there, though prepared all of them in the devotion of their hearts for divine and heavenly glory. You must know that those whom I had sent for the purpose to the City [Rome], so that they could report to us the truth, verified by themselves, about any rescript issued about us, have arrived. There are a great many various and uncertain rumors passing around. The truth is as follows: Valerian has replied to the senate that bishops,

priests, and deacons are to be executed forthwith; senators, those
with the title of honorable (*egregius*), and Roman *equites* are to
lose their rank and be deprived of their property, and if after the
loss of their goods they persist in being Christians, also to be executed, but women to be sent into exile after loss of their goods.
Freedmen of the emperor who previously confessed, or now confess, are to have their property confiscated and be distributed in
chains to imperial estates. The emperor Valerian also added to his
speech a copy of the letter sent to provincial governors about us.
We expect these letters to arrive any day, standing in the firmness
of faith to endure suffering, and awaiting by the help and indulgence of God the crown of eternal life. You should know that
Xistus was executed in the cemetery on the eighth day before the
ides of August, and with him four deacons. The prefects are every
day pressing this persecution in the City; many persons denounced
to them are executed and their goods confiscated. Please let our
other colleagues know this, so that the brotherhood can be
strengthened by their exhortations and prepared for the spiritual
ordeal; so that all our people may think about immortality rather
than death, and, dedicated to God in full faith and courage, may
rejoice rather than fear this trial, in which they know that the
soldiers of God and Christ are not killed but crowned. I wish you,
dearest brother, good health in the Lord.

173. Diocletian's persecution in Palestine

Eusebius here sets out the four successive edicts of Diocletian and his
colleagues against the Christians. The first was issued on February 23,
303, and also included a clause forbidding religious assemblies. The
second followed shortly, and the third before November 20, the
anniversary of Diocletian's accession, when the imprisoned clergy,
having been forced to sacrifice, were released. The fourth edict,
ordering a general sacrifice, followed next spring.

173. *Eusebius*, Martyrs of Palestine, *I, 3*

IT WAS in the nineteenth year of the reign of Diocletian, in the
month Xanthicus, which is called April by the Romans, about the
time of the feast of our Saviour's passion, while Flavianus was
governor of the province of Palestine, that letters were published
everywhere, commanding that the churches be leveled to the

ground and the Scriptures be destroyed by fire, and ordering that those who held places of honor be degraded, and that imperial freedmen, if they persisted in the profession of Christianity, be deprived of freedom.

Such was the force of the first edict against us. But not long after, other letters were issued, commanding that all the bishops of the churches everywhere be first thrown into prison, and afterward, by every artifice, be compelled to sacrifice.

The first of the martyrs of Palestine was Procopius, who, before he had received the trial of imprisonment, immediately on his first appearance before the governer's tribunal, having been ordered to sacrifice to the so-called gods, declared that he knew only one to whom it was proper to sacrifice, as he himself wills. But when he was commanded to offer libations to the four emperors, having quoted a sentence which displeased them, he was immediately beheaded. The quotation was from the poet: "The rule of many is not good; let there be one ruler and one king."

It was the seventh day of the month Desius, the seventh before the ides of June, as the Romans reckon, and the fourth day of the week, when this first example was given at Caesarea in Palestine.

In the course of the second year, the persecution against us increased greatly. And at that time, Urbanus being governor of the province, imperial edicts were first issued to him, commanding by a general decree that all the people should sacrifice at once in the different cities, and offer libations to the idols.

174. Diocletian's persecution in Africa

This is the official record of the execution of the first edict at Cirta in Numidia. It can be seen that the clergy offered only a token resistance to surrendering the scriptures. Having done so, they were condemned as *traditores* and excommunicated by stricter Christians.

174. Optatus Milevitanus, Appendix I

IN THE eighth and seventh consulships of Diocletian and Maximian [A.D. 303], 19th May, from the records of Munatius Felix, flamen for life, curator of the colony of Cirta. Arrived at the house where the Christians used to meet, Felix, flamen for life, curator of the city, said to Paul the bishop: "Bring out the writings of the law and anything else you have here, according to the order, so that you may obey the command."

Paul the bishop said: "The readers have the scriptures, but we will give what we have here."

Felix, flamen for life, curator of the city, said to Paul the bishop: "Point out the readers or send for them."

Paul the bishop said: "You all know them."

Felix, flamen for life, curator of the city, said: "We do not know them."

Paul the bishop said: "The municipal office knows them, that is, the clerks Edusius and Junius."

Felix, flamen for life, curator of the city, said: "Leaving over the matter of the readers, whom the office will point out, produce what you have."

In the presence of Paul the bishop and Montanus and Victor Deusatelius and Memorius the priests, being seated, and Mars and Helius the deacons, standing, Marcuclius, Catulinus, Silvanus, and Carosus the sub-deacons and Januarius, Meraclus, Fructuosus, Miggis, Saturninus, and Victor son of Samsuricus, and the other gravediggers, carried out the following, Victor son of Aufidus entering them on the list: 2 gold cups, 6 silver cups, 6 silver ewers, 1 silver bowl, 7 silver lamps, 2 candle sticks, 7 short bronze lamp-stands with their lamps, 11 bronze lamps with their chains, 82 women's tunics, 38 hoods, 16 men's tunics, 13 pairs of men's boots, 47 pairs of women's boots, 19 rustic belts. Felix, flamen for life and curator, said to Marcuclius, Silvanus, and Carosus, the grave-diggers: "Bring out what you have."

Silvanus and Carosus said: "We have thrown out everything that was here."

Felix, flamen for life, curator of the city, said to Marcuclius, Silvanus, and Carosus: "Your answer is entered on the record."

After some empty cupboards had been found in the library, Silvanus then produced a silver box and a silver lamp, which he said he had found behind a barrel.

Victor son of Aufidus said to Silvanus: "You would have been a dead man if you hadn't found them."

Felix, flamen for life, curator of the city, said to Silvanus: "Look more carefully, in case there is anything left here."

Silvanus said: "There is nothing left. We have thrown everything out."

And when the dining room was opened, there were found there four bins and six barrels.

Felix, flamen for life, curator of the city, said : "Bring out the scriptures which you have, so that we can obey the orders of the emperors and their command." Catulinus brought out an extremely large volume.

Felix, flamen for life, curator of the city, said to Marcuclius and Silvanus: "Why have you given one volume only? Produce the scriptures that you have."

Marcuclius and Catulinus said: "We haven't any more, because we are subdeacons; the readers have the books."

Felix, flamen for life, curator of the city, said to Marcuclius and Silvanus: "Show me the readers."

Marcuclius and Catulinus said: "We don't know where they live."

Felix, flamen for life, curator of the city, said to Marcuclius and Silvanus: "If you don't know where they live, tell me their names."

Marcuclius and Catulinus said: "We are not traitors: here we are, order us to be killed."

Felix, flamen for life, curator of the city, said: "Put them under arrest."

And when they had come to the house of Eugenius, Felix, flamen for life and curator, said to Eugenius: "Bring out the scriptures which you have, so that you may obey the order. And he brought out 4 books. Felix, flamen for life and curator, said to Silvanus and Carosus: "Show me the other readers."

Silvanus and Carosus said: "The bishop has already said that Edusius and Junius the clerks know them all: they will show you the way to their houses."

Edusius and Junius, the clerks, said: "We will show them, sir."

And when they had come to the house of Felix the cobbler, he brought out 5 books. And when they had come to the house of Victorinus, he brought out 8 books. And when they had come to the house of Projectus, he brought out 5 large books and 2 small. And when they had come to the house of the schoolmaster, Felix, flamen for life and curator, said to Victor the schoolmaster: "Bring out the scriptures which you have, so that you may obey the order." Victor the schoolmaster produced 2 books, and 4 sets of 5 booklets. Felix, flamen for life and curator, said to Victor: "Bring out the scriptures; you have more." Victor the schoolmaster said:

"If I had any more, I would have given them." And when they came to the house of Euticius of Caesarea, Felix, flamen for life and curator, said to Euticius: "Bring out the scriptures, so that you may obey the order." Euticius said: "I have not got any." Felix, flamen for life and curator, said to Euticius: "Your statement is entered on the record." And when they had come to the house of Coddeo, his wife brought out 6 books. Felix, flamen for life and curator, said: "Look in case you have any more and bring them out." The woman replied: "I have not any." Felix, flamen for life and curator, said to Bos the public slave: "Go in and look, in case he has any more." The public slave said: "I have looked and not found any." Felix, flamen for life and curator, said to Victorinus, Silvanus, and Carosus: "If anything has been omitted, the responsibility is yours."

175. The edict of Galerius

In the western provinces the persecution very soon lapsed; it is doubtful whether anything was done after the promulgation and execution of Diocletian's first edict. In the eastern parts, Galerius, who succeeded Diocletian as Augustus, was a rigorous persecutor—according to Lactantius he had bullied Diocletian into starting the whole thing—and with his Caesar Maximinus continued intermittently to renew the persecution till 311. Then, having succumbed to a mortal disease, he had second thoughts and issued the edict of toleration given below. In the preamble he expresses the objection which pagans had to Christianity as a wanton breach of the old and established religious order. Galerius may have feared that the god of the Christians had struck him down and wished to placate him; he died a few days after the issue of this edict.

175. *Eusebius*, Ecclesiastical History, *VIII. 17*

IMPERATOR Caesar Galerius Valerius Maximianus, the invincible, Augustus, pontifex maximus, Germanicus Maximus, Egyptiacus Maximus, Thebaicus Maximus, Sarmaticus Maximus for the fifth time, Persicus Maximus for the second time, Carpicus Maximus for the sixth time, Armeniacus Maximus, Medicus Maximus, Adiabeniacus Maximus, of the tribunician power for the twentieth time, imperator for the nineteenth time, consul for the eighth time, father of his country, proconsul; and imperator Caesar Flavius Valerius Constantinus, the pious, the fortunate, the invincible, Augustus,

pontifex maximus, of the tribunician power, imperator for the fifth
time, consul, father of his country, proconsul; and imperator
Caesar Valerius Licinius, the pious, the fortunate, the invincible,
Augustus, pontifex maximus, of the tribunician power for the
fourth time, imperator for the third time, consul, father of his
country, proconsul; to the people of their provinces, greeting:

"Among the other things which we have ordained for the public
advantage and profit, we formerly wished to restore everything to
conformity with the ancient laws and public discipline of the
Romans and to provide that the Christians also, who have forsaken
the religion of their ancestors, should return to a good disposition.
For in some way such arrogance had seized them and such stupidity had overtaken them, that they did not follow the ancient
institutions which possibly their own ancestors had formerly established, but made for themselves laws according to their own
purpose, as each one desired, and observed them, and thus assembled as separate congregations in various places. When we had
issued this decree that they should return to the institutions established by the ancients, a great many submitted under danger, but a
great many being harassed endured all kinds of death. And since
many continue in the same folly, and we perceive that they neither
offer to the heavenly gods the worship which is due, nor pay
regard to the god of the Christians, in consideration of our philanthropy and our invariable custom, by which we are wont to extend
pardon to all, we have determined that we ought most cheerfully
to extend our indulgence in this matter also; that they may again be
Christians, and may rebuild the conventicles in which they were
accustomed to assemble, on condition that nothing be done by
them contrary to discipline. In another letter we shall indicate to
the provincial governors what they have to observe. Wherefore,
on account of this indulgence of ours, they ought to supplicate
their god for our safety, and that of the people, and their own, that
the public welfare may be preserved in every place, and that they
may live securely in their several homes."

176. The edict of Milan

The persecution was revived by Maximin, who succeeded to Galerius
in the east. In 313, Maximin attacked his western neighbor Licinius,
who ruled the Balkans, but was defeated and killed. Constantine had

shortly before conquered Maxentius in the west, fighting under the sign of the Christian god, and at an interview at Milan persuaded Licinius to issue this edict, commonly called the Edict of Milan. It was actually issued by Licinius at Nicomedia on April 30, 313. While proclaiming general toleration, its tenor is clearly monotheistic and pro-Christian. Its motive is unambiguously stated, to secure the favor of the supreme divinity for the empire.

176. Eusebius, Ecclesiastical History, X. *5*

PERCEIVING LONG ago that religious liberty ought not to be denied, but that it ought to be granted to the judgment and desire of each individual to perform his religious duties according to his own choice, we had given orders that every man, Christians as well as others, should preserve the faith of his own sect and religion. But since in that rescript, in which such liberty was granted them, many and various conditions seemed clearly added, some of them, it may be, after a little retired from such observance. When I, Constantine Augustus, and I, Licinius Augustus, came under favorable auspices to Milan and took under consideration everything which pertained to the common weal and prosperity, we resolved among other things, or rather first of all, to make such decrees as seemed in many respects for the benefit of everyone; namely, such as should preserve reverence and piety toward the deity. We resolved, that is, to grant both to the Christians and to all men freedom to follow the religion which they choose, that whatever heavenly divinity exists may be propitious to us and to all that live under our government. We have therefore determined, with sound and upright purpose, that liberty is to be denied to no one, to choose and to follow the religious observances of the Christians, but that to each one freedom is to be given to devote his mind to that religion which he may think adapted to himself, in order that the deity may exhibit to us in all things his accustomed care and favor. It was fitting that we should write that this is our pleasure, that those conditions being entirely left out which were contained in our former letter concerning the Christians which was sent to your devotion, everything that seemed very severe and foreign to our mildness may be annulled, and that now everyone who has the same desire to observe the religion of the Christians may do so without molestation. We have resolved to communicate this most fully to your care, in order that you may know that we have granted to these same Christians freedom and full liberty to observe their own religion. Since this has been granted freely by us to them, your devotion perceives that liberty is granted to others also who may wish to follow their own religious observances; it being clearly in accordance with the tranquillity of our times, that each one should have the liberty of choosing and worshiping whatever deity he pleases. This has been done by us in order that we might not seem in any way to discriminate against any cult or religion. And we decree still further in regard to the Christians, that their places, in which they were formerly accustomed to assemble, and concerning which in the former letter sent to your devotion a different command was given, if it appear that any have bought them either from our treasury or from any other person, shall be restored to the said Christians, without demanding money or any other equivalent, with no delay or hesitation. If any happen to have received the said places as a gift, they shall restore them as quickly as possible to these same Christians: with the understanding that if those who have bought these places, or those who have received them as a gift, demand anything from our bounty, they may go to the vicar of the district, that provision may be made for them by our clemency. All these things are to be granted to the society of Christians by your care immediately and without any delay. And since the said Christians are known to have possessed not only those places in which they were accustomed to assemble, but also other places, belonging not to individuals among them, but to the society as a whole, that is, to the society of Christians, you will command that all these, in virtue of the law which we have above stated, be restored, without any hesitation, to these same Christians; that is, to their society and congregation: the above-mentioned provision being of course observed, that those who restore them without price, as we have before said, may expect indemnification from our bounty. In all these things, for the behoof of the aforesaid society of Christians, you are to use the utmost diligence, to the end that our command may be speedily fulfilled, and that in this also, by our clemency, provision may be made for the common and public tranquillity. For by this means, as we have said before, the divine favor toward us which we have already experienced in many matters will continue sure through all time. And that the terms of this our gracious ordinance may be known to all, it is expected that this which we have written will be published everywhere by you and brought to the knowledge of all, in order that this gracious ordinance of ours may remain unknown to no one.

177. Constantine's benefactions to the African church

This letter was sent shortly after Constantine's defeat of Maxentius in 312 and shows him forthwith bestowing his favors on the ministers of the deity who had given him victory. It also shows that Constantine had already learned from Hosius, bishop of Corduba, his religious adviser, that in Africa the Christians were divided into true Christians, called Catholics, and others, who were to be excluded from the imperial bounty and punished if they attacked the Catholics. The second group included those who refused any accommodation with *traditores*, even if they did penance for their sins; they came to be known as Donatists from their leader, Donatus.

177. *Eusebius*, Ecclesiastical History, X. 6

CONSTANTINE AUGUSTUS to Caecilianus, bishop of Carthage. Since it is our pleasure that something should be granted in all the provinces of Africa and Numidia and Mauritania to certain ministers of the legitimate and most holy Catholic religion, to defray their expenses, I have written to Ursus, the honorable finance officer of Africa, and have directed him to make provision to pay to your constancy three thousand *folles*. You will, therefore, when you have received the above sum of money, command that it be distributed among all those mentioned above, according to the list sent to you by Hosius. But if you should find that anything is wanting for the fulfillment of this purpose of mine in regard to all of them, you will demand without hesitation from Heracleides, the procurator of our estates, whatever you find to be necessary. For I commanded him when he was present that if your constancy should ask him for any money, he should see to it that it was paid without delay. And since I have learned that some men of unsettled mind wish to turn the people from the most holy and Catholic church by a certain method of shameful corruption, you should know that I gave command to Anulinus, the proconsul, and also to Patricius, the vicar of the prefects, when they were present, that they should give proper attention not only to other matters but also above all to this, and that they should not overlook such a thing when it happened. Therefore if you see any such men continuing in this madness, go without delay to the above-mentioned officers and report the matter to them; that they may correct them as I commanded them when they were present. The divinity of the great God preserve you for many years, honored Sir.

178. Constantine's grant of immunity to the clergy

In this letter to the proconsul of Africa, Constantine directs that the Catholic, but not the schismatic, clergy were to be exempted from the charges incumbent upon decurions (see No. 105). The motive is clearly stated, to maintain the favor of the Supreme Divinity whom they worship toward the empire.

178. Eusebius, Ecclesiastical History, X. 7

GREETINGS, OUR most esteemed Anulinus. Since it appears from many circumstances that when that religion is despised, in which is preserved the chief reverence for the most holy celestial Power, great dangers are brought upon public affairs; but that when legally adopted and observed it affords the most signal prosperity to the Roman name and remarkable felicity to all the affairs of men, through the divine beneficence; it has seemed good to me, most esteemed Anulinus, that those men who give their services, with due sanctity and with constant observance of this law, to the worship of the divine religion, should receive recompense for their labors. Wherefore it is my will that those within the province entrusted to you, in the Catholic church, over which Caecilianus presides, who give their services to this holy religion, and who are commonly called clergymen, be entirely exempted from all public duties, that they may not by any error or sacrilegious negligence be drawn away from the service due to the Deity, but may devote themselves without any hindrance to their own law. For it seems that when they show greatest reverence to the Deity, the greatest benefits accrue to the state. Farewell, our most esteemed and beloved Anulinus.

179. Constantine's letter to Aelafius

Constantine was petitioned by the schismatics in Africa (the Dona-tists) to judge their quarrel with the Catholics. He referred the case to the bishop of Rome with other bishops, who ruled in favor of the Catholics against the Donatists. They again appealed to the emperor, and he summoned a larger council of bishops to Arles. This passage is a

postscript to an official letter to Aelafius, an African official, asking him
to send representatives of the two parties to Arles. It shows how
important Constantine thought it was to secure God's favor, and that
he had been taught that any division in the church was highly displeas-
ing to God.

179. Optatus Milevitanus, Appendix III

SINCE I am informed that you, too, are a worshipper of the Highest
God, I will confess to your gravity that I consider it absolutely
contrary to the divine law that we should overlook such quarrels
and contentions, whereby the Highest Divinity may perhaps be
moved to wrath, not only against the human race, but also against
me myself, to whose care He has, by His celestial will, committed
the government of all earthly things, and that He may be so far
moved as to take some untoward step. For I shall really and fully
be able to feel secure and always to hope for prosperity and happiness from the ready kindness of the most mighty God, only when I
see all venerating the most holy God in the proper cult of the
Catholic religion with harmonious brotherhood of worship.

180. Constantine's letter to Celsus

This is the conclusion of a letter written a few years later to Celsus,
the vicar of Africa, when all Constantine's efforts to heal the Donatist
schism had failed, and his penal measures against the Donatists—the
first persecution of Christians by Christians—had resulted in martyr-
doms. He here clearly announces that he considers it his duty as
emperor to enforce unity on the church in order to secure God's favor
for the empire.

180. Optatus Milevitanus, Appendix VII

BUT WHEN you have received this letter you will make it plain to
Caecilianus and to the other party that with the favor of the divine
piety I shall come to Africa and shall most fully demonstrate, by
pronouncing a clear judgment, to all, both Caecilian and those who
appear to oppose him, what kind of veneration is to be rendered to
the Highest Divinity and what sort of worship appears to please
Him. I shall also by a searching examination fully discover and
bring out into the light of day what some people up to now think
that they are concealing with ignorant cunning. I shall disperse and
destroy those same persons who raise such disorders and bring it

about that the Highest God is not worshiped with the veneration which is His due. And since it is obvious enough that no one can gain the blessings of a martyr from that crew who seem to be alienated and divorced from the truth of religion, I shall without any hesitation cause those whom I shall judge hostile to the divine law and to religion itself, and shall find guilty of violence against the proper worship, to pay the penalty which their mad and reckless obstinacy deserves. So they must know for certain what they ought to have for the fullest faith, their salvation being also called to witness. I shall make a searching inquiry both about the common people and about the clerics who hold the highest positions and shall deliver a judgment which will manifestly be the truest and most religious. I am also going to make plain to them what kind of worship is to be offered to the Divinity. For in no other way do I believe that I can escape the greatest guilt, than by refusing to connive at this wickedness. What higher duty have I in virtue of my imperial office and policy than to dissipate errors and repress rash indiscretions, and so to cause all to offer to Almighty God true religion, honest concord, and due worship?

181. Constantine and the imperial cult

Despite his conversion Constantine saw no inconsistency in allowing the imperial cult, with its temples and games, to continue, provided that no sacrifices were offered. This letter was written after A.D. 325, when Constantine presided at the Council of Nicaea.

181. Dessau, ILS, 705

IMPERATOR Caesar Flavius Constantinus Germanicus Sarmaticus Gothicus victor triumphator Augustus and Flavius Constantinus and Flavius Julius Constantius and Flavius Constans.

We embrace in the thought of our watchful care everything which protects the society of the human race, but the greatest task of our providence is that all cities which beauty and elegance distinguish among the lights of the provinces and all regions shall not only maintain their ancient dignity but also be advanced to better condition by the grant of our beneficence. Since, therefore, you state that you were so closely linked to Tuscia that by the rule of ancient custom high priests are created by you and them in alternate years to give dramatic games and a gladiatorial show at the city of Volsinii in Tuscia, but owing to the steepness of the mountains and the forests through which the roads run you earnestly beg that a remedy be granted so that your high priest be not compelled to go to Volsinii to celebrate his games, that is to say, that we bestow a name derived from our own surname on the city which is now called Hispellum, and which you state is near and adjacent to the Flaminian way, and that in it a temple of the Flavian family should rise, magnificently built in view of the grandeur of its title, and that the high priest which Umbria annually appoints should exhibit in that place his display of dramatic games and a gladiatorial show, the custom remaining in Tuscia that the priest created there should according to custom make his display of the aforesaid games at Volsinii. Our assent is readily given to your request and prayer. For we have granted to the city of Hispellum an eternal name and venerable title drawn from our own nomenclature, viz., that henceforth the city shall be called Flavia Constans: in its bosom we also wish to be built with splendid workmanship, as you request, a temple of the Flavian, that is our own, family: it being observed that the temple dedicated to our name must not be polluted with the deceits of any contagious superstition. We accordingly also give you leave to hold shows in the aforesaid city, on condition that the solemn production of shows, at intervals of time as stated above, does not desert Volsinii also, where the aforesaid celebration is to be offered by the high priest created for Tuscia. In this way old customs will not be greatly altered, and you, who have been our petitioner for the aforesaid reasons, will rejoice that what you earnestly requested has been granted.

182. Judicial powers of bishops

In 333 Constantine, in response to a query from his Christian praetorian prefect Ablabius, interpreted this rather vaguely worded law as meaning that in any civil action either party, whether the other objected or not, might invoke the jurisdiction of the bishop at any stage of the proceedings before judgment was given, and the decision of the bishop should be final and enforced by the civil authorities. This remarkable concession to bishops was subsequently withdrawn, and bishops were allowed to judge only with the consent of both parties. They nevertheless continued to hear many cases, as their courts were cheaper, more expeditious, and probably often fairer than the civil courts.

182. Codex Theodosianus, I. 27. 1

EMPEROR CONSTANTINE AUGUSTUS.

PURSUANT TO his own authority, a judge must observe that if an appeal should be made to an episcopal court, he shall maintain silence, and if any person should desire to transfer his case to the jurisdiction of the Christian law and to observe that kind of court, he shall be heard, even though the action has been instituted before the judge, and whatever may be adjudged by them shall be held as sacred; provided, however, that there shall be no such usurpation of authority that one of the litigants should proceed to the afore-mentioned tribunal and should announce his own choice. For the judge must have the unimpaired right of jurisdiction of the case that is pending before him, in order that he may pronounce his decision, after full credit is given to all the facts as presented.

Given on the ninth day before the kalends of July in [the sixth consulship of Licinius] Augustus and the consulship of Crispus Caesar [June 23, 318].

183. Constans forbids pagan worship

Although Constantine suppressed dissident Christian sects, he did not for a long while take any action against paganism. Instead, after he had gained control over the eastern half of the empire by the defeat of his colleague Licinius in 324, he issued an edict in which, while expressing the hope that pagans would see the error of their ways, he expressly granted toleration for their cults. It appears from this law that he banned sacrifice before he died, and his sons maintained the prohibition. The word "deified" had by now come to mean no more than "deceased emperor."

183. Codex Theodosianus, XVI. 10. 2

EMPEROR CONSTANTIUS AUGUSTUS to Madalianus, Vice Praetorian Prefect.

Superstition shall cease; the madness of sacrifices shall be abolished. For if any man in violation of the law of the deified Emperor, Our Father, and in violation of this command of Our Clemency, should dare to perform sacrifices, he shall suffer the infliction of a suitable punishment and the effect of an immediate sentence.

Received in the consulship of Marcellinus and Probinus [341].

184. Theodosius I finally forbids paganism

Julian the Apostate (360–363) revived pagan worship and tolerated Christianity. His Christian successors maintained a policy of toleration until Theodosius I, who prohibited any kind of pagan cult throughout the empire. His laws, though laxly enforced, were never repealed.

184. Codex Theodosianus, XVI. 10. 10

THE SAME Augusti to Albinus, Praetorian Prefect.

No person shall pollute himself with sacrificial animals; no person shall slaughter an innocent victim; no person shall approach the shrines, shall wander through the temples, or revere the images formed by mortal labor, lest he become guilty by divine and human laws. Judges also shall be bound by the general rule that if any of them should be devoted to profane rites and should enter a temple for the purpose of worship anywhere, either on a journey or in the city, he shall immediately be compelled to pay fifteen pounds of gold, and his office staff shall pay a like sum with similar haste, unless they resist the judge and immediately report him by a public attestation. Governors with the rank of consular shall pay six pounds of gold each, their office staffs a like amount; those with the rank of corrector or of praeses shall pay four pounds each, and their apparitors, by equal lot, a like amount.

Given on the sixth day before the kalends of March at Milan in the consulship of Tatianus and Symmachus [February 24, 391].

Selected Bibliography

General Works

The Cambridge Ancient History, Vols. X–XII and Vol. V of Plates. Cambridge, 1934–39

The Cambridge Medieval History, Vol. I, Cambridge, 1924

JONES, A. H. M. *The Later Roman Empire, 284–602*, 3 vols. Norman, 1964

JONES, H. S. *The Roman Empire, 29 B.C.–A.D. 476*, 3d impression. London, 1916

LOT, F. *The End of the Ancient World and the Beginnings of the Middle Ages.* New York, 1931

NILSSON, M. P. *Imperial Rome.* London, 1926

PARKER, H. M. D. *A History of the Roman World from A.D. 138 to 337*, 2d ed. London, 1958

ROSTOVTZEFF, M., and BICKERMAN, E. *A History of the Ancient World.* New York, 1961

ROSTOVTZEFF, M. *The Social and Economic History of the Roman Empire*, 2d ed. by P. M. Fraser, 2 vols. Oxford, 1956

SALMON, E. T. *A History of the Roman World from 30 B.C. to A.D. 138*, 3d ed. London, 1957

Special Periods and Reigns

JONES, A. H. M. *Constantine and the Conversion of Europe*, rev. ed. New York, 1962

HAMMOND, M. *The Antonine Monarchy.* Rome, 1959

HENDERSON, B. W. *Civil War and Rebellion in the Roman Empire, A.D. 69–70.* London, 1908

—— *Five Roman Emperors; Vespasian, Titus, Domitian, Nerva, Trajan, A.D. 69–117.* Cambridge, 1927

—— *The Life and Principate of the Emperor Hadrian, A.D. 76–138.* London, 1923

HOLMES, T. R. *The Architect of the Roman Empire*, 2 vols. Oxford, 1928–31

MARSH, F. B. *The Founding of the Roman Empire*, 2d ed. London, 1927

—— *The Reign of Tiberius*. London, 1931

SYME, R. *The Roman Revolution*. Oxford, 1939

Constitutional

CROOK, J. A. *Consilium Principis. Imperial Councils and Counsellors from Augustus to Diocletian*. Cambridge, 1954

HAMMOND, M. *The Augustan Principate in Theory and Practice during the Julio-Claudian Period*. Cambridge, Mass., 1933

JOLOWICZ, H. F. *Historical Introduction to the Study of Roman Law*, 2d ed. Cambridge, 1961

JONES, A. H. M. *Studies in Roman Government and Law*. Oxford, 1960

MCFAYDEN, D. *The History of the Title* Imperator *under the Roman Empire*. Chicago, 1920

SHERWIN-WHITE, A. N. *The Roman Citizenship*. Oxford, 1939

The Armed Forces

CHEESMAN, G. L. *The Auxilia of the Roman Imperial Army*. Oxford, 1914

PARKER, H. M. D. *The Roman Legions*, rev. ed. Cambridge, 1958

REYNOLDS, P. K. B. *The Vigiles of Imperial Rome*. London, 1926

STARR, C. G., JR. *The Roman Imperial Navy, 31 B.C.–A.D. 324*, 2d ed. Cambridge, 1960

The Provinces

BOUCHIER, E. S. *Spain under the Roman Empire*. Oxford, 1914

—— *Syria as a Roman Province*. Oxford, 1916

BROGAN, O. *Roman Gaul*. London, 1953

BROUGHTON, T. R. S. *The Romanization of Africa Proconsularis*. Baltimore, 1929

CHILVER, G. E. F. *Cisalpine Gaul; Social and Economic History from 49 B.C. to the Death of Trajan*. Oxford, 1941

JONES, A. H. M. *The Cities of the Eastern Roman Provinces*. Oxford, 1937

—— *The Greek City from Alexander to Justinian*. Oxford, 1940

MAGIE, D. *Roman Rule in Asia Minor*, 2 vols. Princeton, 1950

STEVENSON, G. H. *Roman Provincial Administration till the Age of the Antonines*, 2d ed. Oxford, 1949

WARMINGTON, B. H. *The North African Provinces from Diocletian to the Vandal Conquest.* Cambridge, 1954

Social and Economic

BARROW, R. H. *Slavery in the Roman Empire.* London, 1928

CARCOPINO, J. *Daily Life in Ancient Rome; the People and the City at the Height of the Empire.* New Haven, 1940

CHARLESWORTH, M. P. *Trade-Routes and Commerce of the Roman Empire*, 2d ed., rev. Cambridge, 1926

CLAUSING, R. *The Roman Colonate.* New York, 1925

DAVIES, O. *Roman Mines in Europe.* Oxford, 1935

DILL, S. *Roman Society from Nero to Marcus Aurelius*, 2d ed. London, 1905

———— *Roman Society in the Last Century of the Western Empire.* London, 1910

DUFF, A. M. *Freedmen in the Early Roman Empire.* Oxford, 1928

FRANK, T., ed. *An Economic Survey of Ancient Rome*, Vols. II–V. Baltimore, 1936–40

HEITLAND, W. E. *Agricola. A Study of Agriculture and Rustic Life in the Greco-Roman World from the Point of View of Labour.* Cambridge, 1921

WARMINGTON, E. H. *The Commerce between the Roman Empire and India.* Cambridge, 1928

WHEELER, M. *Rome beyond the Imperial Frontiers.* London, 1954

Religion

GLOVER, T. R. *The Conflict of Religions in the Early Roman Empire*, 10th ed. London, 1923

MOMIGLIANO, A., ed. *The Conflict between Paganism and Christianity in the Fourth Century.* Oxford, 1963

Index

Ablabius, 250

Abuse of power, trial for, 192–195; of requisition, 197–198

Achaia, 21, 116

Achilles, 230

Actium, 43; battle of, 108, 148, 318

Acts of the Apostles, 288–289

Adiutor, Aurelius, 305

Adrianople, 174; battle of (378), 6

Aedesius, 100, 101, 103

Aela, 198

Aelafius, Constantine's letter to, 340–341

Africa, 21, 25, 95, 99, 120, 124, 148, 185, 200, 203, 296; benefactions to the church of, Constantine's, 339–340; Christian persecution in, under Diocletian, 332–335; under Valerian, 330–331

Agricola, Gnaeus Julius, 4, 120–124, 125; in Britain, 183–185

Agrippa, Marcus, 16, 20, 75, 207

Agrippina, 104, 106

Alamanni, 85, 87, 96, 97

Alaric, 174

Alavivus, 175, 177

Albani, 22

Albania, 149

Albanum, 36

Albinus, Luccius, 190

Albinus of Etruria, 101

Alexander the Great, 92

Alexandria, 186, 223–226, 230, 232, 257, 321

Alimenta, the, 293–294

Allegiance, oath of, 43–44, 72

Allobrogicus, 113

Allotments for veterans, 173–174

Alps, 3, 21, 93, 107, 110

Ammianus Marcellinus, 6, 85–89, 89–94, 95–100, 100–107, 127, 128–133, 174–177, 209–212, 268–269

Antioch, 257, 306

Antiochus, King, 129

Antistius, Gaius, 18

Antonius Pius, 4, 73, 80, 98, 160; letters to Ephesus, 229–230

Apion, 151

Apodemius, 102, 104

Apollinaris, Sidonius, 6

Apollinarius, Julius, 151, 152

Appeal to Caesar, 289

Appianus, 136, 137

Apronianus, 210

Apuleius, Sextus, 16, 71

Aqueducts, 19, 207–209; curators of, 44

Aquitania, 123, 126

Arabia, 21; road building in, 198

Arabian expedition, 13, 21

Aratus, 92

Arbetio, 95, 100, 101, 102

Arcadius, 146

Aridelus, 142

Ariminum, 19

Arinthaeus, 94

Ariobaranes, King, 21

Aristomenes, 204, 205

Arles, 340–341

Armaturae, 100, 107

Armenia, 3, 13, 21

Armorers, state, 316–317

Arms factories, state, 316

Army, Roman, 50, 80, 148–177; allotments for veterans, 173–174; colony of veterans at Cyrene, 162; at Deultum, 161; distribution of forces, 148–150; draft in the fourth century, 168–170; draft under the principate, 150; Egyptian recruit, letter from, 151; Egyptian soldier, letter from, 151–152; federates, 174–177; foreign cavalryman, discharge certificate of, 160–161; hereditary military service, 170; legionary veterans, discharge of, 158; marriage of soldiers, 155–157; mobile army of Constantine, 167; mutiny in, 162–166; Numidian troops reviewed by Hadrian, 153–155; pay sheet of two legion-